Virginia Woolf and the Essay

Virginia Woolf and the Essay

Edited by
Beth Carole Rosenberg and Jeanne Dubino

St. Martin's Press
New York

VIRGINIA WOOLF AND THE ESSAY
Copyright © Beth Carole Rosenberg and Jeanne Dubino, 1997
All rights reserved. Printed in the United States of America. No part of this
book may be used or reproduced in any manner whatsoever without written
permission except in the case of brief quotations embodied in critical
articles or reviews. For information, address St. Martin's Press, Scholarly
and Reference Division, 175 Fifth Avenue, New York, N.Y. 10010
ISBN 0-312-17233-8

Library of Congress Cataloging-in-Publication Data
Virginia Woolf and the essay / edited by Beth Carole Rosenberg and
Jeanne Dubino.
    p.   cm.
   Includes bibliographical references and index.
   ISBN 0-312-17233-8
   1. Woolf, Virginia, 1882-1941—Knowledge—Literature. 2. English
essays—20th century—History and criticism. 3. Book reviewing-
-England—History—20th century. 4. Criticism—England-
-History—20th century. 5. Woolf, Virginia, 1882-1941—Prose.
6. Essay. I. Rosenberg, Beth Carole. II. Dubino, Jeanne, 1959- .

PR6045.072Z8923   1998
823'.912—dc21   97-21442
                                    CIP

First edition: November, 1997
10 9 8 7 6 5 4 3 2 1

For our sisters,

Lisa Dubino
Carrie Donohoe
Felicia Rosenberg
Paula Rosenberg Harnist

with affection and admiration

Contents

PART I: WOOLF AND HISTORY

PART II: WOOLF AND LITERARY HISTORY

PART III: WOOLF AND READING

PART IV: WOOLF AND GENRE

PART V: THE ESSAY AND FEMINISM

Acknowledgments

We are grateful to our contributors and those whose earlier work on Virginia Woolf's essays made this collection possible. We wish especially to thank Jean Guiguet, B. J. Kirkpatrick, Andrew McNeillie, Brenda Silver, and Elizabeth Steele. We would also like to thank our editor, Maura Burnett, for her support and enthusiasm, and the anonymous reader of our introduction, whose comments were invaluable. The collection as whole would not be what it is without collaborative effort.

Permission was granted by both the Society of Authors as the literary representative of the Estate of Virginia Woolf and the Henry W. and Albert A. Berg Collection (The New York Public Library, Astor, Lenox and Tilden Foundation) for publication of a portion of Virginia Woolf's manuscript version of "How Should One Read a Book?"("Articles, essays, fiction, and reviews" Vol. 1: April 21, 1925, ms. 177-249. Berg Collection, NYPL).

List of Abbreviations

AHH	*A Haunted House*
AROO	*A Room of One's Own*
BP	*Books and Portraits*
BTA	*Between the Acts*
CDB	*The Captain's Deathbed and Other Essays*
CE	*Collected Essays* (4 vols.)
CR 1	*The Common Reader*
CR 2	*The Common Reader, Second Series*
CSF	*The Complete Shorter Fiction*
D	*The Diary of Virginia Woolf* (5 vols.)
DM	*The Death of the Moth and Other Essays*
E	*The Essays of Virginia Woolf* (6 vols.)
F	*Flush*
GR	*Granite and Rainbow: Essays*
JR	*Jacob's Room*
L	*The Letters of Virginia Woolf* (6 vols.)
M	*The Moment and Other Essays*
MEL	*Melymbrosia*
MOB	*Moments of Being*
MT	*Monday or Tuesday*
MD	*Mrs. Dalloway*
ND	*Night and Day*
O	*Orlando*
PA	*A Passionate Apprentice*
RF	*Roger Fry: A Biography*
TG	*Three Guineas*
TTL	*To the Lighthouse*
TW	*The Waves*
TY	*The Years*
VO	*The Voyage Out*

Introduction

As Sonya Rudikoff wrote more than fifteen years ago in "How Many Lovers Had Virginia Woolf?," Woolf studies has turned into a veritable industry. The annual Virginia Woolf conference grows every year. A journal devoted solely to Woolf, *Woolf Studies Annual,* has been inaugurated. The Woolf Society is entering its twentieth year. Many other journals, including *Twentieth Century Literature* and *Modern Fiction Studies,* devote whole issues to Woolf every decade or so (even as they publish many essays on her on a routine basis). The number of book-length studies, biographies, dissertations, articles, conference panels (especially at the annual Modern Language Association meeting) continues to flourish. When copyrights on most of Woolf's work expired in 1991 a number of new editions were produced.[1] Woolf is also entering the computer age, as a panel entitled "Virginia Woolf in the Age of Computers and Microform" at the 1994 Modern Language Association convention can testify. We see from the growing number of panel presentations and articles on Woolf's work that academics are not only writing about her novels and feminist tracts; they are also beginning to recognize her as a prolific essayist.

The popularity of Virginia Woolf's essays is borne out by the fact that editions of her essays—most notably those published during her lifetime, the two volumes of *The Common Reader, A Room of One's Own,* and *Three Guineas;* and those following her death, including *The Death of the Moth, The Moment, The Captain's Death Bed,* and *Granite and Rainbow*—have mostly remained in print since their publication. However, the towering importance of Woolf's fiction has tended to overshadow the fact that from 1904 to 1922, nearly the first two decades of her professional life as a writer and preceding the publication of her first experimental novel, *Jacob's Room,* Virginia Woolf was primarily a reviewer and essayist, writing more than half of her 500-plus articles, essays, and reviews. She continued to write essays throughout her life, though these essays have been considered secondary or incidental to the rest of her oeuvre.

The history of the reception of Woolf's essays reveals how a lack of serious consideration by her critics obscures the important role that nonacademic essays play in literature. Until World War II, the innovative and authoritative essays and articles on literature were generally written outside the academic institutions in both Great Britain and the United States. Muriel Mellown points out in her introduction to *British Literary Magazines* that the 1920s witnessed the flourishing of literary magazines and periodicals that published consciously avant-garde and experimentalist literature that contained manifestos declaring the novelty of literature. Woolf's works were reviewed and discussed in the important British (and sometimes American) literary journals and in the arts and literature section of journals not specifically devoted to literature, namely the *Times Literary Supplement*, the *Nation and Athenaeum*, the *Bookman*, the *Criterion*, the *Dial*, the *Manchester Guardian*, and *Scrutiny*. Serious criticism emerged from the academy following World War II, when the apparatus of criticism was firmly institutionalized both in Great Britain and the United States.

The history of response to Woolf's essays can be chronicled in four stages. The first, contemporary reception from 1923 to 1941, consists mostly of reviews, review-essays, and occasionally a chapter in a book on the novel. Interestingly, contemporary reception set the tone for the next two stages. The next generation extends from 1941 to 1970. During these three decades of backlash against Woolf, critics generally referred to "Mr. Bennett and Mrs. Brown" and "Modern Fiction" and treated her essays only in the context of her fiction. When critics did address her essays at length, it was primarily to diminish them. The third stage, feminist criticism, which has prevailed from 1970 to the present, has tended to focus primarily on *A Room of One's Own*, *Three Guineas*, and scattered essays that address the position of women. A new approach began in 1992 with the first volume of Woolf's entire critical opus, edited by Andrew McNeillie. McNeillie's editions have made it possible for academics to treat the entire body of Woolf's criticism and not separate out feminism from her critical work as a whole.

The first written responses to Virginia Woolf's criticism date to letters to the editor of the *Times Literary Supplement*. However, because Woolf was writing anonymously, these sporadic responses are hardly significant in terms of establishing her reputation as a critic. Moreover, these correspondents use the letter either as a forum in which to declare their own opinions and knowledge or as a place to quibble with the facts of Woolf's review.[2] The most serious critical responses to Woolf's criticism originated from the famous Bennett-Woolf debate that began in 1923. In their collection of contemporary reviews of Woolf's works, *Virginia Woolf: The Critical Heritage*, Robin Majumdar and Allen McLaurin include six review essays by her contemporaries that respond to Woolf's position on the issue of character in fiction as she describes it in the three versions of "Mr. Bennett and Mrs. Brown." Here is not the place to describe the nature of the debate but rather how Woolf's contemporaries treated her as a critic.

The review-essays by Woolf's contemporaries—such as Arnold Bennett, Logan Pearsall Smith, and Frank Swinnerton—did not address Woolf's argument on character itself except to use it as a springboard from which to launch their own opinions. The argument over what constitutes character and how it is most successfully realized in fiction takes precedence over what Woolf herself has to say about it. This debate continued for at least the next decade since its beginning in 1923. In his book *Men Without Art*, Wyndham Lewis devoted one chapter to attacking "Mr. Bennett and Mrs. Brown" for, among many things, being a "highly artificial little piece" (Majumdar and McLaurin 333-34). Stephen Spender defended Woolf in his review of *Men Without Art*. Philip Henderson also saw the debate important enough to address in 1936 in his book *The Novel of To-day*. Unlike Lewis, Henderson describes Woolf's argument in respectful terms.

One might easily see how the Woolf-Bennett discussion continued to inform responses to Virginia Woolf's essays. "Mr. Bennett and Mrs. Brown" in its various forms and "Modern Fiction" continue to receive more critical attention from academic critics than any of Woolf's essays (with the exception of her feminist tracts), and they are the most anthologized. "Mr. Bennett and Mrs. Brown" received—and still receives—more critical attention than the two volumes of *The Common Reader*, and yet it was the first volume of *The Common Reader* that earned Woolf recognition as a critic. All of the four anonymous reviews of *The Common Reader* included in *Virginia Woolf: The Critical Heritage* treat Woolf as a serious literary critic. Interestingly, as we shall see, the reviewers of the first *Common Reader* treat Woolf's criticism more seriously than do the reviewers of the second *Common Reader*. In her four-volume collection *Virginia Woolf: Critical Assessments*, Eleanor McNees includes reviews by critics like Dilys Powell who praised the second *Common Reader* for its novelistic quality and wrote in the *Sunday Times*, "Above all one remembers the elegance with which it is written" (2: 94). Denys Thompson wrote in *Scrutiny*, a journal edited by Woolf's most famous detractors, Queenie and F. R. Leavis, that "*The Common Reader: First Series* was a contribution to criticism and the *Second Series* is not" (2: 95). Gerald Sykes in *The Nation* regards Woolf's criticism as dated; instead of being the champion of a new movement, she is, he writes, "already beginning to be seen as one of a long line of quite orthodox belletrists and bibliophiles" (2: 97). The diminution of Woolf's criticism may result from the fact that her renown as a novelist was nearly on its way toward eclipsing her reputation as a critic.[3] Yet even in the responses to the first *Common Reader* the reviewers link Woolf's critical ability with her artistry. In the most positive of the four reviews, H. I'A Fausset writes that Woolf "has discovered how to write for the newspapers without ceasing to be an artist and how to exalt criticism into a creative adventure which . . . is yet preserved by the finest sense of values from the quixotry of Impressionism" (Majumdar and McLaurin 151).

Critics would continue to argue that in her essays Woolf excels in her ability as both "critic and artist," as one *Times Literary Supplement* reviewer notes (Majumdar and McLaurin 148). However, the frequent tethering of one role to the other in these four reviews tends to distract if not detract from the strength of Woolf's abilities as a critic. Though the reviewers applaud Woolf for transcending "impressionism" (clearly a bugbear word), their use of this word tends to make us remember that Woolf does start out with impressions. Too, there is an element of surprise in these reviews, as Fausset states clearly: "[w]e will confess that until we read this volume we credited Virginia Woolf with more charm and vivacity than vision" (151). We may read the "we" in this quotation not just as a convention but also as a pronoun for the body of reviewers. True, Fausset and other reviewers attempt to correct this earlier "misjudgment" (151). But in mentioning Woolf's "charm and vivacity," these reviewers tend to imprint these kinds of impressions of her criticism in our own minds. Later Woolf's friend and lover Vita Sackville-West would aptly note in her review of *A Room of One's Own*, "Mrs. Woolf has perhaps never been given sufficient credit for her commonsense. Airy, fantastic, brilliant— all these adjectives have been lavished on her, till you might think her work as coloured but as empty as an iridescent bubble" (257). The contemporary reception of Woolf's essays as impressionistic rather than reasoned set the tone for the critical reception of the next seventy years.

The division of Woolf into essayist, feminist, and novelist also began with the contemporary reception of her works. In the same review of *A Room of One's Own* quoted above, Sackville-West begins by separating Woolf's reputation into these three categories: "[T]his little book, which is not a novel, is not pure criticism either. In so far as it is 'about' anything at all, it is a study of women " (257). Sackville-West's comment points to the generic overlapping of much of Woolf's work—it is novel, criticism, and social commentary. However, following the publication of *The Common Reader*, subsequent reviewers of Woolf's novels make only passing reference to Woolf as a critic, even in the review-essays and the obituaries that treat the body of Woolf's work. More significantly, what we see Sackville-West doing in this quotation is separating "pure criticism" from "a study of women."

It is Woolf's "study of women" in *A Room of One's Own, Three Guineas,* and Michèle Barrett's edited collection of essays, *Women and Writing,* that specifically addresses the position of women in society and her feminism as it is manifest in her fiction. It is her feminism that has drawn the most attention to Woolf's critical abilities in the third stage of the critical reception of her work. From the 1970s on it is clear that the feminist criticism Woolf articulated in *A Room of One's Own* and elsewhere has been taken seriously and has been vigorously discussed by feminists practicing criticism today. Indeed, feminists laud her as their forerunner, one with a continuing presence as, Toril Moi writes, a "great mother and sister" (18). Elaine Showalter notes that "it has become important to feminist critics to emphasize Virginia Woolf's strength and gaiety and to see her as the apotheosis of a new literary sensibility" (263), and the title of the book from which this quotation comes, *A Literature of Their Own,* is one example of the many uses to which the title alone of *A Room of One's Own* has been put. As Ellen Bayuk Rosenman writes in *A Room of One's Own: Women Writers and the Politics of Creativity,* Woolf's title "has become part of our modern cultural vocabulary, testifying to the essay's widespread influence. If imitation is the sincerest form of flattery, then *A Room of One's Own* is surely one of the most flattered books in history" (10-11). In the first part of her essay, "T. S. Eliot, Virginia Woolf, and the Future of Tradition,'" Florence Howe also notes the way Woolf's reputation as a literary critic was largely disregarded in the 1950s. Lillian Robinson writes that this "essay is still seminal and remains a logical starting place" (98), and Judith Kegan Gardiner recommends that those who are interested in reading feminist criticism start with *A Room of One's Own* (145).

Yet the notion of Woolf as a critic and essayist, and not just as a feminist critic, was overlooked by academic critics. In part this omission may have to do with Woolf's eschewal of the institution. Woolf had, of course, most famously illustrated women's exclusion from the academy in *A Room of One's Own.* At the beginning of the essay she portrays a woman not only forbidden to walk on the "turf" (6) but also unable to enter the library unless she is accompanied by a man (7-8). Both the door of the male college and the cover of its text—a "treasure" hoarded by the college and protected by "a guardian angel" (7)—are closed to her. In the following chapter Woolf depicts the female narrator going inside the British Museum, which, with its smooth domed top, becomes the personification of a generic professor, Professor von X., who in turn embodies the university. "The swing-doors swung open," Woolf writes, "and there one stood under the vast dome, as if one were a thought in the huge bald forehead which is so splendidly encircled by a band of famous names" (26).

Woolf wants to step over the textual literary terrain of male culture in an effort to arrive at her own conclusions about some male-authored texts. Though Woolf advocated that women shun membership in patriarchal institutions, she realized the importance of analyzing those institutions. Rather than being hampered by critics' opinions, Woolf shows how the female narrator wants to read the manuscripts in the library at Oxbridge directly, unimpeded. As a critic, Woolf was playful and innovative, as some of the articles in this collection will show. However, rather than treating her playfulness and innovation seriously, critics have used these qualities as a reason to exclude Woolf from consideration as a legitimate essayist and critic. In examining their representations of Woolf one might come to the conclusion that she was only an occasional essayist, one who wrote essays primarily to justify her fiction.

The easy dismissal of Woolf's essays by her contemporaries is continued in more current histories of literary criticism. It is illuminating to compare Woolf's fate as an essayist with that of her contemporary and friend, T. S. Eliot. Like Woolf, Eliot was not an academic, and like Woolf, he is known primarily for his artistic rather than his critical output. Yet, because Eliot is closely associated with a critical school, the New Criticism, the critical assumptions that inform his poetry and that he articulates in his essays are themselves canonized. Indeed, on the map of literary critical history, Eliot's presence eclipses Woolf's. A brief overview of critical opinion of the relation of Woolf's essays to Eliot's will reveal her subordinate position as a literary critic in the mainstream history of literary criticism.

A representative attitude can be found in David Lodge's introductions to Eliot and Woolf in *Twentieth Century Literary Criticism*: "Eliot's was a mind cultured and cosmopolitan," Lodge writes, "that ranged widely and confidently over European literature. . . . Almost everything he wrote gave food for thought" (69). Lodge here approaches hagiography in his appraisal of Eliot's influence and importance. Woolf, on the other hand, was part of a circle, the Bloomsbury group, which, Lodge writes, "exerted considerable (some would say excessive) influence over English literary and intellectual life between the wars" (85).[4] The suggestion here is obvious: this influence was undesirable and, unlike Eliot's, time-bound, lasting only twenty years, from 1919 to 1939. Lodge introduces Eliot as "one of the greatest poets and influential critics of our time"; he introduces Woolf as "the daughter of Leslie Stephen, man-of-letters and first editor of the *Dictionary of National Biography*," not as, at least, one of the greatest novelists of our time (69). Woolf's father receives more attention here than Woolf herself. Lodge also includes the names of Vanessa and Clive Bell, Lytton Strachey, Maynard Keynes, E. M.

Forster, James Joyce, Arnold Bennett, H. G. Wells and John Galsworthy, so that Woolf is crowded, even buried, by a host of luminaries. The only cohort of Eliot's whom Lodge includes is Ezra Pound.

Lodge's introductions are typical of contemporary critical opinion of Woolf and Eliot. When Woolf is included in anthologies, her essays are not given the sustained attention that Eliot's receive. For example, in his introduction to selections from Woolf's critical opus in the eight-volume anthology *The Art of the Critic*, Harold Bloom, like Lodge, concentrates on Woolf's biography while providing commentary on Eliot's essays. In *The Rhetoric of Fiction* Wayne Booth falls in line with other critics (namely David Daiches, whom he quotes) who belittle Woolf by arguing that she writes criticism in order to justify her fiction.

Recent histories of literary criticism follow the New Critical highway of literary critical theory and pass other critical byways. John Casey in *The Language of Criticism* examines the post-Romanticism of twentieth-century critics; he devotes a chapter to explaining how Eliot fails to resolve satisfactorily the role of emotion in one's responses to art and omits Woolf altogether. Frank Lentricchia's *After the New Criticism* looks at critics' responses to the New Criticism. Eliot is often mentioned; Woolf, never. Pamela McCallum's *Literature and Method*, Francis Mulhern's *The Moment of "Scrutiny,"* and J. W. Saunders's *The Profession of English Letters* give little or no attention to Woolf's essays although these studies claim to be addressing the role of criticism in the early twentieth century.

It is probably no coincidence that with the feminist impulse in Woolf criticism in the 1970s came a reevaluation of the essays in general. In their essay, "Virginia Woolf's Criticism: A Polemical Preface," Barbara Currier Bell and Carol Ohmann set the tone for more serious treatment of Woolf's essays by examining the essays published in *The Common Reader*. Bell and Ohmann argue that Woolf's criticism "deserves much more attention than it's gotten" (362) and proceed to praise it for the very qualities for which it has been derided. That is, they attend to the way Woolf refuses to totalize or establish an explicit system of her method. Bell and Ohmann endow Woolf's criticism with a humanistic mission when they conclude that she approaches literature sympathetically with the ultimate goal of "humaniz[ing] our lives," and "urg[ing] a liberation and wholeness of self" (371).

The trend set by Bell and Ohmann is continued by two important book-length studies. Mark Goldman's *The Reader's Art: Virginia Woolf as Literary Critic*, published in 1976, and Vijay Sharma's *Virginia Woolf as Literary Critic*, published in 1977, came out at a time when academic criticism as a whole, and particularly the New Criticism, had long been under attack from the

Continental theory that began influencing the institution in the 1960s. These works were the first full-length studies of the methodology and structure of Woolf's body of nonfiction prose. Both Goldman and Sharma trace early responses to Woolf's essays by David Daiches, Louis Kronenberg, Mark Schorer, and Diana Trilling and cite these critics for establishing the view that the essays are "impressionistic," occasional pieces, unworthy of serious consideration as literary criticism. Freed from the constraints of the New Criticism, Goldman and Sharma apply different criteria when evaluating Woolf's essays and have paved the way for a rearticulation of their worth.

Goldman's study takes a philosophical approach to Woolf's essays. In it he discusses the "Nature of Reality" and how Woolf tries to define it through an "historical-traditional approach" to literature (9). He views the essays in *The Common Reader* as working toward a telos, the end of which is the modern sensibility of Woolf herself. This leads Goldman to a discussion of Woolf's essays on fiction, so that in effect he limits his analysis to the same emphasis on the novel that earlier commentary on Woolf's essays had given. In his chapter on "The Critic as Critic," he discusses her theories of the nature and function of criticism and the critic. He does this by looking at the role of the common reader as critic, the influence of Clive Bell's "significant form," the relationship between criticism and creativity, and the function of the critic as reviewer and contemporary. He concludes by trying to account for the balance or merging of critical functions while understanding Woolf as an "artist-critic" who grew disillusioned with contemporary criticism. According to Goldman, Woolf viewed the critic as a person of sensibility who responds to and understands a work of art and who can express that knowledge and experience and communicate it to a reader (121). Thus Goldman establishes Woolf's common reader as more than a dilettante who expresses her mere "impressions" of a work of art.

Like Goldman, Sharma also seeks to establish a clear and identifiable critical methodology in Woolf's essays. Sharma defines her own approach as that of an "historical interpreter" (15) and begins her study with a survey of the intellectual background that informs Woolf's work. She divides the essays into five broad categories: those written as reviews at the request of editors; those that aim at re-creating for the reader an age, period, or portrait of a writer; those that span the works of a writer and that aim at acquainting the reader with the total achievement of that writer; those that initiate a debate on certain literary tendencies; and those in which Woolf builds critical concepts.

For Sharma, the concept of the androgynous mind is most central to Woolf's critical theory. This concept is derived from Woolf's philosophic understanding of the polymorphic mind, in which reality and form merge in the balance between masculine and feminine forms of thought. Woolf's understanding of reality parallels her views on the novel, and so Sharma, like Goldman and earlier critics, spends a great deal of time discussing Woolf's theory of the novel. Sharma also attempts to sketch out the relationship between the common reader and the critic, and like Goldman begins to develop a theory of the reader as informed and knowledgeable, moving beyond the connotation of "common" as untutored, naive. Sharma concludes her study by citing the various critical schools that were burgeoning in the first quarter of the twentieth century—academic critics, reviewers, professional critics, writer-critics—and places Woolf within the category of writer-critic. As such Woolf is shown to share qualities with Forster, Eliot, Lawrence, and Auden.

With Andrew McNeillie's projected six-volume edition of the essays, of which four volumes have been published, the perspective of Woolf as a writer of fiction rather than a serious writer of the essay is changing. McNeillie's edition makes it possible for us to see the body of Woolf's criticism as a whole and trace its chronological development. While Leonard Woolf's four-volume edition, *Collected Essays*, is still very useful in terms of its consolidation of the essays into categories (literary, critical, biographical), he includes only those essays that had already been collected, and he does not annotate them. McNeillie provides a great service by attempting to include all the essays, reviews, and notes that Woolf wrote (still more are being discovered) and by providing an impressively extensive apparatus of introductions, notes, and appendices. In light of McNeillie's edition, the essays, which have been popular with common readers throughout the century, can now be looked at in the more methodical and organized manner practiced by Goldman and Sharma.

Virginia Woolf and the Essay is a case in point. We view this collection in the tradition of Goldman and Sharma, looking at Woolf's essays from the perspective of literary criticism by focusing on the essays in and of themselves and not merely as secondary material to explicate Woolf's novels or her feminism. It is evidence that Woolf is no longer regarded as just an occasional essayist or as an impressionistic reader who dabbled in criticism. Woolf used the essay not only to put forth a theory of the novel or comment on literary history but to comment on experience itself through writing that addresses social, biographical, and historical matters.

Interest in Woolf as an essayist was evinced at the 1993 MLA conference in Toronto. As co-chairs of the well-attended panel "Virginia Woolf and the History of Literary Criticism," we recognized an attentive regard for Virginia Woolf the essayist. Three of the papers chosen for the panel are represented in this collection. These papers—Melba Cuddy-Keane's on Woolf's view of history, Beth Rigel Daugherty's on the history of Woolf's common reader, and Eleanor McNees's on *Scrutiny* and contemporary cultural views on Woolf—represent the different approaches the scholars in this collection take to the topic of Woolf and the essay. While we began this project in the aftermath of the Modern Language Association panel on Woolf and the history of literary criticism, we found that we too easily used the terms "essay" and "criticism" synonymously. When reviewing the contributions to our collection we saw that although the papers dealt with the essays, they did not necessarily address Woolf's literary criticism. This also made us aware of the difficulty of defining the essay in terms of Woolf's writing. As students of her novels know, Woolf was preoccupied with genre and was constantly experimenting with ways to merge and break down various generic forms. This same preoccupation is found in her essays. Sometimes literary criticism, sometimes social criticism, sometimes autobiography, the essays are diverse. The fluid and often idiosyncratic form of her essays might account for her earlier critics' dismissal of the essays as impressionistic. However, within the context of discussions of the essay, this "formlessness" assumes its own significance in Woolf's work.

A study of Woolf's own definition of the essay might begin with a look at her piece, "The Modern Essay." She begins her discussion by disassociating herself from the history of essay writing, telling her reader that "it is unnecessary to go profoundly into the history and origin of the essay." For Woolf, the essay's "present is more important than its past." The present moment lends itself to an openness and possibility that the past does not. The past, like the essay form itself, allows itself to become ossified—and therefore it is robbed of the vitality and life that give pleasure. Woolf's emphasis, as always, is on the reader of the essay rather than the writer. The "principle which controls [the essay] is simply that it should give pleasure" to the reader (*CR* 1: 211). What should not find its way into essay writing is the desire to convey fact, "[l]iteral truth-telling," or polemic, where the writer uses the essay to find "fault with a culprit for his good." Nor, on the other hand, should the essay writer have unclear thoughts and clutch "aimlessly at vague ideas" (*CR* 1: 212). Woolf believes that the essay of her time has "got some way from pleasure and the art of writing." It is in her description of the "art of writing" that we find her definition of form: ". . . the art of writing has for backbone some fierce attachment to an idea. It is on the back of an idea, something believed in with conviction or seen with precision and thus compelling words to its shape" (*CR* 1: 221). The writer who clutches after vague ideas will not find a clear form for his or her essay. This is because the idea *precedes* the form (and this is why an historical understanding of the essay form is useless). The writing is dependent on the idea, abstract and amorphous as that idea might be, because the idea is fixed and precise. In other words, a fixed form does not come before the idea, where the idea is made to fit the form. It is rather the reverse—the idea compels words to its shape, and there the form of each essay finds its life in the particular ideas it is trying to express. The dilemma for the contemporary essayist is the "lack of an obstinate conviction which lifts ephemeral sounds through the misty sphere of anybody's language . . ." (*CR* 1: 222).

If critics on the form of the essay agree with Woolf on anything, it is that the essay is extremely polyphonic and difficult to define in absolute terms. Two landmark essays on the essay, Georg Lukács's "On the Nature and Form of the Essay" and Theodor Adorno's "The Essay as Form," both argue that the essay, as far as we can define it, is an aesthetic form that is not pragmatic nor scientific in nature and does not rely on what Woolf calls "literal truth-telling." Essays are not written to *prove* anything. Lukács, a contemporary of Woolf's writing in Germany, discusses the essay in the same spiritual, metaphysical, and mystical language we find in Woolf. Coming out of the nineteenth-century emphasis on the empirical representation and understanding of the facts of experience, Woolf and Lukács both reevaluate the essay. Lukács writes that "[s]cience affects us by its contents, art by its forms; science offers us facts and the relationships between facts, but art offers us souls and destinies" (3). The essay makes no claim to fact, according to Lukács, and he contrasts this absence of claim to art, which gives us the abstract sense of the soul. In defining the soul, he says there are two realities: "one is *life* and the other is *living*" (4). This same duality is found in the opposition between "image" and "significance" (5). This duality exists between the surface, literal, or denotative meaning of scientific fact and the figurative and connotative meaning beneath the surface, where meaning is found in process and being—Woolf's "present" rather than the "past."

It is the "soul" of the essay with which both Lukács and Woolf are concerned. The "critic's moment of destiny," as Lukács writes, "is that moment at which things become forms—the moment when all feelings and experiences on the near or the far side of form receive form, are melted down and condensed into form." Lukács agrees with Woolf that the idea precedes the form, and that the form of each essay is unique and individual, coming into being from feelings and experience and helping to create the point of view and perspective each essay expresses. The union between soul and form is a "mystical moment," according to Lukács, as transcendent as the "moment" in Woolf's writing. For essay writers "form *is* reality" and it is "the voice with which they address their questions to life" (8). The essay, therefore, does not create form out of nothingness but orders ideas that were already once alive. The essay orders things anew and speaks "the truth" about them. Two essays can never replicate or contradict each other, for each is creating a unique world. For Lukács, the essay is a judgment but not a verdict; the essay is instead about the "process of judging" (18).

Theodor Adorno's essay, "The Essay as Form," also describes the process through which the essay gains its form. As his title indicates, form does not belong to the essay but is the essay itself. He too rejects the notion that the essay communicates empirical fact and that the essay presents the intellect as *creatio ex nihilo*. The form of the essay, according to Adorno, is a function of the "luck and play" essential to it (152). Luck and play are antithetical to the dogma of pragmatic thought. The form of the essay takes "discreetly separated elements . . . into a readable context" where there is "no scaffolding, no edifice" upon which to build. No empirical formula structures the essay. The luck and play of the essay allow the separate elements to "crystallize into a configuration" (161), and each configuration, each essay, is uniquely itself and unlike any other form. It gains its unity "only by moving through the fissures, rather than by smoothing them over. . . . Discontinuity is essential to the essay" (165). Here is the paradox of the form of the essay; its unity is found in its "discontinuity." The lack of a consistent, unified structure helps the essay to find the structure that is appropriate for the content it is trying to express.

Woolf too finds the form of the essay determined by the play and combination of ideas and language, and through language the form or identity of the essay is created. In her essay "Montaigne," Woolf explains the process of writing and finding order in experience:

> Movement and change are the essence of our being. . . . [L]et us say
> what comes into our heads, repeat ourselves, contradict ourselves, fling
> out the wildest nonsense, and follow the most fantastic fancies without
> caring what the world does or thinks or says. For nothing matters except
> life; and, of course, order. (CR 1: 63)

The freedom, flux, luck, and play of life are part of our essence, the soul of our being. What is equally important to Woolf is that we find order and structure in that essence. The essay is a form that allows identity to coalesce, since it is a structure that takes its lead from the idea, essence, or being that comes before.

For Woolf, the essay is art, not science, with a form different from the novel and poetry. It does have logic, form, and structure, though its form is self-reflexive. As a self-reflexive artifact, it strives to represent and imitate the process of thought itself. Its own particular form constructs its content while, at the same time, it tries to articulate it. That is, it neither begins with a thesis that it proceeds to demonstrate, nor is it inductive, building to a formulated and concrete conclusion. The antiempirical and antipositivistic view of the essay, as defined by Woolf, Lukács, and Adorno, runs counter to the emphasis on positivism that the New Critics strove for, and this can help us to understand why it has been so difficult for Woolf's essays to gain authority. With the influence of Saussurian linguistics in the 1960s, and the structural and poststructural theory that followed in the 1970s and 1980s, academic criticism in general has moved away from New Critical precepts. Woolf's brand of essay writing focuses on living rather than life, significance rather than image, ideas rather than form, and can be reevaluated with this new critical apparatus not available to her or her contemporaries.

Influenced by Lukács and Adorno, Graham Good, in *The Observing Self: Rediscovering the Essay*, argues that different types of essays can be distinguished by tone and content. He distinguishes four principle types: the travel essay, the moral essay, the critical essay, and the autobiographical essay (xii). Woolf writes essays that fall into each of these categories, and like Samuel Johnson's *Lives of the Poets*, many of her essays contain elements of more than one category, constantly pressing the bounds of definition and description. The essay itself is not an article, and for this reason the papers in this collection should be considered "articles" about the essay—for these articles are written to function within an academic discourse and are the beginning of methodical study of the nature of Woolf's essays. Both these articles and Woolf's essays deal with literature, though Woolf's essays, like academic articles, are not limited to the subject of literature for their content. And so the first thing we must realize when studying Woolf's essays is that Woolf wrote many kinds of essays: essayistic criticism, such as "Mr. Bennett and Mrs. Brown" and "Modern Fiction"; essayistic memoir, such as "A Sketch of the Past"; essayistic travel writing, such as "Street Haunting" and "To Spain"; essayistic biography, such as that of her father Leslie Stephen and her good friend Roger Fry; essayistic fiction, such as "A Talk about Memoirs"; and what one might call fictional essays, like *A Room of One's Own*.

We have grouped these articles according to the way each author has come to understand Woolf's approach to the essay. We begin with "Woolf and History" because history grounds Woolf in the early twentieth century and helps us to understand how Woolf perceived her writing in relation to her peers and contemporaries. She is, of course, writing in the wake of the Victorian essayist, particularly her father Leslie Stephen, who not only trained her in historiography but in the art of essay writing itself. For this reason, many of Woolf's essays have a strong historical sense.

Jeanne Dubino's paper, "Virginia Woolf: From Book Reviewer to Literary Critic, 1904-1918," marks Woolf's entrance into essay writing through her reviews. Dubino discusses the material and economic aspect of Woolf's reviewing and shows that Woolf was not above writing for money or writing to please her editors. We can distinguish Woolf's essay writing from her reviewing because the self-definition of form that the essay entails is lacking in the reviews. But Woolf's reviewing was an apprenticeship to the writing that followed.

Eventually Woolf would become an accomplished essayist and critic, and her work would inspire the commentary of the academic critic F. R. Leavis and his *Scrutiny* group. Leavis and his followers considered Woolf's essays elitist and detached from a moral and Arnoldian standard. Eleanor McNees shows us in "Colonizing Virginia Woolf: *Scrutiny* and Contemporary Cultural Critics" how, over fifty years later, the cultural critics of the 1980s read a different work than Leavis using the same critical terms. For the cultural critics of today, according to McNees, Woolf is not elitist but rather argues for the oppressed and exploited. McNees concludes that history becomes a function of the point of view that narrates it; it is no longer an unproblematic and unified concept.

The problem of defining history is something with which Woolf was familiar, and it is her understanding of history that Melba Cuddy-Keane addresses in "Virginia Woolf and the Varieties of Historicist Experience." According to Cuddy-Keane, Woolf transposes history from a metaphysical holistic narrative to a pluralistic and experiential model; Woolf is concerned with the different and varied ways in which we experience history in our reading. Cuddy-Keane does not merely look at Woolf through a New Historicist lens but tries to ground Woolf's view of history in the developments of historiography of her own time. Ultimately, Woolf's view of history is intimately connected with the reading process—both hers and our own.

A pluralistic and experiential model of history renders the notion of literary history problematic. But Woolf immersed herself in literary history and was acutely aware of the writers and works that preceded her. She acknowledged that a writer would not be able to write without understanding where she stood in the literary-historical continuum. Woolf's two

Common Reader volumes were attempts not only to write literary history but to redefine the notion of literary historical writing. Literary history also assumes a kind of literary criticism, and many of her essays fall into the category of essayistic criticism. The section titled "Woolf and Literary History" does make some assumptions about the function of literary history as perhaps linear and teleological, but we view this section as a beginning toward some understanding of Woolf's place within, and her views on, literary history itself.

We begin this section with Sally Greene's discussion of literary history in "Entering Woolf's Renaissance Imaginary: A Second Look at *The Second Common Reader.*" Greene's essay follows the work of Alice Fox's *Virginia Woolf and the Literature of the English Renaissance* and explains how Woolf employs her particular understanding of the Renaissance to invite a feminist critique from within the dominant culture. The first three essays in Woolf's second *Common Reader* employ what Greene terms the "Renaissance imaginary." Woolf draws her readers into a "strange" yet vaguely familiar world populated by women and men who are equally capable of self-enlightenment through the power of reading. In Woolf's essays about the Renaissance we begin to see how literary history is redefined and given a more direct connection to its subjects as well as to its readers.

In "'deeply and consciously affected . . .': Virginia Woolf's Reviews of the Romantic Poets," Edward A. Hungerford describes the kind of literary history Woolf wrote when she addressed a genre that was not strictly her own medium: poetry. In her critical approach to four great Romantics— Wordsworth, Coleridge, Shelley, and Keats—Woolf eschewed formalist criticism in favor of biographical and anecdotal remarks. While Woolf did have an awareness of aesthetic criteria, she did not make that awareness explicit but rather implied it through nuance and quotation. Hungerford historicizes Woolf's practice of literary historiography by showing how Woolf's own standards of poetic valuation were very much informed by those of her day. Indeed, her very selection of these four poets, whose stature as "great" was established by the first decade of the twentieth century, indicates the way Woolf's opinions were informed by contemporary critical consensus.

Like Hungerford, Cheryl Mares notes that Woolf believed in the greatness of already established masterpieces. In "'The Burning Ground of the Present': Woolf and Her Contemporaries," Mares explains the way Woolf used these masterpieces—and Proust's work as the most vivid realization of an ideal of writing—as touchstones to evaluate contemporary literature. While Woolf questioned authority, she did not ultimately reject it, nor did she refrain from establishing her own authority (even as she attempted to undermine that authority through irony and parody) as she critiqued the work of her contemporaries. Difficult as it was, as Woolf realized, to judge the present, she attempted to be fair and honest as she confronted its "burning ground."

Woolf's relationship to her contemporaries is important to our understanding of Modernist aesthetics. The battle between Woolf and the *Scrutiny* critics is one example; a comparison of Woolf's and T. S. Eliot's publishing history is another. Eliot's publication in and editorship of various little magazines has determined much of our understanding of Modernism. Michael Kaufmann, in "A Modernism of One's Own: Virginia Woolf's *TLS* Reviews and Eliotic Modernism," explains how the various audiences for whom Woolf and Eliot wrote played important roles in determining their literary practices. While Eliot promulgated the new poetry and his brand of Modernism to several hundred readers in such publications as *The Egoist* and the *Little Review*, Woolf spread her views on literature and Modernism in a forum that included tens of thousands of readers. These publication forums affected the way in which each writer conceived of his or her audience. Eliot preached his doctrine as a poet-critic to other poets and critics; Woolf spoke as a reader to other readers, thereby defining Modernism and literature in general as something available to all, not set apart for a selected few.

If there is a quality that distinguishes Woolf as essayist and literary historian, it is her relentless desire to define, explain, and refine our notions of the common reader and the process of reading. The essays in the third section of *Virginia Woolf and the Essay* address how Woolf's common reader and the process of reading separate her from the traditional essayist, critic, and scholar. Consistent with the form of the essay as one that relinquishes the pragmatic for the experiential, Woolf's views are not descriptions of free and idiosyncratic reading responses; Woolf's essays reveal the articulation of a theory of the reader and reading that is somewhat paradoxical in its attempt to codify "moments of being" and the mood the reader experiences when interacting with a text.

Beth Rigel Daugherty's "Readin', Writin', and Revisin': Virginia Woolf's 'How Should One Read a Book?'" compares three versions of Woolf's essay—Hayes Court draft, *Yale Review* version, and the *Common Reader* essay— to show how her notions of the common reader and her reading process changed according to context and audience. Daugherty's paper illustrates the masks Woolf assumes when revising the essay for each particular audience. In this analysis of Woolf's writing process we find the same shifts and changes that occur in the reading experience she describes.

The fluid quality of the reading experience is marked by places of insight, termed "moments of reading" in Karen Schiff's article on Woolf's literary criticism. Schiff shows how Woolf's "moments of being" become critical moments in the reading process, during which a reader gains deeper understanding by reading a text, watching a character experience a moment, or perceiving an author's attempt to create varied experiences for readers. These moments share a keen sense of vitality and life and can open up the vast network of one's own being. These moments are not critical concepts and cannot be pinned down or explained away; they are very much a function of the pleasure of a text.

The pleasure of reading is what Anne E. Fernald explains for us in her study of Woolf's "Phases of Fiction." In "Pleasure and Belief in 'Phases of Fiction,'" Fernald wishes us to understand how the structure of Woolf's essay is based not on an historical analysis of literature but rather on the concept of mood in the reading experience. According to Fernald, Woolf shows her readers the need to move among fictional worlds in which they believe. Woolf constructs a theory of the novel that offers coherent accounts of individual books while always leaving open the possibility for a new form to be conceived. She shows us the value in our varying responses to reading. Woolf's theory of the novel, as Fernald explains it, opens up a passage for a discussion of a theory of the common reader.

Woolf's struggle to define the role of reading and the reader is intimately connected to the way she experimented and revised the genre of the essay. Our section on "Woolf and Genre" contains two pieces, Sally Jacobsen's "Four Stages in Woolf's Idea of Comedy: A Sense of Joviality and Magnanimity" and George Johnson's "A Haunted House: Ghostly Presences in Woolf's Essays and Early Fiction." Jacobsen's article allows us to view Woolf's understanding of a clearly established literary mode, comedy, while Johnson's article revisits the contention between Mr. Bennett and Mrs. Woolf through an analysis of the supernatural influence in Woolf's conception of the Georgian writer.

Sally Jacobsen offers a categorical definition of Woolf's treatment of comedy in her remarks on the genre itself and in her essays on writers who incorporate elements of comedy into their works. Jacobsen notes how Woolf highlights three aspects: joviality, magnanimity, and intersubjective play. As Woolf addresses these qualities of comedy, she also engages in dialogues with other critics and novelists.

George Johnson argues that the language used by Woolf to describe the Georgian writer is the ethereal terminology of the supernatural rather than the language of psychological realism. The supernatural literature of the nineteenth century influenced Woolf's construction of character in fiction. In the end, Woolf's polemics on fiction should be read as ingenious and strategic essays clearing the field of rivals in the psychological and supernatural approaches she embraces rather than as literary history.

The genre of the essay is itself concerned with the openness of form and the relation of the form to experience. The last section of our collection, "The Essay and Feminism," works toward a definition of the feminist essay by looking at the intersection between gender and form. The discussion of the essay's relation to feminism was initiated by Ruth-Ellen Boetcher Joeres in "The Passionate Essay: Radical Feminist Essays," in which she argues that the feminist essay "marks" its identity as feminist in order to distinguish itself from the conventional masculine essay that presents itself as detached and objective. Woolf's essays, according to Joeres, are not radical-feminist because of Woolf's lack of direct communication with her audience through a considerable time, marking herself and her point of departure (156-58). However, the pieces in *Woolf and the Essay* by Lisa Low and Catherine Sandbach-Dahlström confront the way in which Woolf undermines the illusion of objective rhetoric. These authors illustrate that Woolf's essays, though not explicitly feminist in the terms Joeres would call for, question our understanding of knowledge construction.

In "Refusing to Hit Back: Virginia Woolf and the Impersonality Question," Lisa Low rereads the Modernist notion of impersonality, arguing that Woolf's impersonality is not a flight from her feminist impulse but is rather a way of including a democratic impulse in her criticism. There is a difference between Woolf's version of impersonality and those of her male contemporaries. At the same time, as Low writes, Woolf does not identify with an "impersonal" position—by refusing to settle on one notion of personality or impersonality, she manages to maintain the dynamic quality inherent in meaning.

The second essay of the section and the final essay of the collection as a whole is written by Catherine Sandbach-Dahlström, who places Woolf's essays within the tradition of the essay and thereby brings our collection back to the original problem of placing Woolf as an essayist within the history of nonfiction prose. She argues that what Joeres finds detached and objective is really a carnivalesque parody of the qualities that have been traditionally valued. The traditional essay, from Montaigne to Lamb, Hazlitt, Arnold, and Pater, is a conversation about men and addressed to men. Woolf may appear to be appropriating the form of the traditional male essay, but she uses it to critique the male culture of which it is a product while at the same time valorizing the feminine. The endorsement of the feminine and a new use of the essay form emerge from the evocation of the carnival spirit.

As this collection attests, the approaches to Woolf's essays are diverse. Indeed, the range of our selection identifies one of the troubling aspects that arises when one tries to define the genre of the essay itself. The body of Woolf's nonfiction prose brings to the study of the essay a fresh look at the form and uses of the genre. With a serious consideration of Woolf's essays, we can reevaluate not only Woolf's own concern with genre and form but the criteria by which her essays continue to be judged, understood, and enjoyed.

Beth Carole Rosenberg   Jeanne Dubino
University of Nevada, Las Vegas   Plymouth State College,
                                         New Hampshire

Works Cited

Adorno, Theodor. "The Essay as Form." Trans. Bob Hullot-Kentor. *New German Critique* 3.2 (1984): 151-71.

Annan, Noel. *Our Age: English Intellectuals between the World Wars: A Group Portrait.* New York: Random House, 1990.

Bell, Barbara Currier and Carol Ohmann. "Virginia Woolf's Criticism: A Polemical Preface." *Critical Inquiry* 1.2 (1974): 361-71.

Bloom, Harold, ed. *The Art of the Critic: Literary Theory and Criticism from the Greeks to the Present.* 8 vols. New York: Chelsea House, 1989.

Booth, Wayne C. *The Rhetoric of Fiction.* Chicago: U of Chicago P, 1961.

Casey, John. *The Language of Criticism.* London: Methuen, 1966.

Dubino, Jeanne. "Virginia Woolf as a Literary Critic and Her Relation to the Institution of Literary Critical History." Modern Language Association Annual Convention. San Francisco, December 1991.

Fausset, H. I'A. "The Art of Virginia Woolf." Rev. of *The Common Reader.* Majumdar and McLaurin 151-52.

Gardiner, Judith Kegan. "Mind mother: psychoanalysis and feminism." *Making a Difference: Feminist Literary Criticism.* Ed. Gayle Greene and Coppelia Kahn. New York: Methuen, 1985. 113-45.

Goldman, Mark. *The Reader's Art: Virginia Woolf as Literary Critic.* The Hague: Mouton, 1976.

Good, Graham. *The Observing Self: Rediscovering the Essay.* London: Routledge, 1988.

Henderson, Philip. *The Novel of To-day.* Majumdar and McLaurin 351-55.

Howe, Florence. "Introduction: T. S. Eliot, Virginia Woolf, and the Future of 'Tradition.'" *Tradition and the Talents of Women.* Ed. Florence Howe. Urbana: U of Illinois P, 1991. 1-33.

Joeres, Ruth-Ellen Boetcher. "The Passionate Essay: Radical Feminist Essays." *The Politics of the Essay: Feminist Perspectives.* Ed. Ruth-Ellen Boetcher Joeres and Elizabeth Mittman. Bloomington: Indiana UP, 1993.

Lentricchia, Frank. *After the New Criticism.* Chicago: U of Chicago P, 1980.

Lodge, David, ed. *Twentieth Century Literary Criticism.* London: Longman, 1972.

Lewis, Wyndham. "Virginia Woolf"; ch. 5 of *Men Without Art.* Majumdar and McLaurin 330-38.

Lukács, Georg. "On the Nature and Form of the Essay." *Soul and Form.* Trans. Anna Bostock. Cambridge, MA: MIT P, 1974. 1-18.

McCallum, Pamela. *Literature and Method: Towards a Critique of I. A. Richards, T. S. Eliot, and F. R. Leavis.* Dublin: Gill and Macmillan, 1983.

McNees, Eleanor, ed. *Virginia Woolf: Critical Assessments.* 4 vols. Mountfield, East Sussex: Helm Information, 1994.

Majumdar, Robin, and Allen McLaurin, eds. *Virginia Woolf: The Critical Heritage.* London: Routledge, 1975.

Mellown, Muriel. Introduction. *British Literary Magazines.* Ed. Alvin Sullivan. 4 vols. New York: Greenwood P, 1986. 4: xv-xxx.

Moi, Toril. *Sexual/Textual Politics: Feminist Literary Theory.* New York: Methuen, 1985.

Mulhern, Francis. *The Moment of "Scrutiny."* London: Verso, 1979.

Powell, Dilys. "Virginia Woolf." Rev. of *The Common Reader: Second Series.* McNees 2: 93-94.

Robinson, Lillian. *Sex, Class, and Culture.* New York: Methuen, 1978.

Rosenman, Ellen Bayuk. *"A Room of One's Own": Women Writers and the Politics of Creativity.* New York: Twayne, 1995.

Rudikoff, Sonya. "How Many Lovers Had Virginia Woolf?" *Hudson Review* 32.4 (1979-1980): 540-66.

Sackville-West, Vita. Rev. of *A Room of One's Own.* Majumdar and McLaurin 257-58.

Saunders, J. W. *The Profession of English Letters.* London: Routledge and Kegan Paul, 1964.

Sharma, Vijay L. *Virginia Woolf as Literary Critic: A Revaluation.* New Delhi: Arnold-Heineman, 1977.

Shorer, Mark. "Virginia Woolf." Rev. of *The Death of the Moth.* McNees 4: 257-60.

Showalter, Elaine. *A Literature of Their Own.* Princeton: Princeton UP, 1977.

Smith, H. Maynard. Letter. *Times Literary Supplement* 4 Nov. 1920: 720.

Spender, Stephen. Rev. of Wyndham Lewis's *Men Without Art.* Majumdar and McLaurin 338-40.

Sykes, Gerald. "Ex-Modernist." Rev. of *The Common Reader: Second Series.* McNees 2: 97-98.

Thompson, Denys. "Review of *The Common Reader: Second Series.*" McNees 2: 95-96.

"Virginia Woolf and the History of Literary Criticism." Modern Language Association Annual Convention. Toronto, 30 December 1993.

"Virginia Woolf in the Age of Computers and Microform." Modern Language Association Annual Convention. San Diego, 28 December 1994.

Woolf, Virginia. *The Captain's Death Bed and Other Essays.* New York: Harcourt, 1950.

————. *Collected Essays.* Ed. Leonard Woolf. 4 vols. London: Chatto & Windus, 1967.

————. *The Common Reader.* 1925. New York: Harcourt, 1953.

————. *The Death of the Moth and Other Essays.* 1942. New York: Harcourt, 1970.

————. *The Essays of Virginia Woolf.* Ed. Andrew McNeillie. 3 vols. to date. New York: Harcourt, 1986-.

————. *Granite and Rainbow.* 1958. New York: Harcourt, 1975.

————. *Jacob's Room.* 1922. New York: Harcourt, 1950.

————. *The Moment and Other Essays.* 1947. New York: Harcourt, 1948.

————. *A Room of One's Own.* 1929. New York: Harcourt, 1957.

————. *The Second Common Reader.* 1932. New York: Harcourt, 1960.

————. *Three Guineas.* 1938. New York: Harcourt, 1966.

————. *Women and Writing.* Ed. Michèle Barrett. New York: Harcourt, 1979.

Whitley, William T. Letter. *Times Literary Supplement* 14 Aug. 1919: 437.

Notes

1. However, since the latest rounds of General Agreement on Tariff and Trade (GATT) talks were resumed, much of her work has gone back to being under copyright. Until the GATT agreement has been settled, much of Woolf's literary production may be sold but not reprinted.

2. For example, on 14 August 1919, William T. Whitley sent in a previously unpublished fragment of Horace Walpole's writing after Woolf had reviewed an edition of Walpole's letters. H. Maynard Smith pointed out on 4 November 1920 that John Evelyn lived until he was eighty-six, not eighty-four as Woolf had written in a commemorative essay on the publication of a new biography on Evelyn.

3. Reviewers of posthumous collections of Woolf's essays, *The Death of the Moth* (1942), *The Moment* (1947), *The Captain's Death Bed* (1950), and *Granite and Rainbow* (1958), continued to subordinate her essays to her fiction. Mark Shorer proclaims Forster's statement—"It is as a novelist that she will be

judged"—as if it had become a foregone conclusion (McNees 4: 257). See also reviews by Joan Bennett, Eudora Welty, and Vita Sackville-West (McNees 4: 261-71) for similar assessments.

4. By the 1950s, as Noel Annan describes in *Our Age: Portrait of a Generation*, Bloomsbury was effectively discredited, partly as a result of the Leavis's attack that began in the 1930s. In the 1950s, Annan writes, "[t]hose who sat at Leavis's feet began to move into positions of influence" (322), so that by "the seventies hardly a good word was ever spoken of Bloomsbury" (323).

PART I

WOOLF AND HISTORY

Virginia Woolf: From Book Reviewer to Literary Critic, 1904–1918

Jeanne Dubino

At the beginning of 1905, after Woolf had broken into the field of reviewing by publishing her first two reviews, she wrote to Violet Dickinson, "reading makes me intensely happy, and culminates in a fit of writing always" (L 1: 172). From the beginning of her career Woolf established a lifelong connection between reading and writing. Though she undoubtedly enjoyed reading as an end in itself, reading often meant more when there was another end in view (D 2: 259), an end that saw itself in published print. The desire of Woolf to publish is similar to that of her character Orlando, who had been carrying around a manuscript throughout most of the novel:

> The manuscript which reposed above her heart began shuffling and beating as if it were a living thing, and, what was still odder, and showed how fine a sympathy was between them, Orlando, by inclining her head, could make out what it was that it was saying. It wanted to be read. It must be read. It would die in her bosom if it were not read. (O 272)

As if her own words might miscarry, the young Virginia Stephen eagerly and quickly sought to be published.

The major avenue open to her was through book reviewing. For the first fourteen years of her writing career, from 1904 to 1918, Woolf served her apprenticeship in the trade of publishing as a book reviewer. Toward the end of her apprenticeship she began increasingly to take on the role of a critic, a writer who self-consciously both espouses and shapes opinions in a public forum. In the essays written from the time she began to publish her

short fiction in 1917, Woolf began to articulate critical principles that she
would continue to develop over the rest of her life.

The first decade and a half of Woolf's writing career are important for
us to know about if we are to understand the process by which she became
a professional writer and if we are to realize the influences and forces that
shaped her writing career. Woolf's training as a writer enabled her to enter
another world, outside that of her imagination, a public realm in which she
had to conform to editorial control. In exchange for this control over her
authorial freedom, she received much more, earning money, adapting herself
to the discipline required for a professional writer's life, growing in confidence, entering into a community of other writers, learning how to anticipate audience response, and perhaps most important of all, gaining skill and
experience in writing.

Woolf also became more familiar with a wide range of books, a range
that pulled her away from the mostly canonical literature and history with
which she had nourished her imagination. This familiarity helped to make
her essays, as McNeillie writes, "democratic in spirit: uncanonical, inquisi-
tive, open, and unacademic" (E 1: ix). At the beginning of her career she
accepted all the books she was asked to review, including popular fiction,
travelogues, cookbooks. But she was asked to write on more than the
ephemeral; she was also allowed to write thoughtful pieces about writers
who were important to her. By 1918, with the acquisition of the Hogarth
Press the previous year, her growing desire to pursue her fiction, her
established sense of herself as a professional writer, and her improved
economic state, Woolf was not as compelled to continue her reviewing with
the same drive as she had throughout most of her apprenticeship. Having
learned what she could and accrued what benefits she could, Woolf was now
free to pursue her own writing and to write criticism on her own terms.

1904–1909

The first five years of Woolf's career as a journalist, 1904 to 1909, show how
diligently she pursued her family's social connections in order to realize her
dream as a writer. The social and personal dimensions of her connections
persisted even as these dimensions expanded to include the professional.
Part of her goal to be in print was motivated by a desire to make money,
something that would signify her professional status and, at first, grant her
a modicum of self-sufficiency (her income was to grow considerably by the
time she published *Orlando,* which sold more than 20,000 copies within the

first six months of publication). Another part of her goal was to get a response to her writing: "Oh—for some one to tell me whether it is well, very well, or indifferently done" (*PA* 226). Woolf quickly settled into a pattern of writing, a pattern that was to last her the rest of her life. Though she learned strategies to get around what were to her censorious editors, she soon grew frustrated with having to contend with their often hampering and stifling expectations.

Woolf may have grown up in a house that fostered a love of reading and books, and she may have been exposed to literary giants—especially her father Leslie Stephen—who helped to create an atmosphere that inspired learning, but she did not have the benefit of active assistance. Stephen may have regarded his youngest daughter as his literary heir, and to that end he may have directed his discussions of literature to her, but he did nothing practical—such as providing a university education—in the way of ensuring her success at this or any other vocation. Woolf, notably, did not start to publish until after her father's death. The following oft-quoted passage from her 1928 diary indicates her recognition that his life surely would have prevented her literary life from developing:

> Father's birthday. He would have been . . . 96, yes, today; & could have
> been 96, like other people one has known; but mercifully was not. His
> life would have entirely ended mine. What would have happened? No
> writing, no books;—inconceivable. (*D* 3: 208)

If Julia Stephen had lived, she undoubtedly would have thwarted her daughter's career as well, believing as strongly as she did that a woman's place is in the home.

However, in terms of providing help passively, the Stephens were of immeasurable assistance. In addition to fostering a milieu of high culture, they were possessed of family and social connections that gave Woolf the opportunity to meet people who might help her further her quest to become a published writer.[1] The Stephen family was connected in one way or another to the editors[2] of the first three publications for which Woolf wrote: *The Guardian*, the *Cornhill Magazine*, and the *Times Literary Supplement* (*TLS*).[3] Violet Dickinson, who had been friends with Woolf's older stepsister Stella, was Woolf's most intimate friend while she was in her twenties. Through Dickinson Woolf met Margaret Lyttelton, the editor of the Women's Supplement of *The Guardian*. Reginald Smith was the editor of the *Cornhill Magazine*, which Leslie Stephen had edited for the ten years preceding Woolf's birth. In 1902 Leslie was asked to contribute to the just-founded

TLS but was unable to do so because his health was fading. By the time Woolf met Bruce Richmond, the editor of the *TLS*, in 1905, at a dinner party given by some friends of Dickinson's, she had already submitted several pieces for him to read. Woolf continued to socialize with all of these and other editors during her tenure as a writer for their publications.

It is important to note that apart from F. W. Maitland, who was writing a biography of Leslie Stephen and asked Woolf to contribute a piece on her father, none of these other editors sought her out. It was up to the young Virginia Stephen to take advantage of the opportunities her family and social ties afforded her. Her letters and diary reveal how hard she worked at making the most of these connections, and how she maintained these connections on a social level as well as in the professional sphere.

In November 1904 Woolf proposed the idea to Dickinson of writing an essay for Lyttelton. Woolf wrote to Dickinson that she wanted to show Lyttelton the kind of essay she wrote, and continued, "I only want to get some idea as to whether possibly she would like me to write something in the future" (L 1: 154). Woolf did give an article to Dickinson to pass on to Lyttelton. Anxious over Lyttelton's opinion of this piece, Woolf wrote to Dickinson several times to learn what her reaction was. If Lyttelton wouldn't accept it, Woolf wrote, ". . . I must try and get someone to take it" (L 1: 155), possibly, she would later write, the *Cornhill Magazine* or *The National Review* (L 1: 156). Finally, Lyttelton sent Woolf a book to review, W. D. Howells's *The Son of Royal Langbrith*. Woolf did not stop with this piece. She submitted to Lyttelton an unsolicited article on her visit to the Brontës' home Haworth—written, she boasted to Dickinson, in less than two hours (L 1: 158)—and followed that up with an obituary of Shag, the family dog. These two articles presage Woolf's interest in women writers and the playful, mock-serious tone that characterized many of her pieces and culminated in *Orlando*.

Woolf's letters and diary at this time, from the end of 1904 to late spring of the following year, are filled with a mixture of responses: heady excitement, frustration, anticipation, boasting, and, what is possibly more telling, a desire to make money. Indeed, it would almost seem that the desire to make money prevailed over the desire to get published. She wrote to her friend Emma Vaughan in a postscript, "By the way, I am reviewing novels and writing articles for the Guardian and so hope to make a little money—which was our old ambition" (L 1: 160). When Woolf received another book to review, she wrote in her diary, "so that means more work, & cheques ultimately" (PA 219). She did not make much at first, only a few pounds here and there, which she often used to buy treasured items, such as an "extravagant little table" (PA 235) or "that long coveted & resisted coal scuttle, all of beaten brass," about which, she continues, "This was extravagance—So I must write another article" (*PA* 241). No doubt Woolf enjoyed being able to afford these little purchases.

But making money meant more to her than allowing herself to indulge in household items; it also signified that she was a professional, a real writer. It was one thing to practice writing essays for her eye alone; it was another to enter another money-making sphere, an entry required to legitimatize her calling. After all, as she later wrote in *A Room of One's Own*, "Money dignifies what is frivolous if unpaid for" (68). Even in 1905 Woolf was not unaware that she had adopted the "Grub St. point of view" (*PA* 256), an attitude that regarded the writing of articles as a means to an end—namely, the making of money. In line with her newly won professionalism, Woolf also established a pattern of work that was to last her the rest of her life. In her diary entries dating from 9 January to 26 March 1905, she meticulously records her days' schedules. We see how quickly, in her new calling, she settled into a routine, one that involved writing every morning. She was also learning how it can take, as she wrote in February 1905, "as long to rewrite one page, as to write 4 fresh ones" (*PA* 239), and how there were mornings when she faced blocks, when words just wouldn't come (*PA* 250).

After her initiation at *The Guardian*, it seemed as if nothing could stop her. At a tea held in early 1905, Richmond asked her if she would write a review for a number of other magazines. Yes, she eagerly responded. Then he came to the point—would she write a review for the *TLS*? She wrote in her diary, "So I said yes—& thus my work gets established, & I suppose I shall soon have as much as I can do . . ." (*PA* 234). In 1905 Woolf did have as much as she could do: she published thirty-five reviews and articles in *The Guardian* and in the *TLS*, *Academy & Literature*, the *Cornhill Magazine*, and the *National Review*. For the following three years she continued to publish an average of thirty reviews a year, and after a hiatus of several years (brought about, in part, by her mental breakdowns), she continued to average thirty reviews a year for the next six years. Though most of her earliest publications were reviews, she also was able to write some occasional pieces (for example, "Street Music").

With the writing of her articles she encountered not only the joy of being published but also the frustration of being edited, a process that often felt like censorship. The articles she wrote for *The Guardian* are a case in point. On the first occasion, the obituary of the family dog, when Lyttelton asked her "to cut out certain things," Woolf agreed to, going so far as to say, as she wrote Dickinson, "please do, and always alter my things as you like" (*L* 1: 169). But she was not happy with the way Lyttelton had "cobbled" her article

(*L* 1: 172). Such editing, Woolf indicated here, results in laming, crippling. Woolf next experienced Lyttelton's editing of her writing in her first significant critical project, a review of Henry James's *The Golden Bowl*, a book acclaimed as great by nearly all of James's contemporaries. This time, Woolf was not so accommodating of Lyttelton's criticism, as she wrote to Dickinson:

> I spend 5 days of precious time toiling through Henry James' subtleties for Mrs Lyttelton, and write a very hardworking review for her; then come orders to cut out quite half of it—*at once*, as it has to go into next weeks Guardian, and the Parsonesses, I suppose, prefer midwifery, to literature. . . . Really I never read such pedantic commonplace as the Guardianese: it takes up the line of a Governess, and maiden Lady, and high church Parson mixed; how they ever got such a black little goat into their fold, I cant conceive. (*L* 1: 178)

In her failure to appreciate Woolf's writing, Lyttelton has become a parsoness and a prude. Moreover, she does not recognize her young writer's subversiveness. Woolf soon tired of the priggish and religious ideology informing *The Guardian*, and yearned to uncover her real thoughts and feelings, to make her ideas heard loud and clear: "If only I could attack the Church of England!" she exclaimed to Dickinson in July 1905 (*L* 1: 201). Though she was frustrated from the very beginning of her tenure at *The Guardian* with its narrow focus (*L* 1: 214), Woolf was to continue reviewing for it until 1909.

The essays Woolf wrote in 1908 for Reginald Smith, the editor of the *Cornhill Magazine*, show how she had anticipated the editor's scissors and used this anticipation to her advantage. The *Cornhill Magazine* was a family magazine; as such, it toed the line. Having written for *The Guardian*, and having the first essay that she submitted to the *Cornhill Magazine* in late 1904 (or early 1905) rejected by Smith, Woolf knew in 1908 not to write anything too controversial. Nevertheless, though Woolf wrote her essays for the *Cornhill Magazine* under tight stricture, these are among the most playful from the early part of her career and enjoins us to participate in her rather spirited obliquity, as the following explication of "*A Week at the White House*" shows.

In "*A Week in the White House*," a review of a biography of Theodore Roosevelt by William Hale, Woolf includes some metacommentary. When she writes, "no one can be confused, or subtle, or malicious beneath such a torrent of good humour" (*E* 1: 206), she means the opposite, both of Roosevelt and of her own writing. The surface of Woolf's essay is a torrent of good humor, beneath which flow subtlety and sarcasm. Beneath Roosevelt's good humor, Woolf suggests, lie confusion and maliciousness. Woolf wrote to Dickinson about this review, "'The subtlety of the insinuations is so serpentine that no Smith in Europe will see how I jeer the President to derision, seeming to approve the while'" (L 1: 337). Smith must have been very obtuse because the insinuations are not always serpentine, but obvious. Woolf easily belittles by hyperbole and extreme contrasts when she writes, for example, "Dr Hale is surely speaking the truth when he says that if . . . one could get an 'accurate and realistic' picture of the President (or of the dustman, we might add) nothing could exceed the interest of it" (E 1: 204).

As she does in her other essays, Woolf frequently quotes from the book she is reviewing, not to flatter the author but rather to show how inane he can be. In *"A Week at the White House"* Woolf sets a one-sentence citation from the Roosevelt biography apart from her own text. In this particular citation the biographer describes Roosevelt's appearance; "'close-clipped brachycephalous head'" (E 1: 205) hardly shows Roosevelt at his best. Brachycephalous, a term from physiognomy, a pseudo-science in decline by the first part of the twentieth century, suggests dinosaurs and prehistoric beasts. Woolf also includes a clip from Roosevelt's speech, the flavor of which is apparent in the following line: "'Senator, this is a—VERY great pleasure!'" Woolf's commentary on this clip is blatantly sarcastic: "the remarkable point about these greetings is, not only that they are discriminating, but that with all their emphasis they are sincere" (E 1: 206).

Smith's desire that, according to Woolf, she "become a popular lady biographist, safe for—graceful portrait, and such a lady!" (L 1: 356) was disappointed, for she broke with his editorship within a year after she had begun to write for the *Cornhill Magazine*. The instigating factor was his rejection of her short story "Memoirs of a Novelist" in 1909. But as with Lyttelton, events had been leading in that direction. She grew tired of the *Cornhill Magazine*'s proprieties, which would not allow it, for example, to "call a prostitute, or a mistress a mistress" (L 1: 343). And just as Woolf was a black goat among the flock of writers for *The Guardian,* so she perceived herself as a misfit among those whose articles easily fit into the *Cornhill Magazine*. She was well aware of her deliberate posturing at this early stage of her career, as she wrote to her sister: "Of course, I had been posing as an illiterate woman, who had twice as much difficulty in writing an article as other people" (L 1: 360).

Even if anonymity had not been imposed on Woolf, she would have needed to adopt a disguise as a self-protective measure. She also would have needed to shield herself from criticism. When she first wrote articles she frequently sent them to friends. But from her diary entries and letters, we see how she wilted under their criticism and bloomed under their praise. For example, she wrote in February 1905, "How I hate criticism, & what waste it is, because I never take it really" (*PA* 232). She confided to her diary when her brother Thoby told her that he liked her latest note, "Thoby's approval of the Note gives me great pleasure, as I think he meant it, & I am very glad to have made it good" (*PA* 230).

Even as she continued for a time to send articles for preview—and for praise—to her friends, she looked for a mentor in journalism. She found one in Bruce Richmond, the editor of the *TLS*. Richmond and Woolf developed a working relationship that was to last for most of Woolf's writing career. That Richmond resumed his professional relationship with Woolf after her two-year hiatus from 1914 to 1915 (and one might say possibly longer, for she reviewed only a handful of books from 1910 to 1913), and in full measure, for Woolf averaged thirty articles a year for the *TLS* from 1916 to 1920, is another indication of how helpful he could be. On Richmond's retirement in 1938 from the *TLS* she paid high tribute to him: "I learnt a lot of my craft writing for him: how to compress; how to enliven; & also was made to read with a pen & notebook, seriously" (*D* 5: 145).[4]

As she became more established, she reviewed only for the *TLS*. It is important to note here that although Woolf was critical of Lyttelton and Smith for their censorship, they initially allowed her more space than Richmond usually did at first, and it was in the pages of *The Guardian* and the *Cornhill Magazine* that Woolf published her first nonreview essays, or occasional pieces, most of which were unsolicited. Also, Richmond did not give Woolf important books to review when Woolf was starting to review for him; only with a publication like *The Guardian* did she have at the beginning of her career the opportunity to read something as non-ephemeral as James's *The Golden Bowl*. Moreover, most of her early reviews of contemporary fiction for the *TLS* consisted of notices, or one-paragraph write-ups in which she could do little more than give plot summaries.

During their thirty-three-year relationship Woolf recorded social engagements and the frequent correspondence she and Richmond maintained, a record that shows his stature quickly diminishing in her eyes. In 1908, three years after Woolf started to write for the *TLS*, Richmond paid her a visit, one she missed; "however," she wrote to Dickinson, "nothing would alarm me more than to give him tea" (*L* 1: 337). With the years he seemed to shrink literally. Writing again to Dickinson, she described how she met Richmond at a concert the night before: "He has shrunk, and become a lively little old man [Richmond was born in 1871 and was only eleven years older than Woolf;

in 1908, he was thirty-seven years old]—I thought he was younger and bigger" (*L* 1: 372). By 1919 Woolf describes him as if he were a squirrel, "jumping onto a chair to see the traffic over the blind, & chivvying a piece of paper round the room with his feet" (*D* 1: 263). In September 1925 she devoted a paragraph-long diatribe that she entitled "Disillusionment" to savaging Richmond verbally. The conversation she had with him that night "was practically imbecile" (*D* 3: 39). "And to think," she wrote, "that I have ever wasted a thought upon what that goodtempered worldly little grocer thought of my writing!" (*D* 3: 40). By 1935 he has become a "petrified culture-bug" (*L* 5: 453).

The devolving course of Woolf's relationship with Richmond paralleled those with her other editors Lyttelton and Smith, and also, for that matter, Richmond's wife Elena (née Rathbone), a friend from Woolf's childhood. Part of this disintegration had to do with Woolf's tendency to idolize her friends—including Violet Dickinson—only to become disillusioned. Another had to do with the kind of strictures these editors placed on her writing. At the end of 1921, for example, she commented in her diary how restricted she felt in writing, in this case for the *TLS*: ". . . I wonder whether to break off, with an explanation, or to pander, or to go on writing against the current. This last is probably right, but somehow the consciousness of doing that cramps one. One writes stiffly, without spontaneity" (*D* 2: 152). For someone like Woolf, whose career was marked by one consistency—the desire to change, to seek out new forms—this kind of cramping could be deadly. It is no wonder that she would want to break free from writing for editors, to devise "something far less stiff & formal than these Times articles" (*D* 4: 53).

1910–1915

It is not because of her desire to break out of the stiff and formal format of the *TLS* articles, however, that her journalistic output at this time slowed to a trickle over the next five years. In 1909 she received a legacy of £2500 from her aunt Caroline Emilia Stephen, who had wanted her niece to abandon journalism and devote her attention solely to other, more glorious writing pursuits. Stephen's legacy did enable Woolf to devote more time to her fiction, her first love. Fiction was also a form of writing that allowed her far more freedom than journalism, as she wrote to Dickinson as early as 1905: "I am writing for my own pleasure, which is rather a relief after my Guardian drudgery, and I can assail the sanctity of Love and Religion without care for the Parsons morals" (*L* 1: 206).

3

Jeanne Dubino

Another significant reason for this decline has to do with Woolf's personal circumstances. With her marriage to Leonard in 1912, Woolf's life changed dramatically. Though ultimately this marriage did, I think, empower Woolf in her writing—it is notable that she did not publish *The Voyage Out*, her first work of fiction, until after she married—it initially resulted in one of Woolf's severest breakdowns, from which she did not recover until the end of 1915. Woolf had given up her journalism to write her novel, which, as Mepham points out, was not going anywhere, it seemed, even after repeated drafts, and she could not bring herself to publish it. Without even her journalism to sustain her—in 1914 and 1915 records show that she published no reviews at all—Woolf must have felt like a failure. Mepham writes, "With hindsight it is perhaps difficult for us to realise that her permanent failure was a very serious possibility. It seemed quite likely that she would never become an author. In fact, it was not at all clear that she would even survive" (35).

1916–1918

But survive she did. The sign of her returning health was the resumption of her literary journalism. When Woolf started to review again, it was, over the next few years, solely for the *TLS*. Table 1.1 shows a somewhat significant difference between the kind of reviews that she wrote at this period and those she wrote during the first five years of her apprenticeship.

The table is not meant to be comprehensive. These numbers, for example, do not include the forty-four essays that, according to McNeillie, as reported to John Mepham (20), have been discovered since the publication of his edition. Most of these forty-four were published in 1907. Moreover, the Virginia Woolf Special Issue of the Spring 1992 *Modern Fiction Studies* printed some newly found essays. Nor is this table meant to be exact. Some of the books included under the category of Life-writings could also fit under that of Classics, and vice versa. For example, Woolf reviewed biographies on and letters by authors such as Whitman, Rossetti, and Boswell, and in the course of her review she might also discuss their works. If it appeared that she devoted as much or more attention to their texts, then I included that review under the category of Classics. From 1916 to 1918 she reviewed collections of essays, many of which were combined reflections upon literature and life. When they veered more toward the life end of the pendulum, then I included them under Non-literary-critical essays. Moreover, the line dividing Contemporary popular from Contemporary impor-

Table 1.1

KINDS OF ESSAYS PUBLISHED	NUMBER OF ESSAYS PUBLISHED		
	1904-1909	1910-1913	1916-1918
Life-writing (biographies, autobiographies, letters, memoirs, journals, diaries)	37	6	12
Contemporary popular writers (e.g., romantic)	28	0	10
Contemporary important popular writers (e.g., James and Conrad)	7	1	8
Foreign popular fiction (especially Russian writers, who were becoming popular in England)	0	2	6
Classics (Woolf often wrote commemorative essays when new editions appeared, on, for example, Austen and Brontë)	5	1	9
Literary-critical essays and books	3	0	15
Non-literary-critical essays and literature (including travelogues, social and personal histories, reflections on a place, children's, and even a cookbook)	9	1	19
Contemporary poetry	0	0	10
Contemporary drama	0	0	1
Occasional pieces (Woolf's own essays, not reviews)	10	0	2
Obituaries	2	0	1
TOTAL	101	11	93

Source: The Essays of Virginia Woolf, ed. Andrew McNeillie.

tant popular is problematic at best. The slippery adjective "important" is based on how seriously these authors were taken by the high literary establishment at the time. Henry James clearly was; A. Cunnick Inchbold was not, having published only one other fictional work before she published the novel that Woolf reviewed in 1905. My decision to put the novel by Marjorie Bowen, who had received critical acclaim from other reviewers and whose novel had quickly gone into a second edition soon after the time that Woolf reviewed her *The Glen o' Weeping* (*E* 1: 138-39), under Contemporary Popular is in part determined by Woolf's own evaluation that it belonged in this category rather than the other.

Rather than being comprehensive or exact, this table is meant to give a flavor of the kinds of books that Woolf reviewed so that we can better understand the shape of her early career. Beginning in 1916, we see that Woolf was given a wider range of books to read. Her critical acumen could grow in having the opportunity to review many other kinds of works besides life-writings and prose fiction and nonfiction. It may be surprising to many Woolf critics that she had at this time reviewed at least ten books of and about poetry, so steeped is she in prose, even if that prose took on poetic dimensions. More significantly for her criticism, we see how she read many books of collections of literary critical essays, a form that was clearly in vogue at the time, and most likely planted the seed of an idea in her to compile her own collections in the two volumes of *The Common Reader*, the first volume of which was published in her twentieth year as a reviewer. The collections she reviewed were written by popularizers of classical literature, figures such as Sir Walter Raleigh, J. C. Squire, Arnold Bennett, Alice Meynell, and the then-popular American critic J. E. Spingarn. Woolf also reviewed critical studies of authors, such as Eliza Haywood and Henry James. As a reviewer, Woolf's literary taste could broaden to encompass foreign writers, namely the great Russian triumvirate Chekhov, Tolstoy, and especially Dostoyevsky, all of whose works were currently being translated into English.

Woolf did not have the power to select the specific books she wanted to review, but as early as 1908 she let it be known what kind of books she preferred to review, as she wrote to Dickinson: "I have refused to review any more novels for the Times; and they send me Philosophy" (*L* 1: 331). Apart from reviewing E. M. Forster's *A Room with a View*, from the fall of 1907 to 1916 Woolf had stopped reviewing novels for the *TLS*. She was not exactly, however, reviewing philosophy, but rather, in 1908 and 1909, mostly life-writings; out of the twenty-seven books she reviewed for the *TLS*, seventeen were some form of life-writing. From the kinds of works of fiction that we see Woolf reviewed, it is apparent that at this point in her career she had not quite reached the tastemaker stage. The reputations of the "important" writers—James, Conrad, Galsworthy, Wells—were already established; as a reviewer she was in a position to maintain the status quo and function as a cheerleader. Her own reviews of the popular writers reveal that almost all were, to put it mildly, far from groundbreaking. Indeed, it is amusing to think of the young Virginia Stephen reading a conventional romance, the plot of which sounds little different from today's Harlequins.

It is interesting to read what Woolf wrote, with self-prescience, in a 1906 review: "It is no disparagement to the author to say that we find his volumes of greater interest as a revelation of his point of view than as a criticism of the subjects which he professes to treat" (*E* 1: 83). One consistency that emerges from reading Woolf's reviews in chronological order is, as McNeillie also notes (*E* 1: xv), her growing tendency to focus less on the text and more on expressing her own viewpoints. In her early reviews Woolf carefully describes the plot and outline of the text; later, she feels freer to pay them shorter shrift.

To gain an even clearer sense of the changes in style and emphasis that took place during Woolf's apprenticeship as a reviewer, it is helpful to look more closely at one set of reviews, one that dates to an early period in her career and the other to a later stage. Both reviews— "The Genius of Boswell" (1909) and "Papers on Pepys" (1918)—treat life-writing. In "The Genius of Boswell" Woolf is reviewing a collection of letters by Boswell that had been discovered decades after Boswell's death. Her tone is respectful. Woolf devotes the first long paragraph, or a fourth of the review, to narrating a history—which, as she describes it, is clearly an "adventurous" one, for they were first found as sheets wrapped around a parcel in Boulogne—of the letters and the editors under whose hands they have passed. That is, she foregrounds the physical text itself. We then move from its history to that of Boswell's. Addressed to a college friend, these letters reveal Boswell, as Woolf portrays him, to be a man of many contradictions: self-obsessed yet largely sympathetic and understanding; exuberant toward life but unable to settle down to any one project. This review shows Woolf to be insightful, particularly in her awareness that the true artist, like Boswell, knows to leave "out much that other people put in" and in her understanding that one's strong point may also, as in Boswell's case, be one's undoing. Moreover Woolf even at this early stage is well aware of effective rhetorical strategies. She prefaces her own discussion by referring to what other authorities have said, and then offers her own commentary, which serves in part to supplant if not undermine those whose evaluation could not, as she proclaimed with almost self-acknowledged false modesty, be surpassed: "When a man has had the eyes of Carlyle and Macaulay fixed upon him it may well seem that there is nothing fresh to be said." After we read this review we easily conclude that, yes, there is something more to be added to Carlyle's conclusive summation that Boswell is "'an ill-assorted, glaring mixture of the highest and the lowest'" (E 1: 249).

In "Papers on Pepys" Woolf does not ever bother to cite authorities nor, for that matter, does she even get around to describing the text under consideration—a collection of papers by the Pepys Club—until the end of her review. Rather than referring to an illustrious authority as Carlyle, Woolf instead focuses on the reader. Great must be the number of people "who read themselves at night with Pepys and awake at day with Pepys," but far greater the number who do not read Pepys at all. To that end, the Pepys Club has been formed, as Woolf writes, "to convert the heathen." The tone immediately becomes a recognizably Woolfian one: mock-serious and playful. She takes the desire of the Pepys Club to have the public treat Pepys with respect, and she sends it in orbit: "Lack of respect for Pepys," she writes, "seems to us a heresy which is beyond argument, and deserving of punishment . . ." (E 2: 233). At this point, rather than turning to the arguments presented by the Pepys Club, as she might have if she had written this review nine years ago, Woolf highlights her *own* reasons why Pepys deserves to be read. According to Woolf, Pepys wrote his diary out of a desire to create for himself a private self that his public self as a civil servant and administrator could not accommodate. In his diary he confides not only affairs of state but also his personal weaknesses, weaknesses that continue to draw contemporary readers to him. In his self-consciousness Pepys reveals himself to be a modern, but in his record of the life around him he also shows himself to be a product of his seventeenth-century climate. It is this mixture of the new and the old that will make his diary, while not ranking in the highest echelons of the literary canon, persist in its appeal to readers. Only at the end of this review, when Woolf refers to one of the papers that elaborates on how, if Pepys had only had a pair of reading glasses, he would have continued the diary for the remaining thirty years of his life, does she specifically attend to the text. And then, she refers to this particular paper in an effort to show the tragedy of Pepys's life: in losing the opportunity to write in his diary, Pepys lost "the store house of his most private self . . ." (236). In conclusion, this contrast of an early review to a later one is representative of the way Woolf undermines authorities, takes on the position of the underdog, emphasizes the reader, demonstrates her interest in the private self, and adopts a mock-serious and playful tone while at the same time making her criticism less covert and more explicit.

Woolf's review of "Papers on Pepys" appeared as her first foray into experimental fiction, the short story "The Mark on the Wall." It was because she sought more time to write fiction that she wanted to reduce her reviewing. Even as Woolf had been "writ[ing] articles without end" (*L* 2: 391), even as she had never "been so pressed with reviewing" (*D* 1: 308), "get[ting] 2 or even 3 books weekly from the Times, & thus breast[ing] one short choppy wave after another" (*D* 1: 224), she never lost the desire to write fiction. Before the end of her second decade as a reviewer, she was expressing this desire more frequently and regarding her reviewing as an obstacle. It got in the way of the writing of *Night and Day* and *Jacob's Room*. She confided to her diary, "my private aim is to drop my reviewing . . ." (2: 34). By 1920 she had worked up the nerve to break the review habit, which, as the following quote shows, had become a destructive addiction rather than an empowering discipline; she wrote in August 1920, "[I] feel like a drunkard who has successfully resisted three invitations to drink" (*D* 2: 58). By the next month she was dictating her own conditions: "only leading articles, or those I suggest myself" (*D* 2: 63). Woolf wanted to review initially to prove herself a professional writer. By the end of the second decade of the twentieth century, she clearly had.

Works Cited

Mepham, John. *Virginia Woolf: A Literary Life.* New York: St. Martin's, 1991.

Woolf, Virginia. *The Diary of Virginia Woolf.* Ed. Anne Olivier Bell and Andrew McNeillie. 5 vols. New York: Harcourt, 1977-1984.

———. *The Essays of Virginia Woolf.* Ed. Andrew McNeillie. 3 vols. to date. New York: Harcourt, 1986-.

———. *The Letters of Virginia Woolf.* Ed. Nigel Nicolson and Joanne Trautmann. 6 vols. New York: Harcourt, 1975-1980.

———. *Orlando.* 1928. New York: Harcourt, 1956.

———. *A Passionate Apprentice: The Early Journals 1897-1909.* Ed. Mitchell A. Leaska. New York: Harcourt, 1990.

———. *A Room of One's Own.* 1929. New York: Harcourt, 1957.

Notes

1. From the beginning of her career Woolf also reviewed books written by people who were connected to her family, such as *A Dark Lantern* by Elizabeth Robins in 1905.

2. Woolf also published an essay, "Street Music," in the *National Review*, edited by Leo Maxse, whose marriage to Kitty Lushington was engineered by Julia Stephen. "Street Music" was the only piece Woolf contributed to this review, though, as she wrote to Dickinson in 1907, Leo Maxse had written to her that he was "'constantly trying to think of subjects what [sic] would be likely to appeal to you and is open to any suggestions" (*L* 1: 309).

3. See also McNeillie's introductions to the first two volumes of his edition of the collected essays. Using essentially the same periodizations, he also traces the early history of Woolf's essay writing. But where McNeillie emphasizes the variety and kinds of essays Woolf wrote at this time, I focus here on the nature of her relationships with her editors and the efforts she made to get her material published.

4. Richmond not only supported her journalism. He made sure that the review of *Jacob's Room* appeared when it would get the most publicity, on Thursday, the day on which the *TLS* was out, rather than on Friday, the day on which it was published (*D* 2: 207). Richmond was supportive about giving Woolf release time from reviewing so that she could write *Mrs. Dalloway*, Woolf wrote in her diary, ". . . Richmond rather touch[ed] me by saying that he gives way to my novel with all the will in the world" (*D* 2: 312).

Colonizing Virginia Woolf: Scrutiny and Contemporary Cultural Views

Eleanor McNees

Rival stories about literature derive from alternative positions that are finally political, and the quarrel between them is about who is to define and dominate that cultural apparatus.

—Sinfield 30

In her late essay "Reviewing," Virginia Woolf laments the proliferation of book reviews and sarcastically proposes the "Gutter and Stamp system" whereby a "competent official" called The Gutter "will write out a short statement of the book; extract the plot . . . ; choose a few verses . . . ; quote a few anecdotes," and "The Taster" will signify approval with an asterisk, disapproval with a dagger stamped at the end of the Gutter's statement (*CE* 2: 209). In view of the hundreds of reviews of her own novels and essays by 1939, Woolf, herself a prolific reviewer for the *Times Literary Supplement* (*TLS*), *The Nation and Athenaeum* and other British and American journals, appears unusually defensive. Yet she bases her suggestion on the assumption that reviews, often containing opposite opinions of a work, have begun to cancel each other out and have consequently lost their effectiveness. They no longer persuade readers to buy books:

> Sixty reviewers at once assure [the reader] that it is a masterpiece—
> and worthless. The clash of contradictory opinions cancel each other
> out. The reader suspends judgment; waits for an opportunity of seeing
> the book himself; very probably forgets all about it, and keeps his seven
> and sixpence in his pocket. (*CE* 2: 207)

A survey of the two decades of reviews of Woolf's own writings as they appeared and of the five decades of criticism since her death tends to support Woolf's charge of mutual cancellation. The early reviewers, spear-headed by the Edwardians Arnold Bennett and E. M. Forster, aligned themselves quite evenly either on the "dagger" or on the "asterisk" side. The "dagger-stampers," represented by Bennett and abetted by Forster, criticized Woolf for subordinating character to stylistic cleverness, a complaint that was to be echoed by the *Scrutiny* critics of the 1930s and 1940s and later by the British Marxist critics of the 1950s and 1960s. The "asterisks," led by Desmond MacCarthy and Basil De Selincourt, praised her technique and paved the way for the later, more sophisticated appreciations of Auerbach and Guiguet. Occasionally, especially in the reviews of *To the Lighthouse,* writers like Conrad Aiken tried to bridge the gulf between subject and style (later metamorphosed into a debate between ethics and aesthetics) and thus to heal a division in Woolf studies that has persisted to this day.

If the early reviewers of Woolf's work tended to cancel each other out, subsequent critics have followed suit. Although she severely criticized the critic's profession, especially that of the academic critic, Woolf also respected and feared the critic's verdict. As critical essays began to treat her work retrospectively, she complained in "An Essay in Criticism" about the prospective reader's inability to assess a novel independently:

> He begins to think that critics, because they call themselves so, must be right. He begins to suppose that something actually happens to a book when it has been praised or denounced in print. He begins to doubt and conceal his own sensitive, hesitating apprehensions when they conflict with the critics' decrees. (CE 2: 252)

In retaliation, Woolf published her two *Common Readers,* essays that hover somewhere between reviews and criticism, variously termed "literary essays" (Kronenberger 385), "impressionistic criticism" (Goldman 275; Madison 64; Yaseen 190), and "heuristic" writing (Bishop 574). Few critics of Woolf, however, have adopted the congenial method of her *Common Reader* essays. Rather they have tended to make authoritative pronouncements about the merits or demerits of Woolf's writing and have thus justified Woolf's fear. Bullying the reader has become a popular pursuit. Discussing the conflict between Bloomsbury and the Leavises, Noel Annan questions the anti-Arnoldian trend of twentieth-century criticism when he notes, "The person-ality of the critic and the strength of character that comes through his prose are of equal force in persuading his readers to accept what must, inevitably, be assertions. And, the more powerful the assertions, the more likely the risk of distortion" (37).

Sinfield moves beyond Annan's (and Woolf's) focus on the individual critic's bias to discuss the critical and cultural hegemony of the formerly dominant "idealist" critics who believe that literature rises above "social and political concerns and other such mundane matters" (27). Sinfield aligns himself with the "materialist position" that insists on literature as cultural production. Following Raymond Williams, he argues that any story is political because it tells "a story about the world, and therefore it has a politics" (30). But Sinfield's definition of politics appears to be the flip side of Arnold's definition of culture: the former seeks to subject literature to context and readership; the latter attempts to elevate literature above such time-bound concerns. In both cases then, literary criticism has a specific mission: to raise human consciousness. And in both cases, critics are the prophets who guide the public toward a better world. For Arnold, that world consists (somewhat vaguely) of the best ideas of the time, which the critic and the poet-novelist have promised to identify for the public. For Sinfield (and Williams) the world contains conflicting sets of ideas that can be divided into dominant, subordinate, and radical (34). The materialist critic's duty is to expose the radical position and to oppose the dominant culture that has denied voice to other ideas. As Sinfield admits, here we return to the old conservative/liberal debate:

> When a part of our world view threatens disruption by manifestly failing to cohere with the rest, then we must reorganize and retell its story again and again, trying to get it into shape—back into the old shape if we are conservative-minded, or into a new shape we can develop and apply if we are more adventurous. (37)

Perhaps the primary disagreement between the conservative and "more adventurous" elements Sinfield identifies here is the belief in absolute value. While Arnold laments the waning of consensus as to what constitutes value, he is hopeful that literature and criticism can cooperate to restore or at least redefine value in an increasingly mechanistic and materialistic world. Sinfield and contemporary cultural critics, and indeed many post–World War I writers, see the old Victorian and Edwardian definitions of value as elitist and socially bankrupt. Arnold, and later Eliot, offered culture as a substitute for this lost consensus of value. The Leavises, living in a world that, according to them, had lost sense of literary value, followed Arnold in their attempt to enlighten the debased public and to restore an intellectual culture. As Raymond Williams notes, "The process which Arnold began, when he virtually equated "culture" with "criticism," is completed by Leavis, and had been similarly completed a little earlier, by I. A. Richards" (254). And according to Williams, Leavis faces an even more massive resistance to culture or to the educated mind than Arnold did. While Arnold was confronted with the effects of industrialism, Leavis had to contend with the new mass media—advertising, film, popular press—that threatened the maintenance of all literary standards. Like Arnold, Leavis opposed culture to mass civilization and followed Arnold in his endeavor to elevate criticism to a position of social and cultural authority. This authority Leavis located in the university. The critic's goal then was to combat the leveling effect of civilization with academic culture. Although the Leavises viewed themselves as rebels against dominant institutions—the government and the media—they exhibited an academic elitism that has been the target of much cultural criticism of the past two decades.

According to Tony Inglis, in his recently translated essay, "Virginia Woolf and English Culture," the Leavises and their followers throughout the 1950s are guilty of a typically English tendency toward "positivist ethicizing," a position that stems from an abhorrence of modernism and its tendency toward disintegration as opposed to cohesiveness (qtd. in Bowlby 55). Inglis blames the critical and cultural reaction to Modernism among English literary critics for a too-facile dismissal of Woolf's works. Experiment, as in the Post–Impressionist Exhibition of 1910, becomes either a willful rebellion against traditional standards or an equally culpable withdrawal from current aesthetic expectations. As Chris Baldick suggests, *Scrutiny* strove to dictate the appropriate combination between experiment and tradition in literature: "*Scrutiny*, then, is to take upon itself the preservation of linguistic health. . . . To carry out this task, it must avoid any taking of sides in the phony war of abstractions waged between different political movements" (173). By the politically charged 1930s the *Scrutiny* critics railed against Virginia Woolf's work as elitist; Q. D. Leavis accused it of being "insulated by class" ("Caterpillars" 203), while F. R. Leavis said it expressed a "lack of moral interest" ("After *To the Lighthouse*" 297). This accusation of Woolf's (and Bloomsbury's) elitism, still alive in England today in the essays of, among others, John Bayley and John Carey, has for some time been challenged by an American group, a subset of cultural critics we might term postcolonialists or anti-imperialists. Jane Marcus, Alex Zwerdling, Kathy J. Phillips, and the contributors to the Spring 1992 issue of *Modern Fiction Studies* and to Mark Hussey's edited collection *Virginia Woolf and War* all rescue Woolf's work from the tirades of *Scrutiny* and *The London Review of Books*, but in doing so they risk distorting Woolf's texts by transforming them into politically correct icons of the 1990s. The collection of essays, *Virginia Woolf,* edited by Rachel Bowlby, offers a more measured response while still making a significant case for cultural reevaluation.

In light of the cultural criticism of the 1990s it seems now instructive to recall how the *Scrutiny* critics of the 1930s, headed, of course, by the Leavises, rejected Virginia Woolf for being a highbrow, an elitist, an author who, according to F. R. Leavis, had no "interest in the world 'out there'" ("After *To the Lighthouse*" 297) and who, according to Muriel Bradbrook, subordinated ideas to an "extraordinary fineness and delicacy of perception" (156). Like the cultural critics of the 1980s and 1990s, the Leavises argued for a connection between criticism and culture, although their definitions of criticism and culture were more Arnoldian than postcolonial.

Lamenting the lack of scholarly criticism that allowed best-sellers to thrive indiscriminately, F. R. Leavis founded *Scrutiny* in 1932 at Cambridge University to offer the public a new set of literary (and by implication cultural) standards. In his "Manifesto" in the first issue, he announces that *Scrutiny* will be "a review. . . that combines criticism of literature with criticism of extra-literary activities" (*Scrutiny* 1.1: 1). And a decade later in his editorial "After Ten Years," he credits the journal with helping to provide anxious readers "a humane consciousness; a centre where, faced with the specializations and distractions in which human ends lose themselves, intelligence, bringing to bear a mature sense of values, should apply itself to the problems of civilization" (327). Leavis proceeds to reevaluate literature from a largely Arnoldian perspective. He admires Arnold's touchstones—lines of great classics that for Leavis remind "us vividly of what the best is like" ("Revaluations" 328). Not surprisingly, measured against classically mimetic theories of the novel, Leavis finds Virginia Woolf wanting. Woolf, Eliot, and Joyce impress "only . . . a very small specialised public and are beyond the reach of the vast majority of those who consider themselves educated" (*Continuity* 38-39). But more subtly, Leavis finds in Woolf no affirmation of those values *Scrutiny* has vowed to uphold. The vast majority of "educated" readers have, according to Leavis, no standards by which to judge new works. Literature has ceased to fulfill its moral and social function. Either it has retreated to the hermetic aestheticism Leavis finds in Woolf and Joyce, or it caters to the lowest common denominator in the form of an outrageous thirst after sensation—a charge Wordsworth had leveled against the reading public as early as his *Preface to Lyrical Ballads* in 1800. Leavis intends *Scrutiny* to provide these missing standards and in so doing to narrow the gap between the effete author and the indiscriminate reader.

Contemporary cultural critics, uneasy with Leavis's application of Eurocentric moral values and ethical standards to literary criticism, maintain

that such universal interpretations assert a false hegemony since all interpretation is inevitably based on culture and class. Thus, for example, the
Leavisite search for a balance between form and content becomes a middle-
class demand for a consensus that seeks to suppress disruptive voices within
a text. Furthermore, the Leavises' tendency to locate culture within the
academy presupposes a hierarchical stance and ignores the population who,
for economic and other reasons, do not belong to that academy. These
cultural critics of the 1980s and 1990s seek to reverse *Scrutiny*'s verdict on
Virginia Woolf's writing. The ironic introspection of Woolf's characters,
their fragmented thoughts, and the dispersed narrative voices all appear as
covert responses to the social and political dilemmas Woolf diagnoses more
straightforwardly in *Three Guineas*. In an essay on Virginia Woolf in *Classics
in Cultural Criticism*, Irmgard Maassen admits that Woolf employs "indirect
stylistic devices like irony or imagery to open attack when she aims at
debunking patriarchal power structures" (260). But Maassen goes on, like
Sinfield, to equate the aesthetic with the political in Woolf's writings. Hence
Maassen can identify "the power of the father," the patriarch against whom
Woolf struggles, with "the patriarch who denies the woman creative talent,
and the ruler over the world of letters and signs who interferes with her own
vision and style" (270). Maassen, however, ignores Woolf's distinction
between the aims of the novel and those of the essay or treatise. She judges
the novels from the feminist and political perspectives expressed in *A Room
of One's Own* and *Three Guineas* respectively.

Contemporary cultural critics have chosen to interpret Woolf's novels
as subversive postcolonial texts in which patriarchy and imperialism are
synonymous. The mature novels of Woolf's middle period—*Mrs. Dalloway,
To the Lighthouse,* and *The Waves*—have received close and persistent attention
from postcolonialist critics. *The Waves,* in particular, has undergone a critical
metamorphosis from early accusations of its detached aestheticism to recent
defenses of its political irony. It is helpful to return briefly to the literary and
political climate of 1930s Europe to understand this discrepancy in critical
views.

The 1930s, Virginia Woolf's last full decade of life (she was in her
fifties), saw not only the founding in 1932 of *Scrutiny* in England but also the
rise of postwar fascism in Europe. In her assessment of the new British writers
of the 1930s, "The Leaning Tower," Woolf quite succinctly addresses the
conflict between politics and aesthetics:

> There was communism in one country; in another fascism. The whole
> of civilization, of society, was changing. There was, it is true, neither

war nor revolution in England itself. All those writers had time to write many books before 1939. But even in England towers that were built of gold and stucco were no longer steady towers. They were leaning towers. The books were written under the influence of change, under the threat of war. (*CE* 2: 170)

Woolf suggests that the poems of Auden, Isherwood, Spender, Mac-Niece, and Day-Lewis were too tied to the political and cultural climate to qualify as true works of art.

F. R. Leavis concurs with Woolf when he defends the humanist critic against the Marxist: "There is, then, a point of view above classes; there can be intellectual, aesthetic and moral activity that is not merely an expression of class origin and economic circumstances; there is a 'human culture' to be aimed at that must be achieved by cultivating a certain autonomy of the human spirit" (*Continuity* 9). Leavis deplores the "levelling-down" of criticism and of novel reading among the public. He shares Woolf's distaste for Arnold Bennett and the promulgation of the best-seller through book clubs and circulating libraries. Given their tacit hostility toward a largely anti-intel-lectual, philistine society, why were Woolf and the Leavises at loggerheads throughout the 1930s? In his essay "Bloomsbury and the Leavises," Noel Annan fails to answer this question. Instead he accuses the Leavises of falling prey to conspiracy theory, of believing that Bloomsbury artists and writers were trying to promulgate cultural elitism. Against this presumed elitism Annan blames the Leavises for erecting their own narrow cultural program which was no more viable than that of the Bloomsbury set.

A more plausible reason for the opposition between Woolf and the Leavises, one only briefly mentioned by Annan, is their disparity in class and education. The class distinction—Woolf from the upper middle class, Leavis from the lower middle class—partially accounts for the latter's relegation of Woolf to exclusive highbrow status. On Woolf's part, one senses from her random comments in her letters and diaries on *Scrutiny*, and specifically on Q. D. Leavis, an alternately defensive and condescending attitude. She writes to Ethel Smyth after Q. D. Leavis's attack on *Three Guineas* in *Scrutiny*, that she has received "a drubbing and a scourging from the Cambridge ladies—the professors of Eng. lit," and she goes on to gloat, "I thought I should raise their hackles—poor old strumpets" (*L* 6: 270). In her diary for 1 September 1938, she refers to the review as personal, "about Queenie's own grievances and retorts to my snubs" (*D* 5: 165). And prior to Q. D. Leavis's review of *Three Guineas*, Woolf calls *Scrutiny* a "prigs [sic] manual. All they can do is to schoolmaster" (*D* 165). While the Leavises were, in the

British caste system of the 1930s, socially inferior to Woolf, they had considerably more formal education than she had. They taught at a university Woolf herself was unable to attend, one with which the entire male side of her family was closely connected. *A Room of One's Own,* a compilation of lectures delivered at two women's colleges (Girton and Newnham) at Cambridge, highlights Woolf's hostility to the men's colleges at Oxford and Cambridge. Q. D. Leavis's comment in her review of *Three Guineas* that she herself is "a member of a class of educated women Mrs. Woolf has apparently never heard of" ("Caterpillars" 204) emphasizes Woolf's ambivalent and often openly antagonistic attitude toward university-educated women. Instead, Woolf pointedly refers to herself as an "educated man's daughter," choosing ironically to subordinate her status to that of her father.

The extraliterary reasons that separate Virginia Woolf from the Leavises are largely overlooked by contemporary cultural critics eager to claim Woolf as a political radical. We now are urged to assume that Woolf was a not-so-covert rebel against what Diana Laurenson calls the gentry class (156) and that while lacking a university education, she was probably far more educated in terms of book culture than we are today. Yet perusal of her essay "Middlebrow" (not published in Woolf's lifetime), an unpublished letter to the editor of the *New Statesman,* as well as "Three Characters," first published in *Adam International Review* in 1972, considerably complicates the appropriation of Woolf by contemporary cultural critics. While Woolf reserves her bitterest invective for the middlebrow who is preoccupied with money and status, she exhibits a characteristically English intellectual attitude toward the lowbrow. She praises the lowbrow for his or her vitality, the highbrow for his or her mind. This body-mind opposition recurs throughout her novelistic depiction of the lower and upper classes and suggests an envious but proprietary stance toward the lower class. A lowbrow denotes "a man or a woman of thoroughbred vitality who rides his body in pursuit of a living at a gallop across life" (*CE* 2: 197).[1] Alternatively, the highbrow with whom she wholeheartedly identifies "is the man or woman of thoroughbred intelligence who rides his mind at a gallop across country in pursuit of an idea" (*CE* 2: 196).

In "Three Characters," Woolf elaborates this distinction in cultural and historical terms. Here the lowbrow is "the rock upon which the state is founded" (24) yet is "inarticulate, gross and in many ways obscene and grossly uncivilised" (24). Woolf acknowledges the dependence of the highbrow on the lowbrow and concedes the highbrow's physical ineptness. Again she posits the dichotomy between mind and body in a value-laden analogy: "He [the high brow] works his head as hard as they work their hands." Yet the highbrow is also a hero in a way that neither the lowbrow nor the middlebrow can ever be: "He is a pioneer and uses his mind as an ice axe to shiver and crack the thick stones of ignorance and superstition" (25). In this essay the middlebrow becomes the broadbrow, the Bradshavian advocate of proportion and a target for Woolf's most severe criticism: "And of all persuasions the most contemptible and most unsuccessful and most parasitic and best paid in all the state is the broad brow. And him I most despise and wish to live precisely as he does live, in his Queen Anne villa for ever and ever" (26). Although she narrows Woolf's categories to literary types, Q. D. Leavis defends the highbrow against the best-seller (her version of the lowbrow) and the middlebrow. She accuses the reading public of thirsting after sensation and identification and blames them for their inability to read the highbrow novels of Woolf, Joyce, Lawrence, and Powys.

Leavis's partial defense of Woolf's highbrow status reflects a constant division in Woolf criticism prior to 1980 between praise for Woolf's experimental and elegant style and condemnation of her antirealist tendencies.[2] Woolf herself was aware of this division; she worried about her refusal to merge political and aesthetic concerns in her novels, yet she defends her preference for the aesthetic in a series of letters to Vita Sackville-West's son, Ben Nicolson. She calls her novel public "a little private circle of exquisite and cultivated people" (*L* 6: 420) and asks on the eve of World War II, "ought artists now to become politicians? My instinct says no; but I'm not sure that I can justify my instinct. I take refuge in the fact that I've received so little from society that I owe it very little." She defends this choice in a comparison of her own writing with that of the Romantic poets: "They didn't have anything like the influence they should have had upon 19th century politics. And so we drifted into imperialism and all the other horrors that led to 1914. Would they have had more influence if they had taken an active part in politics? Or would they only have written worse poetry?" (*L* 6: 421). That politics and political agendas contaminate art the Bloomsbury artists and writers agreed. It seems then that a principal difficulty in evaluating Woolf's work from a postcolonial position arises from Woolf's own enunciation of her highbrow and antipolitical precepts in relation to novel writing. Nevertheless, if one surveys the trend in recent Woolf studies one cannot ignore the impact of cultural criticism or postcolonial criticism on Woolf's work. Discussions of *Mrs. Dalloway* from Alex Zwerdling's 1985 essay "Mrs. Dalloway and the Social System" to Reginald Abbott's "What Miss Kilman's Petticoat Means: Virginia Woolf, Shopping, and Spectacle" in *Modern Fiction Studies* insist on the ways the novel undermines the social and political codes of post–World War I England. Though the essays vary in plausibility and accuracy, two—Alex Zwerdling's and Jeremy Tambling's—by placing the novel in a specific historical and social context, help readers to appreciate the tension between Woolf's aesthetic and political goals. This tension, I would argue, is greatest in *Mrs. Dalloway* and progressively less relevant in *To the Lighthouse* and *The Waves*.

Alex Zwerdling's study of Woolf's critique of the dying English aristocracy wisely refuses to simplify Woolf's attitude toward the political and social climate of post–World War I England. He notes that Woolf "works by indirection, subterraneously undermining the officially accepted code, mocking, suggesting, calling into question, rather than asserting, advocating, bearing witness" (132). Zwerdling places Mrs. Dalloway midway between the characters who represent the Establishment and those who are its victims. Occupying this middle ground, Clarissa Dalloway offers both a critique and a reinforcement of the British class system. Zwerdling argues that because of the interior monologue narration (we are largely within Clarissa's consciousness) the reader is forced to sympathize with Mrs. Dalloway and thus cannot be completely critical of her as the wife of Conservative MP Richard Dalloway. But Mrs. Dalloway's interior monologue seems to have a further function in the novel. It tends to override, indeed to overwhelm the public and social life of London. We are far more interested in Mrs. Dalloway's past, in even her most insignificant musings, than we are in the political and social situation of London in 1923. John Mepham notes Woolf's tendency in all her novels, but especially in *Mrs. Dalloway*, "to aesthetisise experience . . . as if no experience could be significant for her unless, as in one of her 'moments of being,' it could be conceived as opening up a vision of ultimate reality" (31). This aestheticization (hostile critics might say anesthetization) of experience was continuously ridiculed by the *Scrutiny* critics, especially by W. H. Mellers in his review of *The Years* and F. R. Leavis in his review of *Between the Acts*. For the *Scrutiny* writers, Woolf's emphasis on aesthetics precludes any focus on ethics. They fault Woolf's characters for being solipsistically concerned with their own thoughts and for lacking a social conscience that would impel them to act.

Of the recent cultural-critical readings of *Mrs. Dalloway*, Jeremy Tambling's 1989 essay, "Repression in *Mrs. Dalloway's* London," is the most historically specific and the most persuasive. Tambling discusses the newly erected empire-affirming military statues in front of which the novel's characters pause throughout their London walks. He sees a "London studded with statues of its nineteenth-century war heroes" (140) as Woolf's way of critiquing "[e]mpire and the war, taking the state as the embodiment of patriarchal power" (138). He believes these statues—and indeed in West-minster one sees them at nearly every turn—represent an ideology against which Mrs. Dalloway secretly rebels. The most obvious landmark, the one that constantly interrupts Clarissa's and Septimus's reveries, is, of course, Big Ben, but Tambling moves well beyond that over-determined symbol to many of the lesser-known statues and memorials, all of which celebrate Britain's imperialist past. As she moves toward the store on Bond Street to buy flowers, Clarissa dissociates herself from these outward symbols of Britain's imperial and military strength. She repeatedly reverts to memories of the pastoral prewar Bourton. Her reveries alienate her from her surround-ings and specifically from modern-day London.

In *Virginia Woolf Against Empire*, entirely devoted to a postcolonial interpretation of Woolf's novels, Kathy Phillips represents a highly political and socially critical Virginia Woolf at the opposite extreme from the Leavises' portrait of Woolf as an aesthetic elitist. Phillips's interpretation of *Mrs. Dalloway*, unlike that of Zwerdling or Tambling, allows for no textual or thematic complexity as it aims to reduce all the characters to representa-tives of a deadened post–World War I British society. Disagreeing with both Zwerdling and Tambling that Clarissa stands in contrast to her "set," Phillips views the novel as forcefully criticizing British imperialist tactics at home and abroad. Instead of focusing on Clarissa, Phillips presents society as "the main character of *Mrs. Dalloway*, with individuals serving as the microcosms of the cultural macrocosm" (5). In this reading Clarissa and her old friend Peter Walsh—a British civil servant recently returned from India—represent a rigid and ultimately vacuous social system in which wives of MPs play hostess to prime ministers, and retired civil servants long for the status they held as Englishmen in the nonwhite colonies.

Postcolonial and cultural-critical readings of *To the Lighthouse*, rarer than ones of *Mrs. Dalloway*, are also more problematic. These readings concur in viewing Mr. Ramsay as the colonialist-patriarch but vary in their assessments of how explicit Woolf's critique of empire really is. Among these, most balanced because most historically researched, is Gillian Beer's "The Island and the Aeroplane: The Case of Virginia Woolf." Here Beer traces Britain's literary preoccupation with the island story as far back as Shakespeare's *Richard II*. While she sees *Between the Acts* as Woolf's final elegy for England's island sanctity, Beer argues that *To the Lighthouse* prophesies the end of the insular British mentality. Significant for Beer in this verdict is the ending of *To the Lighthouse* with the arrival at the smallest island, the rock on which the lighthouse sits. Interestingly, Mrs. Ramsay, an upholder of the old order and civilization and, by implication, of Britain's imperialist past, dies before the journey is completed. Following this reading, and remembering Mrs. Ramsay's connection with the eye or the third stroke of light from the lighthouse, one could see the final boat journey as the surviving Ramsays' last attempt to control a world rapidly slipping away from British domination. Like Tambling, Beer uses a historically specific invention, here the aeroplane, to document Woolf's Modernist aesthetics. By *Between the Acts* the aeroplane has come to represent a complete dispersal of point of view, a loss of single-narrator authority. It has made Britain prone to invasion and has irrevocably destroyed the idea of the island as a little world. Beer's essay wisely links Modernism with historical and political events to justify Woolf's move away from plot and point-of-view-centered narrative. Stipulating the connections between the Modernist aesthetic and the new political atmosphere of post–World War I England, Beer successfully bridges the debate between aesthetics and politics without loosely equating the two.

In a more radical reading, "The Work at the Center of *To the Lighthouse*," Mary Lou Emery presents a Bakhtinian analysis of the cleaning ladies in the "Time Passes" section. In the essay, the "work" is that of Mrs. McNab and Mrs. Bast who lurch through the abandoned house, preparing it for the Ramsays' return. Emery sees Mrs. McNab's inarticulate language as "the 'mumblings' of a counter-discourse" that counterpoints the language of the surrounding two sections. Implausibly, Emery asks if the female outsiders, Lily Briscoe and Mrs. McNab, can (like Clarissa and the old woman in the window opposite) ever bridge their class differences to forge a creative alliance through their work. Though she concludes they cannot, that Lily's vision is finally achieved at the expense of Mrs. McNab's work, making the house again inhabitable so that the Ramsays and their friends may return, Emery still sees Mrs. McNab as a female conduit between the maternal and domestic Mrs. Ramsay and the potentially frigid but now androgynous Lily. It is hard to believe in view of her own descriptions of highbrow and lowbrow that Virginia Woolf intended this symbolic role for Mrs. McNab. The language Woolf uses in her essays to describe the lowbrow fits exactly with her brief description of Mrs. McNab lurching through the empty house. The physicality of the weather and the factual insertion in brackets of the deaths in the "Time Passes" section, together with Mrs. McNab's housecleaning role, support Woolf's description of the lowbrow as predominantly vital and physical as opposed to mental or philosophical. In Woolf's essay, "Three Characters," "She—for he is also she—lights the earliest fires in the land; is up when the mist lies thick upon the fields, lays the breakfast, washes up the crocks, sees the children off to school, is brought to bed between breakfast and dinner of another; is up and about in nine days; goes charring; lurches unsteadily, sits over baskets of carnations in Piccadilly, was once a servant in the house of a peer . . . grows to a great size; has wrinkles in her skin like the cracks of some species of melon . . ." (24).

Woolf clearly distinguishes here between intellectual and physical ability. She never equates these in her work. They continue to define class through her last novel, *Between the Acts*. Most importantly, what separates the charwomen from their female employers and their guests is language. The latter group with whom Virginia Woolf identifies is able to define and thus dominate the other group because of a superior linguistic and grammatical knowledge, a knowledge gained from being heirs of an educated class. The words and accent of this latter class (all "educated men's daughters") create an abyss than can be crossed only if the groups remain silent. Woolf's portraits of these women figure her relation to them. She silences them behind her own dominant and intellectual discourse, a discourse of which, she implies, they are incapable. That work could unite Lily and Mrs. McNab is therefore unlikely unless they could discover a common language. (And here it should be noted that Woolf's "common reader" does not include the common people, the Mrs. McNabs of the world.)

Those cultural critics who admit the ambivalence of Virginia Woolf's role as a writer and as a woman of the upper-middle-class intelligentsia offer the sagest readings of Woolf's novels. They refuse to allow the polemical critical voice to debunk the artistic one, nor do they use the artistic voice to support, however subversively, the political. In a balanced reading of *To the Lighthouse*, Jeanette McVicker, like Zwerdling, insists that Woolf's critique is always indirect and often ambivalent. She instances Mr. Ramsay's frequent citation of fragments from Tennyson's "Charge of the Light Brigade" as evidence of the former's imperialist patriarchal tendencies, but she cautions against viewing Woolf herself as a cultural critic in her own novels: "Woolf's intense aesthetic commitment to the modern and to the redeeming function of art in society were in direct conflict with her impulse to expose and critique the ideology of empire. Thus, for all the sociopolitical awareness in her work, the unified vision so prevalent in modernist art takes priority" (42).

As Jane Marcus states, there have been very few postcolonial readings of *The Waves*, a novel generally thought to represent Woolf's furthest aesthetic reach and thus regarded mainly from a stylistic point of view. Marcus seeks to dislodge apolitical discussions of *The Waves* by reading it as the "submerged mind of empire" (136) or as a western narrative enclosed and critiqued by an eastern one. Marcus specifically accuses F. R. Leavis and Raymond Williams for failing to appreciate Woolf's socialist critique of empire. Marcus aims to resurrect Woolf for contemporary American women from diverse classes. Like Beer's view of *Between the Acts* as an elegy for island insularity, Marcus reads *The Waves* as an elegy for imperialism with Percival's and Bernard's deaths designating final swan songs of the British empire. In Marcus's version, one can read *The Waves* as a "postcolonial carnivalesque" (144) in which Percival, the British colonial imperialist, dies as a result of an almost comic fall from a donkey. Though Marcus's reading is purposely provocative, it is also often reductive as, for instance, in its penchant for such metaphorically definitive statements as, "The body of her text, *The Waves*, is like the corpse of the literary canon, the mausoleum of white male English culture" (154).

In reaction to Marcus's essay, Patrick McGee blames her for presenting a too simplistic equation of Bernard with the white patriarchy. McGee, like McVicker on *To the Lighthouse* and Tambling on *Mrs. Dalloway*, argues for a more complex reading of *The Waves* where indeterminate form combines with indeterminate characters to undermine the traditionally author-centered text. Thus he sees Woolf caught between a desire to criticize imperialism through both form and character and a recognition that she herself is part of that critique. For McGee, ambivalence, an essentially modern characteristic, rules *The Waves*.

Marcus calls her reading "the rescue of the text" and addresses it to "those deeply indoctrinated by the Leavisite legacy of a mythical 'Virginia Woolf,' created to stand for that elite, effete English culture against which the democratic Great Tradition strenuously struggled" (139). Yet that elite, effete aroma of Woolf is still with us in the troubling discrepancy between her public (and published during her lifetime) writings and her private diaries and letters. It is this discrepancy that Hermione Lee addressed at a Virginia Woolf conference at Oxford in the autumn of 1992. Lee concedes that there appear to be at least two Virginia Woolfs: the Bloomsbury snob and the socialist feminist. Lee contrasts Woolf's self-censorship in her fiction with the self-expression in her diaries and letters and concludes that she was torn between her allegiance to and dependence on her upper-middle-class background and her desire to know and by knowing to share the inside lives of other classes.

In her essay, "Virginia Woolf on the Outside Looking Down: Reflections on the Class of Women," Mary Childers addresses the same dichotomy that worries Lee—the snob versus the socialist. Childers suggests that Woolf's emphasis on inner vision marks her as an upper-middle-class writer who has the leisure time to speculate on states of mind. Such a writer is not confined by the practical exigencies of simply earning enough money to survive. Childers argues

This is precisely where Virginia Woolf maintains her class's dominance—through the advocacy of certain forms of consciousness that are largely dependent upon access to ample leisure time inhabited with at least the illusion of self-awareness. Woolf is not defending what the establishment of her time considered their class interests; she is defending the interestingness of her class in order to protect the interest of her subject matter. (76-77)

Childer's criticism of Virginia Woolf's elitism returns us to the harsher dismay of the *Scrutiny* critics and especially to Queenie Leavis's charge that Woolf could only understand and write for "the five-hundred-a-year-by-right-of-birth-as-daughters-of-the-ruling-classes women" ("Caterpillars" 211). Yet Childers, unlike the *Scrutiny* critics, clearly admires Woolf's writing and even appears to respect the political and aesthetic contradictions in her works. Far from dismissing her, Childers calls for a renewed appreciation of the "multivocality" of Woolf's writing and for an openness to the "political contradictions of her texts" (71).

For decades, literary critics have sought either to eliminate Woolf from the critical map or to chart one territory with perfectly clear borders. The borders have been under siege now for over twenty years since the rise of feminist criticism in the 1970s and cultural criticism in the 1980s and 1990s. Has the time finally come to allow for the partition and contradiction without critical and class warfare? If we resist ambivalence and ambiguity, believing, like the *Scrutiny* writers and many contemporary cultural critics, that aesthetic emphasis necessarily excludes ethical action, we reduce Woolf's novels either to beautiful but irrelevant designs or to didactic political position papers. Woolf would have resisted both stances.

Works Cited

Annan, Noel. "Bloomsbury and the Leavises." *Virginia Woolf and Bloomsbury: A Centenary Celebration.* Ed. Jane Marcus. Bloomington: Indiana UP, 1987. 23-38.

Baldick, Chris. *The Social Mission of English Criticism 1848-1932.* Oxford: Clarendon P, 1983.

Beer, Gillian. "The Island and the Aeroplane: The Case of Virginia Woolf." *Virginia Woolf.* Ed. Rachel Bowlby. London: Longman, 1992. 132-61.

Bishop, Edward L. "Metaphor and the Subversive Process of Virginia Woolf's Essays." *Style* 21.4 (1987): 573-88.

Bloom, Harold, and Lionel Trilling, eds. *Romantic Poetry and Prose.* New York: Oxford
    UP, 1973.
Bradbrook, Muriel. "Notes on the Style of Mrs. Woolf." *Scrutiny* 1.2 (1932): 152-57.
Carey, John. *The Intellectuals and the Masses: Pride and Prejudice Among the Literary Intelligentsia
    1880-1939.* London: Faber and Faber, 1992.
Childers, Mary M. "Virginia Woolf on the Outside Looking Down: Reflections on
    the Class of Women." *Modern Fiction Studies* 38.1 (1992): 61-79.
Dollimore, Jonathan, and Alan Sinfield. "Introduction." *Poetry, Language and Politics.*
    Ed. John Barrell. Manchester: Manchester UP, 1988.
Emery, Mary Lou. "'Robbed of Meaning': The Work at the Center of *To the Lighthouse.*"
    Modern Fiction Studies 38.1 (1992): 217-34.
Goldman, Mark. "Virginia Woolf and the Critic as Reader." *PMLA* 80 (1965): 275-84.
Inglis, Tony. "Virginia Woolf and the English Culture." *Virginia Woolf.* Ed. Rachel
    Bowlby. London: Longman, 1992. 46-61.
Kronenberger, Louis. "Virginia Woolf as Critic." *The Nation* 17 Oct. 1942, 382-85.
Laurenson, Diana, ed. *The Sociology of Literature.* London: MacGibbon and Kee, 1971-
    72.
Leavis, F. R. "After Ten Years." *Scrutiny* 10.4 (1942): 326-28.
———. "After *To the Lighthouse.*" *Scrutiny* 10.3 (1942): 295-98.
———. *For Continuity.* Cambridge: Minority P, 1933.
———. "A Retrospect of a Decade." *Scrutiny* 9.1 (1940): 70-72.
———. "Revaluations XI: Arnold as Critic." *Scrutiny* 7.3 (1938): 319-32.
———. "*Scrutiny:* A Manifesto." *Scrutiny* 1.1 (1932): 1-7.
Leavis, Q. D. "Caterpillars of the Commonwealth Unite!" *Scrutiny* 7.2 (1938): 203-14.
———. *Fiction and the Reading Public.* London: Chatto & Windus, 1939.
Lee, Hermione. "Virginia Woolf and Offence." Unpublished conference paper at the
    Virginia Woolf: Women and Writing Conference. Hertford College,
    Oxford. 26 Sept. 1992.
Maassen, Irmgard. "Virginia Woolf." *Classics in Cultural Criticism.* Ed. Bernd-Peter Lang.
    Vol. 1. Frankfurt: Peter Lang, 1990. 245-79.
Madison, Elizabeth C. "The Common Reader and Critical Method in Virginia
    Woolf's Essays." *Journal of Aesthetic Education* 15 (1981): 61-73.
Marcus, Jane. "Britannia Rules *The Waves.*" *Decolonizing Tradition: The Cultural Politics of
    Modern Literary Canons.* Ed. Karen Lawrence. Urbana: U of Illinois P, 1991.
    136-62.
McGee, Patrick. "The Politics of Modernist Form; Or, Who Rules *The Waves?*" *Modern
    Fiction Studies* 38.3 (1992): 631-50.
McVicker, Jeanette. "Vast Nets of Chinese Boxes, or Getting from Q to R: Critiquing
    Empire in 'Kew Gardens' and *To the Lighthouse.*" *Virginia Woolf Miscellanies:*

Proceedings of the First Annual Conference on Virginia Woolf. Ed. Mark Hussey and Vara Neverow-Turk. New York: Pace UP, 1992. 40-42.

Mellers, W. H. "Mrs. Woolf and Life." *Scrutiny* 6.1 (1937): 71-75.

Mepham, John. *Virginia Woolf: A Literary Life.* New York: St. Martin's, 1992.

Phillips, Kathy J. *Virginia Woolf Against Empire.* Knoxville: U of Tennessee P, 1994.

Sinfield, Alan. *Literature, Politics and Culture in Postwar Britain.* Oxford: Basil Blackwell, 1989.

Tambling, Jeremy. "Repression in Mrs. Dalloway's London." *Essays in Criticism* 39.2 (1989): 137-55.

Williams, Raymond. *Culture and Society: Coleridge to Orwell.* 1958. London: Hogarth P, 1993.

Woolf, Virginia. *Collected Essays.* Ed. Leonard Woolf. 4 vols. London: Harcourt, 1966.

———. *The Diary of Virginia Woolf.* Ed. Anne Olivier Bell and Andrew McNeillie. 5 vols. London: Harcourt, 1977-1984.

———. *The Letters of Virginia Woolf.* Ed. Nigel Nicolson and Joanne Trautmann. 6 vols. London: Harcourt, 1975-1980.

———. *Mrs. Dalloway.* London: Harcourt, 1925.

———. "Three Characters." *Adam International Review* nos. 364-366 (1972): 24-26.

Yaseen, Mohammad. "Virginia Woolf's Theory of Fiction." *Aligarth Journal of English Studies* 7.2 (1982): 179-91.

Zwerdling, Alex. "The Common Reader, the Coterie and the Audience of One." *Virginia Woolf Miscellanies: Proceedings of the First Annual Conference on Virginia Woolf.* New York: Pace UP, 1992. 8-9.

———. "Mrs. Dalloway and the Social System." *Critical Essays on Virginia Woolf.* Ed. Morris Beja. Boston: G. K. Hall, 1985. 131-51.

Notes

1. In his study of the attitude of the intellectuals toward the masses, John Carey finds Virginia Woolf thoroughly on the side of the former. He instances Woolf's poeticizing of the masses through the beggar woman's song in *Mrs. Dalloway* as a means of eliminating the reality of the unsavory lower social classes (36-37).

2. In his survey of criticism on Virginia Woolf, John Mepham supports this division when he notes, "By and large . . . the consensus view was that Woolf was not interested in the external world. She did not aim either to depict or, through her writing, to reform, the world of social and political relations and institutions" (25). Mepham goes on to criticize American feminists who claim

Woolf as a socialist or a Marxist on the basis of her Labor Party allegiance. He argues that Americans in general are ignorant of "that complex and exasperating nightmare, the British class system" (29).

Virginia Woolf and the Varieties of Historicist Experience

Melba Cuddy-Keane

The allusion in my title is to William James, whose radical pluralistic approach to religion, *The Varieties of Religious Experience,* was published in 1902. I take James as my starting point, not to posit an influence on Woolf's approach to history but to situate my discussion of Woolf in the context of Modernism and to engage in particular the characteristic turn during this period away from linear teleological definition to explorations of multiple states.[1] *The Varieties of Religious Experience* marks a significant node in the history of religion, shifting discussion from the question of transcendent origin to a focus on experiential contents. In traditional theological discourse, the questions at issue concerned the existence and nature of God and the ethical framework for human action proceeding from such belief. Shifting to a psychological discourse, James focused instead on the physiological and psychological symptoms that he identified as commonly recurring features in records and descriptions of religious experiences. Comparative and inclusive in its approach, James's analysis went beyond accounts of mystical apprehensions of God to include such diverse phenomena as moments of oneness with Nature, hallucinatory visions, automatic writing, and even states of consciousness produced by intoxicants and anesthetics such as alcohol and chloroform. But despite the heretical nature of this approach, James presented his analysis not as a rejection of religion but as a transformation and reconfiguration of the way it was conceived. In rewriting theology as psychology, James preserved the idea of the supernatural by relocating it in the observable realm of human nature—in an unexplored aspect of the mind that he termed the religious consciousness.

The comparative, pluralist approach taken by James was itself part of a massive cultural shift in thinking—evidenced in another area, for example, by Sir James Frazer's comparative anthropological studies in *The Golden Bough*.[2] But James's study is perhaps the more relevant intertext here, since his focus on the varied modes of religious consciousness offers a particularly striking Modernist analogue to Virginia Woolf's multiple versionings of history. In similar fashion, Woolf, I propose, locates her study of history in various states of consciousness, delineating a variety of historicist experience that, to use James's words, reveals "no one essence" but "many characters" (26). And just as James redefines the supernatural by locating it in "A Study of *Human* Nature" [his subtitle, my italics], so Woolf transposes history from a metaphysical explanatory narrative to an exploration of multiple human states—the different and varied ways in which we experience history in our reading.

In a manner thus very similar to James, Woolf's pluralistic and experiential approach marks a radical departure from dominant nineteenth-century views that, in the words of Peter Allan Dale, increasingly construed history, like religion, as a source of "intelligible design and purpose" (5). In his overview, Dale posits that history developed along two distinguishable paths: the theistic strain, in which history elucidates a revelation of providential design, and the positivist strain, in which history illustrates the laws of social development. Yet both approaches, he argues, are characterized by evolutionary or teleological assumptions. More fundamentally, the basic premise underlying traditional history, as Gertrude Himmelfarb states, is that "the natural mode of historical writing is essentially narrative" with the corollary that such narrative is, by definition, chronological (1). Furthermore, as Peter Burke states, "According to the traditional paradigm, History is objective" and "[t]he historian's task is to give readers the facts" (5). While the idea of cultural relativity might come into play in assessing the relation of one age to another, there is little sense of the possible relativity of all knowledge, including that of the historian. Finally, the traditional approach to history can be characterized as "monumental," since its patterns are constructed from certain privileged moments—if biographical history, in the great lives of great men; if political and constitutional history, in the public arena of laws, wars, and treaties. The same general assumptions were as pervasive in the growing body of literary histories as they were in the more established genre of political history. Surveying the history of early English literary historiography, Wellek and Warren identify two main groups: works that present loosely chronological biographical portraitures or appreciations and those that use literature as "mere document for the illustration of national or social history" (252). While in their view neither group adequately manages to be both literary and historical, we can see nevertheless how both participate in traditional historical thinking. The first group supports the monumental approach to history by inscribing, as a series of peaks, the canonized works of major figures, whereas the second reinforces the idea of history as chronological linear pattern, most usually one of development, progress, and evolution.

In numerous ways, Woolf's writings subvert these modes of traditional history—a history she describes in "'Modes and Manners of the Nineteenth Century'" as invented by "gentlemen in tall hats in the Forties who wished to dignify mankind" (*E* 1: 331). Woolf's verbal cartoon deftly mocks the ideologies of class and gender encoded in her cultural inheritance, and she continually directs attention to the silent or silenced voices that an inclusive history must be attuned to hear. In "The War from the Street," for example, she praises a book that presents the common man's view because it helps to supply what has been left out of "historians' histories" (*E* 3: 3); then finding herself still unrepresented by this particular common *man's* view, she goes further to argue that there is yet another occluded history—presumably that of the common *woman*—whose voice has yet to be heard. Exposing the need to question assumptions of historical closure, Woolf foregrounds the difference between "history as it is written" and "history as it is lived." But while it is not uncommon for Woolf to be this explicit about the inadequacy of existing histories, it is her actual historical practice that most effectively overturns the prevailing historiographical assumptions. The significance that she accords to unpublished and noncanonical works; her hybrid conflation of literary, social, and economic history; her focus on historical questions rather than on historical patterns; and perhaps most importantly, her situating of literary judgments in terms of an historical text and an historical reader—all contribute to a sense of history that is various, multiple, dynamic, and complexly interrelational. For Woolf does more than direct attention to the lacunae in existing history; by foregrounding her own thinking as a historicized fallible reader, she avoids any suggestion that she is supplying historical closure herself.

Within a broad generalized framework, it is therefore easy to locate Woolf as a radical Modernist whose break with traditional historicism parallels her significant break with traditional narrative form. And this particular construction of Woolf makes it similarly easy to see her interest in multiple alternative histories as foreshadowing the historiographical concerns of our own time. Discussing the predicament of history today, historian Modris Eksteins writes, "Perhaps, after all the horrors spawned by ideological rigidity in our century, the prospect of a variety of histories, as opposed to a single history, is to be celebrated, not denigrated," and, "We must accept a variety of histories, but we must also accept variety within our history" (279). In their overview to *New Historical Literary Study*, Jeffrey Cox and Larry Reynolds similarly argue that a predominant feature of New Historicist criticism is that it "rejects the idea of 'History' as a directly accessible, unitary past, and substitutes for it the conception of 'histories,' an ongoing series of human constructions, each representing the past at particular present moments for particular present purposes" (4). Janet Levarie Smarr, in her introduction to *Historical Criticism and the Challenge of Theory*, likewise emphasizes current resistance to the single historical model, referring to Frank Lentricchia's criticism of "a history which would deny histories" (17n7), Stephen Greenblatt's rejection of a "single master discourse" (3), and Hayden White's delineations of the various metanarratives that underlie the prevailing constructions of the past (4). Furthermore, like Woolf's historicism, the current suspicion of monolinear narrative precipitates not an abandoning of history but rather a shift to limited and multiple articulations: the writing of history today, as Dominick LaCapra suggests, more commonly seeks "[p]articular studies that simultaneously provide 'local knowledge' and suggest tentative generalizations on the basis of concrete cases— in contrast to massive and massively reductive surveys, as well as [to] hermetically sealed monographs" (7).

Thus situated, Woolf's pluralistic approach to history appears extremely relevant to historicist thinking today. At the same time, as an historically situated reader myself, I need to consider the alternative possibility that this reading of Woolf is largely a projection of late twentieth-century desire. Despite my opening gesture of locating Woolf in the context of Modernism, I run the risk of constructing Woolf's historical approach as the embryo of the present—reading her too much, that is, through the lens of what historicist thinking is later to become and thus inscribing her not in her time but rather before (ahead of) her time, that is, in our time. At this point, however, a contemporary nontotalizing historicism can be invoked, perhaps somewhat ironically, as a way of avoiding an evolutionary reading that culminates in the present moment. The complexities of relations are such that Woolf was arguably both behind and in advance of our current state of historical affairs. On the one hand, we can agree that Woolf's ideas anticipate the concerns of contemporary theory without in any way suggesting that she possessed a poststructuralist theoretical sophistication. On the other hand, despite the prevalence now of theoretical arguments for destabilized and multiple histories, practicing historians still do little to prevent the continued predominance of totalizing and comprehensive history. It is not unreasonable to claim that Woolf was more daring in her practice than most historical writers today. And finally, I suggest that it may be less problematic to identify our contemporary concerns in Woolf's writing than to fail to recognize the long history of unease with traditional practice that lies behind those concerns. To construct the past as only distinct from the present is to practice selective forgetting; monolithic constructions of any era reflect a reliance on partial evidence.

It is therefore important, in our own telling of history, to recognize the heterogeneity of the past. My opening narrative of the Victorian/ Modernist break needs thus to be complicated by acknowledging a diversity within nineteenth-century historiography that challenged its own hegemonic practice. For nineteenth-century historical writing includes numerous examples of the strain of adhering to the prevailing models and the gradual emergence of new and various modes of historical thinking. It includes, for example, Carlyle's defense—*pace* his focus on heroes and hero-worship—of the history of common life and his comparative practice of juxtaposing moments in the past to the present. It includes the challenge to individualist, patriarchal history in the work of the Cambridge myth-ritualists and Jane Harrison who, despite her use of the Darwinian evolutionary model, posited an earlier antithetical origin in a communal, possibly maternal, society. And it includes—although in *Three Guineas* Woolf takes him to task for his masculinist bias—Macaulay's extension of English history into such aspects of daily life as eating and drinking, the culture of coffeehouses, the state of the roads, the romance of highwaymen, and the importance to newspapers of the post.[3] Then, in considering Woolf's more personal inheritance, we need to acknowledge as well the radical elements in the work of Leslie Stephen. For despite the evolutionary and Darwinian frameworks that characterize Stephen's writing and the decidedly non-self-reflexive nature of his prose, many of his *ideas* anticipate dialogic and pluralistic modes. Stephen himself suggested, for instance, that his intention was to connect literary history with "religious, political, social, and economical changes" and thus to foster a different conception of history as "a very complex tissue" made up of intersecting strands (31). And though in large part he attempted to use the "spirit" of each age to trace an evolutionary social and intellectual development, he also argued for the importance of relative and contextual judgments, proposing that each literary form "has its own rules, right under certain conditions and appropriate within the given sphere" (5). I do not suggest that Stephen reflected on his own analysis as relative to a positioned observer or that he eschewed

metanarratives.[4] Nor do I mean to posit a continuous underground coun-
tertradition that develops from the nineteenth century to poststructural-
ism. My point is simply that the nineteenth century was itself a
heterogeneous time and that some diversity of historiographical approach
was already available to Woolf in the legacy of her past.

Then, turning again to the Modernist period, we must add that Woolf's
era was itself heterogeneous, so that her writing must be located diversely
as "like" some Modernist strands and "unlike" others. Woolf's approach to
history contrasts strikingly, for example, with the systematizing and totalizing patterns that, according to Paul Costello, mark the dominant trend in
the works of twentieth-century world historians or macrohistorians such as
Henry Adams, Oswald Spengler, and H. G. Wells. Referring to such
globalizing systems as "metahistory" (after Christopher Dawson) or "mythis-
tory" (after William McNeill), Costello argues that, responding to the crisis
of Modernism and the loss of faith in nineteenth-century notions of
progress, the macrohistorians developed models of world history in an
"attempt to grasp the pattern of the past as a unity" and "to reanimate a
meaningful myth of history" (4, 21). Although tending toward cyclical rather
than linear patterns, such systems—like those too of W. B. Yeats—evidence
the strong propensity within the Modernist period toward overarching
historical narratives and universal explanations.

At the same time, however, other historicist approaches within the
Modernist period emphasized, as did Woolf, the subjectivity and perspec-
tivism at the root of historical knowledge. Woolf's approach has much in
common, for example, with the theory of history that R. G. Collingwood
developed throughout the twenties and thirties, culminating in his posthumous *The Idea of History* in 1946. For Collingwood, each historian sees history
from a discrete point of view and history itself exists as a "space of
perspectives" around a continually shifting and ultimately unknowable
center (54-55). But for Collingwood, as for Woolf, the impossibility of
possessing complete historical evidence and achieving a final and finite
understanding does not leave us simply with subjective idealism—unless,
as he notes in a strongly Woolfian passage, "it is subjective idealism to
maintain that a hundred people looking at the same tree all see different
aspects of it, each seeing something hidden from the rest." Furthermore,
sharing with Woolf a dynamic model of historiography, Collingwood
posits that the meaning of existing historical evidence at any given time
lies in its significance for the historian's own particular present, with the
implication that history must be continually rewritten for different generations and for different cultures (138-39).

In addition, another approach contemporaneous to Woolf paralleled her interest in the recording of ordinary life, in a line of historiography leading forward to more recent practices of microhistory and the history of the everyday. In 1924, for example, Eileen Power's *Medieval People* invoked Carlyle's injunction that history tell "[h]ow men lived and had their being" and proceeded, perhaps more with the sensibilities of George Eliot, to reconstruct imaginatively the lives of six medieval figures, five of whom represented "the obscure lives and activities of the great mass of humanity" (19, 18). In his 1927 essay "The Pageant of History," Leonard Woolf cited Power's book as part of the new history of the common man but then argued that instead of presenting, as Power did, the daily detail of how ordinary people lived, history should seek out what went on in their heads, and should turn for this purpose to "[c]ontemporary accounts of events, old letters, and ancient diaries" (134). An increasing interest in eyewitness accounts can be seen in the Mass Observation project, founded by Tom Harrison and others in 1937, to study "the everyday lives of people in Britain." The project used two distinct methods: "A team of paid investigators recorded people's behavior and conversation in a variety of public situations" and "a panel of volunteer observers around the country kept diaries and responded to monthly questionnaires" ("Mass Observation"). In terms of historical synchronicity, Virginia Woolf's essay "Lives of the Obscure" appeared in January of the year in which Power's book probing the "obscure lives" of medieval people was published. In 1937, Kingsley Martin asked Woolf to review *May 12th: Mass-Observation Day Surveys*, a work that recorded the opinions and responses of ordinary people on the Coronation Day of George VI. Although Woolf declined because she was completely submerged in *Three Guineas*, her reply that the book "certainly sounds as though it ought to be interesting" seems like a genuine response from a novelist midway between the everyday detail of *The Years* and the choric chatter of *Between the Acts* (L 6: 172).

Again, my point is that while the dominant historical paradigm in Woolf's time was still totalizing, linear, political, and monumental, historical writing in its entirety reflected a broad diversification in scope and method. As fleeting as my overview must necessarily be, it testifies to the fact that genuine intellectual culture is a foment of different and differing ideas; only hindsight can identify which of the voices will succeed in engaging majority interest. To see Woolf as anticipating contemporary concerns is thus not to single her out as extraordinarily prescient; her intellectual inheritance was one in which—to use the words of Peter Allan Dale—questions about "the nature of historical knowledge" and "cultural relativity" were "pervasive intellectual concern[s]" (4, 2). At the same time, Woolf was distinctively individual both for the range of ideas encompassed in her historical thinking and in what she did with them; for, unlike many writers, Woolf tended to be modest in her claims but bold in her practice.

It is specifically Woolf's way of writing history that is her most distinguishing characteristic as an historiographer and perhaps the most pertinent aspect of her approach for us today. As I have indicated, given that we are surrounded by sophisticated theories challenging historical metanarratives, it is somewhat remarkable that few practicing historians have been able to develop effective modes for writing alternative histories. What we discover in Woolf's writing, however, is not only an early statement of the need for diversity and multiplicity but also the pursuit of a practice that could put her beliefs into effect. By pressuring the boundaries of conventional historical writing, Woolf offers a provocative example that might well stimulate our own search for less problematic and reductive forms.

A remarkable early work, unpublished during her lifetime, shows Woolf already experimenting in 1906 with ways of representing history as a dialogic relation between the historical text and the historian's understanding. "The Journal of Mistress Joan Martyn" is a two-part sketch: the first part narrating a female historian's discovery of a medieval manuscript, the second presenting the supposed historical document itself. If the first part is read merely as a colorful preface that highlights the human interest factor in the "historical" text, then Woolf's writing will not appear as markedly unconventional.[5] However, this first section—roughly two-thirds the length of the second—does much more. What it presents is a conversation—in fact, a debate—between two different definitions of history: the one privileging objective facts and focused on issues of genealogy, property and ownership, the other giving equal weight to personal, subjective recordings of daily life. The family inheritor of the manuscript collection, Mr. John Martyn, is spokesperson for the first approach; the manuscripts he treasures are the family Estate books, the "Household Books of Jasper," and "the Stud book of Willoughby" (CSF 45). The value of such historical records is not lost on his visitor, Miss Merridew; her considerable international reputation as an historian rests, she admits, on her research into the "system of land tenure in mediaeval England" (33). Yet Miss Merridew has complicated the issue, and engaged in many professional battles on behalf of these complications, by her manner of presenting land tenure material in relation to "the life of the time" (34). In a detail such as Dame Elizabeth Partridge's need for stockings, for example, Miss Merridew marks the "reality of mediaeval legs," leading to the "reality of mediaeval bodies," and finally the "reality of mediaeval brains"—all helping her as an historian to bear in mind that "the intricacies of the land tenure were not always the most important facts in the lives of men and women." And the controversy about historical materials, we see, runs along both common reader and academic lines; the difference of view emerging in her conversation with Mr. Martyn has had its public equivalent, we are told, in the pages of the *Historian's Quarterly.*

But perhaps most significantly, the debate is shown to have a very real consequence for the preservation of historical records and the construction of the historical text: were it not for Miss Merridew's persistence, the particular manuscript in question—a woman's diary—would have been neglected and cast aside. The impact of Miss Merridew as reader highlights what we would now call the textuality of history, for by giving the journal a meaningful reading, Miss Merridew transforms it from a meaningless bit of old paper into an historical document. And its preservation and inclusion as part of history alters the nature of history. Mistress Martyn's diary describes and thus inscribes the history of customs, manners, and the otherwise occluded lives of women. And, perhaps even more significantly, it inscribes both the history of narrative and the role of narrative in history. Joan Martyn's prized ability to read gives her access, through a poem, to the story of Troy; a travelling ballad singer passes on the story of Tristram and Iseult; the final passages in the diary commemorate the old women sitting by the fireside telling of "fights and kings, and great nobles, and stories of the poor people too, till the air seemed to move and murmur" (62). The meaning of stories to Joan Martyn finds its repetition in the meaning of Joan Martyn's writing to Rosamond Merridew, and the sketch as a whole illuminates the role of narrative in connecting our pasts and our presents, the role of narrative in history.

Theoretically, this early work shows Woolf already developing a construct of historical thinking as a function of the present, showing how the past is always reenacted in the present historian's mind. And Woolf not only inscribes the past as mediated through the present observer; her sketch goes further to reveal that not only the meaning of history but the very definition of what constitutes history is a product of the historian's understanding. And though, like Collingwood, Woolf thus theorizes the subjective nature of history, unlike the philosopher-historian, she writes not monologic prose but dialogic fiction—and dialogic not just because the reader is placed in the position of negotiating and examining the relation between the historian Miss Merridew and her subject Mistress Joan Martyn, but also because the debate about historical definition is presented fairly through the juxtaposition of two different but contextually valid views. Through an extended conversation, Woolf performs what she later achieves so effectively in the opening few paragraphs of her essays: she raises theoretical questions in a way that gets the reader to think about the role of our own preconceptions in the actual production of a meaning.

The distinctiveness of Woolf's approach is that she is concerned with historically situating both the actual text under discussion and herself as a specifically located reader. Furthermore—in a manner that may be useful to consider for our own critical practice—she achieves a balance between theoretical speculation and textual discussion: in implication, she addresses many of the issues debated today in historicist theory while, in her focus on the text, she pursues a deliberately nontheoretical style. Woolf suggests a way of raising theoretical questions without writing theoretically, of enacting both an engagement with and an escape from theory. For while Woolf objects to the approach of reading literature *through* theory, her emphasis on what the reader is thinking and why the reader may be thinking it keeps her discussion oriented to theoretical concerns.

Woolf's essay on *Robinson Crusoe*, for example, begins by getting her reader to think about the negative effects of reading literature through the lens of rigid a priori constructs. Beginning with the question of how to read Defoe, Woolf outlines the kinds of historical criticism commonly employed in her time: the genre approach through "the development of the novel" and the biographical approach through "the life of the author" (CR 2: 51). The problem with these approaches for Woolf is in part the irrelevancy of much of their information, and she is mockingly biting about the biographer's obsession with such details as the shape of novelists' chins. More significantly, she raises concerns about the reductiveness of general constructs. Challenging the concept of periodization, Woolf directs her reader's attention to the differences among authors living at the same time. While "textbooks" may group writers into historical periods, what chronological container, she asks, can fit the diverse shapes of Sir Walter Scott, Jane Austen, and Thomas Peacock? But Woolf's main concern is the way such introductory materials produce passive rather than responsive readings by distancing the reader from the text. "There is a piece of business to be transacted between writer and reader," she argues, and a preconceived theory is only too likely to become the obnoxious middleman, complicating and muddying the exchange (CR 2: 52).

Having foregrounded questions of how we read—and specifically how we read an historical text—Woolf then proceeds to discuss her own reading as an historically situated reader. What she achieves by this approach is a reading that is theoretically aware while, at the same time, it negotiates directly with the text. She achieves as well a reading that recognizes both the historicity of the text and the historicity of the reader. For while her discussion resembles formalist criticism in its concern with perspective, the historical nature of her reading is evident in her ongoing commentary on the difference between the text's perspective and her own. And while her reading produces a Defoe that much resembles the Defoe of generic or biographical criticism (in his emphasis on fact and his middle-class values), the consideration she gives to her own positioning clearly affects the way she responds to, interprets, and judges his work.

Woolf's initial impression of Defoe's limiting biases is modified, first of all, by her awareness of the influence of her own biases in shaping her response: her resistance derives from her post–Romantic preference for more poetic and imaginative treatments of solitude and isolation and her Modernist expectation of a psychological treatment of this theme. Woolf furthermore avoids the stance of the objective historian even in representing this difference. Instead, she offers the story of her reading: how Defoe puzzles and annoys her and how she has to struggle to close the gap between his perspective and her own. In the end, the struggle leads to theoretical speculation, but for Woolf this is the right dynamic: the text is not read through the theory; rather, theory arises out of the reading. Thus, on the one hand, Woolf allows full ironic expression of her own distaste for national and class complacency: "There is no greater good fortune we are assured than to be born of the British middle-class" (55); on the other hand, her willingness to see through Defoe's eyes leads her to see and to appreciate the way he illuminates the value of everyday life: "he comes in the end to make common actions dignified and common objects beautiful" (57). Then, too, although Defoe takes "the opposite way from the psychologist's's" and "describes the effect of emotion on the body, not on the mind," she discovers that, because his "fact is the right fact," he manages to convey the effects of desolation and solitude as powerfully as any psychological writer (57). By so exploring her varying responses to the text, Woolf both articulates difference and speculates about the lack of difference. At the end, the critical stance is inconclusive, with Woolf as divided reader unable to drop totally her ironic amusement at Defoe's prosaic faith in facts, unable to assert that her Modernist way is, in the final tally, superior. Even in this one essay, the historicist experience is various, recording not merely the dialectic of difference and similarity but the complex experience of the difficulty of coping with difference. Woolf exposes the way a reader can use amusement and explanation to contain and control the threat of difference, but then she demonstrates the power of the text to unsettle that comfort—in effect, the power of the past to *disturb* the present.

Such a constant turning over of theoretical questions is one reason why it is difficult to go through the essays and select relevant quotations to illustrate Woolf's historical judgments of literature. Lest we assume that Woolf adopts a rigid Modernist resistance to the factual writing of the past, for example, we should note how her difficulty with Defoe's reliance on factual statement is countered, in another essay, by her admiration for Dorothy Wordsworth's calm and exacting recording of nature; indeed, in this instance, Woolf exhibits a marked preference for Dorothy Wordsworth's self-effacing journals over Mary Wollstonecraft's more passionate but excessively self-referential prose (CR 2: 164-72). Or, to take another example, the distance between herself and the historical Other evident in her reading of Defoe is reversed in the essay "The Strange Elizabethans," where the past, which initially appears remote and inaccessible, after a struggle yields "a face like ours—a changing, a variable, a human face" (CR 2: 23). Historical comparison in Woolf thus makes us aware sometimes of difference, sometimes of similarity, but most often of these elements as competing tensions in our constantly shifting reading experience. Reading John Evelyn, Woolf ponders her own era's greater susceptibility to scenes of suffering yet seriously questions any general progress in the area of the humane instincts (CR 1: 78-85); reading a study of Gothic novelists, Woolf acknowledges the modern smile at "the absurdity of the visions which they conjure up" (E 3: 305) yet challenges this sense of difference with a nod to the psychological thriller and the new Gothic of science fiction—different routes for seeking the same shudder of fear; reading Sterne, Woolf negotiates not only with the eighteenth-century context but with his nineteenth-century reception, remarking a change not only in values but in the way the values are conceived. In the twentieth century, she posits, sentimentality has replaced immorality as Sterne's perceived failing; more outrageously, she speaks of morality as a matter of "taste" and philosophy, as an effect of "fashion" (CR 2: 84). By ironically undercutting the seriousness of the Victorians' moral attitudes, Woolf both points to their extreme difference and resituates them within a Modernist pattern of changing ideas of "truth."

Such differences in historical readership frequently inform Woolf's sense of the varieties of reading experience. In the opening paragraph of "'The Countess of Pembroke's Arcadia,'" for example, Woolf positions herself at the end of a long succession of readers, acknowledging an historical tradition that neither overwhelms with its authority nor palls beside the more enlightened present: "Each has read differently, with the insight and the blindness of his own generation. Our reading will be equally partial. In 1930 we shall miss a great deal that was obvious to 1655; we shall see some things that the eighteenth-century ignored" (*CR* 2: 40). In her subsequent reading, Woolf as an exacting Modernist becomes increasingly exasperated by Sidney's lack of narrative control and drifts further and further away from the rapt Elizabethan audience spellbound by his musical and fantastical charm. But, though alert to her own demands, Woolf understands Sidney's appeal for a more luxurious, languorous age and the varied reception of the *Arcadia* accords with her sense of its multiple riches; within it "all the seeds of English fiction lie latent" (49), all equally capable of stimulating the further writing of fiction. Woolf neither privileges nor undervalues her own reading, although what does make her approach perhaps broader than that of previous readers is her ability to read through multiple historical lenses— through historically past as well as historically present eyes. Frequently, as in "Notes on an Elizabethan Play," Woolf urges her reader to "make the necessary alterations in perspective" and to enter "a different but not more elementary stage of [our] reading development" (*CR* 1: 55). Thus historicism serves both to contain the present reading in the relativity of its moment and to expand the present reader with an awareness of historically "other" readings. And by grounding her discussions in the experience of different readings, Woolf is able to illuminate matters of historical difference while resisting any rigid identification of her own era with fixed monolithic views.

Yet, having argued that Woolf's historicism is pluralistic and experiential, my interest in what Ronald Bush calls "a critical as opposed to a totalizing form of literary history" cautions me not to make a totalizing theory out of Woolf's provisional models (59). *A Room of Own's Own*, I must admit, *does* construct a linear narrative: the gradual development, since the sixteenth century, of increasingly restrictive gender roles and the emancipatory counternarrative of the emergence of women's writing. And this linear feminist history has been challenged by new feminist-historicist critics for its imitation and reinscription of the same exclusionary history that characterized the patriarchal model. In *Writing Women's Literary History*, for example, Margaret Ezell argues that in constructing a continuous women's tradition, Woolf privileges fiction and writing for publication, obscuring both the diversity of genres and the circulation of manuscripts by women writers. Ezell further objects to Woolf's claiming Aphra Behn as the first woman writer, as if women's history began in the middle of the seventeenth century. But the contrast between *Room* and the essays warns us not to enshrine *Room* as Woolf's definitive theory; it, too, is an historical work written at a particular time for a specific audience—an audience that, even in the published version, is encoded from the second, if not the first, word.[6] The holistic teleological narrative of *Room* exists as "a piece of business" being "transacted between writer and reader": on this occasion, Woolf sought to validate the presence of women at Cambridge in 1928-29 by constructing an affirmative history for them and to create a space for women within the existing capitalist society by urging them to earn money and achieve financial self-dependence by publishing books. And the success of Woolf's project as cultural work can be seen in the way it has supplied an effective model—until perhaps very recently—for the task of recuperating a lost female history and a silenced female identity. As essentialist history, Woolf's text may well be limiting today; but contextualized in history, its rhetorical power is very clear.

Woolf's last project, "Anon" and "The Reader," functions as alternative history in the same way, offering a more conventionally written history meant to expose the absences in the dominant models. Unfinished at the time of her death, Woolf's historical narrative—of what we might today call the changing methods of production and consumption of the literary text—shaped itself in her mind as a counterdiscourse: "Try to write lit the other way round," Woolf noted to herself, while she considered the possibility—before Borges—of casting her version of literary history as a review of a fictitious conventional history, detailing "[w]hat it omits" (374). Woolf, it seems, wanted to attach her literary history to life, to emotion, to both the "surrounding" and the "inner, current," and above all to writers and readers bound together in a rich dynamic relation—all things "left out in text books." Ordering and structuring this work was a task that plagued Woolf with endless difficulty, as Brenda Silver has demonstrated. But whereas Silver relates this difficulty to the personal and social crisis facing Woolf in 1940, the structural problems in this work may also have resulted from conflicting aims that were not easily resolved. For it is evident from her notes and her drafts of the first two chapters that Woolf wanted both to delineate a linear path from anonymous oral recitation to signed printed publication *and* to range freely and widely, following variously the hints and signs of diversity and continuity between past and present. The work may well have foundered on the tension between consecutive historical narrative and "Reading at Random" (Woolf's original title). If Woolf had lived and continued with this work, perhaps she might have resolved these problems with a third volume of *The Common Reader* series, as Brenda Silver suggests. For in the essay collection, the possibility of chronological ordering gives scope for themes of change and development while the individual character of each essay offers space for contradictory and pluralistic impulses. However, it is important not to accede to the expectation that this work would or should have been like Woolf's earlier essays; we must not forget that this last linear objective history of reading was prompted by a different motive. If we remember to situate "Anon" and "The Reader" as Woolf's antiphonal response to rigidly author- or period-centered studies, then we will see the advantage of continuous narrative in her alternative but complementary history of the reader and of the book. Woolf's more traditionally linear histories need to be read as contextually situated, not essentialist, narratives. They represent yet another of the varieties of history that Woolf tells.

There are, of course, further varieties in Woolf's historicism to explore, since over the range of her numerous essays she approaches historical questions in different and sometimes almost oppositional ways. Thus while Woolf most often resists a teleological history of literature, negotiating as she does in "Notes on an Elizabethan Play" between the strengths and weaknesses of both past and present, her avoidance of an evolutionary metanarrative does not preclude her recognition of developmental patterns: in "'Gold and Iron'" for example she uses the image of photographic development to suggest the gradual emergence of a writer's mature vision and distinctive voice. And yet in "'Robinson Crusoe'" Woolf cautions against biographical and generic approaches, she herself invokes biographical material in "'George Eliot'" and argues for a theory of generic mutation in "'Aurora Leigh,'" in both instances to turn stale critical commonplaces into powerful new valuations. A number of essays, such as "Postscript or Prelude?," imply a canonical and genius-centered view of literature, elevating those works that best articulate a strong and original perspective; however, other essays, such as "The Pastons and Chaucer," "Miss Ormerod," and *A Room of One's Own*, inscribe a communal and collaborative model of writing, in which the language of literature is forged in the smithy of the common tongue and modes of production and consumption are the informing circumstances from which art takes its being. And while in many instances Woolf avoids and even rejects a containing theory of periodization— "No 'periods': No text book," she wrote in "Notes for Reading at Random" ("Anon" 373)—she conveys a strong sense of historical consciousness, seeing the work as always in dialogue with the multiple and multifarious influences of its time. But what might appear as inconsistency directs us instead to complexity; the variations indicate that for Woolf, historical approaches are not absolute but instead function within specific contexts and for particular use. Taken as a whole, the essays—much like the conversation between Mr. Martyn and Miss Merridew—engage the reader in a process of sifting, thinking, and evaluating as the historical lens turns to focus on different objects and in different ways.

My point is not simply that Woolf articulates these multiple and complex perspectives; it is having these different perspectives—and indeed experiencing the shifts among them—that for her is the nature of the reading process, a process that she further historicizes as her own reading in her own time and as therefore differing from the various historical readings that have preceded and will follow her. It is in this light that I see Woolf as anticipating the dialogically oriented historical reading advocated by Dominick LaCapra, who defines his own project in this way: "What is nonetheless evident in my own approach is a conception of historical discourse which is neither presentist nor 'passéist'. I try neither to projectively reprocess the past in the terms of the present through an ahistorical reading technology nor to see the past exclusively in its own putative terms through some kind of total empathetic 'teletransportation'" (9). As an historically situated reader myself, I am motivated, like LaCapra, to read Woolf in a dialogic way, and that means both to link her approach to late twentieth-century historicist theory and yet to situate her practice within the context of the shifts in historical writing taking place in her own time. It means also to acknowledge the dialogic mix of voices and diversity of approaches that existed both in the Modernist period and also within Woolf's own writing.[7] And yet to make this attempt, at the end of the twentieth century, is perhaps only still to respond to the expectations signaled by William James at the century's beginning: to explore, that is, the varieties of our human experience.

Works Cited

Allen, Walter. *The English Novel: A Short Critical History.* New York: Dutton, 1954.
Burke, Peter, ed. *New Perspectives on Historical Writing.* University Park: Pennsylvania State UP, 1992.
Bush, Ronald. "Paul de Man, Modernist." *Theoretical Issues in Literary History.* Ed. David Perkins. Cambridge, MA: Harvard UP, 1991. 35-59.
Collingwood, R. G. *Essays in the Philosophy of History.* Ed. William Debbins. 1921-30. Austin: U of Texas P, 1965.
Costello, Paul. *World Historians and Their Goals: Twentieth-Century Answers to Modernism.* DeKalb: Northern Illinois UP, 1993.
Cox, Jeffrey N. and Larry J. Reynolds, eds. *New Historical Literary Study: Essays on Reproducing Texts, Representing History.* Princeton: Princeton UP, 1993.
Dale, Peter Allan. *The Victorian Critic and the Idea of History: Carlyle, Arnold, Pater.* Cambridge, MA: Harvard UP, 1977.

Eksteins, Modris. "History and Enlightenment." *Queen's Quarterly* 102.2 (1995): 275-81.

Engler, Bernd. "Imagining Her-Story: Virginia Woolf's 'The Journal of Mistress Joan Martyn' as Historiographical Metafiction." *Journal of the Short Story in English* 20 (1993): 9-26.

Ezell, Margaret J. M. *Writing Women's Literary History.* Baltimore: Johns Hopkins UP, 1993.

Frazer, Sir James. *The Golden Bough: A Study of Magic and Religion.* 3rd ed. London: Macmillan, 1913.

Hill, Katherine C. "Virginia Woolf and Leslie Stephen: History and Literary Revolution." *PMLA* 96.3 (1981): 351-62.

Himmelfarb, Gertrude. *The New History and the Old.* Cambridge, MA: The Belknap of Harvard UP, 1987.

Hotho-Jackson, Sabine. "Virginia Woolf on History: Between Tradition and Modernity." *Forum for Modern Language Studies* 27.4 (1991): 293-313.

Isaacs, Jacob. *An Assessment of Twentieth-Century Literature.* London: Secker and Warburg, 1951.

James, William. *The Varieties of Religious Experience: A Study of Human Nature.* 1902. Intro. and appendices Joseph Ratner. New Hyde Park, NY: University Books, 1963.

LaCapra, Dominick. *History, Politics and the Novel.* Ithaca: Cornell UP, 1987.

"Mass Observation." Leaflet. The Mass Observation Archive. The Library, U of Sussex, [c. 1992].

Power, Eileen. *Medieval People.* 1924. 10th ed. London: Methuen, 1963.

Smarr, Janet Levarie, ed. *Historical Criticism and the Challenge of Theory.* Urbana: U of Illinois P, 1993.

Stephen, Leslie. *English Literature and Society in the Eighteenth Century.* London: Duckworth and Co., 1904.

Wellek, René and Austin Warren. *Theory of Literature.* New York: Harcourt, 1956.

Woolf, Leonard. "The Pageant of History." *Essays on Literature, History, Politics, Etc.* 1927. Freeport, NY: Books for Libraries P, 1970. 125-48.

Woolf, Virginia. "'Anon' and 'The Reader': Virginia Woolf's Last Essays." Ed. Brenda R. Silver. *Twentieth Century Literature* 25. 3-4 (1979): 356-441.

———. *The Common Reader.* 1925. Ed. Andrew McNeillie. London: Hogarth, 1984.

———. *The Common Reader: Second Series.* 1932. Ed. Andrew McNeillie. London: Hogarth, 1986.

———. *The Essays of Virginia Woolf.* Ed. Andrew McNeillie. 3 vols. to date. New York: Harcourt, 1986-.

———. "The Journal of Mistress Joan Martyn." *The Complete Shorter Fiction of Virginia Woolf.* Ed. Susan Dick. London: Hogarth, 1985. 33-62.

————. *The Letters of Virginia Woolf*. Ed. Nigel Nicolson and Joanne Trautmann. 6 vols.
   London: Chatto and Windus, 1975-80.
————. *A Room of One's Own*. London: Hogarth, 1929.
————. *Three Guineas*. 1938. Ed. Hermione Lee. London: Hogarth, 1986.

Notes

1. Critics have occasionally proposed that James's formulation of "stream of consciousness" was a direct influence on Virginia Woolf (Isaacs 88). Recent views, however, would more likely approach the ideas of Woolf and James as synchronous and complementary and as part of a growing way of thinking in a whole culture.

2. It should be noted, however, that despite the comparative nature of Frazer's study, his underlying project, as he wrote in the preface to the Second Edition, was "to follow the long march, the slow and toilsome ascent, of humanity from savagery to civilization" (xxv) and "to expedite progress" by exposing the common reliance in all religious beliefs on superstition. Thus expressed, his goals remain teleological and linear.

3. Although Woolf acknowledges that Macaulay extended history to include everyday life, she also notes that he implied that women occupied themselves with trivial things such as cooking dinner, while men engaged in important affairs. Woolf, not surprisingly, suggests a different valuation, being rather more skeptical about the importance of men's occupations: "It must be left to the scientist of the future to tell us what effect drink and property have had upon the chromosomes" (*TG* 169).

4. Katherine Hill sees Woolf as incorporating her father's interest in the lives of the obscure and his sense of the relation between literary production and class structures, but as developing beyond Stephen in her inclusion of the obscure lives of *women* and her belief in the basic immorality of class distinctions. Historicizing each writer, Hill then proposes the deeper connection that both father and daughter were "intent on ushering in a new age in their respective spheres" (360).

5. Sabine Hotho-Johnson reads Miss Merridew as Woolf's mouthpiece, claiming that both character and author endorse an approach to history as a "colourful depiction" of ordinary life along the "reader-oriented" lines of the "Macaulay/ Trevelyan" school (297). But such an interpretation looks at storytelling only as a means for generating readerly interest and not, as I argue, as a subject

matter under interrogation for its role in producing both historical understanding and historical evidence.

   Yet another reading of Woolf's sketch is proposed by Bernd Engler
who, like me, thinks that the reader is asked to reflect on Miss Merridew's
historical method but, unlike me, thinks that Woolf exposes Miss Merridew
as an egotistical fraud who both plagiarizes the Paston letters and inappropri-
ately recasts them as feminist material. But Engler, to my mind, misses the
Miss Marple-like charm of Miss Merridew, Woolf's open-minded probing of
the implications of historical method, and the journal's serious treatment of
the importance of reading and storytelling in women's lives.

6. While the reader/audience is addressed directly in the second word "you," the
    first word "But" has already marked the sentence as a reply.
7. Hotho-Jackson similarly discusses Woolf in relation to changing historiogra-
    phies, but her analysis assumes constructs of Victorian and Modernist histories
    that are more purist and consequently more oppositional than mine. Thus
    Hotho-Jackson locates Woolf as a transitional figure positioned "halfway
    between conventional and modern concepts" (302), whereas I see Woolf as
    foregrounding the controversies—controversies that themselves were part of
    the Modern period—for our reflection.

PART II

WOOLF AND LITERARY HISTORY

Entering Woolf's Renaissance Imaginary: A Second Look at The Second Common Reader

Sally Greene

In the years leading up to *The Second Common Reader*, Virginia Woolf deliberated over the proper style for her increasingly nontraditional criticism. The mind that created such transgressive figures as the protagonist of *Orlando* and Shakespeare's "sister" could hardly continue to mirror the patriarchal biases of the British reading public, as Woolf had done skillfully for some twenty years in the *Times Literary Supplement* (*TLS*) and elsewhere. Woolf herself realized that she had reached a turning point. It was thanks to *A Room of One's Own*, she remarked, that she found herself "able to write criticism fearlessly" (*D* 4: 25). Yet she anticipated that her *Room* would be considered "feminine logic" and therefore its message "not . . . taken seriously" (*D* 3: 262)—a prediction realized in Arnold Bennett's complaint that Woolf "is merely the victim of her extraordinary gift of fancy" (147-48). Her self-confidence as a critic still depended in large measure on the approval of the *TLS* audience. Thus, at the very moment when she was sketching the early contours of *Three Guineas*—a "sequel" to *A Room of One's Own* "for which I have collected enough powder to blow up St. Pauls"—she was concerned with completing the conventional *Second Common Reader*, "by way of proving my credentials" (*D* 4: 77).

Perhaps because of the book's surface resemblance to traditional collections of essays that literary men of Woolf's period specialized in producing (already successfully imitated in *The Common Reader*), *The Second Common Reader* has suffered the benign neglect of the current generation of feminist critics. Carolyn Heilbrun, for example, dismisses it as "the memorial volume to the old Virginia Woolf" (242). Woolf herself declared on its completion, "There is no sense of glory; only of drudgery done" (D 4: 115). But if we become, as she urges in the collection's concluding essay, her "fellow- worker and accomplice" (282)—and if we follow the advice she gives in the first *Common Reader* of reading the book as a whole (advice that, as Georgia Johnston notes, has not always been heeded)—we will find a surprisingly personal, surprisingly feminist subtext. Further, we will find that the force animating this work, like that behind so many other of Woolf's works, is an active engagement with the literature of the Renaissance.

Notable in *The Second Common Reader* is a running debate between two sides of Woolf's mind—on the one hand, a comfortable aesthetic self-image as artistic "butterfly," and on the other, an incipient attraction to the political "gadfly," terms she had set in opposition in "Women and Fiction,"[1] a pivotal essay that anticipates the feminist themes of *A Room of One's Own*. She admires Mary Wollstonecraft's social action in one essay, Dorothy Wordsworth's contemplative writing in the next. William Hazlitt's intellectual side is opposed to his artistic side. Geraldine Jewsbury, possessed of a "speculative imagination," is thrown into passionate relief against the "positive, direct, and practical" Jane Carlyle (213). Elizabeth Barrett Browning is seen as a natural activist forced by circumstance into a life of the mind. To be sure, the first *Common Reader* betrays important signs of Woolf's feminism, as Andrew McNeillie notes (xiv). There, she treats numerous women with the same attentive respect that her Miss Omerod (a nineteenth-century ento-mologist who only reluctantly acknowledged her LL.D.) reserved for boot beetles and the Hessian Fly (CR 1: 122-33). But while emphasizing, as the first volume did, the authority of the common reader (of either sex), the second volume is more interested than the first in exploring the gaps between women's hopes and their realistic expectations—more interested, following Sir Thomas Browne, in asking why.

"But why—his favourite beginning," Woolf remarks in one of many sets of notes she took on Browne's work over years of reading and rereading.[2] Her conversations with this restless figure, whom she envied for his ability to write for his own pure "pleasure" without practical considerations of audience (E 3: 310), offer a way in to her larger view of the Renaissance—a view that, in turn, invites a fuller appreciation of the feminist subtext of *The Second Common Reader*.

Woolf's perception of Browne has more in common with that of Coleridge, who characterized him as a humorist mixed with philosopher "as the darting colours in shot silk play upon the main dye,"[3] than it does with academic critics of her generation, who were engaged in a project of reading him more seriously as a man of science (see, for example, Edmund Gosse's monograph on Browne in the "English Men of Letters" series, 25-26). Like her friend Lytton Strachey, she allows herself to be immersed in the literary effect of the whole; she appreciates, for example, the way in which "[v]ast inquiries sweeping in immense circles of ambiguity and doubt are clenched by short sentences rapped out with solemn authority" (*E* 3: 370). But unlike Strachey, who is persuaded that Browne's work is best read within the walls of "some habitation consecrated to learning, some University which still smells of antiquity and has learnt the habit of repose" (44), Woolf takes him far afield. For example, with her least confined of all characters, Orlando, Browne's arresting influence becomes more of a familiar presence than the memory of blood relatives. The movement of Orlando's fantastical story, which comes to a halt in "the present moment" (*O* 298), is Brownean in its constantly searching effect.

Browne's presiding spirit, as Balachandra Rajan has noted, is Janus, the god of doors (10). Impatient with the systematizing of philosophers, he chooses to keep all answers provisional. "We do but learn to-day what our better advanced judgements will unteach us to morrow; and Aristotle doth but instruct us, as Plato did him; that is, to confute himself." Having "run through all sorts" of philosophers and found "no rest in any," he concludes that "the wisest heads prove, at last, almost all Sceptiks, and stand like Janus in the field of knowledge" (*Religio Medici* 81). From Browne, Woolf could conclude that the mind has many rooms of its own.

The permeability of his thinking, which Woolf recognized for its value to her own habits of thought, reflects in part the unsettled temper of the late Renaissance. Although important historical differences separate the early seventeenth from the late sixteenth century (and would be dealt with in a fuller treatment of the subject), Woolf's writerly imagination tends to obscure such details: she is no New Historicist. Browne, like John Donne, is just one of the many presences in what I have come to think of as her Renaissance imaginary—a mental space that she most often associates with Elizabethans and their voyages (literal and metaphorical) to new worlds. For example, in the 1919 essay "Reading," much of which evolved into the *Common Reader* essay "The Elizabethan Lumber Room," she draws in part on James Anthony Froude's *History of England* and in part on her own creativity to conclude that "Elizabeth, of all our kings and queens, seems most fit for that gesture which bids the great sailors farewell, or welcomes them home to her presence again, her imagination still lusting for the strange tales they bring her." Aware that her construction of this world contains "much

exaggeration, much misunderstanding," she defends these "visions of Elizabethan magnanimity" as stays against the "restlessness" of her own time. "It
is," she writes, "an atmosphere, not only soft and fine, but rich, too, with
more than one can grasp at any single reading" (*E* 3: 149).

By stressing the imaginative quality of her engagement with the
Renaissance, I am distinguishing my own reading from that offered by Alice
Fox in her valuable source book *Virginia Woolf and the English Renaissance* (and
elsewhere), as well as from the theory propounded by Sandra Gilbert and
Susan Gubar in their influential treatment, in *The Madwoman in the Attic*, of
"Milton's bogey."[4] Both of these bodies of criticism tend to consider the
influence of Renaissance writers—who were, after all, overwhelmingly
male—in terms of Harold Bloom's theory of the anxiety of influence. For
Woolf, according to this line of thought, Milton, like all male predecessors
of the Renaissance or otherwise (except possibly Shakespeare), becomes
"'the great Inhibitor, the Sphinx who strangles even strong imaginations in
their cradles'" (Gilbert and Gubar 191, quoting Bloom); hence allusion to
Milton and other male writers becomes little more than a clever rhetorical
tool for subverting the authority of the entire male canon.[5]

These critics are surely right to conclude that Woolf rejects the
patriarchal authority that "Milton's bogey" represents: she dismisses that
concept as thoroughly as she had the authority of the Victorian fathers of
her youth. But as Lisa Low persuasively argues in approaching the "Milton's
bogey" critique from a Miltonist's perspective, the trope of influence is
insufficient to the task of accounting for the complex reworkings of
Renaissance sources—sources that are themselves far from univocal. While
resisting the ever-present undercurrents of militarism and patriarchal
domination in Renaissance England, Woolf was able to find within that
richly literary world a framework for her own longings for new worlds. As
Juliet Dusinberre writes, Woolf's "awareness of intertextuality, of language
as a tissue of inherited discourses," enabled her "to write herself, 'to put
herself into the text,'" as she sought to "remake the language of men in her
own image" (221).[6]

Sensing that the Elizabethans were "intoxicated" with "beautiful
words lying about for the asking," as she puts it in "'The Countess of
Pembroke's Arcadia,'" one of the opening essays of *The Second Common Reader*
(*CR* 2: 41-42), she appreciates what Roland Barthes would later call the
"lavish profusion of literary languages" of the sixteenth and early seventeenth centuries (55). That so much was unsettled and still unknown is not
a drawback but rather a hopeful point of connection to her own period,
which she considers in "How It Strikes a Contemporary" as "an age of

fragments" (*CR* 1: 234). She finds in the explosion of activities in the Renaissance a parallel to the Modernist period, a period she invests with hope for a new age of "infinite possibilities" for the novelist's art, with "no limit to the horizon" (*CR* 1: 154). The Renaissance forms the common ground on which Woolf and her common readers meet to embark on a creative rewriting of their collective story.

In *The Second Common Reader*, Woolf employs her peculiar understanding of the Renaissance to establish the dialectic that the volume enacts—and thus to initiate, or at least to invite, a feminist critique from within the dominant culture. As in the first *Common Reader*,[7] her Renaissance imaginary is the first world that the reader encounters. Repeating the sequence of the previous volume, she begins her roughly chronological survey of English letters with several chapters centered on that remote though historically crucial period. Moreover, a deeper strategy than mere parallel structure is evident here. After the work of completing *A Room of One's Own*, Woolf rewarded herself with a romp among the Elizabethans—a prospect, she wrote, that "fills me with joy—no overstatement" (*D* 3: 270). Two essays on Elizabethans that she planned in late 1929, plus a third on Donne, evolved into the three first essays of *The Second Common Reader*. (All but one of the other essays to appear in the volume had first been published in journals over the seven years since *The Common Reader*.)

In this context, the Renaissance becomes an alternative *locus communes*, or "common place," to use the language of the classical tradition—a mental location to be dwelt upon, foundational to yet far removed from early twentieth-century England. Invoking the wide vistas of the Elizabethan landscape, she invites her readers to think behind and beyond the settled ideologies of the day (reflected, to cite examples she elsewhere made famous, in the empirical realist novels of John Galsworthy, Arnold Bennett, and H. G. Wells). From her earliest conception of the book, she appears to have meant for the Renaissance chapters to have the effect that the Russian formalists have taught us to call "defamiliarization"—*ostranenie*, a word also translatable as "estrangement" or "alienation" (Stacy 3). Her choice to begin with an essay on "The Strange Elizabethans," in which she stresses how little of their everyday lives is known, signals an intent to upset her readers' likely assumptions that the course of literary history was inevitable and indisputable.[8] Concerned to give voice to minor figures as she embraces the power of creative reading, she chooses to begin not with major figures such as Edmund Spenser or Philip Sidney but with their lesser-known friend Gabriel Harvey. In the second essay she focuses on Donne, whose intense and changeable nature colors him "more Elizabethan than the Elizabethans."[9] The third, a transition to Woolf's study of the roots of the English novel, considers Sidney's *Arcadia* as a beautiful but puzzling work within which "all the seeds of English fiction lie latent" (48).

In addition to emphasizing the dialectic between the active and the contemplative life that emerges as a theme of the collection, the volume's first three essays trace Woolf's increasing interest in the women of the Renaissance—a topic that undoubtedly grew out of her exploration of women's literary history in *A Room of One's Own*. The essays depict women contextually, beside their more famous Renaissance brothers and courtiers, in roles ranging from patrons of the arts to a milkmaid struggling to defend her chastity. Woolf acknowledges the depth of the cultural forces that mark women's experiences as inferior to men's, while at the same time she stresses the transformative potential that women share equally with men as common readers.

The first strategy Woolf employs to encourage her readers to consider Renaissance women the equals of men is to begin with the career of one man who was by most of society's measures a failure. The precocious son of a ropemaker, Harvey earned a bachelor's degree from Christ's College, Cambridge; but despite ranking near the top of his class, he was denied a graduate fellowship there. He did secure a fellowship at Pembroke Hall, where he began a famous friendship with Spenser, then an undergraduate. Failure threatened again, though, when after meeting the requirements for the master's degree he was initially denied it out of the ill will of certain other fellows. Although he ultimately obtained the degree, an unfortunate pattern had set in. Successes, such as election to the university-wide position of professor of rhetoric, were overwhelmed by disappointments, including failure to become the university's public orator or master of Trinity Hall.

So great were Harvey's setbacks that at thirty-five "his public career [had] led to nothing and [would] lead to nothing," according to G. C. Moore Smith, whose 1913 book recites the preceding facts. Woolf, who in drafting "The Strange Elizabethans" relied on Moore Smith for biographical detail, substantially concurs with his assessment that Harvey was, for all his public failures, a good man whose wide reading and open-minded scholarship recommended him above contemporary "pedants" "who saw nothing good outside the classical writers of Greece and Rome" (76). But whereas Moore Smith reads Harvey as an opportunist "who can sympathize with the intellectual detachment of Machiavelli," Woolf sees someone else—someone who seems, like herself, to be caught in an internal contradiction.[10]

Basing her judgment, as Moore Smith had, on Harvey's *Commonplace Book*, Woolf discerns a debate between active and passive impulses, "between the Harvey who blundered among men and the Harvey who sat wisely at home among his books" (16). Admitting that "the two halves, for all their counselling together, made but a sorry business of the whole" (18), she refrains from uncharitable conclusions. Rather, she chooses to dwell on what Moore Smith only outlines: Harvey's relationship with Spenser. "In the small, smoky rooms where Spenser and other young men discussed poetry and language and the future of English literature," she writes, "Harvey was not laughed at." On the contrary, "he created for Spenser that atmosphere of hope and ardent curiosity spiced with sound learning that serves to spur the imagination of a young writer and to make each fresh poem as it is written seem the common property of a little band of adventurers set upon the same quest" (14). Harvey thus exemplifies Woolf's ideal common reader: bringing his best critical attention to bear, he not only enjoys reading but also keeps literature alive and open to new directions.

Even more significant than her emphasis on Harvey's love of books "as a true reader loves them" (18), though, is Woolf's treatment of a story involving his sister Mercy. In his *Letter-Book*, Harvey details a threat to her virtue posed by a married lord, whose elaborate overtures involved several proposed assignations (each time, she evaded him) and an exchange of letters. After accidentally intercepting one of the letters, Harvey sent the lord a stern warning that apparently ended the episode. The incident has been variously interpreted. Moore Smith, for example, finds Mercy's "conduct [to have] been somewhat ambiguous" (16). A later scholar has suggested that Harvey's account is fiction, "'a novella in miniature.'"[11] Woolf, in contrast, presents it as an obvious account of a seduction, and she further conjectures that "[t]his is probably no uncommon story" (7).

Evidence from Woolf's drafting of "The Strange Elizabethans" reveals that the sympathetic attention drawn to Mercy Harvey resulted from a deliberate elevation of her position within Gabriel's story. One narrative ploy that evolved through the drafting is Woolf's decision to relate Mercy's story before her brother's. The draft version introduces Mercy's story as little more than a footnote to Gabriel's: "Sure enough as we turn the pages of Gabriels letter book, we come upon the story of his sister who was a milkmaid" (Berg, reel 5, M11). The published version, in contrast, announces that "[t]he first person whom we meet" in the world of the strange Elizabethans "is indeed a milkmaid" (5) and proceeds to tell of her attempted seduction before turning to Gabriel's career. As a result of this ordering, it is difficult to ignore the contrast between Mercy's narrow prospects and the wide world open to her brother at Cambridge. Additionally, Woolf revised her essay to tell Mercy's adventure directly, suppressing in the final draft the fact that it is related only through letters to and from her brother. Like "Shakespeare's sister," Gabriel Harvey's sister at last has a voice.

The companion-piece to "The Strange Elizabethans" is "'The Countess of Pembroke's Arcadia,'" the third essay in the collection. After having read three biographies of Sidney with the idea of writing a biographical essay on him, Woolf settled on discussing the *Arcadia* as a predecessor to the English novel.[12] Because she attempts to judge Sidney's success by her own formalist notions of how a "modern novelist" should handle a plot (44), she is understandably frustrated with his lush and digressive style. Her failure to discuss the political allegory about which Annabel Patterson (32-51) has recently written for a highly receptive audience in Renaissance studies—and about which she herself would have read in Fulke Greville's biography, which she reviewed (*E* 1: 139-43)—illustrates, no doubt, the way in which the larger forces of intellectual history bend to shape personal biases. Within the context of the volume of essays she was crafting, however, two purposes are apparent.

First, she is extending the process of defamiliarizing her readers, opening their minds to a time before the course of literary history was set so that they might imagine other directions it could have taken—and by analogy other directions it still could take in the twentieth century. A second aim seems to have been another shift in attention toward the women who populated the Renaissance landscape, in particular to the role of Sidney's sister Mary, the Countess of Pembroke, as patron and guiding spirit. Late in the drafting, Woolf changed the title from "Philip Sidney's Arcadia" to "The Countess of Pembroke's Arcadia"; and the published version differs from the extant draft in ending with a turn toward the sister (Berg, reel 5, M13). These changes are minor—the change in title, at one level, simply achieves a more accurate reflection of Sidney's title. Yet at a deeper level they offer further proof of Woolf's interest in the lives of Renaissance women.

In "Donne After Three Centuries," the second essay in the collection but last of the three Renaissance essays to be conceived and the one that taxed her energies the most,[13] Woolf finds an opportunity to investigate a couple of women who served as patrons—and thus important readers—for some of the finest literature of the period. Donne himself, who in the words of Edmund Gosse possessed "an independence of opinion which bordered upon eccentricity" (3), becomes for Woolf a fascinating subject, a man who even more than Harvey exhibits the intellectual and artistic restlessness to which she perpetually succumbed; her emphasis on Donne's intensity and volatility matches her self-contradictory frame of mind while completing *The Second Common Reader*. Drawing on Gosse's biography as well as Herbert Grierson's recent edition of Donne, and supplementing them with less familiar books on Lady Anne Clifford,[14] she produces an essay that combines a writerly appreciation for Donne's remarkable style with an insightful feminist glance at the Renaissance system of patronage.

A poem by Donne "is an entity that owes its power to estrangement," she wrote in a draft of the essay (Monk's House, reel 2, 2.3). The final version bears witness both to the arresting immediacy of language in each distinct type of poem and to the dizzying leaps of perspective demanded of the reader as Donne careens from the early satires, to the love poems, to the poems for patronage, to the concluding holy sonnets. With the admiration of a "fellow-worker," she follows his perpetual and uneasy quest for "union" in the face of "so many different desires" (27), citing the tone of relentless searching that marks even the divine poems. In the satires and love poems she finds a sensibility that "brings him closer than his contemporaries" to the modern age: "we may claim to be akin to Donne in our readiness to admit contrasts, in our desire for openness, in that psychological intricacy which the novelists have taught us" (29-30). Especially notable is his boldly unconventional depiction of women in the love poems as characters "as various and complex as Donne himself" (26).

When she reaches Donne's period of seeking favors from "[g]reat ladies . . . with well-spread tables and fair gardens" and "rich men with the gift of rooms in their possession" (29), her reading departs in one significant respect from the settled one. While bemoaning the forces that turned him from his culture's "rebel" to its "slave" (30), she finds more to praise in the two elaborate poems presented to Robert Drury commemorating the death of his daughter than does Gosse—more, even (according to Gosse 1: 277), than many of Donne's contemporaries could find. Rather than dwell on the hyperbolic "absurdities" (Gosse 1: 275) of Donne's flights of fancy as he relates fifteen-year-old Elizabeth's death to "the frailty and decay of this whole World," as the poem is subtitled, Woolf marvels at his ingenuity and intellect, at his grasp of the "much [that] remains for a poet to write about when the season of love is over" (33). This criticism is as subjective as it is astute: as a novelist, she continually sought to "write beyond the ending" of the conventional love plot, as Rachel Blau DuPlessis has pointed out.

Woolf's sympathetic reading of the period of Donne's patronage extends to a curiosity about the world of those "great ladies" who generously provided him with material (in two senses). No matter how particularized his poems to the Countess of Bedford might seem, however, they are at bottom the vehicle of a courtier's ambition. "Poetry," Woolf concludes, "is saluting Rank" (32). Since the poems provide no reliable window into the lives of these women, she turns to a more promising source. The diary of

Lady Clifford—not a benefactor of Donne's but a notable patroness of the period—affords some direct access.

What Woolf finds is that this woman, who financed Spenser's first monument in Westminster Abbey, is an avid reader—of Spenser and Sidney, Jonson (she acted in his masques), Montaigne, and others. "[I]t is proof of the respect in which reading was held that a girl of fashion should be able to read an old corrupt poet like Chaucer without feeling that she was making herself a target for ridicule as a blue-stocking," Woolf remarks (31). Lady Clifford, then, joins a succession of common readers that includes Gabriel Harvey, the Countess of Pembroke, and even John Paston, the young landed gentleman reading Chaucer in the opening essay of the first *Common Reader*. Further, the mention of blue-stockings deftly places the late Victorian professor Walter Raleigh's dismissal of literary studies as an occupation for "spinsters," which Woolf had decried in a scathing review of his letters,[15] in perspective as a historical aberration.

Thus, through her Renaissance imaginary, which she concedes is little more than a tantalizing "illusion" (3), Woolf draws readers of *The Second Common Reader* into a "strange" yet strangely familiar world populated by women and men who, despite widely varying circumstances, are equally capable of self-enlightenment through the power of reading. The emphasis on internal division initiated in her discussion of Harvey and continued across these three chapters introduces a theme that weaves through the volume, distinguishing it from *The Common Reader*. That this work should raise more unanswered questions than the first volume is a logical outcome of Woolf's increasingly restless spirit; during the seven-year interim, her own work as writer and common reader had led her to note with more conscious objection the cultural divide between men and women. What remains constant, however, is her belief in literature, especially Renaissance literature, as an agent through which a culture's highest possibilities are capable of transmission— through active reading on the part of women no less than men.

An illustration of Woolf's faith in literature during the early 1930s, while economic depression threatened the welfare of many, is her reaction to the British government's decision in September 1931 to take its currency off the gold standard. As Malcolm Muggeridge recalls in his memoir of the thirties, the resulting flow of new money was seen as a turning point for the imperiled empire. Comparison to the Armada, among other "triumphs," was common (127). Woolf also invokes the Renaissance, but to a different end. Learning the news while drafting her essay on Donne, she says, "if everybody had spent their time writing about Donne we should not have gone off the Gold Standard— thats my version of the greatest crisis &c &c &c." (*D* 4: 45; see also *L* 4: 392).

This offhand, seemingly flippant remark springs from a deep well. As "Donne After Three Centuries" demonstrates, Woolf senses the power of his psychological complexity; his techniques of "surprise" and "subjugation" (21) call the reader to an honest reckoning that can lead to recognition and change beyond the private sphere. Her comment further recalls a passage in her diary of August 1918, during the height of the first World War. The sight of her brother Adrian talking to a German prisoner, the apparent naturalness of the civil human interchange between two men who "[b]y rights . . . should have been killing each other," prompts her to consider the powerful, potentially transformative effect that literature can exert on sympathetic readers. Recording some impressions about "Milton, the German prisoners, life, & other subjects," Woolf writes that

> the existence of life in another human being is as difficult to realize as a play of Shakespeare when the book is shut. . . . The reason why it is easy to kill another person must be that one's imagination is too sluggish to conceive what his life means to him—the infinite possibilities of a succession of days which are furled to him, & have already been spent. (D 1: 186)

To read the works of Donne, Milton, Shakespeare, and so on (especially, always, works of the Renaissance) is to appreciate "the infinite possibilities" of other people's lives. Practiced seriously and consistently, such reading could reduce conflict and promote understanding—among nations, among the men and women who are their reason to exist.

Although Woolf had reason to regret her attempt to repeat the genteel success of the first *Common Reader*—its very form required a "sidelong approach" that she later attributed to early "tea-table training" ("A Sketch of the Past" 150)—her engagement with the Renaissance ultimately sustained her. More than that, it served her well. At the beginning of summer in 1931, when she was planning the essays that would begin the volume, she promised herself: "I intend to walk; to read, Elizabethans; to be mistress of my soul" (D 4: 24). Reading for these essays clearly energized her; it fed her thoughts about politics, culture, and literature. And though her public voice still yielded to the generic masculine pronoun, this private comment records *in parvo* the most significant transformation that was taking place. The lessons learned from Mercy Harvey and Lady Anne Clifford are encapsulated in this quiet subversion of the most memorable lines of what George Meredith called that most "manful" of poems (quoted in Flora 29-30), William Ernest Henley's "Invictus."

Afterword

While writing this essay, I was given a first American edition of *The Second Common Reader*, a treasure made even more valuable—to me, if not to an antiquarian—by traces of a previous reading. According to the inscription, the book was a Christmas present from a woman to her husband. He evidently fell to reading it immediately, making notes in light pencil when moved to agree or talk back. He observed, for example, that Lord Chesterfield's advice to his son sounds like Polonius, and he took an interest in Woolf's descriptions of Donne's female patrons. As Montaigne advises (305), he recorded on the last page the date he finished reading: 27 December 1932. But he did not, as Montaigne would further advise, render a final judgment on the book. Perhaps, as one of the company of Woolf's common readers, he knew better.

Works Cited

Barthes, Roland. *Writing Degree Zero*. 1953. Trans. Annette Lavers and Colin Smith. New York: Noonday, 1968.

Bennett, Arnold. "Queen of the Highbrows." *Virginia Woolf: Critical Assessments*. Ed. Eleanor McNees. 4 vols. Mountfield, England: Helm Information, 1994. 2: 147-48.

Browne, Sir Thomas. *Religio Medici and Other Writings*. Intro. Frank L. Huntley. New York: Dutton Everyman's Library, 1951.

DuPlessis, Rachel Blau. *Writing Beyond the Ending: Narrative Strategies of Twentieth-Century Women Writers*. Bloomington: Indiana UP, 1985.

Dusinberre, Juliet. "Virginia Woolf and Montaigne." *Textual Practice* 5 (1991): 219-41.

Flora, Joseph M. *William Ernest Henley*. New York: Twayne, 1970.

Fox, Alice. "Literary Allusion as Feminist Criticism in *A Room of One's Own*." *Virginia Woolf: Critical Assessments*. Ed. Eleanor McNees. 4 vols. Mountfield, England: Helm Information, 1994. 2: 199-214.

———. *Virginia Woolf and the Literature of the English Renaissance*. Oxford: Clarendon P, 1990.

Gilbert, Sandra, and Susan Gubar. *The Madwoman in the Attic: The Woman Writer and the Nineteenth-Century Literary Imagination*. New Haven: Yale UP, 1979.

Gosse, Edmund. *Sir Thomas Browne*. ["English Men of Letters."] NY: Macmillan, 1905.

———. *The Life and Letters of John Donne*. 2 vols. 1899. Gloucester, MA: Peter Smith, 1959.

Heilbrun, Carolyn G. "Virginia Woolf in Her Fifties." *Virginia Woolf: A Feminist Slant.* Ed. Jane Marcus. Lincoln: U of Nebraska P, 1983. 236-53.

Johnston, Georgia. "The Whole Achievement in Virginia Woolf's *The Common Reader.*" *Essays on the Essay: Redefining the Genre.* Ed. Alexander J. Butrym. Athens: U of Georgia P, 1989. 148-58.

Low, Lisa. "'Two Figures in Dense Violet Night': Virginia Woolf, John Milton, and the Epic Vision of Marriage." *Woolf Studies Annual* 1 (1995): 68-88.

McNeillie, Andrew. "Intro." *The Common Reader.* By Virginia Woolf. Ed. Andrew McNeillie. New York: Harcourt, 1984. ix-xv.

Montaigne, Michel de. "Of Books." *The Complete Essays of Montaigne.* Trans. Donald M. Frame. Stanford: Stanford UP, 1965. 296-306.

Moore Smith, G. C. *Gabriel Harvey's Marginalia.* Stratford: Shakespeare Head P, 1913.

Muggeridge, Malcolm. *The Thirties: 1930-1940 in Great Britain.* London: Collins, 1940.

Patterson, Annabel. *Censorship and Interpretation: The Conditions of Writing and Reading in Early Modern England.* 2nd ed. Madison: U of Wisconsin P, n.d.

Post, Jonathan F. S. *Sir Thomas Browne.* Boston: Twayne, 1987.

Rajan, Balachandra. "Browne and Milton: The Divided and the Distinguished." *Approaches to Sir Thomas Browne: The Ann Arbor Tercentenary Lectures and Essays.* Ed. C. A. Patrides. Columbia: U of Missouri P, 1982. 1-11.

Rosenbaum, S. P. *Women and Fiction: The Manuscript Versions of* A Room of One's Own. Oxford: Blackwell, 1992.

Silver, Brenda. *Virginia Woolf's Reading Notebooks.* Princeton: Princeton UP, 1983.

Stacy, R. H. *Defamiliarization in Language and Culture.* Syracuse: Syracuse UP, 1977.

Stern, Virginia F. *Gabriel Harvey: His Life, Marginalia and Library.* Oxford: Oxford UP, 1979.

Strachey, Lytton. "Sir Thomas Browne." 1906. *Books and Characters, French and English.* London: Chatto & Windus, 1922. 31-44.

Woolf, Virginia. *The Captain's Death Bed.* New York: Harcourt, 1950.

———. *The Common Reader.* 1925. Ed. Andrew McNeillie. New York: Harcourt, 1984.

———. *The Second Common Reader.* New York: Harcourt, 1932.

———. *The Diary of Virginia Woolf.* Ed. Anne Olivier Bell. 5 vols. New York: Harcourt, 1977-84.

———. *The Essays of Virginia Woolf.* Ed. Andrew McNeillie. 4 vols. to date. London: Hogarth, 1986- .

———. *The Letters of Virginia Woolf.* Ed. Nigel Nicolson and Joanne Trautmann. 6 vols. London: Hogarth Press, 1975-80.

———. *Orlando: A Biography.* 1928. New York: Harcourt, 1956.

———. *A Room of One's Own.* 1929. New York: Harcourt, 1957.

———. "A Sketch of the Past." *Moments of Being.* 2nd ed. Ed. Jeanne Schulkind. New York: Harcourt, 1985. 64-159.

————. *Three Guineas*. 1938. New York: Harcourt, 1966.

————. *The Virginia Woolf Manuscripts from the Henry W. and Albert A. Berg Collection at the New York Public Library*. Microform. Woodbridge, CT: Research Publications International, 1993.

————. *The Virginia Woolf Manuscripts from the Monk's House Papers at the University of Sussex*. Microform. Sussex, England: Harvester Microform, 1985.

Notes

1. "Women and Fiction" first appeared in *The Forum*, March 1929. It is reprinted in Rosenbaum, ed., *Women and Fiction: The Manuscript Versions of* A Room of One's Own.

2. From the Woolf manuscripts in the Berg Collection of the New York Public Library, microfilm ed. (hereafter "Berg"), reel 13, RN1.25, p. 28.

3. Letter to Sara Hutchinson, qtd. in Post 24.

4. The argument, found in Ch. 6 of *The Madwoman in the Attic*, was first articulated in Gilbert's essay "Patriarchal Poetry and Women Readers: Reflections on Milton's Bogey," *PMLA* 93 (1978): 368-82.

5. See Fox's "Literary Allusion," which argues that Woolf's sophisticated use of allusion is calculated to demonstrate that male writers have a tradition of literature to which they may comfortably allude, whereas female writers do not.

6. Dusinberre is quoting Hélène Cixous, "The Laugh of the Medusa."

7. *The Common Reader* begins with "The Pastons and Chaucer," an essay that explores the possibilities of reading that Chaucer opened up. From there, by way of an essay on Greek literature, Woolf proceeds to two essays on the English Renaissance, followed by one on Montaigne. Her draft work shows that the first three chapters originated as one chapter stressing the fertile, creative atmosphere of Renaissance exploration (Berg, reel 6, M20).

8. The essay's title evolved from "Some Elizabethans" to "The Strange Elizabethans," apparently reflecting Woolf's genuine sense of their "strangeness"—a concept that recurs throughout the draft (Berg, reel 5, M11).

9. This phrase is found in a draft of the Donne essay titled "Corrections to Donne" (Virginia Woolf Manuscripts from the Monk's House Papers at the University of Sussex, microfilm ed. [hereafter "Monk's House"], reel 2, 2.e).

10. Woolf's tendencies to sympathize with Harvey even more strongly than had Moore Smith, who was himself correcting the harsher conclusions of an earlier

biographer, are echoed in the most recent biography of him, Virginia Stern's 1979 volume.

11.   Janet Biller, qtd. in Stern 38 n.16.

12.   When Woolf conceived the two essays on Elizabethans, she planned for one to discuss the critical theorists William Webbe, George Puttenham, and Gabriel Harvey; and the other to consist of a sketch of Sidney emphasizing his relationship with Penelope Rich (Berg, reel 13, RN12). Her decision to narrow the first chapter to Harvey appears to reflect her desire to explore the private thoughts of one man rather than the details of Renaissance prosody. As for Sidney, her enthusiasm appears to have waned (see *D* 4: 53).

13.   While correcting the essay on 3 Feb. 1932, Woolf remarks on her absorption in the subject; the same diary entry suggests that she considered placing this essay first in the collection (*D* 4: 70).

14.   One of her sources was Clifford's *Diary*, published in 1923 with an introduction by Vita Sackville-West, a descendant. As Brenda Silver notes (8-9), Clifford continued to inhabit Woolf's imagination; she was to become, for example, a prominent figure in Woolf's late, unfinished essay "The Reader."

15.   "A Professor of Life," review of *The Letters of Walter Raleigh*, ed. Lady Raleigh, *Vogue*, May 1926. Rpt. as "Walter Raleigh" in *CDB* 87-93.

"deeply and consciously affected . . .": Virginia Woolf's Reviews of the Romantic Poets

Edward A. Hungerford

The present essay explores how Virginia Woolf's book reviews and occasional articles provide the evidence for a reassessment of her many uses of Romanticism. A dozen years ago, Eric Warner's collection of essays *Virginia Woolf: A Centenary Perspective* showed that British scholars have been inspired by her interest in the Romantic writers, without by any means exhausting the subject. Hermione Lee, for example, convincingly demonstrates in her formalist essay "A Burning Glass: Reflection in Virginia Woolf" the interpenetration of Romantic images not only in the fiction but throughout Woolf's works. Lee also, later in her essay, reminds us that we have not far to seek if we would explore Woolf's sources in Romantic writers. Her many essays and book reviews dealing with "Hazlitt, Byron, Shelley, Leigh Hunt, De Quincey, Wordsworth, and Coleridge" show that Woolf was "deeply and consciously affected by the patterns of thought and by the language of the Romantic writers" (21). The purpose of my own investigation is to document these patterns of thought, but I confine my study to the reviews and comments about Wordsworth, Coleridge, Shelley, and Keats. The involvement of Woolf with Byron has proved too complex to deal with in the same proportions, and I leave that for a future article. Other articles might well be devoted to the Romantic prose essayists, Hazlitt and De Quincey especially, and to Woolf's interest in the women of the early nineteenth century.

Books, Woolf said, bubbled up in her mind and gave her so many ideas that she could scarcely record them all. Yet, her preparation as literary critic did not lead to the kind of formalist criticism (for example, by the New Critics) that would become the dominant mode in the United

States from the 1950s to the end of the 1960s and beyond. The close reading and analysis of individual lines and images, still practiced assiduously today by some scholars and teachers, seldom forms the basis of her essays and reviews. Woolf was interested in "judging the whole," the whole poem, the complete effect of the novel she had just read, like the common reader she virtually reinvented (following, of course, Dr. Johnson). She will occasionally quote individual lines of poems, but she almost never provides an analysis of any image or individual line of verse. Thus, when we explore what the young Virginia Stephen wrote before her marriage, we find a number of reviews concerned with Romanticism; yet these essays almost invariably make their major points by biographical and anecdotal remarks. She did not move far from that practice even when she came to produce the essays she collected in *The Common Reader*.

I. Wordsworth

Her earliest reviews, in 1904-1905, now available in the first volume of Andrew McNeillie's splendid edition, did not give her a chance to treat the Romantics, but after more than eighteen months of rather routine book reviewing assignments, she had two that allowed her to express opinions about major poets. One of these, commenting on two collections of letters by Robert and Elizabeth Barrett Browning, was a signed review published in *The Speaker*. The other is "Wordsworth and the Lakes," printed anonymously, as were all her reviews in the *Times Literary Supplement (TLS)*. The latter review discusses *Wordsworth's Guide to the Lakes, with an Introduction* and *Months at the Lakes* in *TLS* (*E* 1:105-9).

While the Browning review allows Woolf to display an awareness of the decline in Mrs. Browning's current literary reputation, these are not major works in the Browning canon that she is reviewing. By contrast, the Wordsworth review differs in tactics and result. By approaching Wordsworth's short prose document with great respect and sympathy, the twenty-four-year-old reviewer declares her sympathy with his informed yet transcendent view of the natural world. The Wordsworth *Guide to the Lakes* was written in 1810, at a time when mass tourism had not yet begun, and yet when writing about the English Lake District still suffered from the affected language of the picturesque school of William Gilpin. "Wordsworth," Woolf says, "coming after these somewhat perplexed and perfunctory tourists, wrote with the calm authority of one who had lived for all but three years of his life among the scenes he describes" (*E* 1: 106). She admires his knowledge of scientific data:

> But all through the minute and scrupulous catalogue there runs a
> purpose which solves it into one coherent and increasingly impressive
> picture. For all these details . . . are of such interest to him because he
> sees them all as living parts of a vast and exquisitely ordered system. It
> is this combination in him of obstinate truth and fervent imagination
> that stamps his descriptions more deeply upon the mind than those of
> almost any other writer. (*E* 1: 106-7)

She finds parts of sentences to quote, skillfully working them into her own
viewpoint. A characteristic passage, she says, "is that in which he reflects
why it is that a lake carries you 'into recesses of feeling otherwise impene-
trable. The reason of this is that the heavens are not only brought down into
the bosom of the earth, but that the earth is mainly looked at and thought
of through the medium of a purer element'" (107). Appropriately, the young
reviewer devoted about three-fourths of her 1,400-word review to Wordsworth and the remainder to Canon Rawnsley, whom she rather gleefully
destroyed as an old windbag. She took care to ridicule him, however, not
by personal attack but by citing Rawnsley's own falsely elegant vocabulary.
Running through the seasons with talk of "white galleons that come sailing
into seas of sapphire," Rawnsley's words give her this concluding impression:
"In December, finally, we feel that we have passed a very innocent and
brightly coloured year, although we are not quite sure that we have been at
the Lakes" (*E* 1:108). While her language here is clearly harsh, her language
describing Wordsworth's work contains none of the ridicule and reflects her
reverence for him.

By the spring of 1908, when Woolf next was given a book about
Wordsworth to review, she was already experienced, with more than seventy
articles to her credit. Her next *TLS* review was of *Letters of the Wordsworth
Family. From 1787 to 1855* (*E* 1:183-88). The *Letters* had been collected apparently in the view that a new life of the poet would be unnecessary for some
decades. Again, as she had in her comments on the *Guide to the Lakes*, Woolf
dealt with the great poet in straightforward terms, without a trace of satire.
One senses from the review that Wordsworth's reputation, as well as her
own personal study of the poems, commanded unqualified respect, and that
she was prepared to give no less than that.

Wordsworth, Virginia Stephen says, sees the details of the natural
world "as living parts of a vast and exquisitely ordered system" (*E* 1: 106-7)
with which she sympathizes, even though her own agnostic beliefs did not
agree with his natural supernaturalism. Perhaps, however, she was sympathetic to the tendency toward pantheism in much of his poetry. In William

Wordsworth's letters, "There is no gulf between the stuff of daily life and the stuff of poetry, save that one is the raw material of the other . . ." (E 1: 186). She can find little humor in his work. But he is much aware of the "perplexed lives" of his friends, Coleridge and De Quincey. "He is not blind for a moment to the disastrous weakness underlying the splendid powers of Coleridge, but exposes it with the melancholy insight of a physician" (185-86). Her concluding sentence leaves an indelible impression of respect: "His daily life, exposed to us here so largely, and with such indifference to effect, has thus the same quality that moves us in the deepest of his poems; it points unswervingly, through trials and obscurities, to the most exalted end" (187). It would be difficult to imagine higher praise or more perceptive insight from a reviewer than this. Woolf did not, in fact, lose sight of these high, altruistic values in later life. In 1929, for example, twenty-three years later than the review just cited, we find from her diary that she has been reading Wordsworth's *Prelude* at night before going to sleep. She had become in her forties a major writer, was beginning her novel *The Waves*, and still often had Wordsworth by her bedside. Romanticism had deep roots in her mind.

II. Coleridge

Though it is clear that Woolf also thought highly of Coleridge's lyrics, particularly "Kubla Khan," her book reviews and articles about Coleridge focus only upon his prose: his prose criticism of other writers, and his *Table Talk and Omniana*.[1] Coleridge was regarded by a wide segment of the British public in the mid-nineteenth century as a kind of benign sage. Emerson visited him and wrote about his visit. Other writers such as Matthew Arnold cited him and praised his insights. By the time Virginia Woolf wrote her article for the *TLS* entitled "Coleridge's Criticism," she had absorbed all that adulatory comment from the past, it is true. Yet from her own study she had also come to the conclusion that his criticism is "the most spiritual in the language" (E 2: 222).

The Coleridge article for the *TLS*, "Coleridge as Critic," appeared 7 February 1918 as a review of *The Table Talk and Omniana of Samuel Taylor Coleridge*. That Woolf had thought in a penetrating way, deeply into the question of motives in Coleridge's writing, is shown by her comment late in the article:

> The possibility that one may throw light upon a book by considering
> the circumstances in which it was written did not commend itself to

Coleridge; to him the light was concentrated and confined in one ray—
in the art itself. (*E* 2: 223)

Woolf characterizes Coleridge in contrast to Samuel Johnson as
indifferent to "mere personality" in writers. Coleridge's concentration sometimes on the abstract omitted not only gossip but the kind of concerns with
ordinary human problems that Johnson excelled in recognizing. And this
tendency, Woolf says,

> persuades us, from the fact that even more than Shelley he was 'a
> beautiful and ineffectual angel'—a spirit imprisoned behind bars invis-
> ible and intangible to the tame hordes of humanity, a spirit always
> beckoned by something from without. (222)

Yet the rewards of reading Coleridge are great: ". . . there has been no
finer messenger between gods and men, nor one whose being kept from
youth to age so high a measure of transparency." Woolf calls attention to
"the incompatibility which certainly existed between Coleridge and the rest
of the world" (222). She attempts in this article to summarize the total effect
of his complex mind on her own, that is, on what she claimed was an ordinary
reader's mind. She refers to his interests in painting and music, and she cites
a number of quotations—included "only for their brevity," to give some of
the flavor of his judgments, particularly literary judgments.

As a guide to readers, and for a specific series of the great critic's essays
to explore and to test our own mettle, she says, "His notes upon Shakespeare
are, to our thinking, the only criticisms which bear reading with the sound
of the play still in one's ears" (222). The article gives evidence of admirable
compression in Woolf's thought about the place of literary criticism; she
gives her readers something to grasp, a direction in which to move, and a
certain vision of the whole body of Coleridge's organic and architectonic
writing about literature as well as other related topics. Woolf had chosen
his writing as a model without in any way attempting to imitate her great
predecessor. Coleridge became, I think, the other mentor of intellectual
ideas for her, to counteract the dogmatic and moral tendencies of Johnson,
whom she also admired for different reasons.

In an earlier article, "Mr. Symons's Essays," Woolf stated her views of
some other important critics and writers from the nineteenth century:

> Coleridge and Lamb, Arnold and Sainte-Beuve were all poets, either
> with the right hand or the left. Indeed, it seems impossible for anyone

who is not actually dealing with the problems of art to know the nature
of them; or—and this is of greater importance—to have a lively enough
passion for the artist's view to be in sympathy with the different forms
of it. (E 2: 67)

Woolf respected Coleridge, as she did these other writers, because
they were involved minutely with the problems of art. Yet she does not
attempt to explore further the interaction between the poet's mind and the
critic's in the same writer. However, these complex questions were often
on her mind, since they were the same questions she attempted to solve
in her own writing. The preparation of *The Common Reader* taught her that
she could perform as both poetic novelist and literary critic, and could do
so during the same day when she needed to work on both books, in this
case *Mrs. Dalloway* and *The Common Reader,* issued within a month of each
other in 1925.

If her first important statement about Coleridge was the comment on
"Coleridge as Critic," another easily accessible estimate of Coleridge's power
as a thinker and conversationalist came with her late essay, "The Man at the
Gate."[2] This essay clearly reveals the consistency of Woolf's ideas about
Coleridge as well as her own approach to an understanding of his wonderful
abundance and variety. It is, of course, probable that she reread her 1918
TLS review while she was writing the article of 1940 twenty-two years later.

As in the former review, she places great emphasis upon the character
and in fact, the personality of Coleridge, the man who can be observed by
others. In "The Man at the Gate"

[t]he man was Coleridge as De Quincey saw him, standing in a gateway.
For it is vain to put the single word Coleridge at the head of a page—
Coleridge the innumerable, the mutable, the atmospheric; Coleridge
who is part of Wordsworth, Keats and Shelley; of his age and of our
own; Coleridge whose written words fill hundreds of pages and over-
flow innumerable margins; whose spoken words still reverberate, so
that as we enter his radius he seems not a man, but a swarm, a cloud, a
buzz of words, darting this way and that, clustering, quivering and
hanging suspended. (*DM* 104)

This eighty-seven-word sentence, the second sentence of the essay,
perfectly sets the tone of the entire piece of writing. She knows that each
one of us, as an ordinary mortal, can comprehend only bits and pieces of
this very complex man, the poet-philosopher. So she grounds him in

biographical fact. De Quincey saw him thus in 1807, when Coleridge was "already incapable of movement." But, later to be confined to residence with Dr. Gillman at Highgate after 1816, he lived on until 1834, always talking, attracting miscellaneous listeners from foreign lands as well as the neighbors. Woolf seems interested in setting forth the ultimate strangeness, friendly though benign, of the great writer's personality. Her superb skill in the art of brief biography gives us a precise, limited vignette of a Coleridge who can be observed only in partial glimpses. And like a quatrain from the Greek Anthology, her concluding sentence fixes him forever in our minds:

> Is it for hours or for years that this heavily built man standing in a gate has been pouring forth this passionate soliloquy, while his "large soft eyes with a peculiar expression of haze or dreaminess mixed in their light" have been fixed upon a far-away vision that filled a very few pages with poems in which every word is exact and every image as clear as crystal? (*DM* 110)

Nowhere else in the essay has Coleridge's poetry been mentioned, so that the effect of the final phrases is almost to make us catch our breath, as though we suddenly remembered an intense emotion. A tribute of such magnitude convinces us, the readers, that it *was* a sort of love affair—Virginia Woolf's admiration for the marvelous mind, and too for the poet of "Kubla Khan" and "The Rime of the Ancient Mariner," perhaps a memory of her youth and her reading Palgrave's *Golden Treasury* in the park across from Hyde Park Gate at the age of thirteen.[3]

III. Shelley

I shall not attempt to summarize all the biographical detail that Woolf includes in her book reviews and essays on Shelley, since the reprinting of her reviews has made them readily available. It is worth noticing, however, that she has specific comments to make about Shelley's poetry, albeit in rather quick, darting judgments. She had certainly read most of the works of all four of the poets we are discussing, as can be discerned from a summary of reading notes in Brenda Silver's *Virginia Woolf's Reading Notebooks*. She invariably chose some other way than analysis to discuss the work of poets; and her methods usually meant that she turned first to the life of the poet, to his letters, to an investigation and questioning of his personality.

A rather early example of the method comes in her 1908 article on Shelley—or rather, on one of the female figures of the poet's early acquaintanceship, Elizabeth Hitchener, with whom the poet exchanged many letters before his first marriage. Woolf wrote two book reviews about that poet, which have subsequently been collected; one included in *The Death of the Moth* was Woolf's review of Walter E. Peck's 1927 biography *Shelley: His Life and Work*. But first, a word might be said for the much earlier footnote to the Shelley biography, "Shelley and Elizabeth Hitchener" (*BP* 154-57). The 1908 *TLS* review places her readers within the context of the Shelley, aged nineteen, who was about to marry Harriet Westbrook (contrary to his avowed principles) and was traveling the countryside to awaken others to the need of political and social reform. This is the boy, says Woolf, who would, in five or six years, "write consummate poetry." The reason to read Shelley's letters to his spiritual convert, Hitchener, she remarks, is that "Shelley's character is always amazing." The future poet, by exchanging long and intimate letters with Miss Hitchener, ultimately persuaded her to join him and Harriet in their expeditions: "It was to be a spiritual companionship, in no way inspired by carnal love of that 'lump of organized matter which enshrines thy soul'; and, further, there was the insidious bait which Shelley offered, with his curious lack of humanity . . ." (*BP* 155).[4]

At any rate, Elizabeth Hitchener did join Harriet and Percy Shelley. She helped to distribute pamphlets, was a part of the menage for a few months (until the inevitable jealousies flared out of control), and returned to Sussex. "The spiritual sister and prophetess [whom Shelley had proclaimed in his letters to her] became simply 'The Brown Demon,' 'a woman of desperate views and dreadful passions,' who must be got rid of even at the cost of a yearly allowance of a hundred pounds." Hitchener's story is concluded in an amused tone and slightly satirical glance:

> It is not known whether she ever received it; but there is a very credible tradition that she recovered her senses, after her startling downfall, and lived a respectable and laborious life at Edmonton, sweetened by the reading of the poets, and the memory of her romantic indiscretions with the truest of them all. (*BP* 157)

It is Shelley's life that Woolf seems to be concerned with, the relationships he had and his effect on others' lives. In writing about the obscure Elizabeth Hitchener, Woolf gives the reader insight into the Romantic poet Percy Shelley. One quality that made Woolf an excellent reviewer, especially of the lives of the Romantic writers, is that she had lived in a home in which biography as a craft and art was unquestionably admired, and Sir Leslie's daughter fell heir to a vast knowledge of the circumstances, reputations, and influence of great writers.

So with this constant chatter of literary associations that can be verified by reference to any of the volumes of her diary and letters, she was well equipped to take the measure of the Peck biography of Shelley when it appeared in 1927. Our impression from the review of Walter Edwin Peck's *Shelley: His Life and Work* is a favorable one. Dealing in the first paragraph with the fluctuations over a century of Shelley's reputation, she praises Peck's approach: "He is singularly dispassionate, and yet not colourless. He has opinions, but he does not obtrude them. His attitude to Shelley is kind but not condescending. He does not rhapsodize, but at the same time he does not scold" (*DM* 120). Gradually in the essay, Woolf's opinions narrow and concentrate into her own meditation. She does not simply review routinely the current book at hand. She seizes on a citation from one of Mary Shelley's letters to express her personal vision of Shelley, which sums up twenty or thirty years of her own reading. Her review turns into a personal essay, more like her early 1908 *Cornhill* essays, or resembling the nineteenth-century concept of reviews.

The essay's title, as it appeared in the *New York Herald Tribune* "Books" section, 23 October, was "Not One of Us." Woolf notes that Mary Shelley had mused at a time after Shelley had died, "What a strange life mine has been. Love, youth, fear and fearlessness led me early from the regular routine of life and I united myself to this being who, not one of *us*, though like us, was pursued by numberless miseries and annoyances, in all of which I shared" (*DM* 124). Woolf finds this the key to understanding the poet's strange, unearthly personality: full of idealism, compassionate, a lover of the clouds and mountains, but oddly formal in his private life, without intimacy. But, "The most ethereal of poets was the most practical of men" (125).

In the last third of this 2,700-word essay, Woolf mentions by title and brief evaluations some of the better-known Shelley poems. Quite likely we see here, in 1927, the residue of much conversation between herself, T. S. Eliot, and the Bloomsbury regulars who devalued the Romantics in general, and particularly, even notoriously, the poetry of Shelley.[5] Her antagonism to sentimentality, even sometimes to the mere thought of the sentimental, comes to the fore: "We may not agree with Professor Peck's definition, yet we have only to read Shelley again to come up against the difficulty of which he speaks. It lies partly in the disconcerting fact that we had thought his poetry so good and we find it indeed so poor" (*DM* 125).

The following quotation demonstrates how severely she judged the poems in the middle stages of her literary career (prior to *The Second Common Reader*):

> How are we to account for the fact that we remember him as a great poet and find him on opening his pages a bad one? The explanation seems to be that he was not a "pure poet." He did not concentrate his meaning in a small space; there is nothing in Shelley's poetry as rich and compact as the odes of Keats. His taste could be sentimental; he had all the vices of the album makers; he was unreal, strained, verbose. (*DM* 126)

The paragraph following the one just partially quoted returns us not only to Shelley's biography, but to the modern world of England in which certain social and political conditions prevail. However, let us examine the literary judgments uttered in Johnsonian terms to consider what Woolf thought her own task as an essayist. Certainly it is one important task of the critic to make judgments; Woolf cannot be faulted for that position. She takes her stance as a common reader within the limitations imposed by her own definition—not university-educated but attempting to construct a whole out of fragments; she is the daughter of an educated man, as she sometimes modestly claims.

This common reader, however, has reviewed three or four hundred books and written several books of her own. She has by diligence turned herself into a critic. So she has a double role in the essay. She speaks for the common, less-educated but well-informed American reader of the *Herald-Tribune*. But she also attempts to suggest the rapture of the earlier Virginia Stephen who had so depended on her *Golden Treasury* in Kensington Gardens at the age of thirteen.[6] Is this the side of her critical mind that loved "the lyrics with all their exquisite beauty"? Had she then abandoned that admiration, when she wrote her 1927 essay-review? Or is she attempting to compensate for the recent denigration of Shelley in the twenties and thirties, when he was under attack from the followers of I. A. Richards?

An important thirty-two-year span separates the young Virginia of 1895 from the Virginia of 1927. In her middle years she is still an admirer of Shelley but feels the weight of a great body of reading, of Eliot's attitudes, perhaps, and of the general modern contempt for the sentimental. So she settles for an undefined distinction between "pure poetry" and "impure poetry" in order to allow herself to praise Shelley. That he is a great poet she still does not doubt, but she has found the means to justify her early and continuing taste for Romantic poetry.

If anything specific can be derived from the quoted paragraph about pure and impure poetry, the distinction has been sharply drawn between Shelley's longer poems, *Prometheus Unbound* and *Epipsychidion*, and some of the briefer lyrics. In the longer poems, "where the faults have space to lose themselves, we again become convinced of his greatness" (126). She feels challenged intellectually by the involved thought structure and complexity of the poet's argument, though phrased as verse. Although by contrast the shorter lyrics mentioned ("The Skylark," "Ode to the West Wind") rein-forced her distaste for the sentimental or bad poetry to which she objected, Woolf has paid no tribute to Shelley's excellence of construction in "Ode to the West Wind," nor does she hint that the intricate adaptation of rhymes from the terza rima of Dante is remarkably appropriate for a lyric composed in one of the lovely parks of the city of Florence. Did she really not care about such matters?[7]

IV. Keats

Her evaluation of Keats, like that of Coleridge and Shelley, takes its direction from her impressions of their respective personalities and charac-ters. And though the occasional comment in her diary and letters shows that she continued to admire Keats as a "pure poet," she wrote no book review or article thus far discovered about Keats.[8]

From Silver's record of Woolf's reading notebooks, we do know that Woolf had read Sidney Colvin's biography, *John Keats. His Life and Poetry, his Friends, Critics, and After-Fame.* There are also notes to *Endymion* that show her use of Keats's *Complete Poetical Works.*[9] The same holograph notebook also contains references to works such as Coleridge's *Biographia Literaria* and other standard historical works of literary criticism. Then, too, the name of John Keats emerges frequently as an incidental figure in essays devoted to other writers and other books.

For example, a review of *Romance: Two Lectures* by Sir Walter Raleigh appeared in *TLS* on 18 January 1917. She praises Raleigh, Professor of English Literature, Oxford University, and fellow of Merton College, for his insights and admonishments about Romanticism. The movement is here termed "the revival of Romance," and the brief review shows Woolf meditating on the meaning of the period of literary history that included the Romantic poets: "We mean a great many things when we say that a poem is romantic. We refer to an atmosphere of vagueness, mystery, distance; but perhaps we most constantly feel that the writer is thinking more of the effect of the thing upon his mind than of the thing itself" (*E* 2: 75). By thus directing our attention to the self-reflexive nature of such poetry, Woolf herself is formulating her own definitions of what we term today Romanticism.[10]

In the last few lines of this review devoted to Raleigh's ideas, she takes up as a challenge his claim that the great poets "face the discipline of facts and life" by concluding:

> They may begin as Keats began, with a sense of the wonder of the visible world; of passion and love and beauty; but there comes a time when the passion turns to dream, and only the greatest wake themselves from that and make poetry with their eyes open. For, as Sir Walter says very finely, "the poetry which can bear all naked truth and still keep its singing voice is the only immortal poetry." (*E* 2: 75-76)

Here Woolf uses Keats as an example of the kind of poet who has a "sense of the wonder of the visible world," and though he digresses into dream he manages to make his poetry with open eyes.

Another review from the period prior to *The Common Reader*, during those years when Woolf moved toward seeing herself as a critic, rather than merely as weekly reviewer, is the important (but little known) review she wrote of Edward Thomas's *A Literary Pilgrim in England*.[11] Woolf conducts an agreeable, amiable, and at times admiring conversation with Thomas, who had recently, a few months earlier than her review, died in battle at Arras; in this one essay, perhaps more so than in most of her essays about literary critics and criticism, she seems supremely confident about her views of poets and poetry. It seems likely, also, that Woolf had met Thomas personally through her friendship with Rupert Brooke and the "Neo-Pagans." McNeillie points out that Thomas was not at the time widely known for his poetry in England, though his stature as poet has since that time gradually risen to a rather solid reputation as a Georgian poet.

Many poets and writers come into his discussion and into Woolf's citation of Thomas's critical views on poetry: Blake, Wordsworth, Matthew Arnold, Shelley, and others. The book's incidental views on Keats particularly interest us here. Speaking of several poets' attachment to landscape, Woolf paraphrases Thomas as having said, "You will always find Shelley

near the water; Wordsworth among the hills; and Meredith within sixty
miles of London. . . . It is much less easy to reduce our vision of the landscape
of Keats to something marked upon a map. We should be inclined to call
him more the poet of a season than the poet of a place" (*E* 2: 162). Woolf is
here thinking of Keats's major Odes, particularly "To Autumn," which she
mentions a few lines later in her review. Continuing her dialogue with
Thomas, Woolf paraphrases him thus:

> But although [Keats] began as most writers do by describing what he
> saw, that was exercise work, and very soon he came to 'hate descrip-
> tions'. And thus he wrote some of the most beautiful descriptions in the
> language, for in spite of many famous and exact passages the best
> descriptions are the least accurate, and represent what the poet saw
> with his eyes shut when the landscape had melted indistinguishably
> into the mood. (162)

Thomas appears to be moving toward a theory of unconscious poetic
creation. But, in any case, Woolf concludes: "We have seldom read a book
indeed which gives a better feeling of England than this one" (163). As always
with her best reviews, she inspires us to seek out the original work and to
continue our own conversations with the great poets. Students of the English
poets, and especially the nineteenth-century poets, can learn a good deal from
Virginia Woolf's knowledgeable review of *A Literary Pilgrim in England.*

Woolf's obvious admiration for the poetry of Keats and Wordsworth,
which she insinuates in dozens of places throughout her writing, may
provide a reason for her total omission of the Romantic poets from her
fictional *Orlando.* Perhaps it seemed to her a cleaner stroke, in order to
maintain the satirical stance toward nearly all literary figures in the novel,
simply to leave out Romanticism. Then she would not be obliged to satirize
Keats and Wordsworth, in whose poetry—and indeed whose lives—she
found little to ridicule.

In the context of the Romantic genius, Mark Goldman relates Woolf's
concept of literary history in her essays to the satirical portraits in *Orlando,*
and takes up as prototypical personality the character of Benjamin R.
Haydon, friend of Keats and self-proclaimed painter of genius.[12] Goldman's
summary places the essays of Woolf about the Romantic writers in a helpful
context, though he does not explore the significance of Woolf's near-total
omission of the Romantic writers in *Orlando.*

V. The Visionary Imagination and the Intellectual Imagination

At the conclusion of her last essay in *The Common Reader*, "How It Strikes a Contemporary," she includes a quick checklist of books written in the first two decades of the nineteenth century to furnish the reader with a set of standards when comparing "the present time" (a hundred years later) with that glorious period of the past in which great writers inhabited the earth. The list is a mixed one, composed of poets, novelists, and essayists: "*Waverley, The Excursion, Kubla Khan, Don Juan, Hazlitt's Essays, Pride and Prejudice, Hyperion,* and *Prometheus Unbound* were all published between 1800 and 1821" (CR 1: 235). This list mainly states to us that Scott, Wordsworth, Coleridge, Byron, Hazlitt, Austen, Keats, and Shelley were incontrovertibly great writers. In other words, she has made a judgment that she believes incapable of contradiction; and she rests that judgment upon one well-known work of major importance (for each of the writers) and upon the achievement in general of Scott and Hazlitt. We find ourselves entering the conversation with her, being challenged to defend our own claims and ultimately to agree with the central ideas of her essay. We also find the essay true to her own standards for the common reader: to judge the whole work rather than to concentrate on smaller parts and quibble over fine points as the critics are, she claims, most likely to do. For example, we wonder why she chose *The Excursion* for Wordsworth's representative achievement instead of *The Prelude*. Then we realize, of course, that very little scholarship on *The Prelude* had been published by 1923, the date of Woolf's essay, and it was not generally known that *The Prelude* had been completed for all practical purposes before 1820, though not published in book form until 1850. Though reputations have risen and fallen in the seventy years since "How It Strikes a Contemporary" reached its first printing, for the most part Woolf's list of the great writers represents an established (traditional, mostly male) canon for the Romantic period and an important part of the canon of all English literature.

In December 1919, during a time when she had set for herself an ambitious reading program that included many works of literary criticism, the opportunity presented itself to Virginia Woolf to review *Rupert Brooke and the Intellectual Imagination*, by Walter de la Mare (*E* 3: 134-36). She was planning and preparing for a book tentatively titled "Reading"; and her reading notebooks of 1918 to 1922 might have been collectively entitled, "How to Become a Literary Critic."[13] So the comments of de la Mare helped her to define certain aspects of criticism.

Walter de la Mare's book claimed that "greatest poets, having both the visionary imagination and the intellectual imagination, deal with both sides of life; in the lesser poets either the one kind of imagination or the other predominates" (*E* 3: 134). Woolf agrees and continues with a careful and sympathetic critique applied to Brooke's method of composing poetry, made more vital for the reader by her own personal knowledge of Brooke before his death in World War I. She notes that Keats died younger, and Shelley only a year or two older than Brooke. Yet perhaps the important point here comes not in her evaluation of her contemporary as a poet but in her system of poetic values. For her, Shelley and Keats have written some of the "supreme felicities" of English poetry (*E* 3: 135). Though "the greatest poets, having both the visionary imagination and the intellectual imagination, deal with both sides of life," Woolf writes, paraphrasing de la Mare, she does not refer to any poet who combined both types of imagination. She does cite others: "Blake and Shelley are obvious examples of the visionary; Donne and Meredith of the intellectual" (*E* 3: 134). She appears to have considered the chief Romantics, particularly Wordsworth, Keats, and Shelley, as visionary poets; their visionary imagination transcended (particularly in their longer poems) any work that had been produced by other poets who had only achieved the intellectual imagination.

I have said that Woolf often seems uncomfortable when talking about recent or experimental poetry. Her judgments about any poem, when she concentrates on a single poem, are always interesting and provocative, and are particularly lucid when she is tempering her mind against another artist's own criticism of poetry, such as that of Walter de la Mare, or Swinburne or Coventry Patmore. It may seem odd that at this point in her life it apparently did not occur to her that her new friend T. S. Eliot would become a critical force of equal and even greater influence than Patmore and de la Mare for the middle years of the new century. The difficulty that Woolf had in reviewing the Hogarth Press edition of Eliot's *Poems* in 1919—when she had to confess herself unequal to the task, and handed it over to Leonard—is related in her *Letters* (2: 353, 370). So far as her opinion of Imagism is concerned, there is scarcely a mention of that movement in either her diary or her letters.

When we attempt to assess these meaningful silences in her comments about contemporary poetry, we come to her fine essay "The Leaning Tower" with pleasure to find her in touch with the poets of the 1930s, Auden and Spender and Day-Lewis. We find that Woolf did indeed care about the direction of the poetry of her time, that she had followed the writings of her contemporaries, including the poets, and that she had important things to say to them. To look once again at "The Leaning Tower" is to discover, however, that she made her approach to modern poets through her assumptions about Keats, Shelley, and the earlier generations:

> Considering how much we talk about writers, how much they talk
> about themselves, it is odd how little we know about them. Why are
> they so common sometimes; then so rare? Why do they sometimes
> write masterpieces, then nothing but trash? And why should a family,
> like the Shelleys, like the Keatses, like the Brontës, suddenly burst into
> flame and bring to birth Shelley, Keats, and the Brontës? (M 105)

Woolf's audience for the paper, the Workers' Educational Association
in Brighton, may have suggested this approach through history; it is clear
that she talked about those writers more comfortably, using the Romantic
generation as a point of departure rather than more avant-garde figures who
would perhaps be unknown to her listeners. But, of course, she is working
toward her sociological argument about the "towers of gold and stucco" upon
which the poets and writers have always stood in the past: toward her
metaphor of the leaning tower upon which present-day poets now stand in
1940, the date of her talk. The towers are built upon family wealth and
expensive education.

Once she has established her metaphor of the tower, she introduces
quite casually the group that she has an interest in: "If you read current
literary journalism you will be able to rattle off a string of names—Day-
Lewis, Auden, Spender, Isherwood, Louis MacNeice and so on" (M 113).
Her essay mentions a generation of 1914 writers whose education in the
universities was secure before the 1914 war. Then she skips to the newer
generation of writers prominent from 1925 onwards, a procedure that
conveniently skips over an in-between group: some briefly mentioned, such
as Eliot, and some omitted, such as Pound.

Woolf takes one example from the "string of names," Louis MacNeice,
for quotation and more particular notice. One of MacNeice's poems, *Autumn
Journal*, interests her: "feeble as poetry, but interesting as autobiography" (M
116). And she quotes at intervals more than thirty lines of *Autumn Journal*
(and very little is quoted from any other poet). A page or two farther along,
her standard of comparison for evaluation of poetry is to quote a few lines
from one poet (in this case, it appears, Stephen Spender); and then to place
beside these lines a few of Wordsworth (M 119). We listen to Wordsworth
in solitude, and approve, she says. But the MacNeice and Spender poetry is
"politician's poetry": "We listen to oratory, not poetry" (119).

Virginia Woolf's taste in poetry, as these passages hint, remained a
very severe taste, austere in its attitude to contemporary poetry of nearly all
sorts. Her claims for the contrast of pure and impure poetry seem to rest
upon an almost universal disapproval of short lyric poems for their senti-

mentality and her belief that only in the longer poems (even of the Romantic poets whom she greatly admired) could true poetic values be found. What had happened to those "supreme felicities" of Keats and Shelley in her personal pantheon of taste? Had she excluded the short poems because she felt a kind of superiority, in maturity, to her youthful rapture in these same Romantic lyrics? She could, however, make amends by turning to *The Prelude* for comfort, by placing her Wordsworth by her bedside when in doubt about the state of poetry in the modern world.

Works Cited

Daiches, David. *Virginia Woolf.* Norfolk, CT: New Directions, 1942.

Dictionary of National Biography. "Byron, George Gordon," 3: 584-607; "Wordsworth, William," 21: 927-42.

Goldman, Mark. *The Reader's Art: Virginia Woolf as Literary Critic.* The Hague: Mouton, 1976.

Kirkpatrick, B. J. *A Bibliography of Virginia Woolf.* 3rd ed. Oxford: Claredon P, 1980.

Lee, Hermione. "A Burning Glass: Reflection in Virginia Woolf." Warner 12-27.

Palgrave, Francis Turner, ed. *The Golden Treasury of the Best Songs and Lyrical Poems in the English Language.* World's Classics. London: Oxford UP, 1907.

Rosenberg, Beth Carole. *Virginia Woolf and Samuel Johnson: Common Readers.* New York: St. Martin's, 1995.

Silver, Brenda. *Virginia Woolf's Reading Notebooks.* Princeton: Princeton UP, 1983.

Warner, Eric, ed. *Virginia Woolf: A Centenary Perspective.* New York: St. Martin's, 1984.

Woolf, Virginia. *Books and Portraits.* Ed. Mary Lyon. New York: Harcourt, 1978.

———. *The Common Reader.* Ed. Andrew McNeillie. London: Hogarth, 1984.

———. *The Death of the Moth.* New York: Harcourt, 1942.

———. *The Diary of Virginia Woolf.* Ed. Anne Olivier Bell and Andrew McNeillie. 5 vols. New York: Harcourt, 1977-1984.

———. *The Essays of Virginia Woolf.* Ed. Andrew McNeillie. 3 vols. to date. New York: Harcourt, 1986-.

———. *The Letters of Virginia Woolf.* Ed. Nigel Nicolson and Joanne Trautmann. 6 vols. New York: Harcourt, 1975-1980.

———. *The Moment and Other Essays.* London: Hogarth, 1947.

———. *Moments of Being.* Ed. Jeanne Schulkind. 1976. Harvest, 1978.

Wordsworth, William. *Selected Poems and Prefaces.* Ed. Jack Stillinger. Boston: Houghton Mifflin, 1965.

Notes

1. "Kubla Khan" appears with a list of several masterpieces of Romanticism in "How It Strikes a Contemporary," which is the closing essay in *The Common Reader*.

2. Also written in September 1940, according to Leonard Woolf, was "Sara Coleridge," based on the book *Coleridge Fille: A Biography of Sara Coleridge* (*DM* 111-18).

3. The Virginia Stephen of thirteen, at the time of her mother's death, plays a central role in some sections of Hermione Lee's essay. Lee alerts us to the young Virginia's memories in "A Sketch of the Past" (*MOB* 93) in order to explore the imagery of these reminiscences. Palgrave's *Golden Treasury* was published in 1861 and had many editions in both the nineteenth and twentieth centuries, with additions and alterations down to at least 1944. At that time, the Modern Library took it over in the United States, furnished it with a new introduction by Louis Untermeyer, and kept the venerable anthology in print for several more years.

4. Also collected in *E 1*: 174-78. McNeillie's notes also help in showing what specific letters and passages of the book under review have been used by Woolf.

5. See Goldman, 105-21. David Daiches devotes a perceptive chapter to "The Uncommon Reader" and also addresses the question of aesthetic, impressionist, and judicious (or "systematic") criticism (130-52).

6. The 1907 World's Classics edition of Palgrave contained twenty-two lyrics of Shelley. We have no record at this time of what earlier edition of Palgrave Woolf used.

7. Woolf may be conscious in her 1927 review of addressing male readers in the journals she wrote for, and (unconsciously) crediting Shelley's ideas more than his lyricism. Another possible rationale for her lack of interest in the close analysis of poems may have been that Woolf's home education paid little attention to versification or prosody. In contrast, men educated in the public schools not only received this training but had to write poetry in the styles of Latin and Greek poets. She claimed to be ignorant of iambics and dactyls. Yet, since there is no evidence that she did actually write more than an occasional poem, perhaps we should believe her disclaimer. Leslie Stephen's writings give their attention to the intellectual and moral themes of the writers he discusses, so Woolf had that model, too, for the proper subject matter of her reviews of the poets. There seems a self-contradictory split in her mind between the

marvelous lyricism of her best novels and her inability later in life to believe in, or to admire, the lyrics of contemporary poets.

8.   Kirkpatrick lists no essay or reference directly to Keats. As a convenient way to trace allusions to the poets, especially elusive references and occasional comments rather than extensive essay treatment of the poets, readers can consult the two volumes by Elizabeth Steele.

9.   Silver, 152-54. Silver notes that the group of reading notes from November 1918 to January 1919 "suggests that this is the first of six volumes that pertain to *The Common Reader*."

10.   Woolf thought rather often, it appears, in the years 1916 to 1918, about turning her book-reviewing talents in the directions of becoming a literary critic. As noted above in Silver's comments, Woolf began to think rather specifically about turning to the great critics such as Sidney, Dryden, and Coleridge in preparation for her concept of a book about reading. We can assume that Woolf requested books of literary criticism for her reviews on assignment from her principal editor, Bruce Richmond, editor of the *TLS*. On Richmond's position with regard to reviewing of books by her own presumed friends, see *L* 2: 224, 233.

11.   Review in *TLS*, 11 October 1917 entitled "Flumina Amem Silvasque," which may be translated, McNeillie notes, as "Let me adore the rivers and the woods." The further identifying note states: "(Philip) Edward Thomas (1878-1917), poet, essayist, and critic, had been killed at Arras on 9 April 1917, serving with the Royal Garrison Artillery . . ." (*E* 2: 164).

12.   On Haydon, see *M* 186-92. See also Goldman 22-27. Goldman's perspective is mainly to summarize Woolf's treatment of literary history in this section of his book.

13.   Especially interesting in this regard is "Notebook XXX." Here Woolf lists her brief reading notes for Wordsworth's *Preface to Lyrical Ballads*; Colvin's life of Keats; Coleridge's *Table Talk* & *Omniana*; notes on Keats's *Endymion*; Dryden's "An Essay of Dramatic Poesy"; Sydney's "Apology"; and Shelley's "Defence of Poetry" (Silver 152-55).

"The Burning Ground of the Present": Woolf and Her Contemporaries

Cheryl J. Mares

Certain critics have been quick to point out that Virginia Woolf was often less than kind in her judgments of her contemporaries.[1] Woolf herself would hardly have been surprised by this observation. In her diaries and letters, she repeatedly acknowledges that she is "jealous" and "rather mean always about contemporaries" (D 5: 130). In "How It Strikes a Contemporary," as in many of her other essays and reviews, she repeatedly stresses the difficulties of "pass[ing] judgement on the books of the moment" (E 3: 359). Current estimates of Woolf as a critic of other modern writers vary wildly. Malcolm Bradbury, for example, finds her judgments "exact" (231). Jean Guiguet praises their "fairness" (11). Mary Lyon warns, however, that Woolf's "critical judgment was often less sure in dealing with writers of her own time" (viii). "It is clear," Mark Goldman notes, "that her objectivity will stretch just so far" (97). Indeed, according to Perry Meisel, Woolf simply imposed "the whole and self-contained perfection of her own critical vision" (92) on the work of even "strong contemporaries" (93). Shifting the ground of the debate, Beth Rosenberg contends that when it was a question of contemporary work, Woolf tried to revise the critic's role so that it no longer was "a position from which to give a value judgment," precisely because she "realize[d] that there [was] no way to gauge a masterpiece during the present time" (66).

"It is impossible for the living to judge the works of the living," Woolf wrote in her 1939 essay "Reviewing." "Years, many years, according to Matthew Arnold, have to pass before it is possible to deliver an opinion that is not 'only personal, but personal with passion'" (CDB 137). "It's true," she wryly observed in a letter to Ethel Smyth in 1931, "that death makes judgment easier" (L 4: 316). Although Woolf has been dead now for over half a century, perhaps she—and her "rivals"—are still too contemporary for us to expect much of a consensus on this aspect of her work, or perhaps the expectation of consensus is itself part of the problem, and this state of critical discord and disarray is itself creative and testifies to the ongoing vitality of her views on modern fiction. But Woolf herself, while stressing the importance of remaining open and responsive to change, seems to have believed in continuing to work toward critical consensus, at least as an ideal.

A longing for authoritative criticism repeatedly surfaces in Woolf's work, as does a longing for conditions more propitious for the creation of masterpieces. "[L]et us flatter ourselves," she remarked in "Mr. Howells on Form" in 1918, that even if all that we can do at present is "to frame tentative outlines of belief, always shifting and modifying their terms as we read, we are providing material for the great critic to build with when he comes" (E 2: 324). In "How It Strikes a Contemporary," she claimed that "the risks of judging contemporary works [were] greater than ever before" (E 3: 359), especially since there were no great critics to exercise "a centralising influence" (354). Nevertheless, taking issue with Matthew Arnold, she urged readers not to retreat from "the burning ground of the present" (E 3: 359). Confronted by the chaos, confusion, and frustrations of the present, Woolf seems to have sustained herself in part by a "blessed illusion" (D 4: 221). She suggests in "Mr. Bennett and Mrs. Brown" that her generation is preparing the way for "one of the great ages of English literature" (CDB 119). In "How it Strikes a Contemporary," she portrays her fellow writers as contributing to the eventual emergence of not only "great critics" but also a reading public that would take novels seriously as works of art (E 3: 355). A new world is in the making, she hints in 1929 in A Room of One's Own (114), in which it may prove possible for "Shakespeare's sister" to be born and to flourish, for masterpieces to be written in which "the experience of the mass is behind the single voice" (65). If in "How It Strikes a Contemporary" she counsels writers to give up the hope of creating masterpieces, she immediately extends another hope—that their works will contribute to the making of "the masterpieces of the future" (E 3: 359). Writing to the young Gerald Brenan in 1922, she concedes that "we, in our generation" must "renounce finally" the hope of creating a masterpiece, then hastens to add, "now that I have written this, I doubt its truth. Are we not always hoping?. . . One must renounce, when the book is finished; but not before it is begun" (L 2: 599-600).

Woolf recognized that ultimately a work's "value is constructed by the future," as Rosenberg points out (66); nevertheless, there is a ring of conviction to her judgments on the work of her contemporaries, a sense of confidence in her own "critical sagacity" (D 2: 189). In spite of her self-confessed tendency to be jealous of "rivals," she claimed in a diary entry in 1928 that she would gladly sustain "the superficial pain" of jealousy for the sake of experiencing "the real pleasure" of encountering a modern masterpiece, should one come to light. "Oh yes, I should," she insisted. "I have a mind that feeds perfectly dispassionately & apart from my vanities & jealousies upon literature; & that would have taken a masterpiece to itself" (*D* 3: 209).

The one modern writer who came closest to producing a masterpiece, in Woolf's judgment, was Proust. Nothing in her subsequent writings suggests that she ever altered the opinion she expressed in a letter to Vanessa Bell in 1927: "Proust . . . is far the greatest modern novelist" (*L* 3: 365). Woolf's treatment of Proust strikingly contradicts her own confession that she tended to be "jealous" and "mean . . . about contemporaries." Meisel, who presents Woolf's "ambivalent treatment" of Joyce and Lawrence in her criticism as "determined by her anxiety about a rivalry," deals with the anomaly of her treatment of Proust by discounting its importance: Woolf could allow herself to be generous with Proust, he claims, because Proust was French and therefore not a threat (90). In fact, abundant evidence in Woolf's diaries and letters suggests that in spite of the differences of language, tradition, and nationality, Proust was as threatening to Woolf as the rest of her contemporaries and near-contemporaries, if not more so.[2] Obviously he was not a threat to her standing among novelists writing in the English language. That does not mean, however, that she praised him only or even primarily because he was not a threat in this sense; nor does it necessarily mean that she criticized Joyce and Lawrence, for example, only or even primarily because they were.

Woolf lavished praise on Proust primarily because, apart from her vanities and jealousies, she had a higher regard for his work, even when in some respects it disappointed her, than she did, for example, for *Ulysses*, *Sons and Lovers*, *Pointed Roofs*, Mansfield's short stories, or *A Passage to India*. Meisel argues, however, that in praising Proust, Woolf really is only praising herself, since she "fire[d] out all that is alien to her" in his work and imposed upon it "her own critical vision" (92-93). Woolf's comments on Proust over the years are more complex and contradictory, and therefore more interesting, than Meisel suggests, but it is true that at times she distorted Proust's work in using it as a kind of proxy or stalking horse to advance her own views on the novel. At times she also drew attention to and defended aspects of *A la recherche du temps perdu* that markedly depart from what are generally under-stood to be her own aesthetic ideals. There are, however, recurrent qualities and effects that she looked for and failed to find in contemporary work, that she strove to attain, never to her complete satisfaction, in her own work, and that she suggests were realized, to a considerable extent, in Proust. For a number of reasons, she felt that an achievement comparable to Proust's was beyond her own reach and that of her contemporaries, especially in England. While a detailed examination of the complexities of Woolf's reading of Proust is beyond the scope of this essay, comparing certain comments she made on his work with those she made on Joyce and Lawrence (and, more briefly, on James) will clarify some of the "tentative outlines of belief" that shaped her own fiction and criticism.

Proust was the only modern writer who Woolf thought was "pliant & rich enough to provide a wall for the book from [himself] without its becoming . . . narrowing & restricting" (*D* 2: 14). "Proust," she wrote in her 1929 essay "Phases of Fiction," "is so porous, so pliable, so perfectly receptive that we realize him only as an envelope, thin but elastic, which stretches wider and wider and serves not to enforce a view but to enclose a world" (*GR* 123). By way of contrast, as she notes in "American Fiction," what she found in nearly all contemporary fiction, even by writers who were "otherwise poles asunder," was evidence of an "acute self-consciousness" (*M* 116), writers intent on enforcing their views and clinging to "surface distinctions" between individuals, groups, and whole cultures that block awareness of "profound" differences, including those within the self (124). What these profound differences are cannot be known beforehand and cannot be consciously manipulated; paradoxically, their revelation can free us, however briefly, to imagine ourselves as someone else and give us access to "another world" (*D* 4: 126-27).

It may seem odd to us to see Joyce as a writer who insisted upon "surface distinctions," but that seems to be how Woolf saw him. In an often quoted diary entry she states that what "ruins Joyce," in her opinion, is "the damned egotistical self . . . narrowing and restricting" (*D* 2: 14). In a diary entry that some critics consider scandalous, she denounces *Ulysses* as "an illiterate, underbred book . . . the book of a self taught working man," adding that "we all know how distressing they are, how egotistic, insistent, raw, striking, & ultimately nauseating" (*D* 2: 189). While these remarks have been singled out as an egregious example of class prejudice on Woolf's part, she seems to have been reacting to what she considered a conspicuous display of class prejudice on Joyce's part, a deliberate, clever, and highly self-conscious attempt to shock and impress his readers, who most likely would be middle to upper-middle class, even at the expense of his characters. In her working notes for "Modern Fiction," Woolf seems disappointed by not only Joyce's overly restrictive "method" but also the limitations he places on his characters' minds. "Their minds lack quality and as you get nothing but their minds!—still an effort in the right direction—at least out of the first Class Carriage line. . . ."[3] Woolf is pleased that Joyce has taken us "out of the first Class Carriage line," but she implies that he has restricted his characters' minds in such a way that they cannot sustain the reader's interest (as they must for prolonged stretches in the book), a "failing" that could be viewed as a sign of condescension (and egotism) on Joyce's part. Woolf's remarks may also reflect her sense that Joyce does not allow his characters or the readers access to his "superior" viewpoint as the author, moments when we (or they) become aware of the "outside" or framing perspective on the work, the "background rods" of its "conception" ("A Sketch of the Past," *MOB* 72-73). The characters' minds thus seem to be confined to, and to operate on, an entirely different plane from the author (however effaced), and since "you get nothing but their minds," the reader is similarly subjugated. Again, Woolf seems to suggest that this "method" betrays a certain egotism on the part of the author, a certain contempt for one's characters and one's readers.

Only fragments of *Ulysses* had appeared when Woolf wrote "Modern Novels" in 1919, the first version of "Modern Fiction," which was published in 1925. In the interim, she read a particularly "intelligent" review of *Ulysses*, "the first" that "analyze[d] its meaning," and noted in her diary that the book seemed "very much more impressive than [she] judged." She realized that she "had [her] back up on purpose" because T. S. Eliot had praised *Ulysses* so highly, and vowed to "read some of the chapters again." And yet, she adds, "contemporaries" (presumably, she means other highly accomplished artist-critics) "ought . . . to be bowled over" by a work that is supposedly a masterpiece, even if they cannot realize its "final beauty," and she knows that, apart from her vanities and jealousies, she was not bowled over by *Ulysses* (*D* 2: 200).

Woolf finished reading *Ulysses* in 1922, but she made few changes to the passages on Joyce in "Modern Novels" in revising it as "Modern Fiction." In the latter, she grants that the book is "undeniably important," however "difficult or unpleasant . . . we may judge it" (*CR* 1: 190), a change from "Modern Novels," in which she was willing to say only that it was "undeniably distinct" (*E* 3: 34). In "Modern Fiction" she adds, perhaps as a concession to T. S. Eliot and other Joyce enthusiasts, that "it is difficult not to acclaim a masterpiece" on "first reading" of certain passages in *Ulysses*, such as "the scene in the cemetery" (*CR* 1: 191). (Here Woolf seems at least to exaggerate if not betray her own first impressions; see *D* 2: 188.) Joyce's approach does bring us "close to the quick of the mind," she observes in both versions of this essay, but she knows that in reading this novel she felt "confined and shut in, rather than enlarged and set free." In *Ulysses*, she claims, we find ourselves "centered in a self which . . . never embraces or creates what is outside itself and beyond." This sense of confinement is the result of not only the writer's method but also "the comparative poverty of the writer's mind" (*CR* 1: 191). These comments have bewildered and exasperated many a critic.

In charging Joyce with "poverty of . . . mind," Woolf seems be referring not to his intellectual prowess, which is obviously formidable, but to the "quality" of his mind, which is not a matter of intellect alone. Joyce's "method has the merit of bringing us closer to what we were prepared to call life itself," and, she concludes, "did not the reading of *Ulysses* suggest how much of life is excluded or ignored." In her view, "there are not only other aspects of life, but more important ones into the bargain" (*CR* 1:192). Again, we may find this criticism baffling, and Woolf admits that she (or rather "we") can only "fumbl[e] . . . awkwardly" when pressed to specify what those "more important" aspects are (*CR* 1: 191). But she does seem to be implying that because Joyce focuses too much on "surface distinctions," she does not consider *Ulysses* a "profound" work of the literary imagination. At the time, T. S. Eliot, who greatly admired *Ulysses*, seems to have agreed with Woolf on this point: "Tom . . . said [Joyce] left out many things that were important. . . . [T]here was no 'great conception.' . . . [H]e did not think that he gave a new insight into human nature—said nothing new like Tolstoi. Bloom told one nothing" (*D* 2: 203).

Woolf also may have seen "the emphasis [Joyce] laid, perhaps didac-tically, on indecency" as further evidence that he was largely concerned with "surface distinctions" (*CR* 1: 191). Comments in her letters and diaries suggest that she was not so much shocked by Joyce's "indecency" as bored by it.[4] She grants in "Mr. Bennett and Mrs. Brown" that it took courage on his part to buck these conventions (while noting in "Professions for Women" that society's double standard makes those conventions weigh much more heavily on women than they do on men [*DM* 240]); she sympathizes with his effort to "break the windows" and let in some "fresh air," but on the whole she sees this sort of rebellion as "a waste of energy" (*CDB* 116). Since it attacks only class-based notions of propriety, which are mere "surface distinctions," instead of giving us access to deeper levels of the human psyche, this aspect of Joyce's experiment, Woolf implies, is neither radical nor especially interesting. "[A]fter all, how dull indecency is, when it is not the overflowing of a superabundant energy or savagery, but the determined and public-spirited act of a man who needs fresh air" (*CDB* 116). "Proust [did not] pass that way," she notes in a letter in 1926 to Vita Sackville-West; that is, Proust did not have to take Joyce's way, the way of "jolly vulgarity," in order to advance the art of the novel (*L* 3: 247).

Woolf also may have seen Joyce's experiment as only of interest in terms of technique (a "highly developed" method [*L* 2: 234]; a "gallant approach . . . then the usual smash and splinters" [*L* 2: 598]), since it fundamentally reinstates masculinist values. Joyce "has nothing especially new to say about social or ethical or religious values," S. L. Goldberg observes in *The Classical Temper*. "[I]n many ways he seems old-fashioned."[5] One consequence, as Carolyn Heilbrun points out, is that "[n]owhere do Joyce and Woolf divide so sharply as in their portrayal of women and the destinies of women" (70). In *Ulysses*, "the patriarchal view of women [is] presented in its quintessential form" (73). Joyce was "virile—a he-goat," Woolf declared to T. S. Eliot, expecting him to disagree. To her surprise, Eliot agreed, then went on to suggest that nevertheless *Ulysses* was a "landmark" work, if only because "it destroyed the whole of the 19th century. . . . It showed up the futility of all the English styles" (*D* 2: 203). Woolf could hardly have found this news heartening. As Lyn Pykett and other scholars have noted, Woolf was more concerned with "negotiating and reworking the established [literary] conventions" than with finishing them off (97).

To my knowledge, Woolf never suggests that a deliberate insistence on "the surface distinction" of nationality may have played some part in Joyce's attitude toward the English language and literary tradition.[6] But she was acutely aware of how being an "outsider" can affect one's writing and can give one a different perspective on language, literary traditions, and social arrangements in general. In her diary she complained that she found *Ulysses* "underbred, not only in the obvious sense, but in the literary sense," arguing that "[a] first-rate writer . . . respects writing too much to be tricky; startling; doing stunts." He reminds her of "some callow board school boy . . . full of wits & powers, but so self-conscious & egotistical that he loses his head, becomes extravagant, mannered, uproarious, ill at ease."[7] These comments may call to mind the figure of Stephen Dedalus, "ill at ease" in part because he is a member of a colonized "race," forced to write and speak in the conqueror's tongue, and plotting how he will use the master's tools to dismantle the master's house.

Like Joyce, Woolf suggests in "Phases of Fiction," Henry James was also "ill at ease." In spite of his "magnificent urbanity," James was a foreigner "in a strange civilization" (*GR* 123). In "American Fiction," she charges him with refusing to take "the first step in the process of being an American—to be not English" (*M* 116). Unlike the Irishman Joyce, whose work Woolf found "underbred," James, she suspected, was "[v]ery highly American in the determination to be highly bred, & the slight obtuseness as to what high breeding is" (D 2: 136). She seems to suggest that James and Joyce were too involved in reacting to "surface distinctions" of class and nationality, which she considers a deflection of creative energy. Just as, in her view, Joyce "excluded or ignored" other, "more important" aspects of life in *Ulysses*, James failed to grasp the "profound" social differences within English culture. He was "obsess[ed] with surface distinction," she observes in "American Fiction," with "the age of old houses, the glamour of great names," an obsession that is related, she implies, to James's status as an outsider and especially to his rejection of his own culture. "It is necessary to remember that Henry James was a foreigner if we are not to call him a snob," she concludes (M 124-25). Largely because of their insecurities about being outsiders, Woolf seems to imply, both James and Joyce became merely "excessively ingenious," so "manipulative" that "instead of feeling the artist, you merely feel the man who is posing the subject" (D 2: 136). Although she praises the "distinct and peculiar beauty" of James's fictive "world," Woolf sounds relieved in "Phases of Fiction" when she turns from James to Proust.

> Henry James . . . was an obstacle never perfectly assimilated even by the juices of his own art. . . . To gratify [our] desire ["to be free from the perpetual tutelage of the author's presence, his arrangements, his anxieties"], naturally, we turn to the work of Proust. (GR 123)

Unlike James, she notes, Proust does not have to strain to convince us that we are in the presence of "an immensely civilized and saturated intelligence" (GR 140). Proust's "ease" Woolf attributes in part to his being "the product of the civilization which he describes" (GR 123), of a society she later characterizes, in "Notes on D. H. Lawrence," as "settled and satisfied" (M 97).

Woolf also sounds greatly relieved in a letter to Roger Fry in 1922 in which she notes that having finished *Ulysses* at last, she is now free to return to Proust. She conceded reluctantly that *Ulysses* was a work one could not afford to neglect, even if one disliked it. Out of a sense of professional obligation, it seems, she forced herself to finish the book. The contrast between that experience and her experience of reading Proust is dramatic.

> My great adventure is really Proust. Well—what remains to be written after that? I'm only in the first volume, and there are, I suppose, faults to be found, but I am in a state of amazement; as if a miracle were being done before my eyes. How, at last, has someone solidified what has always escaped—and made it too into this beautiful and perfectly

enduring substance? One has to put the book down and gasp. The
pleasure becomes physical—like sun and wine and grapes and perfect
serenity and intense vitality combined. Far otherwise is it with *Ulysses;*
to which I bind myself like a martyr to a stake, and have thank God,
now finished.—My martyrdom is over. (*L* 2: 565-66)

An atmosphere of pagan delight suffuses her description of the pleasures of reading Proust. By way of contrast, having to finish *Ulysses* seems a
form of medieval torture, with Woolf comparing the experience to being
burned at the stake, as if she were a heretic whose punishment was to be
forced to read what she could not pretend to admire. Jealous of Joyce's fame
Woolf no doubt was, at times, but she did not envy his gifts. Reading Joyce
did not make her wish that she "could write like that." Reading Proust did:

Proust so titillates my own desire for expression that I can hardly set out
the sentence. Oh if I could write like that! I cry. And at the moment such
is the astonishing vibration and saturation and intensification that he
procures—there's something sexual in it—that I feel I *can* write like that,
and seize my pen and then I *can't* write like that. Scarcely anyone so
stimulates the nerves of language in me: it becomes an obsession. (*L* 2: 525)

Woolf's comments on Proust in these letters to Fry, her delight in his
combination of "perfect serenity and intense vitality," her sense that "there's
something sexual" about "the astonishing vibration and saturation and intensification he procures," anticipate comments that she makes on Proust in *A
Room of One's Own* in her discussion of "the androgynous mind":

Coleridge certainly did not mean, when he said that a great mind is
androgynous, that it is a mind that has any special sympathy with women;
a mind that takes up their cause or devotes itself to their interpretation.
Perhaps the androgynous mind is less apt to make these distinctions than
the single-sexed mind. He meant, perhaps, that the androgynous mind is
resonant and porous; that it transmits emotion without impediment; that
it is naturally creative, incandescent and undivided. (98)

In *A Room of One's Own*, while Shakespeare is her classic example of the
androgynous mind, among writers "[i]n our time" it is Proust, and Proust
alone, whom she finds "wholly androgynous" (103). His writing displays
"that curious sexual quality which comes only when sex is unconscious of
itself" (93). "[A] novelist's chief desire is to be as unconscious as possible,"

Woolf told her audience in 1931 in the speech that eventually became "Professions for Women" (*DM* 239). When writing fiction, Woolf tried to induce this kind of "unconsciousness" (*L* 5: 408), the opposite of the "acute self-consciousness" that she thought afflicted most modern writing. In her own writing she manages to procure "an astonishing vibration and saturation and intensification," even if she found that she could not "write like" Proust.

And yet, unlike her version of Coleridge's "androgynous" writer, and unlike Proust, Woolf did have a "special sympathy with women; a mind that takes up their cause [and] devotes itself to their interpretation." "[E]ven in the writing of Proust," Woolf notes, after calling him "wholly androgynous," "it remains obvious . . . that a man is terribly hampered and partial in his knowledge of women" (*AROO* 83). She downplays this "failing" in Proust, however; his work at least does not display the "self-conscious virility" that, she contends in "An Essay in Criticism," "partly spoil[s] . . . for women readers the works of Lawrence, Joyce, Hemingway, and many other male writers." Woolf devised ways in her novels of expressing the "special sympathy" she felt for women, her interest in their cause, and her devotion to their interpretation, ways that would not alert her internalized "Censors" and make her "self-conscious" (*D* 5: 229). "The desire to teach or to help," to be thought clever or heroic, or even the sudden awareness of opposition can bring the imagination "to the top," she observes (*L* 5: 408), when it should be "sweep[ing] unchecked round every rock and cranny of the world that lies submerged in the depths of our unconscious being" (*DM* 240).

Woolf found the perfect serenity and concentration she associated with Proust increasingly hard to come by in the modern world. She notes in "An Essay in Criticism" that "in our time, thanks to our sexual perturbations, sex consciousness is strong, and shows itself in literature by an exaggeration, a protest of sexual characteristics which in either case is disagreeable" (*GR* 90). If, in her view, James was "emasculated" (*D* 2: 136), a "prude," and Joyce was "virile—a he-goat" (*D* 2: 202), Lawrence was "wildly phallic" (*L* 3: 508), though his "savagery" was not "the overflowing of superabundant energy" she longed for in "Mr. Bennett and Mrs. Brown" (*CDB* 116) but was instead based on a certain "theory" he had about sex. In her reading notes on Lawrence's *The Fox*, Woolf observes that while his work may have some "power of suggestion for other people," she finds it "monotonous." The "sex theory" he imposes on people is, she grants, "very vivid— very physical," but it is also, in her opinion, "very unhumorless & stark." It is "not to me interesting."[8] His notion (as Woolf understood it) that "women can only live in the imaginations of men," she dismisses as "damned [,] conceited nonsense" (*L* 3: 508).

Nevertheless, Woolf was more sympathetic toward Lawrence than she was toward Joyce. She claimed that she was "kept . . . off Lawrence" early on by John Middleton Murry's "obscene objurgations" (*L* 4: 315) and by Lawrence's mean-spirited fictional portrait of Lady Ottoline Morrell in *Women in Love* (*L* 3:508). He was "such a cad to Ottoline," Woolf reflected in a letter to Vita Sackville-West in 1932: "My word, what a cheap little bounder . . . taking her money, books, food, lodging, and then writing that book" (*L* 5: 121-22). She also was disappointed by *The Lost Girl*, which she reviewed in 1920 in "Postscript or Prelude," arguing that the work was still too invested in the (for her, outmoded) mode of exterior realism to constitute a significant and original contribution to the art of fiction (*E* 3: 271-73). To judge from her letters, diary entries, and the opening remarks in "Notes on D. H. Lawrence," she was unimpressed by the little that she read of Lawrence's work until, after his death, she went back and read *Sons and Lovers* as well as Lawrence's letters. Although she still had serious reservations about his work, she acknowledged that Lawrence was "a man of genius" (*L* 4: 315) and expressed sympathy for him as a human being and a fellow writer who fell victim to "the brutality of civilised society" (*D* 4: 126).

Both Woolf and Lawrence were strong "oppositional" thinkers who in their own ways tried to intervene in contemporary debates on the meaning of culture and civilization; both of them viewed questions of gender and gender relations as central to the project of cultural renovation, in spite of their markedly different (and in Lawrence's case, especially, quite unstable) positions on those questions. Woolf felt, though, that what she had most in common with Lawrence was a weakness, not a strength: the temptation, as embattled cultural outsiders and visionaries, to get defensive, to become didactic, to indulge in "heroics." As is clear in her 1925 essay "The Patron and the Crocus," neither Woolf nor her ideal reader wanted "to be lectured, elevated, instructed, or improved" (*CR* 1: 265). In her diary in 1932, Woolf noted that she had been reading Lawrence's letters "with the usual sense of frustration." What she and Lawrence had "in common," she observed, was the "pressure to be ourselves: so that I don't escape when I read him; am surfeited; what I want is to be made free of another world. This Proust does."

> [I]t's the preaching [in Lawrence] that rasps me. . . . Art is being rid of all preaching: things in themselves: the sentence in itself beautiful. . . . L[awrence] would only say what proved something. . . . [H]e . . . must give advice; get you into the system too. Hence his attraction for those who want to be fitted; which I don't. . . . What a discovery that would be—a system that did not shut out. (*D* 4: 126-27)

Woolf felt "shut out" by Lawrence; his attempts to "get [the reader] into [his] system" aroused her own ego instead of suspending it. "I'm sure of [Lawrence's] 'genius,'" she wrote to Ethel Smyth in 1933, "what I distrust is the platform; I hate the 'I'm right' pose in art" (L 5: 167).

In contrast to Lawrence, as is clear in "Phases of Fiction," Proust seemed to Woolf "to enclose a world" rather than "to enforce a view." His work approximated the ideal she dreamed of—"a system that did not shut out":

> We are never told [by Proust], as the English novelists so frequently tell us, that one way is right and the other wrong. Every way is thrown open without reserve and without prejudice. . . . Direction or emphasis, to be told that that is right, to be nudged and bidden to attend to that, would fall like a shadow on this profound luminosity and cut off some section of it from our view. . . . [P]erhaps sympathy is of more value than interference, understanding than judgment. (GR 125)

Woolf finds in both Proust and Lawrence an intense vitality and great powers of visualization, but in Proust these qualities are coupled with a "perfect serenity" that allows him to consider things as ends in themselves. By way of contrast, Lawrence seems strident, dogmatic, and restless. "I get no satisfaction from his explanations of what he sees," she complains. "I don't want 'a philosophy'" (D 4: 126). In "Notes on D. H. Lawrence," Woolf objects that in Lawrence "everything has a use, a meaning, is not an end in itself" (M 97).

> There is a scene of course; a character; yes, and people related to each other by a net of sensations; but these are not there—as in Proust—for themselves. They do not admit of prolonged exploration, of rapture in them for the sake of rapture, as one may sit in front of the famous hawthorn hedge in *Swann's Way* and look at it. No, there is always something further on, another goal. . . . We must not look for more than a second; we must hurry on. But to what? . . . Nothing rests secure to be looked at. All is being sucked away by some dissatisfaction, some superior beauty, or desire, or possibility. (M 95-96)

Woolf accounts for the differences she foregrounds in Proust's and Lawrence's work in part by contrasting the writers' "circumstances," resting her argument on assumptions about French society and Proust's position within it that recall her image of him as "the product of the civilization which he describes." Proust she considers a member of "a settled and satisfied society," perhaps reflecting the Bloomsbury tendency to idealize France. By way of contrast, she emphasizes that Lawrence was "anxious to leave his own class and to enter another. . . . [T]he fact that he . . . was a miner's son, and that he disliked his conditions," she argues, "gave him a different approach to writing from those who have a settled station and enjoy circumstances which allow them to forget what those circumstances are" (M 97).

Although Woolf grants that Lawrence has "genius," she sees him as driven, aggrieved, anxious, restless, and deracinated to the point at which he can offer nothing "to rest upon, to expand upon, to feel to the limits of our powers," except some fleeting "rapture of physical being," to which he imparts "a transcendental significance" that she finds unconvincing and ineffective as a means of "stabilizing" his work and giving it "cohesion" (M 96). His restlessness and stridency she sees as consequences of his being an outsider not only in terms of class but also, eventually, in terms of his own country. He "injure[d] his imagination" running up "against convention" (*Pargiters* xxxix), and not just the internalized "censors" and "visionary figures" that haunted Woolf (D 5: 229), but actual government agents who "hoof[ed] him out, like a toad; and bann[ed] his book" (D 4: 126). She notes "the brutality of civilised society to this panting, agonised man," and how, by way of reaction, Lawrence increasingly indulged in heroics, struck the pose of a preacher, a prophet (D 4: 126), and became ever more "shrill and hard and positive" (*Pargiters* xxxix); in the end, she reflects, "how futile it was" (D 4: 126). The example of Lawrence may have been in Woolf's mind in the late thirties when, having "committed [her]self" (D 5: 136) and written her most polemical and unequivocal cultural critique, *Three Guineas* (which she tentatively titled *On Being Despised*), she thought about the "pack"—"reviewers, friends, enemies"—that would soon be "howl[ing]" after her (D 5: 141). Feeling increasingly "detach[ed] from the hierarchy, the patriarchy" (D 5: 347), she told herself what she seems to have wanted to tell Lawrence all along: "[I]f one's an outsider, be an outsider—only don't for God's sake attitudinise & take up the striking[,] the becoming attitude" (D 5: 245).

Woolf saw both Lawrence and Joyce as outsiders in that, unlike other male writers of her generation, they were not "[literary] aristocrats; the unconscious inheritors of a great tradition" (M 139). Lawrence's working class and Joyce's Irish origins exclude them from those ranks. In her 1932 essay "A Letter to a Young Poet," however, Woolf suggests that writers who are not "unconscious inheritors" can and should try to imagine that they are (DM 212). Her complaint, in contrast to Proust, that Lawrence "echoes nobody, continues no tradition" (M 97) is obviously false, but her insistence on this point may be an effort to differentiate between his and her own responses to being "outsiders." Lawrence's contempt and defiance of the system that excluded him (which, to his mind, included Bloomsbury—and Virginia Woolf) drove him to embrace varieties of neo-Romantic individualism and eventually to attempt to escape from "[Western] civilization" altogether.[9] Woolf is committed to working within the system and the culture that, she feels, excludes her (and a great many others), in order to bring about change. In spite of thinking of herself as an "outsider," she is protective toward the "inheritance" that outsiders (in terms of class, gender, race, or nationality) must struggle consciously and against considerable odds to acquire if they are to have any share—or say—in it at all. In "The Leaning Tower," Woolf objects not so much to the "inheritance" itself as to the "criminal injustice" of a system that confers upon a certain group privileged access to that inheritance, exclusive claims to and authority over it (M 152). Nevertheless, that she appreciates the potentially great advantages to a writer of being an "unconscious inheritor" is clear, for example, from her advice to her "correspondent" in "A Letter to a Young Poet." "Think of yourself," she suggests, "as . . . a poet in whom live all the poets of the past, from whom all poets in time will come to spring. You have a touch of Chaucer in you, and something of Shakespeare; Dryden, Pope, Tennyson. . . . In short you are an immensely ancient, complex, and continuous character, for which reason please treat yourself with respect" (DM 212).

What one can sense in the work of "unconscious inheritors," Woolf implies, whatever limitations their work may have in other respects, is the presence of the past. This view makes itself felt in her criticism of Lawrence and in her use of Proust as a counterexample. It also points to the most obvious source of the profound affinity she felt with Proust: their mutual preoccupation with the experience of time. For Woolf, the sense (however fleeting) of the "full present," of "the present . . . backed by the past"(MOB 98) was crucial, both for her own stability and for the temporary "stabilizing" effect it has on her novels, where it provides a sense of "cohesion" (M 96). "The past only comes back," she notes, "when the present runs so smoothly that it is like the sliding surface of a deep river. Then one sees through the surface to the depths" (MOB 98). Hence, there is the potential advantage of the writer "who has a settled station and enjoys circumstances which allow him to forget what those circumstances are" (M 97).

The image of Proust that emerges from Woolf's comments over the years is that of a writer who enjoys all the advantages and possesses all the gifts whose lack or frustration Woolf uses to explain her own and her contemporaries' failure, in her judgment, to produce "masterpieces." He has an "extravagant command of every resource," "an immensely civilized and saturated intelligence," a "porous," "pliable," "wholly androgynous" sensibility; the world he "encloses" is an inclusive one, in part because greater understanding and intimacy were possible among people of different classes in his society (since class divisions were either more "settled" and accepted or more "blurred" and permeable than they were in England—Woolf's indecision here may reflect her own political ambivalence). A privileged inheritor of a great tradition, Proust had the un-self-consciousness, the self-confidence of a literary "aristocrat"; and yet, he was also fundamentally an "outsider . . . writing against the current," which is how Woolf increasingly saw herself (*D* 5: 189). Indeed, Woolf remarked in a 1927 interview with Jacques-Émile Blanche, "Society must have understood little" of what Proust was saying about it in his books ("Interview" 212).

Woolf insists on Proust's inclusiveness: her claims about class relations in French society are vague and inconsistent, and she refuses to dwell at length on what or whom his "system" excludes, aside from a passing reference in *A Room of One's Own* to his "terribly . . . partial" view of women, which she downplays (83). She also refuses to consider why, if Proust enjoyed such advantages and gifts, "the atmosphere" of his work is so often, as she notes in "Phases of Fiction," "permeated with unhappiness" (*GR* 129), with "pain, perhaps . . . despair" (130). This imprecision or equivocation on Woolf's part at length suggests that at times her version of Proust may have been prompted by "some imperious need" to "anchor [her] instability upon [his] security," even if that required some mythmaking on her part ("How It Strikes a Contemporary," *E* 3: 357). Her evocations of the "circumstances" Proust supposedly enjoyed seem to reflect not only a sense of nostalgia on her part but also the residual conservatism that Alex Zwerdling traces in her attitudes toward both literary and social change. The radical kinds of political and economic transformation that her commitments to greater social justice and equality seemed to require conflicted with her sense of the material conditions and social arrangements most likely to bring about a "great age of English literature."

If it is true, as Woolf claims in "Modern Fiction," that it is always easier to feel what a contemporary work lacks than what the writer is trying to give, that may not necessarily be a result of measuring the work against standards appropriate for the past; it may be a result of measuring the work against one's dreams for the future (*CR* 1: 191). "[M]asterpieces," Woolf wagers in *A Room of One's Own*, are "not single and solitary births; they are the outcome of many years of thinking in common, of thinking by the body of the people, so that the experience of the mass is behind the single voice."[10] But this definition of a masterpiece can be seen as more of an evocation of an ideal than an accurate description of any existing work. One could consider it a mystification of particular comfort to liberal-minded members of a cultural elite. Alternatively, one could argue that Woolf is referring to what we might think of as intertextuality or that she is even anticipating current debates about "the death of the author." There may be some merit in that argument, especially since Woolf's philosophy of "anonymity" became increasingly important in her thinking about the creative process and about literary history. And, of course, it is quite true that no book is ever solely "the effort of a single mind" ("Defoe," CR 1: 121). Still, to claim that "the experience of the mass" or "the body of the people" can somehow be represented in a work of art, masterpiece or not, or even in the entire literary tradition seems to beg some important questions. In fact, as suggested by her reference in "The Leaning Tower" to the "criminal injustice" of a system that dehumanizes its elite while culturally and economically disenfranchising the masses, Woolf knew in her bones what Walter Benjamin put so cogently: "There is no document of civilization which is not at the same time a document of barbarism" (256). It is to Woolf's credit that faced with that truth, she did not, in spite of her equivocations and reservations, find it easy to look the other way. If she was often less than kind in judging contemporary work—including, it must be added—her own, it may be in part because she measured that work against the vision of a masterpiece she articulated in *A Room of One's Own*, that is, against her sense of what great works of art should do and be ideally rather than what the realities were and are of their actual production, dissemination, and appropriation, even though she did not delude herself about those realities.

When it seems to us that Woolf has "scamped the virtue" of her critical subjects (D 2: 200) or, as in Proust's case, inflated and in some ways falsified it, we may find that those very distortions open up lines of inquiry that help us to reconstitute a sense of the "complex network of social tendencies and anxieties" to which she was responding and into which she tried to intervene (Pykett 17). Furthermore, if we are willing to take them seriously, even the comments on her contemporaries that now strike us as aberrant, excessive, or ungenerous may prompt us to look at her critical subjects in a somewhat different light, to question how we arrived at "our own" judgments of them, and to realize that there are views we have come to accept uncritically, views that once were contested and perhaps should be contested again. In short, what we may see as errors in Woolf's judgment of contemporary work prove to be far more interesting and worthy of investigation if we resist the tendency simply to privatize or pathologize them by attributing them to her vanities and jealousies. Even when she was less than kind, and less than precise, in her judgments of her contemporaries, there was much more at stake in Woolf's criticism of their work than a merely personal bid for power and prestige among a handful of "rivals."

Works Cited

Adams, Robert. *Afterjoyce: Studies in Fiction After "Ulysses."* New York: Oxford UP, 1977.

Benjamin, Walter. *Illuminations.* Trans. Harry Zohn. New York: Schocken, 1969.

Bradbury, Malcolm. *The Modern World: Ten Great Writers.* New York: Penguin, 1988.

DiBattista, Maria. "Joyce, Woolf and the Modern Mind." *Virginia Woolf: New Critical Essays.* Ed. Patricia Clements and Isobel Grundy. New York: Barnes and Noble, 1983. 96-114.

Gillespie, Diane Filby. "Political Aesthetics: Virginia Woolf and Dorothy Richardson." *Virginia Woolf: A Feminist Slant.* Ed. Jane Marcus. Lincoln: U of Nebraska P, 1983. 132-51.

Goldman, Mark. *The Reader's Art: Virginia Woolf as Literary Critic.* The Hague: Mouton, 1976.

Guiguet, Jean. Preface. *Contemporary Writers.* By Virginia Woolf. London: Hogarth, 1965. 7-12.

Heilbrun, Carolyn G. *Hamlet's Mother and Other Women.* New York: Columbia UP, 1990.

Lyon, Mary. Preface. *Books and Portraits: Some Further Selections from the Literary and Biographical Writings of Virginia Woolf.* By Virginia Woolf. Ed. Mary Lyon. New York: Harcourt, 1977. vii-x.

Marcus, Jane, ed. *Virginia Woolf: A Feminist Slant.* Lincoln: U of Nebraska P, 1983.

McLaughlin, Ann L. "An Uneasy Sisterhood: Virginia Woolf and Katherine Mansfield." *Virginia Woolf: A Feminist Slant.* Ed. Jane Marcus. Lincoln: U of Nebraska P, 1983. 152-61.

Meisel, Perry. *The Absent Father: Virginia Woolf and Walter Pater.* New Haven: Yale UP, 1980.

Pearce, Richard. "Who Comes First, Joyce or Woolf?" *Virginia Woolf: Themes and Variations.* Ed. Vara Neverow-Turk and Mark Hussey. New York: Pace UP, 1993. 59-67.

Pykett, Lyn. *Engendering Fictions: The English Novel in the Early Twentieth Century.* London: Edward Arnold, 1995.

Rosenberg, Beth Carole. *Virginia Woolf and Samuel Johnson: Common Readers.* New York: St. Martin's, 1995.

Siegel, Carole. *Lawrence Among the Women: Wavering Boundaries in the Women's Literary Tradition.* Charlottesville: U of Virginia P, 1991.

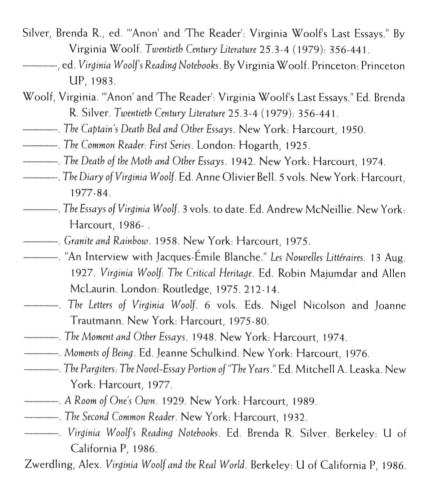

Silver, Brenda R., ed. "'Anon' and 'The Reader': Virginia Woolf's Last Essays." By Virginia Woolf. *Twentieth Century Literature* 25.3-4 (1979): 356-441.

———, ed. *Virginia Woolf's Reading Notebooks.* By Virginia Woolf. Princeton: Princeton UP, 1983.

Woolf, Virginia. "'Anon' and 'The Reader': Virginia Woolf's Last Essays." Ed. Brenda R. Silver. *Twentieth Century Literature* 25.3-4 (1979): 356-441.

———. *The Captain's Death Bed and Other Essays.* New York: Harcourt, 1950.

———. *The Common Reader: First Series.* London: Hogarth, 1925.

———. *The Death of the Moth and Other Essays.* 1942. New York: Harcourt, 1974.

———. *The Diary of Virginia Woolf.* Ed. Anne Olivier Bell. 5 vols. New York: Harcourt, 1977-84.

———. *The Essays of Virginia Woolf.* 3 vols. to date. Ed. Andrew McNeillie. New York: Harcourt, 1986- .

———. *Granite and Rainbow.* 1958. New York: Harcourt, 1975.

———. "An Interview with Jacques-Émile Blanche." *Les Nouvelles Littéraires.* 13 Aug. 1927. *Virginia Woolf: The Critical Heritage.* Ed. Robin Majumdar and Allen McLaurin. London: Routledge, 1975. 212-14.

———. *The Letters of Virginia Woolf.* 6 vols. Eds. Nigel Nicolson and Joanne Trautmann. New York: Harcourt, 1975-80.

———. *The Moment and Other Essays.* 1948. New York: Harcourt, 1974.

———. *Moments of Being.* Ed. Jeanne Schulkind. New York: Harcourt, 1976.

———. *The Pargiters: The Novel-Essay Portion of "The Years."* Ed. Mitchell A. Leaska. New York: Harcourt, 1977.

———. *A Room of One's Own.* 1929. New York: Harcourt, 1989.

———. *The Second Common Reader.* New York: Harcourt, 1932.

———. *Virginia Woolf's Reading Notebooks.* Ed. Brenda R. Silver. Berkeley: U of California P, 1986.

Zwerdling, Alex. *Virginia Woolf and the Real World.* Berkeley: U of California P, 1986.

Notes

1. See, for example, Bradbury 231; DiBattista 96, 99; Adams 68; Meisel 92-93; McLaughlin 152, 156, 158; and Gillespie 136, 138-39.

2. Meisel does acknowledge in a footnote that Woolf felt "some anxiety" in reading Proust, but he claims that that occurred only when she first began to read his work (91n6). In fact, as her diary entries and letters testify, Woolf continued to feel threatened by Proust's example at least up until the mid thirties, when she writes the following to Ethel Smyth: "Proust . . . is of course

so magnificent that I can't write myself within its arc; that's true; for years I've put off finishing it; but now, thinking I may, and indeed so they say must die one of these years, I've returned, and let my own scribble do what it likes. Lord what a hopeless bad book mine [*The Years*] will be!" (*L* 5: 304).

3. "Modern Novels (Joyce)" Holograph Notebook, unsigned and undated, iv: Henry W. and Albert A. Berg Collection in the New York Public Library (Astor, Lenox, and Tilden Foundations), qtd. in DiBattista 99.

4. For expressions of Woolf's "boredom" with *Ulysses*, see her letters to Lytton Strachey, Roger Fry, and Lady Ottoline Morrell in *L* 2: 233-34, 548, to Gerald Brenan in *L* 3: 80, and her diary entry in *D* 2: 188. In 1941, two days after Joyce's death and a few months before her own, Woolf reached back nearly twenty years to recall how she had read *Ulysses* "one summer . . . with spasms of wonder, of discovery, & then again with long lapses of intense boredom" (*D* 5: 353).

5. S. L. Goldberg, *The Classical Temper: A Study of James Joyce's " Ulysses"* (London: Chatto & Windus, 1966) 35, qtd. in Heilbrun 66.

6. Woolf does tease Nicholas Bagenal about whether the indecencies in a manuscript submitted to the Hogarth Press by "a compatriot of yours, called James Joyce" might be "an Irish quality" (*L* 2: 231). (She is referring to the manuscript of *Ulysses*.)

7. *D* 2: 199. Richard Pearce's remarks cast light on Woolf's characterization of Joyce as "a callow board school boy." Joyce "requires that we admire the way he parodies and undermines canonical writers," Pearce points out, adding that this "is one reason Woolf saw him as egoistic." Pearce also maintains that Joyce's way of "flaunting his defiance of the fathers" was in keeping with "a form of modernism characterized by rebellion [and] coded male." Further-more, Pearce contends, Joyce "constructs the reader as male, not only privi-leged by having a classical education, but driven by what Walter Ong describes as its 'agonistic' pedagogy of ceremonial combat, which governed the classroom as well as the playing field and the dormitory." In contrast to Joyce, Pearce observes, "Virginia Woolf does not show off her knowledge or take on the canonical fathers" (60-61). I would argue, however, that in regard to "the canonical fathers" Woolf in fact created her own strategies of resis-tance, subversion, and transformation.

8. A 1923 entry in Woolf's reading notebooks (XXV, B.11) qtd. in Silver 29n25.

9. Carole Siegel also considers some of the complexities of Woolf's response to Lawrence and concludes that in Woolf's view, Lawrence "could not make a virtue of marginality but instead succumbed to what she believed were the worst temptations facing a nonprivileged writer" (98).

10. *AROO* 65. Woolf's definition of a masterpiece in *A Room of One's Own* elaborates on the one that appears in her 1919 essay on Defoe, revised for inclusion in her first *Common Reader* under the title "Defoe." There she observes that *Robinson Crusoe* "resembles one of the anonymous productions of the race, rather than the effort of a single mind" (*CR* 1: 121). This impression can be explained in part, she suggests, by "the fact that we have all had *Robinson Crusoe* read aloud to us as children," when the idea that books have authors who are or were actual people was a matter of indifference to us or was even perhaps strangely "disturb[ing]." In *A Room of One's Own*, however, it is the idea that a book is "the effort of a single mind" that is the illusion, at least when the book in question is a masterpiece; there Woolf suggests that a masterpiece is in truth "one of the anonymous productions of the race." The so-called child's view of great books as being somehow communally owned and anonymously produced has triumphed over the "adult's" narrow, proprietary perspective. This notion that masterpieces are somehow produced by and belong to "the people" is also reflected in Woolf's famous (and controversial) declaration at the end of "The Leaning Tower" that "literature is common ground" (*M* 154) and in the new "kind of critical book" (*D* 5: 180) she was working on during the last years of her life, the notes for which have been edited by Brenda Silver and published as "'Anon' and 'The Reader': Virginia Woolf's Last Essays."

A Modernism of One's Own: Virginia Woolf's TLS Reviews and Eliotic Modernism

Michael Kaufmann

On 13 March 1921 Virginia Woolf pondered the possibility of closer acquaintance with T.S. Eliot. "Will he become 'Tom'?" she wondered. And "What happens to friendships undertaken at the age of 40? Do they flourish & live long? . . . Not that Tom admires my writing, damn him" (D 2: 100).[1] Critics have long corrected Eliot's shortsightedness concerning Woolf's novels, but Woolf's critical views and formulations continue to be seen through the lens of Eliot's criticism (Howe 3). This is true despite the fact that while Pound and Eliot promulgated the new poetry and their Modernism to several hundred readers centered in London and New York through such "organs" as *The Egoist* and the *Little Review*, Virginia Woolf spread her views on literature and Modernism in a forum that included tens of thousands of readers all over England and abroad.[2] The difference in their respective audiences, both in size and composition, played an important part in the very different critical personas these writers created and reflected the differences in their own literary practices. Further, and perhaps even more important, it affected the way in which each writer conceived of his or her audience. Writing for the "small and select" body of *Egoist* subscribers, Eliot preached his doctrine to a limited audience, as a poet-critic to other poets and critics; Woolf spoke to a much wider audience, as a reader to other readers, thereby defining Modernism and literature in general as something available to all, not set apart for a select few.[3]

Though the *Times Literary Supplement* (*TLS*) appealed predominantly to the upper- and upper-middle-class reader, it enjoyed a much broader and more varied readership than any of the "little" literary magazines of the day simply by virtue of its much larger circulation. At its most successful, *The*

Egoist had four hundred subscribers but averaged closer to two hundred or fewer for most of its years. The *TLS's* subscribers numbered around twenty thousand. Simply put, it *was* the literary establishment of London. The paper had no competitor in either the authority it commanded or the esteem it garnered.[4] To write successfully and continually for not only "the best but the most respected and most respectable" literary periodical of the time, as Eliot later referred to it, one had to know how to appeal to an audience— as Virginia Woolf did for over two decades (*Selected Essays* 325).[5] Later, when renown brought Woolf wider popularity, she occasionally even had articles in mass-market publications such as *The Forum* and *Vogue*, publications that counted their readers in the hundreds of thousands. A similarly wide appeal for Eliot as an essayist is difficult to imagine.

In fact, it is clear from the correspondence section of *The Egoist*, which focuses as much on egoism and suffragism as Imagism, that even *The Egoist's* audience was too broad for Eliot, who disregarded the periodical's original subscribers in favor of a new audience of poet-critics he envisioned. Though it is true that the review, which technically called itself a newspaper, had become more of "a literary periodical" under Harriet Shaw Weaver and had picked up notable international readers such as Marianne Moore, William Carlos Williams, and John Quinn, it retained a sizable contingent of its readers from its earlier incarnation as *The New Freewoman*.[6] If one judges from the correspondence, which predominantly commented on or took issue with Dora Marsden's philosophical section, a large portion of the audience may have only skimmed the back pages designated for the literary editors. Even by the time Eliot took over the editorship from Hilda Doolittle in 1917, what little correspondence there was more often commented on feminist or political issues. Clearly, Eliot's writings (which elicited no comments in the correspondence section) took no account of his actual readership. He aimed his remarks at a select few who could save literature, but they seemed too few to take much notice—at least in the pages of *The Egoist*.

Eliot's audience in *The Egoist* was not strictly of his choosing. He was on the outside of the London literary circles, trying to break in as a foreign and as yet unknown critic. He would have to take his opportunities as he could get them. From Eliot's perspective, *The Egoist* was simply the first place he could get his foot in the door. He was also placing regular critical reviews with the *Athenaeum*; its wider circulation afforded him "a certain notoriety" he would not "have got from *The Egoist*" (*Letters* 315).

And yet it was more than an absence of opportunity that led Eliot to define his as a small and select audience. Eliot was obviously interested in having a wider influence and more readers, but he trusted only a certain kind of reader. Eliot's remarks on Henry James say much about his situation:

> The current of English Literature was not appreciably altered by his work during his lifetime. . . . The "influence" of James hardly matters: . . . [T]here will always be a few intelligent people to understand James, and to be understood by a few intelligent people is all the influence a man requires. ("In Memory" 1)

In a 29 March 1919 letter to his mother, Eliot prides himself on "a small and select public which regards me as the best living critic, as well as the best living poet, in England." He continues by explicitly comparing himself to James, though he reveals that he thinks a select audience yields greater influence—his position will allow him to "have far more *influence* on English letters than any other American has ever had, unless it be Henry James" (italics in original—*Letters* 280).[7]

When Eliot was looking to get his foot in the door, Woolf was already established as a regular reviewer for the *TLS*. Such a vantage offered her a clear sense of the complex situation a mass readership created. In "The Patron and the Crocus," Woolf details the fractured state of the modern writer's audience:

> There is the daily Press, the weekly Press, the monthly Press; the English public and the American public; the best-seller public and the worst-seller public; the high-brow public and the red-blood public; all now organized self-conscious entities capable through their various mouthpieces of making their needs known and their approval or displeasure felt. (*CE* 2: 149)

Eliot spoke, then, through a "mouthpiece," first *The Egoist* and then his *Criterion*, designed to make the "needs" of a small, select populace known. Woolf reached out to a much broader and more varied cross-section of the reading public, one that encompassed more of the various factions she enumerates. Eliot's ignorance of and insensitivity to what little audience he could command in the late teens contrasts markedly with Virginia Woolf's attempt to speak to the large and various audience she had. Ironically, it is precisely her place in the mainstream of literary journals of her day that has led to the comparative lack of serious attention to her literary criticism.

However, the relative prominence of her position (at least in comparison to Eliot's) did not create in her a correspondingly inflated sense of self. Eschewing the mantle of literary pontiff that her two male contemporaries so eagerly sought, Woolf disavowed the authority of her insights in her reviews. In "Charlotte Brontë," an article commemorating Brontë's centenary, Woolf wrote "I do not want to attribute to the world at large the opinions of one solitary, ill-informed, and misguided individual" (169). She addressed her audience as her familiars and as her equals. Part of Woolf's excessive and somewhat ironic modesty here can be attributed to her consciousness of her place as a woman in a largely male journalistic world. Nevertheless, Woolf continued to offer her readers a place equal to her own. She would not try to assign a "final position" on the novel, for herself or for her readers. Woolf insisted that *Jane Eyre* is a work that changes as one grows, that she "offers merely . . . [her] little hoard of observations, which other readers may like to set, for a moment, beside their own" (*E* 2: 27). Unfortunately, the unassuming tone that Woolf cultivated in her essays has led others to overlook their significance.

Woolf's unassuming critical persona in her *TLS* reviews contrasts markedly with the suave acerbity or splenetic bluster that Eliot and Pound project in their critical incarnations.[8] It is hard to imagine Eliot offering the same generous place for the reader's observations that Woolf does. In "Mr. Symons's Essays," Woolf praises critics who write "without display of knowledge or chain of argument" (*E* 2: 67). As for Eliot, one might extend his view that obscurity in twentieth-century poetry was inevitable, even necessary, to literary criticism.[9] Eliot made this claim to contravene Samuel Johnson's condemnation of obscurity in the imagery of metaphysical poets. Woolf, following Johnson's notion of literature, held that enlightenment, not mystification, was the critic's aim. The proof of her critical views shows in her choice of the title for her collections of reviews and essays—*The Common Reader*. The title attests that Woolf envisions her readers as Samuel Johnson did—as "common" ones, "uncorrupted by literary prejudices . . . and the dogmatism of learning" (a view that no doubt grew out of her own unstructured learning—*CR* 1: 1). They read strictly for their "own pleasure rather than to impart knowledge or correct the opinions of others" (*CR* 1: 1).[10] In fact, learning, or aspiring "to become a specialist or an authority, is very apt to kill what it suits us to consider the more human passion for pure and disinterested reading" (*E* 2: 55). The major question that she thinks readers need to answer, as she remarks in "How Should One Read a Book?," is how to "get the deepest and widest pleasure from what we read" (*CE* 2: 1). Despite her focus on pleasure, Woolf feels readers profoundly influenced writers.

Indeed, the reader's effect is wider—since it is anonymous, part of the writer's "general atmosphere," and more valuable because it is "disinterested," the opinion of one who reads merely "for the love of reading, slowly and unprofessionally" (*CE* 2: 11). Woolf prefers enlightened readers to offer writers advice. In her essay "Reviewing" she details the ideal reader further, creating a disinterested critic who advises his "clients" privately on their work (*CE* 2: 212).

Eliot envisions a much different system, one predicated on professionalism. New writing should be distributed to "a private audience of the two hundred people who are most likely to be interested in them." Professional critics, through periodicals such as *The Egoist*, provide a necessary means of communication among various artistic communities:

> Let the practitioners of any art or of several arts who have a sufficient community of interests and standards publish their conversation, their theories and their opinions in periodicals of their own. They should not be afraid of forming "cliques," if their cliques are professional and not personal. The friction will be stimulating. ("A Brief Treatise" 9)

One could say that the literary community presented in this 1920 essay merely describes Eliot's idealized view of his previous role as *The Egoist* assistant editor. In order to conduct the business of literature properly, one needs "a small and select" audience of like-minded individuals.

While Eliot sees such "professional" societies as the answer, Woolf sees "professionals" as the problem. In her view, professional readers answer to others, have axes to grind, reputations to protect (so that they might maintain their profession). They cannot be disinterested. In fact, Eliot also worried about this. In a 29 March 1919 letter to his mother, Eliot describes the respect his bank position affords him. Since the salary provides him independence from any one paper, he is "known to be disinterested" (*Letters* 280). He was therefore not subject to the pressures that Woolf sees as endemic to the professional critic.

In Eliot's view, however, professionalism provided the conditions necessary for disinterestedness. Without professionalism, no one would "learn to take literature [and by implication, criticism] seriously" ("Professionalism" 61). It would remain merely "aimless appreciation" and continue to be something one might aim at "a University Extension audience" ("Observations" 70; "Professionalism" 61). In other words, criticism was serious business. Eliot no doubt considered Woolf's criticism as so much "aimless appreciation." Certainly others of Eliot's mind, such as H. P. Collins, in a *Criterion* review of *The Common Reader*, implied as much. Collins derides Woolf's unwillingness to accept any "impersonal standards of aesthetic value" (156). Further, the readers she conceives of are much closer to the "University Extension" class Eliot sniffs at.

Eliot and Woolf, therefore, both prize the critic's disinterestedness. Her consultant critics are for authors; Eliot fuses authors, critics, and audience into professional societies that will serve as arbiters of public taste. Eliot's emphasis on professionalism, as Gail McDonald has pointed out in *Learning from Modernism*, derives in part from a broader cultural impulse (headed by the Modern Language Association) to professionalize literary studies and clear "the humanities from the taint of gentility and femininity" (viii). Eliot famously "distrust[ed] the Feminine in literature." During his tenure as assistant editor of *The Egoist*, his complaint about the independence of women typists, who are not "wholly dependent on their salary," as being "irritating to men who are dependent on their[s]" sounds suspiciously like a reference to women writers like Amy Lowell, Dora Marsden, and Virginia Woolf (*Letters* 204).[11] These women insist on writing even though they do not, in Eliot's view, *need* to write.

Eliot's emphasis on professionalism is of a piece with the metaphor of scientific research with which he tends to view critical work: "If the critic has performed his laboratory work well, his understanding will be evidence of appreciations; but his work is by the intelligence not the emotions. The judgment also will take place in the reader's mind, not in the critic's explicit statement" ("Studies" 113). Here, Eliot offers the critical equivalent of the "objective correlative" of his literary practice, only here the critic's "facts" are affecting the reader's judgment. The critic, like the artist in Eliot's "Tradition," is the isolated, "disinterested" platinum shred catalyzing the reader's judgment on a given work. Eliot's critic contrasts markedly with Woolf's. Under the cover of impersonal principles, his critic wills the formation of *his* interpretation into the readers' minds; Woolf, in her essay "Hours in a Library," simply offers readers her "hoard of observations . . . to set . . . beside their own," and advises against "read[ing] on a system, to become a specialist or authority" (*CE* 2: 34).

Unlike Woolf, Eliot prefers readers filled with the "dogmatism of learning," though they must be filled with the dogmatism of *his* learning (Woolf preferred readers "uncorrupted" by such). In "Tradition and the Individual Talent" he assumes his readers find "criticism . . . as inevitable as breathing" (*Selected Essays* 3). In "The Function of Criticism" Eliot reveals more overtly his sense of his role as an instructor to critics. He recounts his experiences as an Extension school teacher and, holding forth as he must have done there, insists that the only legitimate role for critics "is not interpretation at all, but merely putting the reader in possession of facts which he would otherwise have missed." He attempts to perform the critical equivalent of the objective correlative—leading his student-readers to "the *right* liking" simply by putting them in "possession of facts" (*Selected Essays* 20).[12] The critic-readers that he aims his writing at are somewhat more advanced versions of his Extension students. Those who graduate from Eliot's class are better equipped "to correct some of the poetical vagaries of the present age" (*Sacred Wood* xvi). They write to guide other critics and artists.

Woolf does not write to advise critics. She does not present or presume herself in so grand a role as literary guide. Her audience does not need such a guide to be useful. Unlike Eliot, whose knowing air sets him apart from his readers (at the head of the class), Woolf includes herself with those in her audience. "We must remain readers," she says in "How Should One Read a Book?," "[and not try to be] critics. But still we have our responsibilities as readers. . . . [Our] judgments become part of the atmosphere which writers breathe as they work" (*CE* 2: 11). Thus Woolf's untutored readers perform the learned role that Eliot envisions for critics.

Woolf's and Eliot's very different senses of their audiences correspond to their differing attitudes toward literary form and feeling. Woolf believed feeling must somehow comprise the form; Eliot insisted feeling must be strictly subordinated to form, associating too overt a display of emotion in literature with adolescent and feminine excess. In "On Re-Reading Fiction," a 1922 review of Percy Lubbock's *The Craft of Fiction*, Woolf protested Lubbock's praise of the form of James's novels, suggesting that "James lost as much by his devotion to art as he gained. We will not silence that protest, for it is the voice of an immediate joy in reading" (*E* 3: 343). She drives home the point that "among all this talk of methods . . . both in writing and in reading it is emotion that must come first" (*E* 3: 341). What stays with readers when they read a work is not its form but its feeling, "which remains in our minds as the book itself" (*E* 3: 340).

Unlike Eliot's learned dogmatism, emotion is available to all of Woolf's readers. Moreover, such indulgence in feeling is important because readers must educate their feeling, not their minds: "[O]ur taste, the nerve of sensation that sends shocks through us, is our chief illuminant; we learn through feeling; we cannot suppress our own idiosyncrasy without impoverishing it. But as time goes on perhaps we can train our taste; perhaps we can make it submit to some control" (*CE* 2: 9-10). Eliot however believes it is facts that educate taste—not feeling.[13]

While Woolf feels emotion must somehow be fashioned into form, Eliot sees it as inimical to form. Eliot believes that for emotion to be admitted into art it must be something else.[14] In describing the perfect critic (a form of the perfect reader), Eliot insists that the "literary critic should have no emotions except those immediately provoked by a work of art—and these . . . are, when valid, perhaps not to be called emotions at all" (*Sacred Wood* 12-13).

These critical judgments reflected their own literary practices in fiction and poetry. Eliot did eventually find a place for the emotions in form in his famous (or notorious) "objective correlative": "a set of objects, a situation, a chain of events which shall be the formula of that *particular* emotion; such that when the external facts, which must terminate in sensory experience, are given, the emotion is immediately evoked" (*Selected Essays* 124-25). He criticized *Hamlet* because Shakespeare failed to find such a correlative. He fell prey to emotion he could not "drag to light" or "manipulate into art." It stayed obstinately mere emotion, "an unmistakable tone" (124). For Woolf, the response to the form of *Hamlet*, like the response to *Jane Eyre*, grew as the individual's ability to respond grew. Woolf wished to create such a form, one that relied on emotion that was otherwise difficult to "drag to light," more "an unmistakable tone," and she struggled with ways of achieving it in her fiction and in her essays throughout the twenties. Her struggle ultimately resulted in *The Waves* and in *A Room of One's Own*.

In his review of Woolf's *Monday or Tuesday*, Eliot perceptively recognizes what Woolf hoped to achieve—the creation of feeling in her readers. Apparently, Eliot felt the force of her art, but he misjudged it. He praises it, after a fashion, but in an equivocal manner that smacks of concealed distaste. He ostensibly compares Woolf neutrally to Joyce—though anyone familiar with his terms can clearly see his censure.[15] Eliot writes that unlike a stronger writer like Joyce, who can make his feeling into "an articulate external world," the "more feminine type" (Eliot's phrase)

> makes its art by feeling and by contemplating the feeling, rather than the object into which the feeling has been made. . . . A good deal of the secret charm of Mrs. Woolf's shorter pieces consists in the immense disparity between the object and the train of feeling which it has set in motion. ("London Letter" 215)

The "immense disparity between the object and the train of feeling which it has set in motion" makes Woolf (in Eliot's view) Shakespeare's sister, unable to find sufficient form for her emotions. Like Shakespeare, she is "dominated by an emotion which is inexpressible, because it is in *excess* of the facts as they appear" (emphasis in original; *Selected Essays* 101). She does not transmute her feelings into the external structure of her art, and lets her feeling run away with her fictional form. She adulterates her "poetic emotions with human emotions," failing to create the "emotions of art" ("Reflections" 133). Eliot's remarks suggest that he does not find her work Modernist.

Eliot's assessment, however, reveals more about his limited notions of form and of Woolf's very different ideas about the sort of form she attempts than any failure on her part to be sufficiently Modernist. In Eliot's scheme of things structure must have a "factual" basis; Woolf conceived of her novelistic form as a unifying mood or emotion that impressed itself on the reader and sought to escape action altogether. In her diary entry for 3 January 1923, Woolf meditates on how "one's life is made up, superficially, of . . . moods; but they cross a solid substance" (*D* 2: 222). She determined to "search out & identify . . . feelings" (*D* 2: 268) as the basis of her novelistic form; the novel of the future would offer not only "people's relations to each other and their activities together . . . but it will give the relation of the mind to general ideas and its soliloquy in solitude" (*CE* 2: 225).

Woolf found models for such a form by looking backward at a different tradition than Eliot's for the source of her Modernism. In "Phases of Fiction" (written in 1929 for *The Bookman*), Woolf asserts that the intense emotion (she refers to it as "poetry") of *Wuthering Heights* "deepens and controls the wild, stormy atmosphere of the whole book. By a master stroke of vision, rarer in prose than in poetry, people and scenery and atmosphere are all in keeping" (*CE* 2: 96). Feeling is not the enemy of form for Woolf but a means of providing unity in novelistic form. Eliot could never understand, much less agree with, what Woolf might have in mind by such a statement. Form for Eliot must be based on what he calls "intelligence" or what we might more generally refer to as a concept (such as Joyce's schema for *Ulysses* or Forster's plan for *A Passage to India*). The treacherous base of emotions could never support the solid structure of form that Eliot feels true art requires. Eliot would consider such reliance on emotion as tantamount to the "kind of daemonic possession" that Romantic writers such as Shelley incite in readers.[16]

It is tempting to see Woolf's description in "Women and Fiction" of a woman's perspective as a reply to Eliot's imperceptive complaint about the overwrought feeling in her work:

> both in life and in art the values of a woman are not the values of a man.
> Thus, when a woman comes to write a novel, she will find that she is

perpetually wishing to alter the established values—to make serious
what appears insignificant to a man, and trivial what is to him important.
And for that, of course, she will be criticized; for the critic of the
opposite sex will be genuinely puzzled and surprised by an attempt to
alter the current scale of values, and will see in it not merely a difference
of view, but a view that is weak, or trivial, or sentimental, because it
differs from his own. (CE 2: 146)

Woolf points out that the world she sees and seeks to invest with life
will not appear to "him," the male critic, to be a world worth exploring.
"Important" books, as Woolf points out in A Room of One's Own, focus on war,
"insignificant" ones on "the feelings of women in a drawing room" (80).
Woolf attempts in her writing to "alter the established values," to give greater
weight to emotions over "facts." Eliot only sees the "immense disparity"
between the narrative and the emotions Woolf invests it with. Similarly, in
her literary criticism, her emphasis on the common reader's response and
construction of meaning over literary historical criticism (Eliot's "facts")
condemns her to the great New Critical sin of impressionism. In the passage
above, Woolf correctly predicts that critics like Eliot will not understand
her different approach to literary criticism; they will see it merely as
"charming"—that is, "weak" or "sentimental."[17] Because she chose to base
the form of her fiction on emotion rather than fact, her fiction seemed
insubstantial to Eliot. Eliot's blindness proves the truth of Woolf's observation that "women submit less readily to observation than men" (CE 2: 146).
Or to adapt the phrase—"women [Modernists] submit less readily to observation" by male Modernists.

The novelistic form she was attempting connects with her view of the
proper relation between critics, readers, and literature. As Woolf wrote
Roger Fry on 22 September 1924, she envisioned an entirely new form,
consisting not of the "factual" structure Eliot theorized but of "emotion put
into the right relations" (L 3: 132). When she had objected in "On Re-
Reading Novels" (a review of Lubbock's The Craft of Fiction) to Lubbock's
definition of novelistic form as a "defined shape . . . interposed between us
and the book" (E 3: 340), her objection corresponds to her complaints about
critics' impositions on readers, interfering with their "intimate" relationship
with the work so that they feel the form more than the work itself. Eliot's
conception of literary form follows his view of critics as readers' guides. For
Eliot the purpose of form is precisely to "interpose" itself between the reader
and the work. The form of the work serves as "the formula of . . . [a] particular
emotion" that the work generates—hence his championing of Joyce's Hom-

eric scaffolding for *Ulysses* (and subsequent invention of his "mythic method"), hence his footnotes to *The Waste Land*.

Not surprisingly, the abstract scaffolding that Eliot found so admirable in *Ulysses* made Woolf decry it. Eliot's insistence on form corresponds to his privileging of facts over emotions and places him with Galsworthy and Bennett whom Woolf so famously chides for their "symmetrical gig lamp" depiction of reality comprised of surface facts. Woolf's dissatisfaction with *Ulysses* (a novel that Eliot championed to her time and time again), then, originates not strictly in what seems to be Woolf's distaste for crudity (though that is part of it, as her characterization of Joyce as a "queasy undergraduate scratching his pimples" suggests) but in its too minute depiction of surface reality.[18] Even Joyce's attempt to depict consciousness relies too much on what Woolf considered the "surface" reality of the individual "centered in a self which, in spite of its tremor of susceptibility, never embraces or creates what is outside itself and beyond" ("Modern Novels" *E* 3: 34).

The Modernism one finds Woolf defining for her readers is one that seeks freedom from convention in order to express emotion and feeling with the widest possible range, a form shaped by emotion itself. Eliotic Modernism seeks to limit feeling through convention and fact. Woolf looks ahead to a new form that would explore the uncharted region of feeling. "For under the dominance of the novel," she writes in the "The Narrow Bridge of Art," an article published in the *New York Herald Tribune*, "we have scrutinized one part of the mind closely and left another part unexplored. We have come to forget that a large and important part of life consists of our emotions focused toward such things as roses and nightingales, the dream, sunset, life, death, and fate" (*CE* 2: 225). She would add that what appears insignificant and trivial to some critics is in fact serious and important. Similarly, it is often forgotten that a significant segment of Modernism and Modernists attempted to give form to this hitherto unexplored area. It is the region Dorothy Richardson and Djuna Barnes explored in their fictional works and H. D. and Mina Loy in their poetic ones. The "large and important part of life" that Woolf saw as demanding a new novel form for its exploration intersects with the intangible and invisible lives of women she describes in "Women and Fiction" for their lives too are like a "dark country . . . beginning to be explored in fiction" (*CE* 2: 146). "The extraordinary woman depends on the ordinary woman"; the extraordinary writer depends on the common reader (*CE* 2: 142). No one's life could truly be seen until these forgotten lives were.

Eliot's statement in "Tradition and the Individual Talent" that "No poet, no artist of any art, has his complete meaning alone" sounds similar, but it means something completely different. Woolf spoke of unexplored lives; Eliot of the artist's "relation to the dead poets and artists" (*Selected Essays* 4). For Eliot, the masses, ordinary lives, and common readers remained a "dark country" that needed to be controlled and shaped by the critic's carefully presented "facts," and he constructed his forbidding critical persona, "the eternal pedagogue" that Woolf mentions, as protection against them (*AROO* 81).[19]

Similarly, Woolf's view of consciousness in "Modern Novels" as a "luminous halo, a semi-transparent envelope surrounding us" (*E* 3: 33) would trouble him with the vague shape it presents of the mind. Woolf's and Eliot's views differ completely on what constitutes consciousness. Woolf believes the mind imbued with emotion; Eliot admits only facts and rationality. In "Tradition and the Individual Talent" Eliot images "the mind that creates" as a chemical process, suggesting its purely rational operation, which answers not to vague shifts of the wind but to the immutable laws of the elements. Admitting the influence of emotion on perception and the mind as Woolf does would have seemed to Eliot to provide a dangerous opening for those dark forces of "daemonic possession" and "the mob in the mind" that he felt needed controlling (Tratner 101). Their views of what constitutes consciousness correspond almost directly to their notions of literary form. The lack of rigid structure and boundaries in Woolf's sense of the mind and in novelistic form eventually led to the consciousness depicted in *The Waves* (Booker 35). In short, she creates finally a novel that has, by her lights, the very "form" of consciousness itself. Not only have the boundaries between parts of the mind disappeared but those between different minds, different characters. In the free flow of consciousness the individual selves of the characters lose their definite edge and merge into one another. This is Woolf's Modernism.

Had Eliot deigned to comment on Woolf's criticism, he would no doubt have deplored her tendency to neglect the boundary between fiction and criticism. This disregard for genre led to *The Years*, a book she originally called "a novel-essay." It almost led her to fictionalize her *Common Reader*, grounding each essay in a conversation between a fictional common reader, Penelope Otway, and her friend, thereby foregrounding the role of the reader (Johnston 150-51). Others have noted Woolf's mixing of fictional and critical boundaries, but few mention Woolf's fluid view of the boundaries between readers and authors.[20] Rather than Eliot's strict hierarchy of extraordinary artist-critics ordering the unruly minds of common readers, Woolf envisions a communal structure of artists and reader-critics. The standards and judgments of readers "pass . . . into the air and become part of the atmosphere which writers breathe as they work. An influence is created which tells upon them even if it never finds its way into print" ("How Should One Read a Book?," *CE* 2: 11). Woolf ultimately recommends that the best way for readers to "understand the elements of what a novelist is doing is not to read, but to write" (*CE* 2: 2). All readers, then, would be not only critics but writers as well. Eliot, in one of his last essays for *The Egoist*, also came to the conclusion that "artists would become their own premier critics. Thus, creation, exposition and criticism would and should all spring firsthand from one source" ("Commentary" 71). Tellingly, Woolf's and Eliot's intents are precisely the opposite here: Woolf advises all readers to become writers so that they might become better reader-critics, and Eliot asserts that *only* practicing writers should be critics if literature is to possess its authority. For Woolf, creation and criticism are goods that should be more widely available; for Eliot, they must be concentrated into "one source" or lose whatever potency they retain.

The pedagogical hierarchy that Eliot describes between critics and readers reverses entirely in Woolf. Rather than artist-critics who will master and control the fragmentary and diffused literary world, Woolf makes the best of a difficult situation—of "writ[ing] for busy people catching trains in the morning or for tired people coming home in the evening"—and instead envisions an audience of critic-reader-artists ("The Modern Essay" *CE* 2: 48). She allows her readers the final say as critics. It is writers who must learn from their readers, for "masterpieces are not single and solitary births, they are the outcome of many years of thinking in common, of thinking by the body of the people, so that the experience of the mass is behind the single voice" (*AROO* 71). Though critics have typically disregarded Woolf's criticism as slight and old-fashioned impressionism, properly seen, Woolf's critical views and attitudes are actually revolutionary. She would hand over criticism to readers themselves and do away with the need for literary journalism, anticipating reader-response criticism by several decades.

This lies behind Woolf's determination to give up the ego. It is not, as some fear, a silencing of the self but rather of a way of avoiding the lecturing style of criticism that Eliot favored. Such lecturing derives from the pretensions of "the eternal pedagogue" decried in *A Room of One's Own* (81; 112). Only by giving up the single voice—which being only a single voice is really no voice—can a writer be heard. Modern writers, as Woolf notes in "The Modern Essay," must admit to the fact that they are no longer an "I" but "the 'we' of public bodies" (*CE* 2: 49). In fact, this surrender is a way of finding her voice, a communal voice, one that requires *every* voice to join in—reader, critic, writer alike. Understanding this communal "we" properly as the we of the writer-reader-critic makes clearer Woolf's strategy in *A Room of One's Own*. The many fictional selves she splits her narrator into is not a denial of her anger, as it is sometimes interpreted, but a means and an opportunity for reader-critics to construct their own anger.[21]

Once the writer and the critic and the reader have addressed and redressed their common wrongs they can move toward constructing Woolf's vision of literary work, with writer-critic-readers "engaged upon some vast building . . . being built by *common* effort" (emphasis in original; "How It Strikes a Contemporary" *CE* 2: 160), for nowhere is equality between reader and critic more evident, for Woolf, than in contemporary literature. In the present, critics and readers occupy the same "burning ground." As with the fellow writers she writes of in "How It Strikes a Contemporary," whose novels are notebooks for future masterpieces, ultimate critical judgement awaits until a later date. Only then, by dint of common effort, will those dark countries come to light.[22]

Works Cited

Ackroyd, Peter. *T. S. Eliot: A Life*. New York: Simon and Schuster, 1984.

Allan, Tuzyline Jita. "A Voice of One's Own: Implications of Impersonality in the Essays of Virginia Woolf and Alice Walker." In *The Politics of the Essay: Feminist Perspectives*. Ed. Ruth-Ellen Boetcher Joeres and Elizabeth Mittman. Bloomington: Indiana UP, 1993. 131-47.

Bergonzi, Bernard. *T. S. Eliot*. New York: Macmillan, 1972.

Bush, Ronald. *T. S. Eliot, A Study in Character and Style*. New York: Oxford UP, 1983.

Collins, H. P. Rev. from *Criterion*, July 1925. *Virginia Woolf: The Critical Heritage*. Ed. Robin Majumdar and Allen McLaurin. Boston: Routledge and Kegan Paul, 1975.

Eliot, T. S. "A Brief Treatise on the Criticism of Poetry." *The Chapbook* 2 (March 1920): 9.

————. "Commentary." *The Egoist* 6.5 (1919): 71.

————. "In Memory of Henry James." *The Egoist* 5.1 (1918): 1-2.

————. "Introduction." *The Use of Poetry and the Use of Criticism*. London: Faber & Faber, 1964.

————. *The Letters of T. S. Eliot*. Ed. Valerie Eliot. Vol 1. New York: Harcourt, 1988.

————. "London Letter." *Dial* 71.2 (1921): 213-17.

————. "Observations." *The Egoist* 5.5 (1918): 69-70.

————. "Professionalism, Or . . . ?" *The Egoist* 5.4 (1918): 61.

————. Rev. of Clive Bell's *Potboiler*. *The Egoist* 5.6 (1918): 84-85.

————. "Reflections on Contemporary Poetry." *The Egoist* 4.9 (1917): 133-34.

————. *The Sacred Wood: Essays on Poetry and Criticism*. London: Methuen, 1920.

————. *Selected Essays*. New York: Harcourt, 1960.

————. "Studies in Contemporary Criticism." *Egoist* 5.9 (1918): 113-14.

Garner, Les. *Dora Marsden, A Brave and Beautiful Spirit*. Aldershot, England: Avebury, 1990.

Hoffman, Frederick J., Charles Allen, and Carolyn F. Ulrich. *The Little Magazine: A History and a Bibliography*. Princeton: Princeton UP, 1947.

Howe, Florence. "'T. S. Eliot, Virginia Woolf, and the Future of Tradition.'" *Tradition and the Talents of Women*. Ed. Florence Howe. Urbana: U of Illinois P, 1991.

Johnston, Georgia. "The Whole Achievement in Virginia Woolf's *Common Reader*." *Essays on the Essay: Redefining the Genre*. Ed. Alexander J. Butrym. Athens: U of Georgia P, 1989.

Kenner, Hugh. *The Invisible Poet: T. S. Eliot*. New York: McDowell, Obolensky, 1959.

————. *The Pound Era*. Berkeley: U of California P, 1971.

Lidderdale, Jane, and Mary Nicholson. *Dear Miss Weaver: Harriet Shaw Weaver*. London: Faber & Faber, 1970.

McDonald, Gail. *Learning to Be Modern: Eliot, Pound, and the American University*. Clarendon: Oxford UP, 1993.

MacKendrick, Louis K. "T. S. Eliot and *The Egoist*: The Critical Preparation." *Dalhousie Review* 55 (1975): 140-54.

Marcus, Jane. *Art and Anger: Reading Like a Woman*. Columbus: Miami UP, 1988.

Marek, Jayne. *Women Editing Modernism: "Little" Magazines and Literary History*. Lexington: U of Kentucky P, 1995.

Pound, Ezra. *The Selected Letters of Ezra Pound to John Quinn, 1915-1924*. Ed. Timothy Materer. Durham: Duke UP, 1991.

————. *Pavannes and Divigations*. New York: New Directions, 1958.

Rosenberg, Beth Carole. *Virginia Woolf and Samuel Johnson: Common Readers*. New York: St. Martin's, 1995.

Rosenman, Ellen Bayuk. *A Room of One's Own: Women Writers and the Politics of Literary Creativity*. New York: Twayne, 1995.

Tratner, Michael. *Modernism and Mass Politics: Joyce, Woolf, Eliot, Yeats*. Stanford: Stanford UP, 1995.

Sharma, Vijay L. *Virginia Woolf as Literary Critic: A Reevaluation*. New Delhi: Arnold-Heineman, 1977.

Showalter, Elaine. *A Literature of Their Own: British Women Novelists from Brontë to Lessing*. Princeton: Princeton UP, 1977.

Woolf, Virginia. "Charlotte Brontë." *Times Literary Supplement*, 12 April 1916, 169.

————. *The Collected Essays of Virginia Woolf*. Ed. Leonard Woolf. 4 vols. New York:
        Harcourt, 1967.
————. *The Common Reader*. London: Hogarth; New York: Harcourt, 1953.
————. *The Diaries of Virginia Woolf*. Ed. Anne Olivier Bell. 5 vols. New York:
        Harcourt, 1978.
————. *The Essays of Virginia Woolf*. Ed. Andrew MacNellie. 4 vols. to date. London:
        Hogarth, 1986-.
————. *The Letters of Virginia Woolf*. Ed. Nigel Nicholson and Joanne Trautmann. 6 vols.
        New York: Harcourt, 1977.
————. *Moments of Being*. Ed. Jeanne Schulkind. New York: Harcourt, 1976.
————. *A Room of One's Own*. 1929. New York: Harcourt, 1991.

Notes

1. As I note below, Eliot did later publicly praise Woolf's short story writing.
    However, he tellingly favors her more conventional work to her experiments
    (*D* 2: 125; 96).
2. Hoffman, Allen, and Ulrich's *The Little Magazine: A History and a Bibliography*
    offers an overview of the importance of small magazines to early Modernist
    writing. Though they do mention notable women editors such as Margaret
    Anderson at *Little Review*, they tend to highlight the activities of the male
    Modernists involved—most notably Ezra Pound (20-21). Hugh Kenner's *The
    Pound Era* follows out such suggestions to their logical extent, recasting the
    entire early history of Modernism as Pound's doing. Jayne Marek's *Women
    Editing Modernism: "Little" Magazines and Literary History* takes large strides in
    recovering a more balanced view of women Modernists and their contribu-
    tions to Modernism.
3. Eliot used the phrase "small and select public" in a letter to his mother
    describing his position in English literary society (*Letters* 280). While I do not
    limit the material examined exclusively to the works of each writer that
    appeared in those periodicals, I argue that each of those outlets formed in
    important ways these writers' approach to their audiences. Consequently,
    even when Eliot later wrote some reviews for the *Times Literary Supplement*, he
    retained—as Kenner and Bergonzi note—much the same stance he had while
    writing for *The Egoist* (Kenner 99; Bergonzi 81). Woolf, on the other hand, did
    move to the less widely circulated (though still not as limited as *The Egoist*)
    Nation and Athenaeum when Leonard Woolf took up editorship there but kept
    her much broader sense of audience. Further, while both writers switched their

venues, Woolf wrote mainly for larger circulation periodicals (including the *New York Herald-Tribune* and the *Bookman*) and Eliot stuck more often to smaller circulation periodicals such as his own *The Criterion*.

4. For information on *The Egoist*'s circulation, see Jane Lidderdale and Mary Nicholson, 460. Peter Ackroyd states that in its best days *The Criterion* sent out eight hundred copies an issue, which fell to around two hundred near its demise (248).

5. Eliot writes the praise in 1931, in "After Lambeth," after his situation became more comfortable (*Selected Essays* 325).

6. Weaver continued to find Dora Marsden's work of interest (unlike Eliot and Pound) and had no intention of abandoning the political and philosophical roots of the periodical. As H. D.'s apologetic letter to Amy Lowell about the 1 May 1915 Imagist issue of *The Egoist* makes clear, both H. D. and Aldington "fought hard" to put the poetry first, "but Miss Weaver runs the paper for Dora Marsden—swears by her" (qtd. in Marek 106).

7. Interestingly, in a review of Clive Bell's *Potboilers*, Eliot mildly chided Bell for preaching "to a small and select public" (87). The remark suggests the strength of Eliot's ambitions for wider influence of his own.

8. In *T. S. Eliot: The Invisible Poet* Hugh Kenner notes the coterie tone of Eliot's reviews: "It was not for a cross-section of The Times reading British public that Eliot with a little quotation assisted Amy Lowell to display her Chautauqua sensibility." He further shows how Eliot sneers at Lowell's popularizing (99). Kenner notes that "the pages of *The Egoist* have a familial intimacy" as "Eliot with incomparable deftness of phrase maneuvers into the light cliché after cliché which he is confident thirty or forty readers will find amusing" (as in Eliot's fake letters to the editors) (99).

9. Eliot's exact words are: "we can only say that it appears likely that poets in our civilization, as it exists at present, must be *difficult*" (emphasis in original; *Selected Essays* 248).

10. Beth C. Rosenberg details the depth of Johnson's influence on Woolf's conception of criticism and readers.

11. He does have the good grace to continue somewhat apologetically, noting that "of course such women are a minority, as there are very few incomes which don't need supplementing nowadays, but there is a certain number" (*Letters* 204).

12. Anthony Powell described Eliot's "manner . . . [as] rather like that of a headmaster talking to the more intelligent boys. . . . 'if not exactly intimidating, at least restraining'" (qtd. in Bush).

13. Eliot says this in his typically roundabout way. He insists that "[a]ny note . . . which produces a fact even of the lowest order about a work of art is a better

piece of work than nine-tenths of the most pretentious critical journalism . . ."
(*Selected Essays* 21).

14.   This redefinition occurs also in Eliot's comments on the part personality plays
        in a poet's work. Personality becomes something else finally when the readers
        come to the work.

15.   Apparently Woolf chose to take it as praise—at least on 7 June 1921 Woolf
        glows, "astounded" and "delighted" at Eliot's praise of *Monday and Tuesday*:
        "'Very good' he said, & meant it, I think." Woolf's hesitation at the end reveals
        her awareness of Eliot's slippery statements.

16.   Eliot uses the same phrasing as he does for Woolf's review. Romantic writers
        like Shelley *"set in motion* these new and delightful feelings [creating] . . . a kind
        of daemonic possession" (emphasis added; "Introduction" 33-34). In describ-
        ing Woolf's work he writes of the "immense disparity between the object and
        the train of feeling which it has set in motion" ("London Letter" 215). The
        turmoil of emotion does not belong in the static form of art.

17.   Proof of the subtle obloquy attached to "charm" in the British lexicon comes
        from Quentin Bell's attack on Jane Marcus's views on Woolf in which he calls
        Marcus "a person of great charm and ability." In *Art and Anger*, Marcus rightly
        senses the insults and takes umbrage at his clever insult (209).

18.   Eliot remarks on at least two occasions about Joyce's accomplishment in
        Ulysses, finding it "extremely brilliant" in September 1920 (much to Woolf's
        unease, because she was starting her own experimental novel) and later in
        September 1922.

19.   Michael Tratner details the change effected on Modernist writers by the
        growing political power of the masses and reflected in Modernist work. The
        masses were imaged as alien and monstrous "Others"—racially, ethnically,
        sexually—as a "dark country" (83).

20.   Beth C. Rosenberg and Ellen Bayuk Rosenman, for example, discuss Woolf's
        fictional techniques in *A Room of One's Own* (Rosenberg 72-77; Rosenman 91-
        102). Rosenberg also insightfully points out Woolf's conflation of "the reading
        and writing processes" in her criticism (67).

21.   Elaine Showalter feels that Woolf deplored "passionate responses . . . because
        she thought that they distorted the artist's integrity." However, the cost, in
        Showalter's view, was "a denial of feeling, and not a mastery of it" (285).
        Following Showalter, Rosenman points out Woolf's ambivalence toward overt
        expression of anger (108-9). Similarly, Tuzyline Jita Allan sees Woolf as
        gaining her voice but losing authorial presence in doing so (145). Rosenman
        points out a similar ambivalence in Woolf toward overt expression of anger
        (108-9).

22. I would like to thank this essay's critics and readers: Sally Jacobsen, Melba Cuddy-Keane, Jeanne Dubino, Beth Rosenberg, and especially Patricia Morse contributed numerous helpful comments and suggestions for improvement on various drafts.

PART III

WOOLF AND READING

Readin', Writin', and Revisin': Virginia Woolf's "How Should One Read a Book?"

Beth Rigel Daugherty

Critics often cite Woolf's common reader, quoting her definition and recasting it to support their interpretations of her work as an essayist. For example, she has been criticized for using the common reader to "disguise heterodox values under the veneer of charm" (Zwerdling 8), to create a mask for herself (Manuel 29), and to maintain modern impersonality (Allan 132-36). She has been praised for assuming a more democratic stance (McNeillie ix), anticipating reader-response criticism (Ferebee 357-61), and using the common reader as the "philosophical basis for her critical method" (Madison 63). Woolf's role as an essayist, in other words, has depended partly on how the critic interprets Woolf's use of the common reader.[1] When attention shifts to how Woolf revised for that reader, how she changed the essays originally published in *Times Literary Supplement*, *The New Republic*, *The Yale Review*, and so on for her two *Common Readers* (1925 and 1932), yet another common reader and essayist emerge.[2]

Out of the fifty-two essays in the two volumes entitled *The Common Reader*, Woolf reprinted only fifteen, wrote thirteen new ones, and revised twenty-four, some extensively.[3] For example, in the essay that ends *The Second Common Reader*, "How Should One Read a Book?," Woolf not only defines the common reader again, thus subtly pairing it with "The Common Reader" that opens her first volume,[4] but also clearly revises for the reader she defines. Woolf's revisions of "How Should One Read a Book?" reveal an acute awareness of audience, a common reader strongly grounded in students, and a teacher at work. What Woolf says about the relationship between the writer and reader in this essay and what she does as she moves from draft to final version also demonstrate the crucial role the common reader plays in her revising process.

"How Should One Read a Book?" begins as a talk Woolf gives to sixty girls at Hayes Court School in Kent on 30 January 1926; a thirty-seven-page holograph draft of the Hayes Court talk, dated 18 November 1925 exists in the Berg Collection, along with a few stray pages located in the *To the Lighthouse* manuscript, Woolf's diary, and another notebook.[5] Although we cannot assume Woolf said at Hayes Court exactly what she wrote in the draft, we can see her earliest thoughts about, and earliest approach to, the subject of how to read. The talk then becomes an essay that appears in *The Yale Review* in October 1926. A seventeen-page holograph draft (quarto pages) of this essay exists in the Berg Collection, and a thirty-one-page typescript (octavo pages) resides in the Beinecke Library at Yale. Woolf edits both this draft and typescript, but they do not differ greatly from the published version.[6] Finally, Woolf revises "How Should One Read a Book?" to appear as the concluding essay in her *Second Common Reader*, published in October 1932. This *Second Common Reader* version is so strikingly different from the *Yale Review* version that we can clearly see her revising for the common reader.

In all three stages—Hayes Court draft, *Yale Review* version, and *Second Common Reader* essay[7]—Woolf uses the same basic ideas: a reader must be the writer's friend first and then the writer's judge; three kinds of books—fiction, biography, and poetry—must be read in three different ways; three novelists, Defoe, Austen, and Hardy, show us three different approaches to fiction; readers read for pleasure, yet it's a difficult skill; rigid laws do not govern reading, and readers must be free to develop their own methods; any book deserves to be compared with the best of its kind. Some statements appear in all three versions, too; for example, the claim that facts are "only an inferior form of fiction" appears in the margin of the Hayes Court draft (ms. 227) and is published, with slight variations, in both *The Yale Review* (40) and *The Second Common Reader* (264). Yet the three versions also differ—in content, purpose, tone, and relationship with reader—because the *audiences* for these versions differ.

At Hayes Court, Woolf's audience consisted of young female students, who were *there*, real, and listening; they were in a private school whose headmistress, Miss Katherine Cox, valued literature (Avery 251). Her draft reveals the Woolf we see in other talks—witty, encouraging, informal. She enjoyed preparing it, writing to Vita Sackville-West in what the editors think was early November 1925 that "I have to write a lecture, for school girls: 'how should one read a Book?' and this, by a merciful dispensation, seems to me a matter of dazzling importance and breathless excitement" (*L* 3: 220). Her draft also shows a teacher at work. Near the beginning, for example, Woolf reassures her young audience about their abilities by slyly claiming to have met "very learned men who cannot read" (ms. 179). Her most obvious teaching occurs, however, when she suggests that a student must become the writer's "fellow worker. And the best way of doing this is to write something oneself." She continues: "Shall we then try, very quickly, to write a story here & now? It will be a very bad one; but never mind; . . . that will make us understand other writers [sic] difficulties; & admire their successes" (ms. 193-95; ellipses added).

In a wonderfully layered presentation covering the next fourteen pages, Woolf proceeds to do exactly that, "writing" a story about Miss Eliza Pelt's con game (Eliza claims to have lost her purse on the top of a London bus and asks for a "loan" of seven and sixpence to get back home, a loan she promises to return in a postal order the next day); creating Mary, Elizabeth, and Helen, each of whom falls for Eliza's scam and then sees Eliza using the same story with another victim; inventing scenarios in which each girl tries to write a story about her experience (Mary wants to write down what happened, Elizabeth wants to record the dialogue, and Helen wants to communicate the cosmic forces operating against Eliza); and then comparing their writing to that of Defoe, Austen, and Hardy (ms. 195-221). Their frustration at not being able to convey clearly what they had experienced (papers get balled up, impulsively thrown in the fire, and labeled embarrassingly bad) shows them (and the girls at Hayes Court) how difficult it was for Defoe, Austen, and Hardy to use plot, dialogue, and fate to create their worlds. It's a delightful strategy, geared toward young students.

The *Yale Review* audience, on the other hand, was distant—new ("How Should One Read a Book?" was the first essay she placed there), American, unknown, academic—and the resulting essay seems cold, vague, and abstract. The *Yale Review* was *not* a purely academic journal at the time (in 1929, before the Crash, its circulation had reached 18,000 [Mott 338]), but Woolf may have associated it with English universities, not a happy association for her.[8] She begins her Hayes Court draft, for example, by saying, "In the first place I am going to confess a crime—not my own doing however—I have never been to school" (ms. 179). When Cambridge University don G. Lowes Dickinson wrote to tell her that her first *Common Reader* was "the best criticism in English—humorous, witty and profound," Woolf replied that she had been "very nervous as to what people like you might think, as I have so little education" (*L* 3: 182). In the face of this audience, perceived as academic, Woolf's "crime" makes her nervous, fearful, and protective. We can hear the difference right away; the essay begins, "At this late hour of the world's history, books are to be found in almost every room of the house"

(*Yale Review* 32). Passive voice, no human presence, and Woolf's version of "Throughout history"! She did not enjoy working on the essay, writing in her diary on 6 June 1926, "I grind out a little of that eternal How to read, lecture, as the Yale Review has bought it " (3: 89), and although the essay has its moments, it *sounds* ground out, at least in comparison to the much more lively Hayes Court draft.

When Woolf returned to her essay six years later for her *Second Common Reader*, she returned to a wider, more familiar audience. She had succeeded in reaching more readers through her first *Common Reader*, not only through libraries but also through increased, steady sales.[9] In fact, by the time Penguin brought out its cheap edition of the first *Common Reader* in 1938, it did so in an issue of 50,000 copies (Mepham 131). For these readers, Woolf could not simply reprint her *Yale Review* essay: "the CR I confess is not yet quite done," she writes in her *Diary*. "But then—well I had to re-write the last article, which I had thought so good, entirely" (4: 113-14). Rewriting "entirely," moving from *The Yale Review* to *The Second Common Reader*, meant restoring many of the Hayes Court draft's features: the relaxed, personal tone, including the sense of language as it is spoken; the trust and exploration and questions; the humor (especially the mockery of learned men); and most important, the collaborative writer-reader relationship. Rewritten for common readers, this essay begins, "In the first place, I want to emphasise the note of interrogation at the end of my title" (*CR* 2: 258). Note the similarity to the Hayes Court draft ("In the first place I am going to confess a crime"): she uses the same opening phrase, immediately employs a strategy to put readers at ease, and uses the pronoun "I." The *Second Common Reader* opener sounds "spoken," uses active voice, and attempts to establish a relationship, in great contrast to the *Yale Review* essay's distancing of the reader.

The *Second Common Reader* essay does not duplicate the Hayes Court draft, and not all of Woolf's revisions rely on it. Some ideas, for example, grow progressively from version to version: critics are not mentioned in the Hayes Court draft, receive two sentences' worth of attention in the *Yale Review* version (43, 44), and receive part of a long paragraph in the *Second Common Reader* essay (268-69). Reading provides more pleasure than any other school activity does in the Hayes Court draft (ms. 249); it causes civilization to be built in the *Yale Review* version (44); and by the time Woolf reaches *The Second Common Reader*, reading is heaven on earth and outdoes God (270)! In addition, Woolf occasionally uses *Yale Review* material for her *Second Common Reader* essay. For example, the idea that "to go from one great novelist to another . . . is to be wrenched and uprooted" (*CR* 2: 260) does not exist in the Hayes Court draft but is almost a direct quotation from the *Yale Review* essay (37). Repeatedly, however, in content, in purpose, in tone, and in its relationship with the reader, the "How Should One Read a Book?" written for *The Second Common Reader* either recalls or literally returns to something in the Hayes Court draft that was dropped or muted in the *Yale Review*. As a result, an almost palpable common reader emerges from the great contrast between the essay written for "furred and gowned" authorities (*CR* 2: 258) and the essay written for "[h]asty, inaccurate, and superficial" readers (*CR* 1: 1), common readers who gain their reality from Hayes Court students.

Content in the Hayes Court draft often goes underground in the *Yale Review* version and turns up again in the *Second Common Reader* essay. For example, although all three versions contain Woolf's suggestion that a reader should try writing in order to understand a writer's work, in the *Yale Review* version, she switches quickly to how Defoe, Austen, and Hardy would write a story and never mentions the reader's writing again. In contrast, Woolf sustains the focus on the reader's attempt to write in the *Second Common Reader* essay, advising readers, "turn from your blurred and littered pages to the opening pages of some great novelist" (260), before she names those great novelists. Eliza Pelt and the three girls taken in by her are gone, but the "blurred and littered pages" recall the girls' frustrating attempts to write about a vivid experience. In another example, books have shape in all three versions, but in the Hayes Court draft, "words are more like fire than they are like clay" (ms. 191) and in *The Second Common Reader*, "words are more impalpable than bricks" (259). In both the Hayes Court draft and the *Second Common Reader* essay, Woolf brings herself into the essay by mentioning reviewing and then reminds her readers that their value lies in *not* being reviewers. In the draft, they do not have to "shoot out an opinion" quickly (ms. 243); in *The Second Common Reader*, they do not have to participate in the carnival where the "books pass in review like the procession of animals in a shooting gallery" (270).

Similarly, in the *Yale Review* essay, history appears only in the deadly first sentence and in a question about how the eighteenth century might have affected Richardson's writing (43). In the Hayes Court draft, Woolf discusses history in a much more personal way, reminding her listeners, "Your grandmothers read Pride & Prejudice, & so do you; but you are reading different books"; that is why "[e]ach generation must read everything over again for itself" (ms. 193). In one long section of the *Second Common Reader* essay, Woolf literally summarizes the contents of *both* of her loosely chronological *Common Reader* volumes and then describes her historical method—"merely by going from friend to friend, from garden to garden, from house to house, we have passed from one end of English literature to another" (*CR* 2: 261-62).[10] As she did in the Hayes Court draft, then, she makes English literary history personal and accessible.

In both the Hayes Court draft and the *Second Common Reader* essay, Woolf has a clear purpose for discussing the topic: she's answering an often unasked but real question that students and amateur readers have. As a result, she puts her readers at ease, talks casually about the topic, and reassures her readers about their ability to learn. For example, in the Hayes Court draft, she says, "The older you grow & the more books you have read the more of these wholes will be hanging in your mind, so that when a new book comes along you can have a [*sic*] many to compare with it. And you will become more & more skilled to bring out the one against the other" (ms. 245). At the end of the *Second Common Reader* essay, the reassurance is somewhat different, yet Woolf indirectly recalls the Hayes Court point—it takes time to develop this ability to compare: "to have read widely enough and with enough understanding to make such comparisons alive and illuminating" is difficult (267-68). In the *Yale Review* version, she assumes professional status in her readers, does not believe they need to be reassured, and so has no real reason to discuss how to read in the first place. She thus sets up a "situation": she "strolls" into a library filled with books and asks herself, "How am I to read these books? What is the right way to set about it?" She continues, "I will lay before you some of the thoughts that have come to me on such an occasion as this" (*Yale Review* 32). But the "occasion" is bogus and the writing pompous. In the Hayes Court draft, she thinks her talk is important and exciting; her *Second Common Reader* essay functions as a summary of reading tips and literary subjects and as a conclusion to her two volumes. In both cases, Woolf tries to illuminate a mysterious process. The *Yale Review* version, lacking a specific purpose, sounds like an artificial writing exercise.

In both the Hayes Court draft and the *Second Common Reader* essay, Woolf's tone is relaxed and occasionally humorous or bantering ("Can you imagine [Jane Austen's] Mr Woodhouse on the top of Stonehenge at midnight?" in the draft [ms. 219]; "[Critics] can do nothing for us if we herd ourselves under their authority and lie down like sheep in the shade of a hedge" in the essay [*CR* 2: 269]). The *Yale Review* version is much more serious; even when Woolf uses the same idea, she drains the humor from it: "If Jane Austen's characters are real in the drawing room, they would not exist at all upon the top of Stonehenge" (36). Woolf's forms of address in the draft and *Second Common Reader* essay vary between "I" and "we," along with the "you" that occurs more frequently in the draft than in the essay. She uses "I" occasionally in the *Yale Review* version, too, but rarely to mean herself;

the references go back to "one" or to "ourselves," and the essay is filled with the impersonal "one." As a result, the *Yale Review* "we" sounds forced. In the Hayes Court draft and the *Second Common Reader* essay, a sense of dialogue prevails.[11] In the draft, Woolf anticipates dialogue, commenting, "I expect you are saying to yourselves. [sic] This is nonsense—Reading is not difficult" (ms. 221), predicts her listeners' boredom (ms. 187), and compares the pleasures of reading to the other pleasures students might mention (ms. 249). In the *Second Common Reader* essay, the dialogue is not as overt, but because Woolf follows the title question with an "I" statement and is willing to make suggestions only if the reader first *agrees* not to let that advice "fetter" her "independence" (258), the remaining questions and answers in the essay seem real and conversational. In effect, however, the *Yale Review* essay silences the Hayes Court students by asking rhetorical or evaluative questions: "how are we to teach people so to read 'Paradise Lost' as to see that it is a great poem, or 'Tess of the D'Urbervilles' so as to see that it is a good novel?" (33). In the Hayes Court draft and the *Second Common Reader* essay, she and the student-readers work together; in the *Yale Review* version, she labors to answer fake questions for fake readers. Ironically, Woolf's aside to Helen McAfee in the letter of 13 July 1926 accompanying the essay—"(it is, by the way, really a lecture)" (*L* 3: 279)—applies much more to the essay sent to Yale than to the lecture she seems to have presented at Hayes Court.

In both the Hayes Court draft and the *Second Common Reader* essay, Woolf works to establish a relationship with the reader; in the *Yale Review* essay, she works to distance herself. The latter seems stiff, formal, artificial. Spending only two sentences on the reader's imaginative power, Woolf uses passive voice and a throwaway line to describe it: "but to read something after this fashion is to be a reader whom writers respect. It is by the means of such readers that masterpieces are helped into the world" (44). In contrast, the Hayes Court draft and the *Second Common Reader* essay are casual, easy-going; writers and readers are partners. Further, Woolf spends more space on the idea that writers depend on readers who read intelligently and talk. In the Hayes Court draft, for example, if the girls read *and* talk about what they read, their voices will reach writers' ears and they will control literature, which is much more important than controlling armies and navies: "Really I believe that if every one in this room were to read intelligently [first sympathetically and then severely] we should soon have another Shakespeare" (ms. 249).[12] In the *Second Common Reader* essay, the references to masterpieces are gone, but the reader's responsibilities and importance are not: "The standards we raise and the judgments we pass steal into the air and become part of the atmosphere which writers breathe as they work. An influence is created which tells upon them even if it never finds its way into print" (269-70). At the end of both the Hayes Court draft and the *Second Common Reader* essay, then, Woolf describes a process by which students and readers actually converse with and affect the writer.

Writing for the common reader in her last version of "How Should One Read a Book?," Woolf consistently revises by using what she had drafted for students six years earlier. Although no proof exists that Woolf sat with the earlier draft as she worked on the *Second Common Reader* essay, her revisions, including the ones for *The Yale Review* that prove by negative example, bring Hayes Court students back into the essay. This move reinforces Woolf's definition of the common reader, which uses words that could describe students: "worse educated," less generously "gifted," "[h]asty, inaccurate, and superficial," reading for pleasure, attempting to make some sense of it all (CR 1: 1). As Susan Stanford Friedman has pointed out, Woolf uses "not knowing" or ignorance as "the privileged base from which the 'common reader' constructs 'a portrait of a man, a sketch of an age, a theory of the art of writing'" (119). Woolf as teacher in "How Should One Read a Book?" sets goals students can reach—be an amateur; read for pleasure rather than for knowledge, power, or money; wander around in books, including ones on the rubbish heaps, without method or direction; try to make connections among works and ideas and writers—while at the same time demanding active, difficult work from them: "To carry out this part of a reader's duty [deciding which books succeed and which books fail] needs such imagination, insight, and learning that it is hard to conceive any one mind sufficiently endowed" (CR 2: 268). Woolf removes reading from the giving of prizes, from competition, from hierarchy (from grades?), and trusts students, if they simply keep reading, to recognize worth when they see it. She is also delighted that they will all define such worth differently. Woolf both respects and likes her readers for their abilities, questions, and common sense. Using self-fulfilling prophecy as a teacher might, Woolf assumes her readers can meet the expectations she has for them. We, in turn, can imagine being her readers, can *be* her readers. She thus creates the readers she wants.

In her *Common Readers*, Woolf works as a teacher might in the class-room, providing her student-readers with a context for understanding liter-ature, and her own generation of writers. Her *Common Readers* are English Literature courses that motivate us to read primary sources, persuade us that literature lives and breathes, and provide us with material for numerous conversations. But the teacher who emerges from the revisions and final version of "How Should One Read a Book?" can also teach us about the teaching of reading and writing.[13]

Woolf, through her description of the writer-reader relationship and through her revision process, implies that teachers and students work together to create meaning and that students must actively contribute to their education if it is to become "stronger, richer, and more varied" (CR 2: 270). Woolf also suggests that teachers should see their students as writers when she says in the margin of her Hayes Court draft, "But we are all poets" (ms. 235), and when she implies in her *Second Common Reader* essay that a reader can at least momentarily become a writer's "fellow-worker and accomplice" (259). In portraying literature as a conversation anyone can enter, at any time and at any point, with no prior preparation or prerequisites required, she describes a pedagogy more concerned with welcoming students into a community than with gatekeeping.[14]

Taking student questions seriously, no matter how basic, Woolf recalls for her readers, as a teacher can for students, how she herself learned how to do something. Those who love reading surely identify with the stages (and the amount of space given to each one) she outlines in her essay: 1) feeding "greedily and lavishly upon books of all sorts" (268) and identifying with everything read (eight pages); 2) comparing and contrasting, making judgments (two pages); and 3) reading critics to discern larger patterns and learning about "literature as an art" (one page). Most important, she insists that critics can only "help us if we come to them laden with questions and suggestions won honestly in the course of our own reading" (269). This description of how readers develop has implications for our pedagogy, particularly when we are working with students who have *not* read indiscriminately and who do *not* identify reading with pleasure. Woolf's description of reading development suggests that when we focus our teaching on analysis and ask our students not only to go to critics before they are "laden with questions" but also to *become* critics, we are skipping major stages in their reading development. By implication, her essay asks us to inject some of the freedom, pleasure, and wandering (even in the "rubbish-heap" [263]!) she describes into classrooms and curricula geared mainly toward analysis and criticism.

Woolf's reading assignment, to understand a writer by writing, "to make your own experiment with the dangers and difficulties of words" (259), implies that reading and writing are similar processes.[15] Asking students to write something *in* the genre they are reading (Woolf later makes the same point about poetry [264]) helps them see not only the writer's craft but also the nature and limits of genre. Perhaps asking students to write an essay like Woolf's "How Should One Read a Book?" would help them see the essay as exploration instead of just thesis and support. Certainly Woolf's assignment reminds us to make experimentation and imitation part of our pedagogy, even as we work to teach "academic writing."

Revising for a common reader grounded in students, then, Woolf emerges in the *Second Common Reader* essay as a teacher who can teach us how to read *and* how to teach. These same revisions, along with the writer-reader relationship she describes, can also teach us more about Woolf's revising process. Critics have generally described this process in two ways. The first grew out of the convergence of feminist criticism and the availability of Woolf's manuscripts in the late 1960s and 1970s. Carefully examining how Woolf revised her manuscripts, Louise DeSalvo, for example, concluded that the later draft of *The Voyage Out* "was *not* an improvement" (154)—"[t]he later version . . . revealed less" (157-58)—and Grace Radin concluded that "during the long period of revision and compression that preceded [*The Years'*] publication, Woolf's original intentions lost their force" (xvii). Neither of these critics claimed that Woolf only cut as she revised, but the critical commonplace that grew out of these and other critics' work on the manuscripts was that Woolf, in revising *any* of her writing, tended to cut what Brenda Silver calls "the explicitness of [her] cultural critique, including her expression of anger" ("Textual Criticism" 210). Sue Roe, for example, in her book on Woolf's writing practice, starts from the premise that Woolf self-censors (6-8). Based on a psychoanalytic paradigm, with repression and suppression at its center, this portrayal of Woolf revising agrees on what is lost, sees her revising *as* loss, and implies a negative relationship with the reader, one based on fear. Ironically having the effect of showing Woolf either at the mercy of forces within and without or in control of her own silencing, this model, as Silver points out, is a "unidirectional view of the revisions as self-censorship and loss" (215).

The second way of describing Woolf's revising process, seen in more recent work, does not so much reject the earlier work as complicate it. It has focused on Woolf's revisions as moving in *two* directions. For example, Susan Stanford Friedman, using Freudian theories of repetition and recollection, reads Woolf's revisions as *both* repression and transformation and thus shifts the emphasis away from loss (114-17; see also Silver 215-16); Kate Flint, examining Woolf's inability to tell the truth about her body in the context of lesbian social history between 1894 and 1931, suggests that her "censorship, whether unconscious or deliberate, may be seen to have the potential for gain as well as for loss" (129-30); Edward Bishop, studying the reading notes and drafts of Woolf's essays, discovers that the "images around which the argument crystallizes most often come in at a later stage of composition" (576); and S. P. Rosenbaum, examining the recently discovered manuscripts of *A Room of One's Own*, points out that Woolf's "criticism of the patriarchy's sexual standards" is actually stronger in her published version than in her draft (xl). In other words, these more recent studies, though often taking a "bi-directional" view, emphasize Woolf's revising as gain, imply a more positive relationship with the reader, and portray Woolf as having more agency.

Woolf's path through her versions of "How Should One Read a Book?" reveals the validity of both these portrayals. Composition theorists Lisa Ede and Andrea Lunsford might explain these two portrayals by saying that writers both accommodate actual readers external to the text and create the readers they want within the text; they simultaneously address an audience and invoke one (167). Early studies of Woolf's revisions, in their focus on the addressed audience, emphasized the harmful, negative voices Woolf internalized (and that she herself named)—the parents who haunted her, the birds singing in Greek, the Angel in the House, patriarchal critics, academics, "tea-table training" ("Sketch" 150). Some of these voices certainly seem to have been talking to her as she revised for *The Yale Review*. Those revisions accommodate an academic audience, and the essay suffers as a result. Woolf's sense of humor, her conversational tone, her purpose, her delight in the reader all disappear.

Later studies of Woolf's revisions have suggested that a countermovement against such loss occurs, and in this essay (and perhaps in all the *Common Reader* essays), when Woolf *invokes* an audience of common reader-students, she triggers the revising movement toward gain. Both creating these readers and revising for them, she hears more positive, supportive voices, voices she describes as permeating the atmosphere in which she works, helping her improve. Louie Mayer did not have to imagine that Woolf must have talked with such voices—she heard her do so! She describes how she was startled, when she first went to work as the cook at Monk's House, at hearing Woolf talk to herself in the bathroom before breakfast—"On and on she went, talk, talk, talk: asking questions and giving herself the answers," a conversation that had become so routine Leonard no longer heard it ("Louie Mayer" 155-56). When Woolf invokes the common reader, with its strong ties to students, she revises to recover and add, not cut, and the final version of her essay gains humor, voice, conversation, partnership with readers, and thus a sense of students and teachers working together in mutual respect and freedom.

Woolf's revisions of this essay, then, fit both portrayals of Woolf revising, with the *Yale Review* revisions leaning more toward loss and accommodation and the *Second Common Reader* revisions leaning more toward gain and invoking. But they also show that the movement toward gain depends on Woolf's sense of the common reader. Woolf's deliberate choice of Samuel

Johnson's term and her revision of his definition is certainly the "profound critical and theoretical act" permeating her other formal decisions that Robert DeMaria claims an author's creation of an ideal reader must be (qtd. in Ferebee 345). It is also the crucial personal decision to look to Samuel Johnson and the eighteenth century rather than to Leslie Stephen and the nineteenth century for a "rhetorical technique that, like dialogue, allows for flux, freedom, and the lack of stable meaning" (xxi) that Beth Rosenberg claims for it.[16] It is also the significant social and political act that Vijay Sharma claims for it (89): after all, at a time when the reader was scorned, attacked, ignored, and divided into classes, the barriers between "art" and the "masses" were getting higher and higher ("Twentieth Century" 1683), and "high Modernism" was practicing detachment and disdain, Woolf chose to invoke and address "common" readers.

Perhaps more important, however, Woolf's creation of the common reader has enormous practical consequences for her as a writer. When Woolf invokes an audience of common readers, she gains exactly what theorists in composition say our student writers need to gain, someone to talk to while revising— a voice. What Robert Roth calls the "best self," composed of other writers, real readers, and ideal readers (50), what Donald Murray calls "the other self speaking" (qtd. in Berkenkotter 163), what Nancy Sommers describes as inner authority that can respond to the voices of mentors and peers (29). As Woolf notes in her Hayes Court draft, we should think of a book as a "dangerous & exciting game, which it takes two to play at" (ms. 189). The common reader gives Woolf her conversational partner, someone who talks back to the voices demanding accommodation, someone who moves her toward gain, excitement, even danger in revising. When she returns to the Hayes Court draft and restores some of what she cut for *The Yale Review*, when she invokes and then revises for the common reader, Woolf adds students to her internal conversation and gains a collaborative writer-reader relationship. Because the active, participating, creative common reader she invokes is grounded in those students, she also provides her readers with a model for the teacher-student relationship. Although Woolf's conversation with students makes her essay more exciting and implicitly critiques teacher-student relationships based on hierarchies, the portrayal and presence of the common reader in "How Should One Read a Book?" ultimately moves beyond critique as Woolf challenges us to reconsider how we teach readin', writin', and revisin'.

Works Cited

Allan, Tuzyline Jita. "A Voice of One's Own: Implications of Impersonality in the Essays of Virginia Woolf and Alice Walker." *The Politics of the Essay: Feminist Perspectives.* Ed. Ruth-Ellen Boetcher Joeres and Elizabeth Mittman. Bloomington: Indiana UP, 1993. 131-47.

Avery, Gillian. *The Best Type of Girl: A History of Girls' Independent Schools.* London: Andrew Deutsch, 1991.

Berkenkotter, Carol. "Decisions and Revisions: The Planning Strategies of a Publishing Writer." *College Composition and Communication* 34 (1983): 156-72.

Bishop, Edward L. "Metaphor and the Subversive Process of Virginia Woolf's Essays." *Style* 21.4 (1987): 573-88.

Daugherty, Beth Rigel. "Virginia Woolf Teaching/Virginia Woolf Learning: Morley College and the Common Reader." *New Essays on Virginia Woolf.* Ed. Helen Wussow. Dallas: Contemporary Research Press, 1995. 61-77.

DeSalvo, Louise. *Virginia Woolf's First Voyage: A Novel in the Making.* Totowa, NJ: Rowman and Littlefield, 1980.

Ede, Lisa, and Andrea Lunsford. "Audience Addressed/Audience Invoked: The Role of Audience in Composition Theory and Pedagogy." *College Composition and Communication* 35 (1984): 155-71.

Ferebee, Steve. "Bridging the Gulf: The Reader In and Out of Virginia Woolf's Literary Essays." *College Language Association Journal* 30.3 (1987): 343-61.

Flint, Kate. "'The pools, the depths, the dark places': Women, Censorship and the Body, 1894-1931." *Essays and Studies* 46 (1993): 118-30.

Friedman, Susan Stanford. "Virginia Woolf's Pedagogical Scenes of Reading: *The Voyage Out, The Common Reader,* and Her 'Common Readers'." *Modern Fiction Studies* 38.1 (1992): 101-25.

Johnston, Georgia. "The Whole Achievement in Virginia Woolf's *The Common Reader.*" *Essays on the Essay: Redefining the Genre.* Ed. Alexander J. Butrym. Athens: U of Georgia P, 1989. 148-58.

"Louie Mayer." *Recollections of Virginia Woolf by her Contemporaries.* Ed. Joan Russell Noble. 1972. Athens: Ohio UP, 1994. 154-63.

Madison, Elizabeth C. "The Common Reader and Critical Method in Virginia Woolf's Essays." *The Journal of Aesthetic Education* 15.4 (1981): 61-73.

Manuel, M. "Virginia Woolf as the Common Reader." *The Literary Criterion.* 7.2 (1966): 28-32.

McNeillie, Andrew. Introduction. *The Essays of Virginia Woolf, Volume 1: 1904-1912.* By Virginia Woolf. San Diego: Harcourt, 1986. ix-xviii.

Mepham, John. *Virginia Woolf: A Literary Life.* New York: St. Martin's, 1991.

Mott, Frank Luther. "The Yale Review." *A History of American Magazines, Volume 5: Sketches of 21 Magazines, 1905-1930.* Cambridge: Harvard UP, 1968. 329-40.

Noble, Joan Russell, ed. *Recollections of Virginia Woolf by Her Contemporaries.* 1972. Athens: Ohio UP, 1994.

Radin, Grace. *Virginia Woolf's* The Years: *The Evolution of a Novel.* Knoxville: U of Tennessee P, 1981.

Roe, Sue. *Writing and Gender: Virginia Woolf's Writing Practice.* New York: St. Martin's, 1990.

Rosenbaum, S. P. Introduction. *Women & Fiction: The Manuscript Versions of* A Room of One's Own. By Virginia Woolf. Oxford: Blackwell, 1992. xiii-xlii.

Rosenberg, Beth Carole. *Virginia Woolf and Samuel Johnson: Common Readers.* New York: St. Martin's, 1995.

Roth, Robert G. "The Evolving Audience: Alternatives to Audience Accommodation." *College Composition and Communication* 38 (1987): 47-55.

Sharma, Vijay L. *Virginia Woolf as Literary Critic: A Revaluation.* New Delhi: Arnold-Heineman, 1977.

Silver, Brenda, ed. *Virginia Woolf's Reading Notebooks.* Princeton: Princeton UP, 1983.

———. "Textual Criticism as Feminist Practice: Or, Who's Afraid of Virginia Woolf Part II." *Representing Modernist Texts: Editing as Interpretation.* Ed. George Bornstein. Ann Arbor: U of Michigan P, 1991. 193-222.

Sommers, Nancy. "Between the Drafts." *College Composition and Communication* 43 (1992): 23-31.

"The Twentieth Century." *The Norton Anthology of English Literature.* Ed. M. H. Abrams et al. 6th ed. Vol 2. New York: Norton, 1993. 1683-91.

Willis, J. H., Jr. *Leonard and Virginia Woolf as Publishers: The Hogarth Press, 1917-1941.* Charlottesville and London: UP of Virginia, 1992.

Woolf, Leonard. *Downhill All the Way: An Autobiography of the Years 1919 to 1939.* 1967. New York: Harcourt, 1975.

Woolf, Virginia. "The Common Reader." *The Common Reader.* Ed. Andrew McNeillie. Annotated ed. 1925. San Diego: Harcourt, 1984. 1-2.

———. *The Diary of Virginia Woolf.* Ed. Anne Olivier Bell and Andrew McNeillie. 5 vols. New York: Harcourt, 1977-1984.

———. *The Essays of Virginia Woolf.* Ed. Andrew McNeillie. 3 vols. to date. San Diego: Harcourt, 1986- .

———. *The Essays of Virginia Woolf.* Ed. Andrew McNeillie. Vol. 4. London: Hogarth, 1994.

———. "How Should One Read a Book?" "Articles, essays, fiction, and reviews." Volume 1: 21 April 1925, ms. 177-249. Berg Collection, New York Public Library.

————. "How Should One Read a Book?" *The Second Common Reader*. 1932. Ed. Andrew
    McNeillie. Annotated ed. San Diego: Harcourt, 1986. 258-70.

————. "How Should One Read a Book?" *The Yale Review* Oct. 1926: 32-44.

————. *The Letters of Virginia Woolf*. Ed. Nigel Nicolson and Joanne Trautmann. 6 vols.
    New York: Harcourt, 1975-1980.

————. "A Sketch of the Past." *Moments of Being*. Ed. Jeanne Schulkind. 2nd ed. San
    Diego: Harcourt, 1985. 64-159.

————. *To the Lighthouse: The Original Holograph Draft*. Ed. Susan Dick. Toronto: U of
    Toronto P, 1982.

Zwerdling, Alex. "The Common Reader, the Coterie and the Audience of One."
    *Virginia Woolf Miscellanies: Proceedings of the First Annual Conference on Virginia
    Woolf*. Ed. Mark Hussey and Vara Neverow-Turk. New York: Pace UP,
    1992. 8-9.

Notes

1. I would like to thank Jeanne Dubino and Beth Rosenberg for the opportunity
    to present these ideas for the first time at the 1993 MLA Convention in
    Toronto. I would also like to thank Philip Milito; Stephen Crook; Frank
    Mattson, Curator at the Berg Collection in the New York Public Library; and
    Kathleen McGrath at the Beinecke Library, Yale University, for their help.

2. In "Virginia Woolf Teaching/Virginia Woolf Learning," I argue that Woolf's
    experiences as a teacher at Morley College from 1905-1907 influenced her
    later characterization of the common reader, which in turn influenced the
    shape of her *Common Reader* volumes, the nature of the essays included, and the
    revisions she made for the volumes. As a result, we see a teacher at work in
    the *Common Readers*.

3. These numbers rely on Andrew McNeillie's conscientious work in his anno-
    tated *Common Readers* and the first three volumes of the projected six-volume
    The Essays of Virginia Woolf.

4. Georgia Johnston notes that "When we read [*The Common Reader*] as a whole,
    circularly, the last essay, 'How It Strikes a Contemporary,' informs the first,
    'The Common Reader,' as if Woolf had conceived of the volume as a loop"
    (153). When Woolf adds *The Second Common Reader* to her first, she enlarges the
    loop, seeing the *two* volumes as a whole.

5. Passages from the holograph Hayes Court draft quoted in this essay are based
    on my transcription of the thirty-seven-page "How Should One Read a Book?"
    manuscript located in the Berg Collection of the New York Public Library. I

wish to thank the Society of Authors, the literary representative of the Estate of Virginia Woolf, and the Henry W. and Albert A. Berg Collection, Astor, Lenox and Tilden Foundations, for their permission to quote from this manuscript. A fragment of the "How Should One Read a Book?" manuscript is included in Susan Dick's transcription of *To the Lighthouse* (282), and she publishes another two-page fragment in Appendix C (55-56) of that volume. The two pages located in the *Diary XIV* manuscript have been published in Appendix III (597-98) of *The Essays of Virginia Woolf*, Volume 4, edited by Andrew McNeillie. Both internal evidence and the dating of *Diary XIV* and the *To the Lighthouse* manuscript suggest that the pages in the diary are part of the Hayes Court draft, while the pages in the *To the Lighthouse* holograph are part of Woolf's *Yale Review* revision. The one-page fragment located in Volume 18 of the Holograph Reading Notes (ms. 5) seems related to the Hayes Court draft in tone, and Brenda Silver suggests 1925 for its dating in *Virginia Woolf's Reading Notebooks* (96-99).

6.   Woolf also abridges the *Yale Review* essay for a preface entitled "The Love of Reading" in *Company of Books 1931-32*, a booklist published by The Hampshire Bookshop, Northampton, MA.

7.   For ease of citation, I have abbreviated the Hayes Court draft as ms. For ease of reading, I have not duplicated passages from the Hayes Court draft as in a formal transcription. Thus, quotations from the Hayes Court draft do not show Woolf's deletions or interlinear additions. My transcription of the holograph Hayes Court draft, the "How Should One Read a Book?" manuscript, is scheduled for publication in *Woolf Studies Annual*, Volume 4 (1998).

8.   Woolf's ambivalence about academics stemmed from her anger at not having been allowed to go to school and her simultaneous belief that the "great patriarchal machine" of English education had a terrible influence on men: "Every one of our male relations was shot into that machine at the age of ten and emerged at sixty a Head Master, an Admiral, a Cabinet Minister, or the Warden of a college. It is . . . impossible to think of them as natural human beings" ("Sketch" 153).

9.   J. H. Willis, Jr. notes that the five-shilling Uniform Edition of the first *Common Reader* sold 1,200 copies of its 3,200-copy press run in the first six months of 1929 (114), and Leonard Woolf says that when *The Second Common Reader* appeared, it sold twice in six months what the first *Common Reader* had sold in a year (143-44). Woolf recalls consciously attempting to reach a wider audience through her *Common Reader* in a draft letter to Ben Nicolson in 1940 (*L* 6: 420).

10. Both Johnston (153) and Beth Rosenberg (65) note *The Common Reader's* chronology.

11. See Rosenberg's discussion of how conversation "as a rhetorical strategy" came to structure *The Common Reader*, 58-64.

12. Surely a glimmer of the conditions necessary for the birth of Shakespeare's sister in *A Room of One's Own*?

13. See Susan Stanford Friedman, 103-05, for how Woolf's texts "compel pedagogical self-reflexivity."

14. Steve Ferebee notes her reader's "cooperative identity," the "sense of reciprocity" created by Woolf's use of pronouns, the establishment of "communal activity," and Woolf's treatment of the reader "as an independent, thinking partner" (349-52).

15. Rosenberg notes that for Woolf the reader and writer "are one and the same," both participating in "creation and interpretation" (xxi).

16. See also Ferebee's comparison of Woolf with eighteenth-century essayists, 345-49.

Moments of Reading and Woolf's Literary Criticism

Karen Schiff

The trope of "the moment" is central to Virginia Woolf's thought and writing.[1] As critic Morris Beja writes, "despite her many experiments with widely differing fictional forms, the technical device of the moment of vision appears in all her work, from first to last" (138). While Beja develops his statement with reference to moments in Woolf's fiction when characters suddenly apprehend a new reality, his point applies to other genres of her writing as well. Woolf's literary reviews often focus on moments when a character or an author experiences a moment of new vision.[2] Woolf uses the phrase "moments of being" as the title of a short story, "Moments of Being: Slater's Pins Have No Points," and as a working title for the book that later became *The Waves*.[3] The phrase is perhaps most familiar to Woolf's current readers as the title of her posthumously published memoir collection.

For Woolf, a "moment" is generally a quality of experience rather than a unit of time. In the 1939-40 essay "A Sketch of the Past" that serves as the backbone of the *Moments of Being* volume, Woolf defines a moment of being as a "violent shock" of "instant understanding." This perceptual jolt yields a wondrous view of a pattern that is usually shielded by a "veil" that keeps people from feeling aware and awake. Moments of being stand out from an undifferentiated background of "non-being." Most of each day is spent in non-being, which Woolf describes as "a kind of nondescript cotton wool" (*MOB* 70). A moment of being occurs when something pulls back the wool and creates an unexpected and overwhelming apprehension of "reality."

As soon as Woolf makes this distinction between moments of being and the general state of non-being, she applies it to literature she has read:

"The real novelist can somehow convey both sorts of being. I think Jane Austen can; and Trollope; perhaps Thackeray and Dickens and Tolstoy" (*MOB* 70). Woolf's impulse to turn to criticism shows how closely she connects moments of being with acts of reading.[4] And just as Woolf's discussion of states of being prompts her to comment upon books she has read, her reviews of books often provide opportunities for her to explore how reading provokes the experience of a "moment of being." She often remarks on a book's ability to evoke experiences of intense awareness that bear a striking resemblance to her descriptions of moments of being. Even though her explicit definition of moments of being appears toward the end of her life—after she has written all of the critical essays I will discuss in this paper—the qualitative similarities between Woolf's descriptions of reading and her later account of moments of being lead me to call these encounters with literature "moments of reading."

I do not mean to imply that Woolf deliberately uses the idea of the "moment" as a litmus test for deciding whether a piece of writing is worthwhile. Though she does praise works that contain or evoke this experience, her return to the topic of the reading process has the flavor of an obsessive rumination. In essay after essay, Woolf focuses on a point in the reading process when something interrupts the flow (either of the narrative or of the experience of reading) to expose an enriching new complex of realizations or sensations. Thus her critical writings explore her fascination with reading even more than they expose her opinions about specific books. Woolf uses these essays to reflect on the qualities that make particular moments of reading—and hence of being—so gripping and so basic.

Since Woolf's main definition of "moments of being" appears in "A Sketch of the Past" ("Sketch"), that document will serve as the backbone of this essay. The fact that the "Sketch" is unfinished is advantageous in this context because a Woolfian moment deals with the raw, unprocessed material of perception. When I analyze the ingredients of Woolf's examples of "moments of being" as she describes them in this work, I operate on the assumption that the examples from "Sketch" sum up the ways that Woolf has characterized a moment of being during her lifetime. They can therefore serve as a template for evaluating the moments of reading that appear in her criticism. Other works by Woolf (fiction, impressionistic essays) that deal with moments supplement this template occasionally. As I elucidate the qualities that structure the experience of a moment, I juxtapose each with excerpts from Woolf's literary criticism. This framework shows that Woolf's essays about books and reading grapple with the characteristics of intense moments.

The central discussion of "moments of being" focuses on three events from Woolf's childhood. She lists them dispassionately, like an all-too-familiar litany, in "A Sketch of the Past":

> The first: I was fighting with Thoby on the lawn. We were pommelling each other with our fists. Just as I raised my fist to hit him, I felt: why hurt another person? I dropped my hand instantly, and stood there, and let him beat me. I remember the feeling. It was a feeling of hopeless sadness. It was as if I became aware of something terrible; and of my own powerlessness. I slunk off alone, feeling horribly depressed. The second instance was also in the garden at St Ives. I was looking at the flower bed by the front door; "That is the whole," I said. I was looking at a plant with a spread of leaves; and it seemed suddenly plain that the flower itself was a part of the earth; that a ring enclosed what was the flower; and that was the real flower; part earth; part flower. It was a thought I put away as being likely to be very useful to me later. The third case was also at St Ives. Some people called Valpy had been staying at St Ives, and had left. We were waiting at dinner one night, when somehow I overheard my father or my mother say that Mr Valpy had killed himself. The next thing I remember is being in the garden at night and walking on the path by the apple tree. It seemed to me that the apple tree was connected with the horror of Mr Valpy's suicide. I could not pass it. I stood there looking at the grey-green creases of the bark—it was a moonlit night—in a trance of horror. I seemed to be dragged down, hopelessly, into some pit of absolute despair from which I could not escape. My body seemed paralyzed. (*MOB* 71)

While Woolf goes on to analyze these moments herself, she is mainly concerned with why they end as they do: "Two of these moments ended in a state of despair. The other ended, on the contrary, in a state of satisfaction" (*MOB* 71). My focus here is on the beginnings and middles of these moments. What conditions make it possible for a moment to arise? What are the subjective qualities of a moment? How do these qualities shed light on the moment–like experiences in reading literature or of perceiving moments of being in a literary work?

One thing seems clear about Woolf's moments: they cannot be planned or anticipated. Though all three take place outside, for instance, there is no sense that Woolf deliberately goes outside in order to experience a heightened state of aliveness. On the contrary, she notes that she does not recall other events that took place outdoors that seem to be more conventionally memorable. She asks, "Why remember the hum of bees in the garden going down to the beach and forget being thrown naked by father into the sea? (Mrs. Swanwick says she saw that happen)" (MOB 70). Conventionally dramatic events do not necessarily make lasting impressions.

A difference between listening to bees and getting thrown into the sea is instructive for interpreting moments of being and also of reading. Playing with one's father is a raucously social activity that leaves little room for introspection, while hearing the bees' hum has the air of a solitary reverie. Each of the moments of being that Woolf describes in her litany has a solitary air about it, even the moment when she is fighting with Thoby. Though they are fighting together—a social (or antisocial) act—the moment that Woolf remembers so vividly is when she breaks away and suddenly feels alone with her thoughts. Being outdoors may help to trigger such a moment, since standing under an open sky, on a large lawn, or in a garden (or anywhere) at night can make one feel alone in vast space.[5] But the aloneness, again, is not a prearranged feeling. Perhaps it is not even a feeling at all but more of a state of being.

Whatever the ontological status of aloneness may be, solitude lays the foundation for the surprising jolt to come. Suddenly aspects of a situation coalesce (such as the memory of Valpy's suicide plus the richly fertile scene of the dark garden) to suggest a new constellation or understanding. As Woolf writes in a 1918 review of Pearsall Smith's book Trivia, "without bidding things come together in a combination of inexplicable significance" (E 2: 250-51). I imagine that this process is like forming a snowflake out of a speck of dust. The most unremarkable detail—the flotsam and jetsam of life—instantly becomes the unwitting center of an organically systematic matrix. Just as dust motes spawn snowflakes with regular geometries, moments of being give Woolf a view of a general order in the universe. As she muses in the "Sketch," "behind the cotton wool is hidden a pattern; that we—I mean all human beings—are connected with this; that the whole world is a work of art; that we are parts of the work of art" (MOB 72). Moments of being or reading connect us to a wholeness that is not so accessible in daily life. And just as each snowflake is different from all others, moments of being stand out distinctly and represent unique realizations. The moment halts the usual dusty trains of thought and creates glistening new ones: the "real flower" is made of blossom and soil.

So moments of being are preconditioned by a sense of solitude and bring about a sense of connection to a larger pattern. The same could be said of reading: one sits alone (or breaks away mentally) to read and uses the book as a bridge to a new world beyond oneself. But there are several intermediate steps between these two points, and it is their peculiarities—violence, paralysis, an emphasis on the visual and on the smallest detail—that the rest of this paper aims to unravel and explore.

Woolf introduces her three examples of moments of being with a sentence that shows how surprising it was to have these experiences: this element of her description bears investigation. In the "Sketch," she writes, "there was a sudden violent shock; something happened so violently that I have remembered it all my life" (*MOB* 71). Certainly her descriptions show that moments of being occur with no forewarning, and that they have an immediate effect: the young Woolf "dropped [her] hand *instantly*" when she was just about to punch her brother, and her new apprehension of the flower "seemed *suddenly* plain." But her commentaries continually call the experiences "violent moments of being" (*MOB* 79, emphasis added)—surprise or suddenness is conflated with violence in Woolf's account. Passages from her critical essays explain why something as seemingly innocuous as looking at a flower could be perceived as violently shocking.

Pulling back the cotton wool of non-being can cause searing pain, like stripping a bandage away from raw flesh, and perhaps it will succeed only if done quickly. Woolf's criticism demonstrates that authors routinely touch raw sensibility. But pulling back the cotton wool is only one way to get to the rawness on the other side; it can also be pierced. In "De Quincey's Autobiography," Woolf quotes a passage from De Quincey's preface to his *Autobiographic Sketches* in which he writes about being "'able to pierce the haze which so often envelops . . . his own secret springs of action and reserve'" (*CR* 2: 135). Woolf returns to this image when she later quotes another passage from De Quincey and reflects, "Nobody after that could maintain that the whole truth of life can be told without 'piercing the haze'" (*CR* 2: 139). The similarities between De Quincey's "haze" and Woolf's "cotton wool" are evident, but De Quincey's formulation introduces a new wrinkle. The word "piercing" indicates violation of a barrier; the haze is like a veil of protection that gets abruptly broken.

An abrupt piercing creates a conduit between one's consciousness and the outside world. It builds a perceptual bridge at the same time that it violates a protective barrier. Thus a piercing shock can feel delightful as well as violent. Seeing that "the real flower" includes both the flower and the earth in which it grows is a gratifying rather than despairing surprise (as Woolf herself observes in the paragraph following her description of the moments quoted above). Being jolted from one's moorings can be pleasantly unsettling because the experience opens up new visions. Authors, like certain events in life, can pierce through habitual thought patterns by bringing a fresh perspective to readers. Though the experiences of the violent shocks and gratifying joys of reading might seem contradictory, they share a sense of vitality.

This vitality could explain why Woolf implies that people read books because they like shocks. She does not specify whether these shocks are terrifying or delightful, most likely because they are both simultaneously. In "Byron & Mr Briggs," an unfinished essay planned to begin the volume *Reading*,[6] she writes, "The truth is that reading is kept up because people like reading. . . . How many thousands I know not, but certainly there are many thousands who never pick up a book on a bookstall for half a minute without getting some kind of shock from it" (329). "Some kind of shock" can be pleasant, exhilarating, stimulating. Though the specific qualities of the "shock" are difficult to articulate,[7] the peculiar pleasure comes from a limited jolt that is not overwhelmingly shocking. The word "shock" itself can refer to the power of electricity, both to energize matter and to debilitate it. A small amount of electricity can be exhilarating, as with an "electric" connection between people, but too much of it can be physically dangerous.

Sometimes the shock of the moment is too much, and one can feel electrocuted. Woolf writes in the "Sketch" that "many of these exceptional moments brought with them a peculiar horror and a physical collapse" (*MOB* 72). For instance, when she felt suddenly that the apple tree was connected with Mr. Valpy's suicide, she could not walk past it. "My body seemed paralysed" (*MOB* 71). It is as if the "flash" that struck her was actually a flash of lightning that had struck her temporarily dead.

Paralysis and other physical side effects of electrocution can also result from moments of reading. In the review "Fishing," of Major Hills's book on the same topic, Woolf writes,

> All books are made of words, but mostly of words that flutter and agitate thought. This book on the contrary, though made of words, has a strange effect on the body. It lifts it out of the chair; stands it on the banks of a river, and strikes it dumb. (*M* 220)

In this description, Major Hills's text acts like a bolt of lightning: the text paralyzes the body and also repositions it. Significantly, the body reappears "on the banks of a river," a vantage point from which it would be easy to watch the fishing that is the book's subject. Looking down over the river is not just a good perspective; the shock creates a physical break from the flow of the "river" of life. A moment of reading or being propels the body onto the banks, from which life is suddenly seen from a new perspective.

Paralysis implies a separation both from the drill of daily life and from the direct experience of an intense moment. It is possible that the strong emotion associated with a moment of being or reading can be experienced only when one's body is paralyzed or metaphorically cut off.[8] Paradoxically, then, one can feel intensely only if one is separate enough from a moment to experience it fully. The experience of reading also involves a slip into a world that is text-based and therefore distant from "reality." That is, in order to experience the full effect of the text, one must concentrate and distance oneself from the immediate physical context. This can extend to becoming separate from one's body so that the consciousness is free to receive the impressions that the text offers. The distance creates the opportunity to activate faculties of apprehension.

Paralysis is also the physical condition of the dead or tortured, as in the two violent moments of being from Woolf's childhood. Intense feeling is closely connected to its opposite: the lack of any feeling at all. Thus Woolf praises Major Hills's ability both to paralyze Woolf's sensibility ("strikes it dumb") and to make her go beyond regular thoughts (this book's words do not merely "flutter and agitate thought"). But perhaps being struck "dumb" is just getting absorbed in the book, since by Woolf's time silent reading was a common practice. Reading, also, has "a strange effect on the body." One must remain motionless, temporarily paralyzed, to read the words on the page.

The violent surprise and occasional paralysis of a moment of being or reading create a sense of unreality that makes possible a new vision, in terms of both something new to see and a new way of looking or thinking. An outstanding quality of Woolf's moments of being in the "Sketch" is that they are intensely visual. The sight of the flower and of the tree, especially, give Woolf intimations of larger understandings. The flower leads her to ponder the interconnection of all things—the flower always exists in the context of the soil in which it grows—and the tree bark mysteriously connects to mortality. The fact that the smallest details create the most vague and profound musing is an aspect of Woolf's moments to which I will return later. For now, I wish to probe the significance of the visual.

A moment of being causes one's perceptions, especially visual perceptions, to become acute, subtle, and incisive. While sensations are heightened, the experience is not purely sensual; sight gives way to "insight." This visually oriented word for wisdom aptly characterizes Woolf's moments of both being and reading: a "moment of vision" connotes a widening sense of understanding. A good illustration of this insight appears in Woolf's critical essay, "The Perfect Language." In her discussion of W. R. Paton's *The Greek Anthology*, she writes that "occasionally [the amateur reader of Greek] would be rewarded with one of those moments of instant understanding which are the flower of reading" (*E* 2: 114-15). The flower image, in addition to being associated with the flower in the garden, represents a blossoming process that indicates an ever-growing sphere of wisdom. Perhaps even the light of the "moment of vision" helps the flower of understanding to grow.

In her 1917 review of Joseph Conrad's *Lord Jim*, Woolf writes that Conrad "has a 'moment of vision' in which he sees people as if he had never seen them before; he expounds his vision, and we see it, too. These visions are the best things in his books" (*E* 2: 142). Woolf uses the word "vision" ambiguously here: it refers both to Conrad's overall plan for his book or view of the world ("his vision") and to the moments when Conrad looks at a character insightfully. The ambiguity implies that seeing a character in a "moment of vision" is actually the same thing as having a shift in world view. The moment of renewed visual perception, as when Woolf looks at the flower in the soil, is contemporaneous with a moment of being. Or, in the case of Conrad, the author's moment of vision simultaneously creates a moment of reading for the reader. As "he expounds his vision, . . . we see it, too" (*E* 2: 142).

Woolf supports her claim that Conrad's visions are the best things in his writing by quoting a passage; it is the only passage she quotes from the novel. Conrad's *Lord Jim* could be describing Woolf's own distinction between being and non-being when he says,

> "It's extraordinary how we go through life with eyes half shut, with dull ears, with dormant thoughts. . . . Nevertheless, there can be but few of us who had never known one of these rare moments of awakening, when we see, hear, understand, ever so much—everything—in a flash, before we fall back again into our agreeable somnolence." (*E* 2: 142)

Conrad's "agreeable somnolence" corresponds to Woolf's "non-being," and his "rare moments of awakening" are directly analogous to Woolf's "moments of being." The close affinity explains why Woolf quotes from the same passage in *Lord Jim* for her essay "Joseph Conrad," which she published on the occasion of Conrad's death in 1924. But while Conrad is careful to include many faculties (seeing, hearing, and thinking) in this passage, Woolf generally focuses on sight.

When Woolf echoes Conrad's use of the term "flash" in her 1923 essay, "Mr Conrad: A Conversation," she gives the flash a decidedly visual bent. She writes, "'He sees once and he sees for ever. His books are full of moments of vision. They light up a whole character in a flash'" (*E* 3: 378). A quick flash of light makes a person look paralyzed, but for Woolf and Conrad it also penetrates to the personality pattern beneath the skin or veil. The loss of mobility occasioned by the visual freeze-frame is perhaps the inevitable price to pay for a paradoxically infinite psychological perspective. As Woolf writes in "The Novels of E. M. Forster" about Forster's technique, "Thus when the moment of illumination comes we . . . feel simply that the thing we are looking at is lit up, and its depths revealed. It has not ceased to be itself by becoming something else" (*DM* 168). Although a person looks different when immobilized by a flash of light, nothing has really changed about the personal "depths." The external perspective has simply shifted; the "moment of illumination" reveals personalities to readers.

The more global understanding of a character that is possible through just one glimpse is an example of Woolf's tendency to extrapolate generalities from details, or to think of the detail as the key into the whole. The "flash" always occurs in the context of daily life. The two together comprise a "whole" moment of reading, just as the "whole" flower is both the flower and the earth in which it grows. As Woolf observes about Siegfried Sassoon's writing in her review "Mr. Sassoon's Poems," "To call back any moment of emotion is to call back with it the strangest odds and ends that have become somehow part of it, and it is the weeds pulled up by mistake with the flowers that bring back the extraordinary moment as a whole" (*E* 2: 121). The same process occurs with Woolf's own moments of being from childhood: Woolf observes in the "Sketch" that her "violent moments of being" were "always including a circle of the scene which they cut out" (*MOB* 79). A moment is situated in time and space, even if it seems cut off from the flow of time.

A writer's words also include a larger web of association, for which they function as an entry point. As Woolf writes in "On Re-reading Novels" about Flaubert's "Un Coeur Simple," "A sudden intensity of phrase, something which for good reasons or for bad we feel to be emphatic, startles us into a flash of understanding" (*M* 160). The understanding is larger than the immediate words; in this case, the flash brings with it the "conviction that we know why the story was written" (*M* 160). Words are catalysts for forging a connection with a general order that lies behind the veil. This seems tautological: if we sense this connection through reading, words have necessarily contributed to the experience, since reading always involves words. But an author can use words specifically and deliberately to articulate the hidden pattern. For example, Woolf senses that Spenser creates an effect that is akin to what she hopes to achieve in her own works. She notes in her meditation on *The Faery Queen*,

Yet as we read, we half consciously have the sense of some pattern
hanging in the sky, so that without referring any of the words to a
special place, they have that meaning which comes from their being
parts of a whole design, and not an isolated fragment of unrelated
loveliness. The mind is being perpetually enlarged by the power of
suggestion. Much more is imagined than is stated. (M 26)

Spenser's art, or any writer's challenge, is to find the precise words that
will enlarge the mind enough to encompass ever-widening matrices of
understanding. The reader, then, provides the dark garden in which the
writer's words can be the seeds that blossom into flowers—or the dust motes
that crystallize into snowflakes—of imagination and understanding.

Woolf demonstrates the power of small words to trigger larger apprehensions in two shorter works that directly address moments as themes:
"Moments of Being: 'Slater's Pins Have No Points'" and "The Moment:
Summer's Night."[9] In "Slater's Pins," the title sentence (which also served as
the original title for the story [see Leonard Woolf, AHH vi]) begins the essay
when Miss Craye says to her piano student Fanny Wilmot, "Slater's pins have
no points—don't you always find that?" Characteristically, "The words gave
[Fanny] an extraordinary shock," and she stands "transfixed for a moment"
as she asks herself, "Did Miss Craye actually go to Slater's and buy pins then"
(AHH 103). This one line of spoken dialogue touches off many pages of
speculations about Miss Craye's love life and psychological states. Fanny's
mind drifts far from the present situation, though it occasionally touches
back to wonder where a pin has fallen, and ultimately it returns when Miss
Craye repeats the title sentence. This small phrase, then, occasions a
complex and poetic personal history.

"Slater's Pins" reads like a less complex version of "The Moment."
Woolf creates a narrative to answer a question that she asks in its first
paragraph: "Yet what composed the present moment?" (M 3). Though
unfinished, the piece is central enough to her thought that Leonard Woolf
chose it to title the posthumous collection of her nonfiction in which it
appears, The Moment and Other Essays. A group of nameless people gather
outdoors at dusk, taking in multisensory impressions of the surrounding
countryside as the light wanes, and talking until they go inside. The
narrator's focus soon settles on the people who speak to each other. Their
words "hit the mind with a wad, then explode like a scent suffusing the whole
dome of the mind" (M 4). Words themselves create moments of being, not
just from their immediate meanings but from the unarticulated experiences
and the shared frameworks toward which they point. After they "hit the

mind with a wad"—recalling the "sledgehammer blow" (*M* 8) of a moment of being[10]—they create a multisensory understanding.

To explore the words' effect, both on the characters and on us as readers, Woolf writes long speculations after each line of dialogue. For instance, one character remarks, "'He'll do well with his hay'" (*M* 6), and Woolf writes over a page of reflections that stem from those few words (*M* 4-6). The web of associations is complex, just as a moment of being (or of reading) resonates on many levels. Judging, flying, sucking, sighing—all of these activities spring from a simple sentence about hay. The final image especially shows the large perspective that can arise from just a few words. "We" (readers, writers, perhaps "lookers" in general) are invited to look down over the enormity of the world, and to take in all of its patterns without diminishing them through judgment.[11]

In her reviews, Woolf focuses on how different authors make use of expanding webs of association that expand from solitary words or other small details. In her 1919 essay, "Dostoevsky in Cranford," Woolf sums up Dostoevsky's philosophy, "In short, once you are alive, there is no end to the complexity of your connections" (*E* 3: 115). She reports that in a book of his short stories, Dostoevsky describes complexities of connections in great detail.

> He is incapable, even when his story is hampered by the digression, of passing by anything so important and loveable as a man or a woman without stopping to consider their case and explain it. Thus at one moment it occurs to him that there must be a reason why an unfortunate clerk could not afford to pay for a bottle of wine. Immediately, as if recalling a story which is known to him down to its most minute detail, he describes how the clerk had been born and brought up; it is then necessary to bring in the career of his brutal father-in-law. . . . (*E* 3: 114-15)

A moment—here triggered by the detail of an event instead of a phrase—can be the occasion for an enormous network of reflections and commentaries.

Woolf praises De Quincey in her essay "De Quincey's Autobiography" for keeping his detailed digressions from spoiling the overall effect of the narrative. She insists that De Quincey's success comes from his ability to balance "the two levels of existence . . . the rapid passage of events and actions; the slow opening up of single and solemn moments of concentrated emotion" (*CR* 2: 139). Here the detailed information that Dostoevsky uses to surround any insignificant event instead takes on the foggy, nonspecific character of Woolf's "non-being." De Quincey is therefore able to balance descriptions of non-being with moments of being:

> For page after page we are in company with a cultivated gentleman who describes with charm and eloquence what he has seen and known—the stage coaches, the Irish rebellion, the appearance and conversation of George the Third. Then suddenly the smooth narrative parts asunder, arch opens beyond arch, the vision of something for ever flying, for ever escaping, is revealed, and time stands still. (CR 2: 139)

Quotidian and seemingly haphazard details give way in an instant to a "vision"—which here sounds like a tantalizing promise or a quasi-religious revelation, in addition to a sudden, comprehensive understanding—of "something" that is in the air (like Spenser's "pattern hanging in the sky") and never wholly in one's grasp.[12]

The point of reading is analogous to that of a moment of being—to glimpse the intractable wholeness behind the veil of everyday life. As Woolf writes in "How Should One Read a Book?," "It may be one letter—but what a vision it gives! It may be a few sentences—but what vistas they suggest" (CR 2: 263)! In reading, as in moments of being, it is possible to be surprised by a condensation of experience that is exceedingly vivid and provocative. Alternatively, the act of reading itself can be a memorable moment. Woolf's essays remind us of the unexpected pleasures of reading—those moments with books that are, after all, life experiences (and not just bookish escapes from "reality"). She writes in "Hours in a Library," for instance, "For days upon end we do nothing but read. It is a time of extraordinary excitement and exultation" (CE 2: 36). In Woolf's essays, the experience of reading can be as overwhelming, physically affecting, and intellectually transformative as a moment of pure being.

But reading is not identical to being. Reading offers the opportunity to return to moments repeatedly, since the words on the page do not change over time. Unlike a moment of being, one can deliberately re-create a moment of reading by pulling a book back off the shelf for another "shock" to remind one of one's passions and perceptions. Of course the return yields different experiences, since people change over time and perceptions of a moment will likewise change. Several of Woolf's essays mention books that get pulled from shelves over and over so that readers can return to favorite passages and feel again the thrill of being transported. Moments of being are always unexpected, but moments of reading are almost guaranteed (as in "Byron & Mr. Briggs")—

reading itself produces the "shock." Though it is impossible to predict what the book will provoke or when, it is clear that a jolt often occurs when readers browse books from sidewalk stalls; reading can intensify being.

Reading is also slower than being—or else it is more subject to the usual laws of time. Readers can process text at their own pace, while a moment of being takes one by surprise (with a fast visual impression) and allows the person little flexibility. Woolf concurs in "How Should One Read a Book?" that "reading is a longer and more complicated process than seeing" (CR 2: 259). But the characteristics of both are still analogous: solitude (or at least a sense of quiet) preconditions a moment of reading or being, and both varieties of moments are characterized by a surprising jolt that can be violent, paralyzing, visually focused, and simultaneously miniscule and immense. And though "being" and "reading" have generally been used in this paper as gerunds, they both function equally well as verbs. Moments temporarily create a stasis that removes one from the flow of time, but they also create the "direct shock[s] of emotion" ("Byron & Mr Briggs" 338) that move us.

Woolf discusses moments least obliquely in her essays, which themselves can be considered moments of reading. The essay is the most periodic of genres: each can be processed in a single sitting or moment. Perhaps Woolf was conscious of the self-reflexiveness inherent in writing critical essays about essays; Carl Klaus notes that "three out of twenty essays in *The Common Reader* were about essayists and the essay" (28). In her criticism about the essay form, Woolf advises essayists to emphasize formally the natural capacity of the essay to envelop the reader in a moment of reading. "The essay must lap us about and draw its curtain across the world" (CR 2: 41), she writes in "The Modern Essay." She expands upon the curtain image in the final sentence: "Vague as all definitions are, a good essay . . . must draw its curtain round us, but it must be a curtain that shuts us in, not out" (CR 2: 50). By bracketing off the world, the essay (or the moment of being or reading) encloses us in a smaller world. After shutting out the larger world, the essay can create and reveal a new view of it. We need the veil of cotton wool in order to cast it aside or get it ripped away.

I hope that this essay, though it is of a slightly different genre than the essay Woolf was describing in "The Modern Essay," has effectively encapsulated the connections between Woolf's moments of being and reading. I have drawn the "curtain" around this theme in order to make the larger point that reading a book, even though it might seem removed from the world, can provoke a multilayered experience that is as "real" as any other, and can offer fresh glimpses of the larger patterns that often are shielded from view.

Works Cited

Beja, Morris. "Matches Struck in the Dark: Virginia Woolf's Moments of Vision."
   Critical Quarterly 6 (1964): 137-52.
Graham, J[ohn]. W., ed. *The Waves: The Two Holograph Drafts*. Toronto: U of Toronto
   P, 1976.
Hungerford, Edward A. Introduction. "Byron and Mr. Briggs." By Virginia Woolf.
   Ed. Hungerford. *The Yale Review* 67.3 (1979): 321-24.
Klaus, Carl H. "On Virginia Woolf on the Essay." *Iowa Review* 20.2 (1990): 28-34.
McNeillie, Andrew. Introduction. *The Essays of Virginia Woolf*. Vol. 2. New York:
   Harcourt, 1987.
Silver, Brenda, ed. *Virginia Woolf's Reading Notebooks*. Princeton: Princeton UP, 1983.
Woolf, Virginia. "Byron and Mr. Briggs." Ed. Edward A. Hungerford. *The Yale Review*
   67.3 (1979): 325-49.
———. *The Death of the Moth and Other Essays*. 1942. New York: Harcourt, 1970.
———. *The Essays of Virginia Woolf*. Ed. Andrew McNeillie. 3 vols. to date. New York:
   Harcourt, 1986-.
———. *The Moment and the Other Essays*. Ed. Leonard Woolf. New York: Harcourt,
   1948.
———. *Moments of Being*. Ed. Jeanne Schulkind. 2nd ed. New York: Harcourt, 1985.
———. "Moments of Being: 'Slater's Pins Have No Points.'" *A Haunted House*. 1944.
   New York: Harcourt, 1966. 103-11.
———. *The Common Reader, Second Series*. 1932. Ed. Andrew McNeillie. New York:
   Harcourt, 1986.
———. *Orlando*. London: Hogarth Press, 1928.
———. *The Waves*. 1931. New York: Harcourt, 1959.
———. *Women and Writing*. Ed. Michèle Barrett. New York: Harcourt, 1979.
Wordsworth, William. "Preface 1800 version (with 1802 variants)." *Lyrical Ballads*. By
   Wordsworth and Coleridge. Ed. R. L. Brett and A. R. Jones. London:
   Methuen, 1963. 235-66.
Zamora, Bobbie Jean. "The Connecting Moment: Woolf, The Reader, and The Act
   of Reading." Diss. U of Pittsburgh, 1993.

Notes

1.   Thanks to Professors Vicki Mahaffey (University of Pennsylvania), Laurence
     Davies (Dartmouth College), and Barbara Hochman (Ben Gurion University)

for their helpful feedback on drafts of this article.

2. Woolf even uses the phrase "moments of vision" in some critical essays, though of course she did not borrow the phrase from Beja.

3. See Graham 1.1.

4. In fact, the definition of moments of being itself arises in the context of a discussion about literature. Woolf portrays her struggles as a writer: "Often when I have been writing one of my so-called novels I have been baffled by this . . . problem; that is, how to describe what I call in my private shorthand— 'non-being'" (*MOB* 70).

5. Later in "A Sketch of the Past," Woolf characterizes pure visual memories by saying that "these points are enclosed in vast empty spaces" (*MOB* 78).

6. Woolf's title for her critical anthology proves her to be more interested in readers' experiences than in specific books or literary judgments. The words of the title, "The Common Reader," place emphasis on the people who experience a book rather than on the texts being discussed. While planning the collection, Woolf focuses even more on reading as an active process: she considers using the titles "Reading," and later, "Reading and Writing" (Hungerford 321; McNeillie xvi; Zamora 83).

7. In draft form, this passage reads, ". . . certainly there are many thousands who never pick up a book on a bookstall for half a minute without getting a shock of one kind or another"(*E* 3: 478).

8. The physical separation from an event is similar to Wordsworth's "emotion recollected in tranquillity" (260), in which the poet can capture the fullness of an experience only by recalling it later, when there is some distance from the event (see also Schulkind 21 on relations between Woolf and Wordsworth). A difference, however, is that Wordsworth's recollections are deliberate—"the emotion is contemplated till . . . the tranquillity gradually disappears, and an emotion, kindred to that which was before the subject of contemplation, is gradually produced" (260)—while Woolf's moments of being, whether in the present or in memory, are seldom foreseen or expected. Wordsworth emphasizes that poets can achieve this creation without the perceptual triggers that we have seen are essential to Woolf's experiences: "the Poet is chiefly distinguished from other men by a greater promptness to think and feel without immediate external excitement" (255). Also, Wordsworth seeks emotions having to do with "rural life" and "the beautiful and permanent forms of nature" (239), while Woolf's random memories are not prescriptively connected to nature.

9. Though "Slater's Pins" appears in a collection of Woolf's short stories and "The Moment" is classified as an essay, the difference between the two lies in their state of finish rather than their genre. Leonard Woolf categorized them after

Virginia Woolf's death, so we cannot be sure how—or whether—Woolf herself would have distinguished the pieces from each other. If we take stock in Leonard Woolf's distinction, however, the limited significance of the assigned genre difference supports the idea that Woolf was blurring the boundaries between fiction and nonfiction. Certainly she deals with moments of being (and the general state of non-being) in both—or all—kinds of writing.

10. See *MOB* 72 on the "sledge-hammer force of the blow" of a moment of being.

11. The idea that a perception should remain uncompromised by "judging" or "overseeing" recalls the passage from *"The Faery Queen"* in which Woolf warns against "referring any of the words to a special place" (*M* 26). Apprehending a complex whole hinges upon the willingness to refrain from systematizing it in any way.

12. When Woolf describes De Quincey's way of recounting a moment of being, she seems to contradict her conclusion that these encounters make time stand still. Also in "De Quincey's Autobiography," she writes that De Quincey is "capable of being transfixed by the mysterious solemnity of certain emotions, of realising how one moment may transcend in value fifty years" (*CR* 2: 138). When time moves that quickly, perhaps it does indeed feel as if it were standing still. Nonetheless, it is significant to note that Woolf contextualizes De Quincey's technique in terms of a transformation of the arts of autobiography and biography (*CR* 2: 139). Woolf is developing this assertion at a time (late 1927) when she is also working on drafts for *Orlando* (see Silver 84, 89), a new kind of biography in which one moment literally "may transcend in value fifty years" (*CR* 2: 139).

Pleasure and Belief in "Phases of Fiction"

Anne E. Fernald

*The central fact remains stable, which is the fact of my own
pleasure in the art.*

—Virginia Woolf, Diary, 12 May 1919

*It is to be lamented that we judge of books by books,
instead of referring what we read to our own experience.*

—Samuel Taylor Coleridge, "Lectures on Shakespeare"
Epigraph to Woolf's "Notes of a Days Walk"[1]

Instead of representing or anticipating a method of criticism, Virginia
Woolf's "Phases of Fiction" (1929) proposes a theory of the novel based on
the pleasure of reading. It is her most sustained theory of fiction; nonetheless, this essay, over fifty pages long, has received little critical attention.
In focusing on pleasure, Woolf ignores the formal, moral, and political
questions that typically preoccupy professional criticism, and indeed, without ever making a case for pleasure, Woolf's literary essays present a model
of reading that would dismiss any other scale of judgment as irrelevant. In
a recent essay, David Bromwich argues that "the cause of our interest in art
is psychological before and after it is moral" (11), and "Phases of Fiction"
exemplifies what it could mean to take such a claim seriously and build a
theory around it.

Any defense of pleasure must dodge the interference of appeals to its
use. In doing so, my account of Woolf's literary essays has strayed from
other accounts of Woolf as a literary theorist. For example, Susan Stanford
Friedman discusses the feminist purpose behind scenes of reading in the

novels while Pamela Caughie places Woolf among the theorists, an activity she performs before and instead of analysis of Woolf's performance as a critic. What continually stalls Caughie is her need to find the use of literature. So she writes, "At the end of 'Phases of Fiction,' Woolf asks a pragmatic question: what do we gain by such comparison [of novels]? One benefit is our awareness of the flexibility and the potentiality of fiction" (176). Here, Caughie overlooks a much more interesting question: why, in "Phases of Fiction," does Woolf abandon any appeal to the use of literature?

Woolf's literary essays do attempt to teach readers how to read even as they work to preserve reading as a pleasure. Doubtless Woolf learned from her reading, and doubtless she believed others might do the same. However, the conclusion to be drawn is not that Woolf's books teach this or that particular political or social lesson, but that they show us again and again how completely she had absorbed her father's practical wisdom: "To read what one liked because one liked it, never to pretend to admire what one did not—that was his only lesson in the art of reading" (CDB 74). For Woolf, pleasure comes from the satisfaction of our need for change and the gratification of our desire to believe. In her literary essays, she often writes as if the very craving that produces the momentum of our passage from one book to another will itself explain the pleasures and deficiencies of each.

At the end of "How Should One Read a Book?" Woolf articulates the double feeling that literature is both somehow useful and an importantly useless pastime through an appeal to the writer's sense of her audience:

> If behind the erratic gunfire of the press the author felt that there was another kind of criticism, the opinion of people reading for the love of reading, slowly and unprofessionally, and judging with great sympathy and yet with great severity, might this not improve the quality of his work? And if by our means books were to become stronger, richer, and more varied, that would be an end worth reaching.
>
> Yet who reads to bring about an end, however desirable? Are there not some pursuits we practise because they are good in themselves, and some pleasures that are final? (CR 2: 270)

Once she has expressed the hope that serious reading will improve literature, she must explain *how*. Here, it is through the perception of a serious audience that writers will be inspired to write better books. The uneasiness surrounding the word "improve" leads Woolf to emphasize the benefits for the reader: more books. However, as Woolf's self-conscious hesitations reveal, it is nearly impossible for us to posit an aesthetic advantage without hinting at a moral one. But Woolf can work to insure that pleasure gets its due, that it is seen as a sufficient good. Thus, her essays lengthen the pause between reading and judgment, blurring the connection between enjoyment of a work of art and its point. This *use* of reading has little in common with what Pamela Caughie claims for Woolf. Furthermore, no sooner does Woolf articulate it than she retracts it in favor of a vision of reading as a final pleasure, leading nowhere.

This vision of reading raises a new problem, one emphasized by Woolf's nomination of reading as a final pleasure. Reading has never been a final pleasure: all of literature contradicts that proposition. Readers want to write, to respond to what they have read. Novels and poems speak obliquely to this desire, letters and journals speak privately to it, and the essay is a genre about and inspired by the desire to continue the pleasure of reading by writing about it. But even if these aesthetic responses make clear that reading is not a final pleasure, they certainly do not make it a useful one.

To refine our sense of Woolf's appeals to pleasure in the literary essay, I turn to two very different texts on reading and pleasure: Lionel Trilling's "The Fate of Pleasure," which offers a history of the idea's decline, and Roland Barthes's *The Pleasure of the Text*, which attempts to effect its resuscitation. Tracing the idea of pleasure from Wordsworth through Keats to Dosto-evsky, Trilling identifies its current association with luxury and moral decay, our consequent suspicion of it, and our reluctance to see it as a fundamental good. He then argues that this idea of pleasure is "a contingent and not a necessary mode of thought. This opens the way to regarding it as a mode of thought which is received or established and which is therefore, like any other received or established mode of thought, available to critical scrutiny" (79). For Trilling, seeing pleasure as "contingent" makes it valuable precisely because it is unfixed, changeable. Thus, there are types of pleasure, not a hierarchy but an abundance, each one meeting a different mood, fulfilling a different aspect of the reader's appetite. Trilling, however, demonstrates that since Keats, writers explicitly concerned with pleasure have had to write in the face of a general cultural ambivalence toward this idea.

This cultural ambivalence is the context in which we hear Woolf's defenses of the pleasure of reading; to understand them we may turn to Roland Barthes with interest. Both Barthes and Woolf occasionally under-took to defend their taste for unfashionable, censored, or right-wing writers, though neither felt his or her interest in literature to be compromised by political commitments. Barthes wants to account for the unpredictability of what gives us pleasure, to separate pleasure in writing from pleasure in reading and even to separate pleasure from the text. Barthesian pleasure is always in danger of becoming ornamental. However, in separating it from secondary moral benefits, Barthes also frees pleasure from any responsibility. His jokes cut to the heart of defenses by critics on behalf of Woolf's obvious pleasure in reading books outside of, or even antithetical to, her feminist project. Woolf shares Barthes's mischievous enjoyment of sheer transgressiveness in literature (of which arcaneness is a variety), but where this taste leads Barthes to Sade, it leads Woolf to the biographies of aristocratic ladies.

The source of our pleasures must be the final criterion by which we distinguish Woolf from these other writers. Much more than Woolf, Wordsworth focuses on the writer and his role as a giver of pleasure. For Wordsworth, pleasure lies in knowledge, and in "the perception of similitude in dissimilitude" (610). Keats and Barthes are more likely to find their pleasures in an eroticized idea of luxury. Woolf is neither as severe as Wordsworth nor as sensuous as Barthes, but it is not enough to say that she takes pleasure somewhere between the two extremes. It is the movement from one to the other that excites her, and this often restless sensibility characterizes her essays.

Woolf's most extensive picture of relations among books organized according to a reader's pursuit of pleasure is "Phases of Fiction." This long essay was written for the Hogarth Press but appeared instead in the New York *Bookman* of April, May, and June 1929. "Phases" divides fiction into six types (or phases), each one discussed according to the mood it satisfies. Beginning with the Truth-Tellers, Woolf tests her sense that, among the reader's appetites, "perhaps, the simplest is the desire to believe" (94). The naturalism of the novels of Defoe, W. E. Norris, Maupassant, and Trollope makes us "aware of another desire . . . making its way into those cracks [of] the great monuments of the truth-tellers. . . . A desire for distance, for music, for shadow" (103), so we move to the Romantics—Scott, Stevenson, and Radcliffe. Then, after a surfeit of emotion, Woolf turns to the Character-Mongers and Comedians, not for a violent change but for "a return to human faces; a sense of walls and towns about us" (110). This section takes us through Dickens, to Austen, and then to George Eliot. With Eliot, we have left broad comedy behind and, "if we consult our own difficult and mixed emotions as we read, it becomes clear that we are . . . moving . . . into a far more dubious region" (120), that of the Psychologists (James, Proust, and Dostoevsky). Again working on the principles of checking the reader's mood and seeking to satisfy it, Woolf finds that this excursion into the details of the soul has left us "saturated" and desiring "the sense that the satirist gives us that he has the world well within his grasp" (130). Thus, we leave *A la recherche du temps perdu* and *The Possessed* for, of all things, *Crotchet Castle* and the

Satirists and Fantastics. In this section, Woolf discusses Sterne, and, just as George Eliot's novels bridge the gap between Comedians and Psychologists, Sterne takes us from the Satirists to the final section of the essay: the Poets.

This brief summary of "Phases of Fiction" demonstrates how thoroughly Woolf relies upon an organizing principle of contrast rather than development. In "Byron and Mr. Briggs," Woolf describes this movement among types of books, this voracious need to sample literature in all its variety:

> Consider the zigzagging of natural [reading done?] in youth. . . . the emotion roused in us by each play poem or story must be so strong that it has the power first to absorb us and then to send us, by a natural reaction, in search of a different sensation—of a sensation which appears to complete the one originally felt. (339)[2]

This "zigzagging" is twice called "natural" and is implicitly contrasted with a set curriculum. Woolf transforms the haphazardness that, if we are honest, characterizes most of our reading, into a virtue and asks us to interest ourselves in why one book might send us back to the library "in search of a different sensation."

Compared to Woolf's other essays depicting a reader's mind at work, "Phases of Fiction" keeps the identity of the reader fairly anonymous. Thus, the strong narrative organization, the essay's interest in following one mind's movements, proceeds with a subject who is almost a blank. It has been suggested that Woolf constructed her common reader without explicit gender to hide her own anxiety about being a woman critic.[3] While this may answer part of the question, it is also evident that Woolf cannot resist the impulse to satirize her characters who read; their pleasure in reading is a bit embarrassing, their judgments unreliable and useless. So reading Augustine Birrell is like being "caught drinking champagne in the middle of the morning—a proceeding too pleasant to be right" ("Augustine Birrell" 755), John Paston's reading causes him to neglect to erect a tombstone for his father (*CR* 1: 10), and "Mrs. Briggs (who was a Grant from Dundee) knew the Waverley novels by heart but she could never abide George Eliot" ("Byron and Mr. Briggs" 330). There is considerable wit and a cunning self-depreciation in these portrayals of what it is to be carried away by reading, but the caricatures cannot carry the weight of any serious argument about reading.

In contrast, "Phases of Fiction" presents an unnamed reader-narrator whose personal eccentricities are viewed as the normal effects of reading.

Like so many of Woolf's literary essays, "Phases in Fiction" opens with a trip
to the library. The reader in the essay is not a person but a mind that explores
the contents of a library shelf but "was not pressed to make a choice. It was
allowed to read what it liked":

> Yet . . . nobody reads simply by chance or without a definite scale of
> values. . . . Hence, an ordinary reader can often trace his course through
> literature with great exactness and can even think himself, from time
> to time, in possession of a whole world as inhabitable as the real world.
> . . . [A]ny such record of reading, it will be concluded, is bound to be
> limited, personal, erratic. (93-94)

This account of an individual's reading is more abstract than many
such passages to be found elsewhere, which perhaps speaks to Woolf's desire
to fulfill the task of writing "some theory" of fiction. Yet, compared to most
other theories, it is hardly abstract at all. Woolf presents all of this with the
nervy confidence of one sure of her readings and equally sure that she is
reading against the grain of most criticism. Her terms become, according to
the conventions of the time, increasingly negative as the paragraph
progresses, until we are left with a criticism that is "limited, personal, erratic,"
a set of terms that, strangely enough, may look like an intelligent and canny
admission of the conditions of literary judgment to us, nearly seventy years
later. In fact, these terms, though they would not have been so obviously
appealing in 1929, do suggest a set of opposites to which Woolf was ardently
opposed. Objecting to a criticism that was broad, impersonal, and interested
in fixing boundaries, Woolf accepted and even rejoiced in a criticism that
would necessarily be limited, personal, and erratic. By describing her method
in terms of its disadvantages, Woolf forces her critics to defend an impersonal reading of literature, if they can. This method preserves the romance
of reading, the way books create the illusion of a whole world, and the way
in which that world is "always in process of creation" (93).

Woolf's more anonymous readers are serious and avid, self-educated
and curious. But it is also to be noted that in reading for pleasure, they often
turn to books they will not and do not enjoy, books that are pleasurable for
their ability to show something about the world. Thus, in "Phases of Fiction,"
we begin with Defoe and the Truth-Tellers not because Defoe is her favorite
but because his writing helps satisfy her hypothesis about the connection
between reading fiction and the desire to believe.

Though the idea of belief remains important to "Phases of Fiction,"
its fullest articulation resides in a twenty-three-page typescript draft

entitled "Notes of a Days Walk." Unlike any other existing draft or typescript of "Phases of Fiction," "Notes" is imbedded in a single extended narrative, opening in a city church where a little old lady is selling cards and lavender in the doorway and two young men pray. In such an atmosphere, Woolf writes:

> It was natural to think about belief. To try to pin down and describe this profound human instinct. What did it spring from—this universal desire to believe in something that cannot be seen or touched? . . . But owing to the extreme age of the human mind, and the consequent weakness of its memories, we find it necessary to support this belief upon something actual; hence the emblems hung up in churches; pictures of saints and madonnas. Hence too our habit of writing words upon tombs. (2)

The church provides an occasion for a meditation at once spiritual and secular. Faith does not enter; belief is as much an object of investigation as a compelling need. Woolf's interest here is very like William James's: "As a matter of fact we find ourselves believing, we hardly know how or why" (18).[4] However, while in 1896 James can still connect belief to the choice between Christianity and agnosticism, Woolf's interest, even in a church, is almost wholly secular. Indeed, the church setting flouts the difference between Woolf and thinkers of her father's generation; it announces her modernity. Even the discussion of belief as an instinct, with its vague musings about a kind of racial memory, suggests an interest more generally scientific (be it biological, psychological, or anthropological) than personal.

Woolf seeks to balance the instinct to believe and the reality in which that belief is grounded. In this, she can sound like one of many Modernists, caught between a fascination with science and a nostalgia for religious faith. However, the immediate and unself-conscious way in which she consistently turns to art, and especially writing, as the obvious place in which that balance is to be found is special to Woolf. It is natural for an artist reluctant to accept a secular world to claim that art can be spiritual. However, while other writers—Joyce, Lawrence, and Eliot, for example—argue for this claim, Woolf accepts it as a given. We need to believe; we write epitaphs. In her treatment of belief as a fact of our psychology, she is a descendant of James, who writes, "Objective evidence and certitude are doubtless very fine ideals to play with, but where on this moonlit and dream-visited planet are they found?" (22).

Once a desire for an object of belief has been expressed, Woolf's essay immediately turns to literature: "the church is known to be the burial place of some of Shakespeare's actors" ("Notes" 2). Doubting that the tomb in question contains an actor's bones, Woolf spins a tale about his life, interrupting it with suggestions as to what evidence she feels to be lacking. As "Notes" continues, "a ray of sun came through the window," revealing the tomb to be that of "Frek. Cripps, Hair merchant of this parish, died Decr. 1705" (3). This fact affects the direction of the essay in two important ways: it confirms the pleasure of connecting belief to knowledge "(drop a fact in and all these ideas coalesce)" (4), and, through a list of what was contemporary to Mr. Cripps, she arrives at Defoe, the first novelist whom she discusses.[5] But Defoe is mentioned here only in passing, and the narrative takes several more turns before considering his fiction. In this, "Notes" has the same meandering form as "Kew Gardens," "The Mark on the Wall," or parts of *A Room of One's Own* (which she was writing at this time): a metonymic shape in which each successive landmark on a walk permits Woolf to comment on a new aspect of belief, until she and her readers are ready to consider belief in relation to fiction.

The narrative structure of "Notes of a Days Walk" promises to answer a question that Woolf cannot answer fully, here or elsewhere: why do some books come to seem as real as our experience? Thus, before Woolf considers Defoe, she gives an account of a minor accident on the street, in which a taxi nearly collides with a boy on a bicycle, causing some bottles of milk to break and spill in the street. Here is Woolf's account of the accident's effect on the crowd, with her transition to Defoe's novels:

> The sight of the accident had caused such a strong feeling that it was natural to ask what the nature of it was—Had it given so much pleasure because it supplied a drama; because it banished all other thoughts so masterfully; because it was heaven sent, provided without our own effort; without any pain to us, or the actors. Most of us would have liked to see another accident. . . . It was rather flat to walk on without an accident. . . .
>
> Partly to prolong the pleasure, partly to try to explain it, I thought, stopping at a bookstall . . . how the same sort of experience was provided by the great truth tellers—Defoe for example, one of whose books—Roxana—happened to be on sale in a cheap edition. Was there not some likeness between reading Defoe and seeing an accident? (9-10)

I have quoted at length to show the trouble Woolf took, in this version, to connect each link in her argument to an external event, which leads to the striking comparison between reading Defoe and seeing an accident. However, here the narrative takes on its own momentum, equally interested in describing the pleasures of spectatorship and surprise as it is in developing the idea of belief and fiction with which it began. The penned addition, ("One would have liked to stop . . . and say, I have just seen an accident") speaks to our frustration at having an experience that is not shared. Indeed, it is the nature of events in the world that, once past, they can never be shared. This is not the case with reading. Not only can we check our sense of life against Defoe's, we can also ask a friend to read Defoe and see what she thinks. In this way, the knowledge that books offer might be superior to life. But the very randomness of spotting an accident lends life a kind of delight and surprise that reading can seldom match. Thus, the sentences in pen on the typescript amplify the thrill of seeing the accident, further delaying the discussion of Defoe. Even when she finally gets to the bookstall, Woolf's sentence labors under the weight of nine modifying phrases. She does not simply say, as she does in "Phases of Fiction," "The novels of the great truth-tellers, of whom Defoe is easily the English chief, procure for us a refreshment of this kind" (95).[6]

In the completed version of "Phases of Fiction," Woolf no longer tries to connect each book to an external event. Instead, she links them to moods of the mind. This change eliminates the burden of constantly justifying her pleasure in reading. Instead, it explores the moods and desires that reading can satisfy. We cannot make life suit our moods, we cannot manufacture minor accidents to gratify a desire for a moment of clarity, but we can turn to Defoe when such a mood is upon us. The Truth-Tellers section of "Phases" also begins with a description of witnessing an accident, but there the relation between the accident and Defoe is metaphoric rather than met-onymic: Defoe offers the "same sort of refreshment and delight that we get from seeing something actually happen" (95). In "Phases," examples from experience are subordinate to discussions of the novels; in "Notes," the examples dominate. The metaphoric organization of the final version is not only swifter, it also seems to do a better job of answering Woolf's desire to write a theory of fiction. Even Virginia Woolf might have become discour-aged at the thought of continuing the narrative through discussions of Scott, Dickens, Proust, Peacock, and Melville. How many more bookstalls, librar-ies, and restaurants would she have to visit?

Woolf's reader does not remain satisfied for long; she cannot be held to chronology nor does she want to bother with some writers ("it [the mind] skipped, by chance or negligence, some of the most celebrated books in English fiction" [93]). In fact, her desire for change is almost as strong as her desire to believe. Woolf sought change in her writing as well, moving from lighter to more serious novels, from essays to fiction. She wrote in her diary,

"No critic ever gives full weight to the desire of the mind for change" (*D* 4:145), a failing that "Phases" begins to redress. The idea of reading as a relief, as providing the opposite of what we live, puts the matter somewhat differently from a discussion of escapism or wish-fulfillment. Reading not only offers a world as real as our own, it also offers us a chance to correct or control our world by turning to a book that gives what our life cannot. In assessing the effect of Woolf's story, it is thus not enough merely to correlate her story to a typology of reading practice. Such moves overlook the significance of choosing to present the idea of escapism in terms of a specific example of escape.

This principle of relief controls the broad movements of "Phases" and it ensures that no one mood or scale can come to dominate. The frame narrative, although diminished from what "Notes of a Days Walk" imagined, makes a significant return as Woolf moves from the Truth-Tellers to the Romantics. Soon enough, Woolf tires of the unencumbered narrative and criticizes Defoe's "obdurate deafness to all the voices which seduce and tempt him to gratify other moods" (96). Though Defoe may be deaf to other moods, Woolf is not, and after reading too many books by the Truth-tellers, she reintroduces the vision of the accident with which the essay began, only now "the dustman has picked up his broken bottle; he has crossed the road; he begins to lose solidity and detail over there in the evening dusk" (103). Noting the deficiencies of the Truth-Tellers' method, Woolf next notes a compensating desire. Only then does the essay look outside, correlating that change with the change in the scene below. What was an exciting accident has become a quiet aftermath. True to novelistic uses of the pathetic fallacy, the relation between the darkening day and her softer mood remains implicit. Thus, while allowing her temperament to control the discussion, she maintains the conceit of reading in time: while we have been reading about Defoe, the sun has set. Once again, the narrative permits Woolf to suggest what would take much longer to argue formally: that as surely as midday turns to dusk, there are books to satisfy the change.

For Woolf, those books are the ones written by the Romantics, especially the novels of Walter Scott. In the case of her numerous references to Walter Scott in particular, we can retrace Woolf's own method of reading by mood. The assessment of Scott in "Phases" sounds merely dutiful in light of the conclusion of "Indiscretions": "no woman can read the life of this man and his diary and his novels without being head over ears in love with Walter Scott" (92). In a different spirit, Mr. Ramsay's reading of Scott in *To the Lighthouse* only complicates the picture, for we must see his enjoyment through the lens of his character, an often affectionate picture of a domineering and selfish man: "He was reading something that moved him very much. He was half smiling and then she knew he was controlling his emotion. He was tossing the pages over. He was acting it—perhaps he was thinking himself the person in the book. She wondered what book it was. Oh, it was one of old Sir Walter's" (117-18). We could continue this catalog, perhaps with a quotation from "Gas at Abbotsford" or "The Antiquary." One could perform a similar exercise with Woolf's references to a number of other authors: my point here is that "Phases" permits and even encourages such changes of mood and mind. Finding contrasting judgments of an author in two Woolf essays, we do not feel, as Mr. Ramsay does, that we "had been arguing with somebody, and had got the better of him" (*TTL* 120). Instead, her emphasis on reading with a fresh eye each time makes such changes into things of value and confirms the seriousness of Woolf's own changing individual responses.

With a tactical psychology that has seldom been justly appreciated, Woolf's novels also rely on a dramatic sense of the necessity of sometimes closing off scenes of pathetic identification with scenes of comic disengagement. This practice is most pointed in *Between the Acts*, where Miss LaTrobe's interpolated play imposes the change, but we also see it in *Mrs. Dalloway*, where chance encounters gesture toward another kind of novel, just below the surface of the one we are reading. Thus, as she tries to distract the shell-shocked Septimus Smith from his reverie, his wife is interrupted with a question: "The way to Regents Park Tube station—could they tell her the way to Regents Park Tube station—Maisie Johnson wanted to know. She was only up from Edinburgh two days ago" (26). Woolf's transitions in "Phases" follow a similar pattern. Change is never imposed from the outside; it is organic. And we understand Woolf's move from the Romantics to the Character-Mongers and Comedians as the *effect* of a change in the reader's mood.

After discussing *Bleak House*, Woolf moves, somewhat restlessly, to Tolstoy, who is quickly passed over in favor of Austen. Here is how she completes the transition:

> Dickens has, himself, given us a taste of the pleasure we derive from looking curiously and intently into another character. He has made us instinctively reduce the size of the scene in proportion to the figure of a normal man, and now we seek this intensification, this reduction, carried out more perfectly and more completely, we shall find, in the novels of Jane Austen. (114)

Here the reader does not seek a contrast but an intensification of an unforeseen pleasure. After the wide expanses of the Romantics, she turns to

Dickens for scaled-down characters and only then remembers the pleasure of a kind of psychological intensity that Dickens does not quite provide. Not only does Austen suit a different mood, but the manner in which we arrived at it is unlike other transitions thus far. It is as if the move from Dickens to Austen teaches us to feel the emotion that Austen satisfies.

Thus far, each book has lead the reader to a new one, but Jane Austen elicits a pause. After several pages on *Pride and Prejudice*, concluding with a repetition of Woolf's persistent interest in the degree to which Austen left her personality out of her novels, Woolf writes:

> It may be the very idiosyncrasy of a writer that tires us of him. Jane Austen, who has so little that is peculiar, does not tire us, nor does she breed in us a desire for those writers whose method and style differ altogether from hers. Thus, instead of being urged as the last page is finished to start in search of something that contrasts and completes, we pause when we have read *Pride and Prejudice*.
>
> The pause is a result of a satisfaction which turns our minds back upon what we have just read, rather than forward to something fresh. (116)

Even Woolf's prose pauses here, the new paragraph gently repeating the assertions of the one before. The word "pause" contrasts sharply with the restless analysis that surrounds it. "Phases" doubles back for two long paragraphs, the first of which returns to *Pride and Prejudice*, insisting that satisfaction is complete in itself. When Woolf concedes that a comparison to something else may help make her point, she returns to *Bleak House*. Shuttling thus between Dickens and Austen, the essay seems in danger of coming to a halt.

Then, repeating the language that first began the pause, Woolf lifts us out of it: "Not to seek contrast but to start afresh—this is the impulse which urges us on after finishing *Pride and Prejudice*" (117). Pamela Caughie is also drawn to the pause at this point in "Phases of Fiction." She claims that "her remark on Austen could fit any of the authors she considers" (175-76). Although Woolf's reading of Austen resembles other readings in its attempt to see the author on her own terms and characterize the particular experience of reading her, what is special about Austen is that she, unlike any of the other writers considered here, provokes a desire to stop and reflect, to turn "our minds back upon what we have just read, rather than forward to something fresh" (116). That is Austen's greatness and her difficulty: Austen's novels match her powers so exactly that it takes some effort to remember that one might want something else. It is too easy to say that her world is limited, thereby dismissing her as if she were a miniaturist. Instead, Woolf repeats this charge as a cliché, which, by its very inadequacy, leads to a fresher observation: "we are about to frame the familiar statement that this is a world which is too small to satisfy us, a prosaic world, a world of inches and blades of grass, [when] we are brought to a pause by another impression which requires a moment of further analysis" (115). This gives way to a reprise, familiar from "Jane Austen" and *A Room of One's Own*, of Austen as a writer who left herself out of her art. Even Woolf's account of the cliché about Austen's limitations has its fanciful side (inches and blades of grass), as if no bit of prose can go unadorned.

Woolf's assessment of Austen provides some clues to her sense of herself as a writer. In spite of her interest in and praise for Austen's sentences, Woolf's own sentences are not very like them. Austen's style itself did not excite Woolf's imitation; her ability to work—to write masterpieces—within her limitations did. In "Jane Austen" she writes, "She knew exactly what her powers were, and what material they were fitted to deal with as material should be dealt with by a writer whose standard of finality was high" (*CR* 1: 142). Although Woolf took quite different situations and emotions as her subject, she was like Austen in that some emotions, scenes, and characters were quite out of her province, and one of her continual challenges as a writer was to work around these limitations. For example, while change in Austen's narratives tends to come about through dialogue, misunderstandings of precise and highly formal conversation, Woolf's narratives often depend for their movement on how objects trigger a character's memories. But neither writer tries her hand at a battle scene, as much as *Mansfield Park* and, to a much greater extent, *Jacob's Room* are colored by an awareness of war elsewhere.

Woolf notes at the end of this section, "it becomes clear that we are fast moving out of the range of pure character-mongering, of comedy, into a far more dubious region" (120). With this, she closes one section and begins her account of the Psychologists (James, Proust, and Dostoevsky). Thus, the pause that Austen created has also removed the need for the framing narrative of the first two sections. For the second half of the essay, the transitions from one writer to another seem calculated as much to reveal unexpected connections as to provide contrast. The essay slides from Austen to Eliot to James as our eyes might slide across a spectrum. Where Eliot might belong in any of several categories, with James we are clearly among the Psychologists, just as, at a certain moment, it is clear that we are no longer looking at blue but violet. Woolf reminds us of the gravity and interest

206 Anne E. Fernald

of her pleasures, of the distinction between them and mere leisure, again when she describes the pleasure to be gotten from reading Henry James as "a pleasure somewhat akin, perhaps, to the pleasure of mathematics, or the pleasure of music" (122).

From James, Woolf moves to Proust, to intensify the psychological investigation. After a few pages on the overwhelming significance with which objects, relations, and feelings are laden, she writes:

> As a consequence of the union of the thinker and the poet, often, on the heel of some fanatically precise observation, we come upon a flight of imagery—beautiful, coloured, visual, as if the mind, having carried its powers as far as possible in analysis, suddenly rose in the air and from a station high up gave us a different view of the same object in terms of metaphor. (125-26)

Proust himself satisfies Woolf's desire for change, and this quality accounts for the preeminence of *A la recherche du temps perdu* in Woolf's judgment of the novel. The word "metaphor" interests me here. Woolf seldom refers to literary terms in her writing, generally preferring a quick imitation, quotation, or a metaphor of her own describing the style that she characterizes. The unusual restraint here signals the imaginative saturation brought on, even for Woolf, by reading Proust.

But, she turns from the Psychologists to the Satirists and Fantastics (Peacock and Sterne) because "the mind feels like a sponge . . . ; it needs to dry itself, to contract upon something hard" (130). This move through Peacock to Sterne and then to the Poets is more subtle and more unexpected in what it reveals of Woolf's own tacit affinities. Although she has turned to Peacock for his satire, she ends by discussing the way his personality pervades his book, an observation that, naturally enough, leads her to Sterne, "a much greater writer, yet sufficiently in the family of Peacock to let us carry on the same train of thought uninterruptedly" (133). If Austen creates a masterpiece by expressing almost no idiosyncrasies, Sterne does the opposite. *Tristram Shandy* is a labyrinth of idiosyncrasy and digression, and to enjoy it we must dive into Sterne's mind:

> So, finally, we get a book in which all the usual conventions are consumed and yet no ruin or catastrophe comes to pass; the whole subsists complete by itself, like a house which is miraculously habitable without the help of walls, staircases, or partitions. . . . [C]an we not escape even further, so that we are not conscious of any author at all?

Can we not find poetry in some novel or other? For Sterne by the beauty
of his style has let us pass beyond the range of personality into a world
which is not altogether the world of fiction. It is above. (135)

The terms of praise in this remarkable passage are familiar; the usual
conventions recall her praise of Shakespeare's mind in *A Room of One's Own*,
which "consumed all impediments," and the house without walls recalls the
odious house-making of Bennett as described in "Modern Fiction." The novel
that frees itself from the more plodding requirements of narrative is poetic;
it rises above the common idea of novels, and it is no stretch for Woolf to
find poetry in the comic. But Woolf's connection of this with poetry and
beauty offers insight into her own particular debt to Sterne. As she writes in
the opening to the Poets, "certain phrases have brought about this change
in us" (135). Here we find another advantage of Woolf's method: unfettered
by the need to give a full account of Sterne's prose, she can find in it the
seed of another kind of novel as yet unwritten.

We also see quite directly here what Woolf's literary essays can teach
us about her goals as a novelist. A more ordinary three-page account of *Tristram
Shandy* would be unlikely to allow itself to end on this note of poetry—it seems
tangential to the spirit of the novel. Academic convention calls for us to explain
Sterne in terms of a critique of Lockean empiricism or perhaps more generally
of the sentimental. But as Woolf wrote in her notes for "Phases," this is not a
critical study but "a writer's way of looking at literature."[7] Woolf was not a
writer able to erase her personality from her prose; nonetheless, she cannot
abandon the desire for a kind of transcendence. Sterne represents the possibility of a mind so involved with itself that it moves beyond. Woolf cannot
find this in Proust, whose shadow haunts the last half of the essay. In contrast
to Sterne, Proust's emotional excursus leave us "numb with exhaustion" (128).
The problem with Proust (and George Eliot, for that matter) is that they are
humorless, full of amour propre. Sterne's tireless catalog of his own mind never
shrinks from showing all of itself.

Woolf herself suggests the connection between Austen and Sterne in
"Mr. Bennett and Mrs. Brown," where she writes, "*Tristram Shandy* or *Pride and
Prejudice* is complete in itself" (*CDB* 105). It has never been satisfactory to
trace Woolf's origins as a novelist to Austen alone; comparisons of Woolf
to Austen invariably neglect the things most special about her prose.
However, when we think of Woolf as a novelist who consistently reserved
special praise for *both* Austen *and* Sterne, we begin to see the imaginative
complexity of her project. E. M. Forster sensed this early when he compared
Woolf to Sterne in *Aspects of the Novel*:

> She and Sterne are both fantasists. They start with a little object, take
> a flutter from it, and settle on it again. They combine a humourous
> appreciation of the muddle of life with a keen sense of its beauty. There
> is even the same tone in their voices—a rather deliberate bewilderment,
> an announcement to all and sundry that they do not know where they
> are going. (19-20)

For Woolf, these expressions of bewilderment are part of a practice of
using literature to characterize the full range of moods of the mind. As such
they are poetic, and thus Sterne is a poetic novelist.

Not surprisingly, reading Sterne in this way creates a desire for more
poetry, this time less mixed with comic interruptions. For this we turn to the
Poets, the final section of "Phases." In the spirit of poetry, Woolf does not
treat each novelist in turn but all at once. We move among Brontë, Tolstoy,
Melville, and Proust, who, in returning, dominates this section as he dominated the Psychologists. Then, just as the pause over Jane Austen marked a
turn in the middle of the essay, "Phases of Fiction" ends with a pause:

> And here we pause, not, certainly, that there are no more books to read
> or no more changes of mood to satisfy, but for a reason which springs
> from the youth and vigour of the art itself. We can imagine so many
> different sorts of novels . . . that we break off in the middle with Emily
> Brontë or with Tolstoy without any pretence that the phases of fiction
> are complete or that our desires as a reader have received full satisfac-
> tion. (139)

In the end, the pause itself is the crucial moment in Woolf's accounts
of reading. It is the moment of satisfaction, the moment just before judgment.
For Woolf, this middle moment, this space before a decision is reached, is
more important than the decision itself. She describes this same space in
"How Should One Read a Book?" in which reading is divided into a series of
discrete stages: "The first process, to receive impressions, is only half the
process of reading; . . . We must pass judgment upon these multitudinous
impressions; . . . But not directly. Wait for the dust of reading to settle" (CR
2: 266). The pause is essential to this method of reading, for it creates the
space in which the reader judges for herself. Only then is it proper to
compare, and these comparisons are first made against our experience or
other works of fiction. Coleridge's opinion, or that of any other authority, is
not to be consulted because criticism stands between us and the text,
threatening to block our response. We may "desire synthesis" ("Phases" 145),

but we cannot have it yet. For this reason, Woolf ends "Phases of Fiction" not with a summing up but with another pause, asking readers to form their own conclusions not only about the books themselves but about the shape of the essay that has discussed them.

The logic of Woolf's method of reading relies equally upon another, quite different idea of space: not of perceiving the structures built by another but of clearing a space for new ones. In accounting for some of the many phases of fiction and presenting them as the beginning of an infinite series, Woolf creates a map of discovery, suggesting much about what is yet unknown as it traces the uncertain boundaries of what is. As an account of fiction, it deliberately resists definitive appropriations, even though elsewhere in her writing, Woolf did have strong reasons to advocate certain authors and books. This is not a contradiction, nor is either mode a betrayal of the true Woolf. Woolf did not ask herself to choose, and we need not choose. When one addresses a girls' school (as in "How Should One Read a Book?") or a women's college (as in *A Room of One's Own*), certain things about the uses of literature need to be said. When one proposes an imaginative and speculative survey of the novel, quite different claims must be made.

While art is always central to Woolf, its power lies in its flexibility and the impossibility of ever pronouncing the last word. Other students of narrative focus on origins and endings, but Woolf will always be at her best in the middle, forcing herself and her readers to pause for a moment between their initial reading and judgment. By focusing on the wide variety of fictional worlds in which we believe and the causes of our need to move among them, Woolf constructs a theory of the novel that offers precise and lucid accounts of individual books while simultaneously leaving open the possibility that any new kind of novel may yet be born. In so doing, she also makes a strong case for the variety of pleasures of reading.

Toward the conclusion of "The Fate of Pleasure," Lionel Trilling is frankly discouraged by his sense that "the ideal of pleasure has exhausted itself" (85), an anxiety that, in their very different ways, Woolf and Roland Barthes attempt to counteract. But while Barthes's proposal of "a typology of the pleasures of reading" immediately dissolves into one of "the readers of pleasure" (63), Woolf, as we have seen, believes that these pleasures are somehow in—not of—the text. The distinctions Woolf makes among the various phases of fiction never diminish the appeal of any one type of pleasure. In the end, Woolf's theory of the novel harmonizes with Barthes's enthusiastic claim: "to judge a text according to pleasure . . . the text . . . can wring from me only this judgment, in no way adjectival: that's it!" (13). But as "Phases of Fiction" demonstrates, such judgments can be as precise, accurate, and true to the experience of reading as judgments made on another scale. Most importantly, Woolf's method shows us the worth of our own varying responses to our reading. In the end, "Phases of Fiction" extends the pleasure of reading into the pleasure of judgment, almost imperceptibly bridging the gap between reading and criticism. And with that, we may return to the question of use: a theory of the novel such as Woolf's provides an entry into theory for the common reader.

Works Cited

Barthes, Roland. *The Pleasure of the Text*. Trans. Richard Miller. New York: Hill, 1975.

Bromwich, David. "How Moral Is Taste?" *The Yale Review* 82: 1 (1994): 1-23.

Caughie, Pamela. *Virginia Woolf and Postmodernism*. Urbana: U of Illinois P, 1991.

Forster, E. M. *Aspects of the Novel*. 1927. New York: Harcourt, 1985.

Friedman, Susan Stanford. "Virginia Woolf's Pedagogical Scenes of Reading: *The Voyage Out, The Common Reader*, and Her Common Readers." *Modern Fiction Studies* 38.1 (1992): 101-26.

James, William. *The Will to Believe*. Cambridge, MA: Harvard UP, 1981.

King, James. *Virginia Woolf*. New York: Norton, 1995.

Trilling, Lionel. *Beyond Culture*. New York: Viking, 1965.

Woolf, Virginia. "Augustine Birrell." *The Yale Review*, 19: 4 (1930): 754-61.

———. "Byron and Mr. Briggs." Ed. Edward A. Hungerford, *The Yale Review*, 68: 3 (1979): 321-49.

———. *The Diary of Virginia Woolf*. Ed. Anne Olivier Bell. 5 vols. New York: Harcourt, 1977-84.

———. *The Captain's Deathbed and Other Essays*. New York: Harcourt, 1950.

———. *The Common Reader: First Series*. Ed. Andrew McNeillie. New York: Harcourt, 1984.

———. *The Common Reader. Second Series*. Ed. Andrew McNeillie. New York: Harcourt, 1986.

———. *The Essays of Virginia Woolf*. Ed. Andrew McNeillie. 3 vols. to date. New York: Harcourt, 1986-.

———. *Granite and Rainbow*. 1958. New York: Harcourt, 1975.

———. "Indiscretions." *A Woman's Essays*. Ed. Rachel Bowlby. New York: Penguin, 1992. 89-92.

———. *The Letters of Virginia Woolf*. Ed. Nigel Nicolson and Joanne Trautmann. 6 vols.New York: Harcourt, 1975-80.

————. *Mrs. Dalloway.* 1925. New York: Harcourt, 1990.

————. "Notes of a Days Walk." Monk's House Papers, Sussex, B7e.

————. "Phases of Fiction." *Granite and Rainbow.* New York: Harcourt, 1975.

————. *To the Lighthouse.* 1927. New York: Harcourt, 1989.

Wordsworth, William, "Preface to *Lyrical Ballads,*" *Wordsworth: The Oxford Authors,* ed. Stephen Gill. Oxford: Oxford UP, 1984, 595-615.

Notes

1. I thank Quentin Bell for permission to quote from the typescript of "Notes of a Days Walk."

2. This essay was published posthumously; the square brackets are those of Edward Hungerford, the editor.

3. For example, Susan Stanford Friedman writes: "Woolf's heavy use of the generic 'he' for her 'common reader' screens the gendered dimension of her persona and the critique of reading it embodies" (118).

4. James's lecture "The Will to Believe" opens with a quotation from Leslie Stephen's *Life* of his brother Fitzjames and closes with a quotation from Fitzjames Stephen himself. This coincidence indicates how fully Woolf was involved in a tradition—literary, philosophical, and familial—of examining the causes of our beliefs.

5. The list is as follows: "Queen Anne, Marlborough, Blenheim, full bottomed wigs, Pepys, the lice that Mrs Pepys found on her husbands body when she combed his hair, Defoe, Moll Flanders—according to the lumber previously stored in the mind" (4).

6. The accident reported here and Woolf's comment in "Notes" that after reading Defoe "Everything had come under his sway" ("Phases" 12) is a transformation of an observation Woolf made ten years earlier in her diary and essay. Reading Defoe for her article, Woolf writes of "yielding to a desire to stop reading & go up to London. But I saw London, in particular . . . palaces from Hungerford Bridge through the eyes of Defoe" (*D* 1: 263). In "Defoe," she writes: "the view of London from Hungerford Bridge, grey, serious, prosaic . . . brings him to mind" (*CR* 1: 93). Woolf's first written mention of *Orlando* conceives of it as a "Defoe narrative for fun," which shows the imaginative license with which she treated her literary precursors (*D* 3: 131).

7. Manuscript note, Monk's House Papers, Sussex, B6b, 1.

PART IV

WOOLF AND GENRE

Four Stages in Woolf's Idea of Comedy: A Sense of Joviality and Magnanimity

Sally A. Jacobsen

Virginia Woolf devoted wholly to comedy only the brief 1905 essay, "The Value of Laughter" (*E* 1: 58-60), in which she did not attempt to formulate a theory of comedy. Nevertheless, Woolf's idea of comedy can be seen to develop in four cumulative and overlapping stages. First, in "The Value of Laughter" Woolf advances a distinction between humor and comedy, one that she will subsequently abandon until the late 1930s. The second, transitional stage of her idea of comedy emerges in Woolf's several essays about Jane Austen and includes definitive observations she makes about the comic novel of manners. Writing *To the Lighthouse* immediately after *The Common Reader* with its "Jane Austen" essay, she teases her reader by playing deliberately with the conventions of the comic novel of manners. "Phases of Fiction" in 1929 ushers in a third stage, in which Woolf articulates a theory of the grotesque that goes beyond the effect of the grotesque in Aristotle's famous theory of comedy in *The Poetics*. Woolf's most original thinking about comedy also appears in "Phases of Fiction," in the "fantastic" category of wit she defines. Finally, in "Congreve's Comedies" in 1937 Woolf advances a more mature idea of the "humor of the heights" she had described in "The Value of Laughter" in 1905. Here the "joviality" she had distinguished as a desired effect of comedy in her earlier essay "Modern Fiction" becomes "pure joy," in the effect of a Congreve play. The tolerant, beneficent humor uniting the community in Woolf's last novel, *Between the Acts*, may be seen as her playing with the ideas and effects she describes in the Congreve essay. It would be false to Woolf's scattered statements about comedy to try to formulate those remarks into a coherent theory of comedy, but it is appropriate to trace their development and discuss them in the context of theories of comedy Woolf had read and of ideas about art that surrounded her in Bloomsbury.[1] An important contribution to Modernism is Woolf's own resistance to established forms. She continually reinvents form in the novel, and her ideas about comedy are similarly fluid.

We turn then to the first stage in Woolf's idea of comedy. In "The Value of Laughter" in 1905, Woolf defines humor as a kind of well-being requiring a sense of distance: "The value of laughter in life and in art cannot be overrated. Humour is of the heights; the rarest minds alone can climb the pinnacle whence the whole of life can be viewed as in a panorama" (E 1:59). This Olympian sense of benignity seems to be the same as the sense of "all's well" that is widely thought of as the emotional effect of Shakespeare's late comedies.[2] It is the same as the "mood of tolerant joviality" that Woolf mentions as a "test of humour" in "Loud Laughter" in 1918 (E 2: 260) and the sense of joviality and magnanimity that she identifies as the desired effect of fiction in "Modern Novels" in 1919, when she says that the failure to produce this effect is the only major defect of James Joyce's Ulysses (E 3: 34). Magnanimity is the Aristotelian virtue of judiciousness with generosity of spirit (or tolerance). The geniality of its even-handedness is its connection with comedy.

Woolf values the comic effect of joviality and magnanimity throughout her career, but she draws a distinction in "The Value of Laughter" that she subsequently ignores between high-minded, genial "humour" and comedy, which "reflects the trivial and accidental—the venial faults and peculiarities" (E 1: 59). She is too fond of the trivial and accidental to classify them below "humour" for long, as she shows in "Character in Fiction" in 1924, when she extols the interest, for example, of a character of a cook asking "advice about a hat" and of the hypothetical Mrs. Brown's "clean little boots" (E 3: 422-23).

Woolf, in opposition to adopting a stance of pretentious intellectualizing, first invokes the principle of common sense that characterizes all her reviews and is the hallmark of The Common Reader. Using George Meredith's term, she says that "the comic spirit" is the enemy of pretentiousness and solemnity: "Women and children . . . are the chief ministers of the comic spirit, because their eyes are not clouded with learning nor are their brains choked with the theories of books" (E 1: 60), and they are able to see things as they are. This dislike for solemnity and the pretentious "dogmatism of learning" shows Woolf to be steeped in Bloomsbury's rejection of received dogma of any sort and to be, like the Bloomsbury writers and artists, an enthusiast for what Leonard Woolf called the "pure light" of common sense (161). Common sense was an essential part of turn-of-the-century philosopher G. E. Moore's aesthetic, in which Virginia Woolf and Bloomsbury shared, and it impacted Woolf's whole concept of the "common reader."[3]

Virginia Woolf's emphasis upon common sense also suggests that she is thinking of George Meredith's nineteenth-century comic theory in "An Essay on Comedy and the Uses of the Comic Spirit," since Meredith calls comedy "the fountain of sound sense" (92). Woolf follows Meredith, too, in "The Value of Laughter" when she establishes a contrast with the feminine comic spirit, claiming that the "spirit of solemnity" ("in a chimney-pot hat and long frock-coat") "is masculine" (*E* 1: 58). The comic spirit is feminine for Meredith as well. Woolf coyly echoes his term "comic muse" by noting, "Comedy is of the sex of the graces and the muses"(*E* 1: 58).[4] What Meredith describes as comedy's civilizing influence (118, 141) would be consistent with the effect of joviality and magnanimity for which Woolf calls in "Modern Novels" and "Loud Laughter."

We turn next to the second stage in Woolf's idea of comedy, roughly grouped around her various essays that discuss Jane Austen's comedy and including Woolf's definition of the comic novel of manners. The comic effect of joviality and magnanimity, constant through all four stages of Woolf's idea of comedy, becomes a judicious magnanimity in Woolf's view of Austen's comedy. When Woolf merges "Jane Austen Practicing" with "Jane Austen at Sixty" to produce the Austen essay in *The Common Reader* in 1925, she says,

> The discrimination is so perfect, the satire so just, that . . . it almost escapes our notice. No touch of pettiness, no hint of spite, rouse us from our contemplation. Delight strangely mingles with our amusement. Beauty illumines these fools. (*E* 4: 151)

Austen's effect is that we are "exalted" (*E* 2: 11), or filled with the sense that "all's well." The passage quoted also illustrates again Woolf's use of Meredith's idea of comedy's power to "civilize" readers. Austen rises above spite, and she lends "beauty" to "these fools" in the perfection of her characterizations.

In "Jane Austen Practicing" in 1921, there seems at first glance no difference between the girl Jane's lofty perspective, "laughing . . . at the world," even in her early *Love and Friendship*, and the laughter of the heights (as opposed to mere comedy) described earlier in "The Value of Laughter":

> One of those fairies who are said to attend with their gifts upon cradles must have taken her on a flight through the air directly she was born. . . . She had agreed that if she might rule over that territory she would covet no other. . . . Whatever she writes is finished and turned and set in its relation to the universe like a work of art. (*E* 3: 333-34)

However, Jane Austen's novels break down the distinction Woolf had drawn in "The Value of Laughter" between high "humour" and the triviality of comedy. In *The Common Reader* essay Woolf says that Austen offers only trifles, triviality. There, however, she says that such "deviations from kindness, truth, and sincerity . . . are among the most delightful things in English literature" (*E* 4: 149, 152)—as opposed to what she had thought the highest kind of humor in 1905.

Absent from Jane Austen's novels is a kind of "triviality" that Woolf relishes in the second and third stages of her idea of comedy—indecency and coarseness. Woolf's specification that indecency is appropriate to comedy is surprising, in view of the unfailing decorum she observes in her own fiction, but it does make her idea compatible with the origin of comedy in the highly indecent ancient Greek "satyr" plays that offered Greek audiences a release after a day of watching trilogies of tragedy. In "Restoration Comedy" in 1924 (the year before publication of *The Common Reader*), Woolf praises comedy leavened in the English way with honest Anglo-Saxon coarseness, as opposed to a narrowly fastidious Victorian version of reality. Woolf prefers Wycherley's muscular particularity to the tendency to generalize in French eighteenth-century comedy: "The English give us a burly sea captain who is far better fitted to polish off a Dutchman with his own fists than to stand apart and meditate the worthlessness of mankind" (*E* 3: 447). Woolf also relishes the "indecency" that is part of Laurence Sterne's fantastic wit, as we shall see, in "Phases of Fiction" (*CE* 2: 93), but she finds in "Restoration Comedy" that indecency for its own sake, like Wycherley's, quickly becomes boring: It "loses its savour sooner, is less fertile and profound, than more normal topics once the shock of novelty has worn off" (*E* 3: 446). In the 1937 essay on "Congreve's Comedies," too, Woolf includes "coarseness" and indecency with the "trivialities" that are part of her definition of comedy from its second stage onward (*CE* 1: 79). In "The Value of Laughter," by contrast, she had assigned "the trivial and accidental, the venial faults and peculiarities" to "comedy" as a lower type than "humour" (*E* 1: 59). However, as we have seen, she valorizes the "trivial and accidental" in the second stage, which is represented by the essay "Jane Austen." Jane Austen's "unfailing good taste" of course leaves out not only indecency and "vice," but "adventure" and "passion" too (*E* 4: 152, 150). Woolf evidently does not consider the extremes of sensibility that Austen portrays as "passions."

Woolf's observations on comedy in the novel of manners in her remarks on Jane Austen anticipate more recent handbooks and could constitute a handbook guide to the genre. Her "Oliver Goldsmith" essay in 1934 confirms these principles. Woolf's definition of the comic novel of manners provides a basis for her to play with and hilariously overturn its conventions in *To the Lighthouse*. Humor is not a defining characteristic of the novel of manners. Bege K. Bowers and Barbara Brothers note, however, that handbooks often represent the novel of manners as "an 'adopted' form of the comedy of manners" and that the terms are sometimes used interchangeably (3).[5]

In the "Jane Austen" essay in *The Common Reader*, Woolf defines the range of the comic novel of manners. She says that in Austen's novels, "life was hedged in by valuable connections and adequate incomes." The incomes of the gentry and country squires support the life they lead in Austen's novels, along with their "consequence" in society and the "education commonly enjoyed by upper middle-class families" (*E* 4: 150). Harmon and Holman's *Handbook to Literature* agrees with this as a description of the novel of manners generally, saying that the genre is "dominated by social customs, manners, conventions, and habits" (354) of an upper social class. Woolf finds in "Phases of Fiction" that the limitations of "personal relations" lead Austen to stress "their comedy" (*CE* 2: 76): "A suitable marriage is, after all, the upshot of all this coming together and drawing apart. A world which so often ends in a suitable marriage is not a world to wring one's hands over" (78). Similarly, the definition the novel of manners given by Fred Millet is "a genre in which the characters' chief business [is] . . . social duties; their chief interest . . . matrimony'" (Bowers and Brothers 2).[6]

The ending of the "Jane Austen" essay shows Woolf thinking simultaneously of Austen's novels in terms of the conventions and witty dialogue of the novel of manners and her own playful stream-of-consciousness method: If Austen had lived longer, traveled more, and resided in London, Woolf says, "her comedy would have suffered. She would have trusted less (this is already perceptible in *Persuasion*) to dialogue and more to reflection to give us a knowledge of her characters" (*E* 4: 154-55). Like Woolf herself, Austen "would have devised a method . . . deeper and more suggestive, for conveying not only what people say, but what they leave unsaid; not only what they are, but what life is. . . . Her satire, while it played less incessantly, would have been more stringent and severe" (*E* 4: 155)—as Woolf's is in her portraits of Mr. Ramsay and Charles Tansley in *To the Lighthouse*. Woolf called the dinner scene near the end of "The Window" section of *To the Lighthouse* "the best thing I ever wrote" (*L* 3: 373). I believe that she was thinking of the hilarious misunderstandings in her characters' streams of consciousness that substitute for the witty repartee in the novel of manners—what she calls in the "Jane Austen" essay "a method . . . deeper and more suggestive, for conveying not only what people say, but what they leave unsaid" (E 4: 155). Woolf surely included such comic aspects in what she triumphantly viewed as her "haul," while she was revising the novel (D 3: 109).

Failures in characterization in the comic novel of manners are unforgivable for Woolf. Capturing depths of character and feeling are her first principles of excellence in a novel. "There is nothing that interests us more than character," Woolf says in "Mr. Bennett and Mrs. Brown" (E 3: 387), and in Jane Austen's novels of manners, she says in The Common Reader, "Always the stress is laid upon character" (E 4: 149). In the comic novel of manners, our delight in the characterization arises from our acknowledging the accuracy of the satire of the characters. It is important, however, that satire not overpower the characterizations, for in order for readers to be involved beyond the level of casual amusement, they must sympathize deeply with the central characters. Woolf says that in Austen's novels, "the satire [is] so just, that . . . it almost escapes our notice. . . . Delight strangely mingles with our amusement. Beauty illumines these fools" (E 4: 151). Woolf adds the criterion of depth of feeling when she observes that "Jane Austen is . . . a mistress of much deeper emotion than appears upon the surface. She stimulates us to supply what is not there" (E 4: 149). Here Woolf recognizes as part of comedy an intersubjective playfulness that realizes the female reading process described by Patrocinio Schweickart. For Woolf, Jane Austen's ability to engage us in the reading transaction makes her brand of comedy one that involves us as her playfellows, and this engagement mutes the satire of the characters so that we can take them seriously while at the same time we laugh at them. Woolf's view of Austen's comedy, "something that expands in the mind" (E 4: 149), implies the active participation of the reader's "mind" and imagination. Woolf sees our ability to have fun as contributing imaginatively to the characters' roundness and as necessary to the "delight" that "mingles with our [mere] amusement," a response that is necessary for satire.

Since Woolf insists upon roundness in character and depth of feeling, in "The Novels of George Meredith" in 1928 she is especially critical of Meredith's failings in characterization, perhaps because he set himself up as an expert in "An Essay on Comedy," which was the basis for much of her thinking about comedy from the beginning. Woolf takes Meredith to task for reviving neoclassical character types in The Ordeal of Richard Feverel, saying that "there is an indescribable conventionality about" his baronets and butlers, good women and bad (E 4: 527). By contrast, she finds in "Oliver Goldsmith" that Goldsmith's characters in his novels "gain vigour and identity by standing before us in the round" (CE 1: 111). Harmon and Holman say that in the comedy of manners "satire is directed . . . against the follies and deficiencies of typical characters," but that the novel of manners abandons neoclassical "types" as a defining characteristic and instead, "the mores of a specific group, described in detail and with great accuracy, become powerful controls over characters" (108, 354). Thus, in Goldsmith's comedy of manners for the stage we expect abstract character types, but Woolf disagrees and thinks that the stereotyped names mislead the audience and may prevent them from appreciating his stage characters' depth. She says, "Goldsmith did himself a wrong when he followed the old habit of labelling his people with names—Croker, Lofty, Richlands. . . . His observation, trained in the finer discriminations of fiction, worked much more cunningly than the names suggest" (*CE* 1: 111).

Common sense is the basis of character satire in the novel of manners and in the comedy of manners for Woolf, as it is for her idea of comedy generally and her idea of the common reader. Woolf credits the operation of the reader's common sense with detecting comic deviations from the norm, and she links the perception of comic triviality to "taste," or the civilizing power of comedy. In the "Jane Austen" essay she says, "The wit of Jane Austen has for partner the perfection of her taste. Her fool is a fool, her snob is a snob, because he departs from *the model of sanity and sense* which she has in mind, and conveys to us unmistakably even while she makes us laugh" (*E* 4: 151; emphasis added). One of Goldsmith's virtues, in the "Oliver Goldsmith" essay, is that like Austen, he does not offend "realistic common sense": In *She Stoops to Conquer*, "nothing is too far-fetched or fantastical to dry up the life blood in the characters themselves" (*CE* 1: 111).

In the category of common sense in the novel of manners, Woolf again finds particular fault with George Meredith's characters, not only for being neoclassical stereotypes but for lacking this "plain common sense." She says in describing "The Novels of George Meredith" that "though we may be able to see these people, very brilliantly, in a moment of illumination," they do not grow gradually upon us, as do Jane Austen's (*E* 4: 527, 529). In criticizing the lack of "common sense" in Meredith's characterizations, Woolf is hoisting Meredith on his own petard, for in "An Essay on Comedy and the Uses of the Comic Spirit" Meredith calls comedy "the first-born of common sense" and also "the fountain of sound sense" (119, 92). Woolf admits using Meredith's own principles to condemn his failure to appeal to common sense: "Had Meredith . . . lived in an age . . . where comedy was the rule, he might never have contracted those airs of intellectual superiority, that manner of oracular solemnity which it is, as he points out, the use of the comic spirit to correct" (*CE* 1: 230). Meredith's disadvantage in living in the Victorian age is no excuse for this defect in his fiction, however: a novel "full of dead characters, even though it is also full of . . . exalted teaching, is not achieving its aim as a novel" (CE 1: 230).Woolf says that her point of departure in the 1928 Meredith essay is dissatisfaction with E. M. Forster's treatment of Meredith in *Aspects of the Novel*, published the year before (E 4: 525-26). Forster gives Meredith eight pages in the "Plot" section of his book, but Woolf (for whom "plot" is not among the principles of novelistic excellence) attempts to pin down Meredith's qualities more exactly.

"Phases of Fiction" contains some of Woolf's most original thinking about comedy and may be viewed as a third stage in her idea of the genre. That Woolf wrote "Phases of Fiction" in playful dialogue with E. M. Forster's *Aspects of the Novel* is evident from her discussion of Forster's categories in "Phases of Fiction," from her review of his *Aspects of the Novel*, and from her clinging to the project, recasting it in dialogue form long after its viability as a book of criticism had ended. Forster classifies Woolf with Laurence Sterne as a "fantasist" in the Introductory Lecture in *Aspects of the Novel* (40), the Clark Lectures he had delivered at Trinity College, Cambridge in 1927, and Forster's classification likely prompted Woolf to include "Fantastics" with "Satirists" in "Phases of Fiction."[7] In her review of Forster's book, Woolf complains that his judgments are arbitrary, he lays down no principles for excellence, and he scants authors' achievements in language, their medium (CE 2: 53-54). The structure of and the choice of authors discussed in "Phases of Fiction" two years later suggest that Woolf was trying to do a better job than Forster, particularly in appreciation of authors' unique artistic accomplishments.

In "Phases of Fiction" Woolf enlarges the concept of the comic grotesque, adding a depth that is not present in Aristotle's discussion of the grotesque in the *Poetics*. She also breaks new ground in her discussion of the "fantastic" in comic fiction, no less complex than her idea of the grotesque. She defines the fantastic as a kind of comedy that takes its shape from the zany personality of the author, and she may be seen to be theorizing about the kind of comedy she wrote in *Orlando*. Two of the six sections of "Phases of Fiction"[8] discuss what we commonly view as the "comic": the third section, "The Character-mongers and Comedians," and the fifth, "The Satirists and Fantastics."

In "The Character-mongers and Comedians" section, Woolf recognizes an unusual close relationship between the Romantic and comedy, an affinity between the appeals of the exotic and the sublime in Romanticism and the grotesque in comedy, and she discusses the principle of comic relief in this context. Woolf focuses for the first time on minor characters, as opposed to the major characters for whom she had demanded roundness and depth, in defining the comic novel of manners, and she says that the comic grotesques of Dickens fulfill the function of comic relief. Moving away from Scott, Stevenson, and Mrs. Radcliffe at the end of the second section, "The Romantics," Woolf defines a Romantic novel as one that realizes "an emotion which is deep and genuine," but she says that the "danger of romance" (she uses "romance" and the "Romantic" as synonyms) is that "it needs the relief of comedy" (CE 2: 71). Then, in "The Character-mongers and Comedians" section, Woolf says that the grotesque characters of Dickens extend into comedy the exotic strangeness that is an important appeal of Romanticism generally and that she had acknowledged in "The Romantics" section. At the beginning of "The Character-mongers and Comedians" she defines Dickens's grotesques as "characters of extravagant force and character in keeping with our romantic mood":

> If the characters satisfy us by their eccentricity and vigour, London and the landscape of the Dedlocks' place . . . are in the mood of the [Romantic] moor, only more luridly lit up. . . . A great part of the delight of Dickens lies in the sense . . . of wantoning with human beings twice or ten times their natural size or smallness, . . . odd figures seen casually through the half-opened doors of public houses, . . . slinking mysteriously down little alleys. (CE 2: 71-72)

Gone is "the spirit of comedy" which Woolf frequently invokes, like Meredith, in discussing the novel of manners. Dickens's grotesques, she says instead, share "the spirit of exaggeration" (CE 2: 72). Woolf calls these character grotesques of Dickens's "gargoyles."

In her discussion of the grotesque in comedy Woolf uses principles from both Aristotle's theory of comedy and the aesthetics of the Bloomsbury art critic, Roger Fry. Woolf had invoked Aristotle's *Poetics* (without naming it) as early as 1905 in "The Value of Laughter," saying, "The old idea was that comedy represented the failings of human nature, and that tragedy pictured men as greater than they are" (E 1: 58). If we think of Dickens's Mrs. Jellyby and Mr. Turveydrop, Woolf's examples of the comic grotesque in "Phases of Fiction," we see how apt Aristotle's definition of comedy is: "an imitation of characters of a lower type, . . . the Ludicrous being merely a subdivision of the ugly. It consists in some defect or ugliness which is not painful or destructive" (21). Distinguished by their exaggerated "smallness," Woolf adds to Aristotle, "it is impossible to imagine that the Jellybys and the Turveydrops are ever affected by human emotion or that their habitual routine is disturbed" (CE 2: 72).

Woolf goes beyond Aristotle's idea of the grotesque in that she assigns Dickens's "gargoyle" characters an almost mystical role. For Aristotle, the ugly is comic because of its shock effect. We laugh in surprise (and embarrassment) when confronted with a shocking distortion of the normal. Woolf raises Aristotle's example, "the comic mask is ugly and distorted, but does not imply pain" (21), to the level of intuition. Her description of the grotesque makes more understandable to a modern viewer what may seem to be an almost fiendish distortion on ancient Greek comic masks. She sees in the sudden, shocking grotesque actions that define Dickens's "gargoyles" an emblematic power of suggestion like the inscrutability of the comic mask:

> Often we . . . wander off down some strange avenue of suggestion. . . .
> A door is flung open in the misty purlieus of London; there is Mr.
> Tulkinghorn's friend, who appears once and once only, . . . [who]
> "hanged himself." (CE 2: 73)

A good illustration of Woolf's idea of the emblematic grotesque from her own works is Miss Kilman in Mrs. Dalloway. One cannot imagine Doris Kilman being deflected by sympathy for Elizabeth or Clarissa Dalloway from her melodramatic self-absorption or her grotesque religious groveling. Woolf reinforces the idea that the almost mystical reverberations of the grotesque in comedy are akin to the awe that is the effect of the Romantic sublime:

> This sense that the meaning goes on after the words are spoken, that
> doors open and let us look through them, is full of romance. But
> romance in Dickens is impressed on us . . . through extreme types of
> human beings, not through castles or banners, not through violence of
> action, adventure or nature. Human faces, scowling, grinning, malignant, benevolent, are projected at us from every corner. (CE 2: 73)[9]

Since Woolf also says that Dickens's grotesques "have a force, a sublimity" (72), she thinks their effect is analogous to that of the awe-inspiring wild scenes of nature that are part of the Romantic aesthetic of the sublime.

Whenever Woolf identifies a literary effect that depends upon intuition, like the mythic sublimity of Dickens's comic grotesques, she strives either to reconcile the effect with or to distinguish it from Bloomsbury aesthetics of the visual arts, in which intuition is very important. In "Phases of Fiction" she compares the effect of Dickens's comic grotesques to the intuitive pleasure in the design a viewer senses behind the details in a painting. In Roger Fry: A Biography Woolf discusses this principle of intuited design. Quoting Fry's *Vision and Design*, she notes that the Post-Impressionists "do not seek to imitate form, but to create form." They "make images which by the clearness of their logical structure . . . appeal to our disinterested and contemplative imagination" (*RF* 177-78). Woolf says in "Phases of Fiction" that Dickens's emblematic comic grotesques analogously "serve as stationary points in the flow and confusion of the narrative. . . . They uphold the extraordinary intricacy of the plot in whose confusion we are often sunk" (*CE* 2: 72). Woolf goes on to describe the intuited mythic or primal permanence of Dickens's comic grotesques in terms of visual structural support: "The prevailing impression is one of movement, of the endless ebb and flow of life round one or two stationary points" (*CE* 2: 73). Thus, in her treatment of the grotesque Woolf transforms into a literary function Fry's idea that an artist *creates* rather than imitates a form whose primal appeal must be intuited.

Some of Woolf's most original thinking about comedy appears in her definition of the humor of a quirky zaniness of personality in the "The Satirists and Fantastics" section of "Phases of Fiction," where she contrasts the appeal of Thomas Love Peacock and Laurence Sterne, both of whose comic effects keep the author as wit and jokester in the forefront of the reader's consciousness. Woolf does not deal with satire definitively in discussing "Satirists" any more than she dealt definitively with "comedy" or "character" in the second section; she ignores bitter satire like Swift's, for example. Instead, she uses Peacock's qualities as a satirist the more clearly to highlight Sterne's differences from him, as a "Fantastic." Peacock's "satire" is more gentle parody: "it is close enough to be a parody of our world and to make our own follies and the solemnity of our institutions look a little silly" (*CE* 2: 90). Outwardly, Peacock's world would seem to have the simplicity of the world of the comic novel of manners, except that we are not immersed in his world, as we are in Jane Austen's (or in Woolf's in *To the Lighthouse*). Instead, we have a keen "sense of his own personality" (*CE* 2: 91). Peacock the satirist "has the leisure to play with his mind freely, ironically. His sympathies are not deeply engaged"—and neither are ours. "His sense of humour is not submerged" (*CE* 2: 90).

In discussing Peacock's characters, Woolf qualifies her rejection in "The Novels of George Meredith," published the year before "Phases of Fiction," of characters that are neoclassical stereotypes—a condemnation that is part of the second stage of her idea of comedy. Peacock's humor inheres in his characters that are "ridiculously and grotesquely simplified out of all knowledge"; they have "the sharpness of a caricature" (*CE* 2: 90). Since the oversimplification of characters into stereotypes is a trait for which

Woolf castigated Meredith, she seems to mean here that pleasure in a caricature that exaggerates the *uniqueness* of the original is justifiable. Woolf's examples are from Peacock's *Crotchet Castle*, but one also thinks of his caricatures of Shelley and Byron in *Nightmare Abbey*. Oversimplification into character "types," in the manner of eighteenth-century stage comedy, however, is a flaw. In this same paragraph Woolf admits the pratfall-level humor of farce, confirming that for her, this satirical "phase" of the novel combines an entertainment level of comedy with artistry in the style: Peacock's world always offers "some amusing contretemps, such as the cook setting herself alight and being put out by the footman, to make us laugh" (*CE* 2: 90).

The planning notes for what became "Phases of Fiction" in the Monk's House Papers suggest that Woolf from the start conceived of a kind of comedy in which the reader is so charmed by the fantastic wit of the writer that she relaxes her expectations of believability in character and coherence in plot. Peacock was in Woolf's plans from the beginning, in a category called "Satire" in an informal list headed "Different things" to be considered. In Woolf's early plans the "Satire" category is alternately called "The Stylists." An unnumbered manuscript page headed "The Stylists" (between Monk's House B6b.4 and 5) has nothing directly to do with comedy or satire, but there Woolf mentions *Tristram Shandy* for the first time and develops the idea that writers whose style is remarkable inscribe their personalities in it—as she manages to inscribe both Vita Sackville-West's and her own personalities in *Orlando*. This notion persists in the published "Satirists and Fantastics" section: "Peacock pervades his book" and "Laurence Sterne is the most important character" in *Tristram Shandy* (*CE* 2: 92, 93).

In "Phases of Fiction," Woolf's "fantastic" category of humor subject to no controls but the personality of the writer goes beyond Forster to incorporate T. S. Eliot's admiration for metaphysical wit in poetry, which he defines as elaborating a conceit "to the furthest stage to which ingenuity can carry it . . . by rapid association of thought" requiring "considerable agility on the part of the reader" (Eliot 282). The breadth of Sterne's content and the ludicrousness of his digressions are similar to the vast "field of play" of the metaphysical poets. Perhaps Woolf's respect for the complex wit of Modernism leads her to say that Sterne's is "a much subtler mind, a mind of far greater reach and intensity" than Peacock's (*CE* 2: 92). Moreover, it is not a giant leap from Sterne, fascinated with his own mental associations and spawning outrageous digressions, to the streams of consciousness of Stephen Dedalus and Septimus Smith, also manifestations of "metaphysical" wit, one might say.

Woolf accepts Sterne's own words to describe his achievement in characterization, her prime criterion for excellence: "His claim is just when he says that however widely he may digress, . . . still 'the drawing of my Uncle Toby's character went on gently all the time . . . so that you are much better acquainted with my Uncle Toby now than you were before'" (*CE* 2: 92; Sterne has "than you *was* before" 55). Eliot's idea of metaphysical wit is analogous to the complexity with which Woolf says Uncle Toby's "modesty" and Sterne's personality highlight one another: "One relishes the simplicity, the modesty, of Uncle Toby all the more for comparing them with the witty, indecent, disagreeable, yet highly sympathetic character of the author" (*CE* 2: 93).

The Sterne paragraphs bring to light a relationship Woolf seems to recognize between the complexity of characterization by way of stream of consciousness and the wit of capturing a real person's personality in a fictional character, while showing the author's amusement with facets of that personality. Having successfully deployed stream of consciousness in *Jacob's Room, Mrs. Dalloway,* and *To the Lighthouse,* Woolf may have thought of *Tristram Shandy* as a model for developing *Orlando*'s freer, more playful kind of Modernism in characterization. Just as Sterne's "own mind . . . fascinates him, its oddities and its whims," may it not also be said that Vita's own mind fascinates Virginia, "its oddities and its whims," and that it colors *Orlando* and "gives it walls and shape"?

A more mature "humor of the heights" than in "The Value of Laughter" marks the fourth stage of Woolf's idea of comedy, from 1935 to 1941. Her earlier desired effect of joviality and magnanimity now becomes "joy." Meredith's civilizing influence of the comic spirit now seems realized most completely for Woolf in William Congreve's stage comedies; from them we receive the joviality and magnanimity that Woolf finds wanting in most of her contemporaries, even James Joyce (*E* 3: 34). Woolf says in the 1937 essay, "Congreve's Comedies," that the sheer "beauty" of Congreve's plays issues from a miraculous synthesis of inclusiveness and completeness, which seems to be a development of the "humour of the heights" and "the whole of life viewed as a panorama" in "The Value of Laughter" thirty-two years earlier. She writes the aging Lady Ottoline Morrell, convalescing after a stroke, "I'm doing Congreve now. If you want sheer joy, read him" (*L* 6: 141).

Woolf still insists upon artistry in the fourth stage of her idea of comedy, but beauty of design is not enough. The large panoramic view of "The Value of Laughter" now must produce complexity of vision and inclusiveness in the portrayal of society. As with Shakespeare, Woolf says in "Congreve's Comedies," "the more slowly we read" Congreve, "the more meaning we find, the more beauty we discover" (*CE* 1: 82). She loses interest in the "satire" that had interested her in Peacock and reflects in her *Diary* on 6 May 1935, "the more complex a vision the less it lends itself to satire; the more it understands the less it is able to sum up & make linear. For example: Shre [Shakespeare] and Dostoevsky neither of them satirise" (D 4: 309). Similarly, a novel of manners that aims no higher than following the conventions, even if artistically crafted, cannot keep her interest, because of its superficiality. In the same 1935 journal entry, while reading Howard Sturgis's 1904 novel *Belchamber*, Woolf writes, "If a writer accepts the conventions, . . . he can produce an effect of symmetry: very pleasant, suggestive; but only on the surface. That is, I cant care what happens yet I like the design" (D 4: 309).[10]

In "Congreve's Comedies" the complexity of vision Woolf now prefers combines her permanent comic value of an appeal to common sense with some of the outrageousness she had relished in the "fantastic" of Sterne. In reading Congreve, she says, "Tossed up on the crest of some wonderful extravagance of humour, . . . we come slap against hard common sense" (CE 1: 78). Going beyond the drawing room to include the common people is also a requirement for the best comedy. Woolf says that Congreve surpasses eighteenth- and nineteenth-century comedians of manners in the completeness and inclusiveness of the world he magically summons up:

> We have only to compare Congreve's comedy with Goldsmith's or with Sheridan's, let alone with Wilde's, to be aware that if . . . we confine him to a room, not a world, that room is not the drawing room. . . . Drays roar on the cobbles beneath. . . . There is . . . an extravagance of humour . . . which cast[s] us back to the Elizabethans. (CE 1: 79)

The whole of a Congreve play is "not merely dazzling": "We notice here a sudden depth beneath the surface, a meaning not grasped but felt. . . . It has a coarseness, a humour something like Shakespeare's . . . a lightning swiftness . . . that snatches a dozen meanings and compacts them into one" (CE 1: 78).

As Melba Cuddy-Keane eloquently demonstrates in "The Politics of Comic Modes in Virginia Woolf's *Between the Acts*," in her last novel Woolf exercises a subversive kind of comedy by moving from a conventional model of society with respected leaders to a more communal, all-encompassing model. This reading of the novel is consistent with the facets of the fourth stage of Woolf's idea of comedy in "Congreve's Comedies"—complexity of vision, depth of understanding, and a model of society in which all are tolerated and all participate. Further, I suspect that the "extravagant" element Woolf relishes in Congreve may be the source of her impulse to portray an undisciplined pageant instead of a polished play and to privilege what happens *between* the acts,[11] just as, inspired by Sterne's ability to turn *Tristram Shandy* to the shape of his own personality, Woolf inscribes *both* her personality and Vita Sackville-West's in the form of *Orlando*.

Of course, there is a world of difference between a Congreve stage comedy and *Between the Acts*. "Ludic comedy" is the term Cuddy-Keane proposes for Woolf's last novel because of its resistance to closure in the plot or in the model of society (283). It remains to be completed by us, the audience. This seems the very antithesis of the "completeness" of the world Woolf praises in Congreve. However, in *Between the Acts* perhaps Woolf is playfully revising Congreve's "completeness" in comedy, just as in *To the Lighthouse* she teases us by reminding us of the conventions of the novel of manners, then overturns them. In drawing in readers to contribute to the vision of an inclusive society in *Between the Acts*, Woolf redefines the "completeness" that is a criterion of her fourth stage of comedy.

Works Cited

Aristotle. *The Poetics*. Trans. S. H. Butcher. *Aristotle's Theory of Poetry and Fine Art* by S. H. Butcher. 2nd ed. London: Macmillan and Co., 1898.

Bell, Quentin. *Virginia Woolf: A Biography*. 2 vols. New York: Harcourt, 1972.

Bieman, Elizabeth. *William Shakespeare: The Romances*. Boston: Twayne-G. K. Hall, 1990.

Bowers, Bege K., and Barbara Brothers. "Introduction: What Is a Novel of Manners?" *Reading and Writing Women's Lives: A Study of the Novel of Manners*. Ed. Bowers and Brothers. Ann Arbor: UMI Research P, 1990. 1-17.

Cuddy-Keane, Melba. "The Politics of Comic Modes in Virginia Woolf's *Between the Acts*." *PMLA* 105.2 (Mar. 1990): 273-85.

Dimock, Wai-Chee. "Feminism, New Historicism, and the Reader." *American Literature* 63.4 (1991): 601-22.

Eliot, T. S. "The Metaphysical Poets." 1921. *Selected Essays*. London: Faber and Faber, 1951. 281-91.

Forster, E. M. *Aspects of the Novel*. 1927. New York: Harcourt, 1955.

Fry, Roger. *Vision and Design*. 1920. Ed. J. B. Bullen. London and New York: Oxford UP, 1990.

Greenblatt, Stephen. "Towards a Poetics of Culture." *The New Historicism*. Ed. H. Aram Veeser. New York and London: Routledge, 1989. 1-14.

Harmon, William, and C. Hugh Holman. *A Handbook to Literature*. 7th ed. Upper Saddle River, NJ: Prentice-Hall, 1996.

Heilman, Robert Bechtold. *The Ways of the World: Comedy and Society*. Seattle and London: U of Washington P, 1978.

Hussey, Mark. "'I Rejected; We Substituted': Self and Society in *Between the Acts*." *Reading and Writing Women's Lives*. Ed. Bege K. Bowers and Barbara Brothers. Ann Arbor: UMI Research P, 1990. 141-52.

Little, Judy. *Comedy and the Woman Writer: Woolf, Spark, and Feminism*. Lincoln: U of Nebraska P, 1983.

Mares, Cheryl. "Reading Proust: Woolf and the Painter's Perspective." *The Multiple Muses of Virginia Woolf*. Ed. Diane Gillespie. Columbia: U of Missouri P, 1993. 58-89.

Marshall, Denise M. "Intimate Alien: Virginia Woolf and the Comedy of Knowledge and the Comedy of Power." Ph.D. Diss. Bowling Green: Bowling Green State U, 1985.

Meredith, George. *An Essay on Comedy and the Uses of the Comic Spirit*. 1897. Ed. Lane Cooper. Port Washington and London: Kennikat, 1972.

Michaels, Walter Benn. *The Gold Standard and the Logic of Naturalism: American Literature at the Turn of the Century*. Berkeley: U of California P, 1987.

Rosenberg, Beth Carole. *Virginia Woolf and Samuel Johnson: Common Readers*. New York: St. Martin's, 1995.

Schweickart, Patrocinio P. "Reading Ourselves: Toward a Feminist Theory of Reading." *Gender and Reading: Essays on Readers, Texts, and Contexts*. Ed. Elizabeth A. Flynn and P. P. Schweickart. Baltimore: Johns Hopkins UP, 1986. 31-62.

Sterne, Laurence. *The Life and Opinions of Tristram Shandy, Gentleman*. New York: Liveright, 1942.

Thomas, Brook. *The New Historicism and Other Old-Fashioned Topics*. Princeton: Princeton UP, 1991.

Woolf, Leonard. *Sowing: An Autobiography of the Years 1880-1904*. New York: Harcourt, 1960.

Woolf, Virginia. *Collected Essays*. Ed. Leonard Woolf. 4 vols. New York: Harcourt, 1967.

———. *The Diary of Virginia Woolf*. Ed. Anne Olivier Bell. 5 vols. New York: Harcourt, 1979-85.

———. *The Essays of Virginia Woolf*. Ed. Andrew McNeillie. Vols. 1, 3, and 4. London: Hogarth, 1986-94.

———. *The Essays of Virginia Woolf*. Ed. Andrew McNeillie. Vol. 2. San Diego: Harcourt, 1987.

———. *The Letters of Virginia Woolf.* Ed. Nigel Nicolson and Joanne Trautmann. 6 vols. New York: Harcourt, 1975-80.

———. Manuscripts of "Phases of Fiction." Monk's House Papers. University of Sussex. Falmer, Sussex, England.

———. *Moments of Being.* Ed. Jeanne Schulkind. 2nd ed. San Diego: Harcourt, 1985.

———. Reading Notebooks. Monks House Papers. University of Sussex. Falmer, Sussex, England.

———. *Roger Fry: A Biography.* 1940. New York: Harcourt, 1968.

———. *To the Lighthouse.* 1927. New York: Harcourt, 1989.

———. *Walter Sickert: A Conversation.* London: Hogarth, 1934.

Notes

1. My New Historical approach is appropriate to discussing Woolf's developing idea of comedy throughout her life, but I do not try to write cultural history or cultural poetics out of Woolf's scattered remarks on comedy in the sense of Stephen Greenblatt or Walter Benn Michaels's widely familiar New Historicism. Brook Thomas is helpful in warning against the tendency toward such global models in their New Historicism (6-10). My focus on Woolf's concern for the common reader guards against the danger Wai-Chee Dimock usefully warns against in New Historicism—that of ignoring feminine realities. Denise Marshall's feminist approach documents Woolf's use of comedy to serve the concerns of feminine readers.

2. Elizabeth Bieman says that "all's well that ends well" characterizes the effect of Shakespeare's late romances (2). Robert Heilman observes that comedy can produce a subtle "sense of well-being" (248).

3. Leonard Woolf credits G. E. Moore with removing from the eyes of his generation of young men in the "Cambridge Apostles" the "cobwebs" of Victorian values, "substituting" for the philosophical "delusions . . . in which . . . Christ, . . . Kant, and Hegel had entangled us, the fresh air and pure light" of common sense (161). Virginia Woolf's description in "Character in Fiction" of a Georgian writer's cook character being "a creature of sunshine and fresh air" (*E* 3:422) echoes Leonard Woolf's diction in his description of Moore's shaping of the Bloomsbury Cambridge men's outlook.

   Beth Carole Rosenberg analyzes Woolf's transformation of the concept of the common reader from Samuel Johnson, through Leslie Stephen's *Hours in a Library*, into her own practice of criticism (1-22).

4.   Woolf begins the review that immediately follows "The Value of Laughter" in
     Andrew McNeillie's edition of her *Essays* and was written the same month with
     this reference to *Diana of the Crossways*: "'A witty woman', says George
     Meredith, 'is a treasure; a witty beauty is a power'" (*E* 1:61).
5.   Harmon and Holman's *Handbook to Literature* describes the comedy of manners
     as "the realistic, often satirical, comedy of the restoration" and also its "revival
     in modified form . . . a hundred years later by Goldsmith and Sheridan" and
     again "late in the nineteenth century" by Wilde. They say that its social arena
     seems almost indistinguishable from that of the novel of manners (107-8).
6.   Mark Hussey gives examples of the novel of manners from Woolf's own work,
     saying in his study of *Between the Acts* that characters like Mrs. Manressa and,
     in *To the Lighthouse*, Mrs. Ramsay, "smooth society's rough edges" and "promote
     moments of harmony" (142).
7.   E. M. Forster also classes Sterne and Woolf together in his "Fantasy" lecture,
     along with Peacock, Melville, Joyce, Lawrence, and Swift—novelists for
     whom the "fantastic-prophetical axis" is "essential" (158). In Forster's "Intro-
     ductory" lecture he compares *Tristram Shandy* and "The Mark on the Wall" as
     the writings of "fantasists," and he also mentions *To the Lighthouse* (34-41).
         The intensity with which Woolf felt involved in playful dialogue with
     Forster no doubt contributed to her difficulty in refusing her own "full term"
     series of Clark Lectures when Cambridge University offered them in 1932.
     She envisioned the six sections of "Phases of Fiction," where so much of her
     thinking about comedy occurs, as capable of being transformed into the
     lectures. (The fact that Woolf's father Leslie Stephen gave the first Clark
     lectures in 1881 also contributed to her reluctance to give them up: "Father
     would have blushed with pleasure could I have told him . . . that his
     daughter—my poor little Ginny—was to be asked to succeed him" [*D* 4:79].)
     Woolf had decided logically to refuse the lectures because accepting would
     have meant "giving up a year to criticism, . . . perhaps shelving another novel,"
     but four days later she was still "upset because the devil whispered . . . that I
     have six lectures written in Phases of Fiction; & could furbish them up &
     deliver the Clark lectures, & win the esteem of my sex" [it was "the first time
     a woman has been asked"], with a few weeks of work (*D* 4:79). Leonard Woolf
     dissuaded her, perhaps unaware of the intense appeal to Virginia of the
     chance to continue her interplay with Forster in the same forum in which he
     had opened it. Clinging to the idea of "Phases of Fiction" as a conversation,
     she labored on for another two years and eight months; in October 1934,
     she gave it first the form of a dialogue and then entitled it "A Discourse for
     4 Voices" (*D* 4: 251n; Monk's House B2m).

8. "The Truth-tellers," "The Romantics," "The Character-mongers and Comedians," "The Psychologists," "The Satirists and Fantastics," and "The Poets."

9. Judy Little recognizes the ancient, "mythic" figures of the Ramsays in *To the Lighthouse* as having an emblematic power and sees Woolf's parody of Ramsay as part of a comic undercutting of their mythic patriarchal roles (58-61). However, the Ramsays are too fully realized to fit Woolf's description of exaggeratedly small grotesques, whose emblematic suggestiveness comes rather from the sketchiness of their characterizations.

10. This insight into inadequacies of Fry's formalism as a measure of the excellence of a literary work ("I like the design" D 4: 309) may have developed as a result of Woolf's writing "Walter Sickert: A Conversation" the year before. There she defended the "human interest" and story-telling qualities of Sickert's paintings against the formalist charge that such qualities were irrelevant to aesthetic excellence. Cheryl Mares notes that by the 1930s Woolf "clung to a distinction between form in painting" and in the novel that allowed portrayal of the fictional self "engaged in human relationships, in a community, in history" (89, 81), unlike the abstract formal considerations of Post-Impressionist painting.

11. Cuddy-Keane observes parenthetically that the scenes of the pageant in *Between the Acts* depict "the history of English comedy" (280).

A Haunted House: Ghostly Presences in Woolf's Essays and Early Fiction

George M. Johnson

Virginia Woolf's most famous essays are those polemical ones in which she attacks her Edwardian predecessors, evolves her own aesthetic position, and ostensibly champions a Modernist aesthetic. The number of times that Woolf elaborated on these topics and the number of venues in which she placed these essays confirm the seriousness of her purpose in promulgating her views. Subsequently, these essays, particularly "Modern Novels," "Mr. Bennett and Mrs. Brown," "Character in Fiction," and "Modern Fiction," have been taken up by innumerable critics and literary historians as the keystone to discussions of drastic changes in the novel; as Douglas Hewitt claims, her statements have become a *locus classicus* of Modernist criticism (7). However successful in galvanizing opinion about the novel, these essays and the ways in which they have been used have contributed to the distorting of literary history. In them, Woolf severely misrepresents the fiction of her immediate predecessors, whom she labels the Edwardians, by making generalizations about them that cannot be substantiated.

Admittedly, Woolf shows some awareness of her manoeuvre, claiming in "Mr. Bennett and Mrs. Brown" that she will "reduce Edwardian fiction to a view" (*E* 3: 385). This she proceeds to do by reducing the Edwardian camp to Arnold Bennett, principally, along with H. G. Wells and John Galsworthy,[1] and ranging them against the Georgians, limited to Forster, Lawrence, Strachey, Joyce, and T. S. Eliot. Provocatively she asserts in "Character in Fiction" that "on or about December 1910 human character changed" and that "the men and women who began writing novels in 1910 or thereabouts had this great difficulty to face—that there was no English novelist living from whom they could learn their business" (*E* 3: 421, 427).

Rather flippantly she excludes Conrad because of his Polish origins and Hardy because he ceased writing novels in 1895 (*E* 3: 427). For the purposes of her argument, Woolf's limited view of the Edwardians is crucial, but she never admits of alternatives to this view. However, examination of several of her relatively obscure essays on the supernatural demonstrate that she was aware of alternatives to the Bennett-Wells-Galsworthy type of realism in the fiction of her immediate predecessors and provide evidence that she drew on these forms of expression in her own work, beginning with her early fiction and continuing into her Modernist works. In particular the essays "Before Midnight," "Across the Border," and "Henry James's Ghost Stories" provide insight into the evolving aesthetic aims later achieved in her fiction.

But first it is necessary to summarize the nature of Woolf's criticism of the Edwardians, as well as some of the motivations prompting them. Most significantly, Woolf certainly objected to the methodology of the Edwardian novel, though she found it difficult to state precisely what she meant by that, terming it variously ill-fitting design, inadequate outline of form, generalized characters, and outmoded conventions of character creation.[2] In only one, later version of the essays— "Character in Fiction"—does she draw a single novel of Arnold Bennett's to illustrate her criticism. Citing passages from *Hilda Lessways* to demonstrate that Bennett spends more lines in describing his character's surroundings and the house in which she lives than in providing insight into her psyche, Woolf clarifies what she views as the problem here—the Edwardians' use of an outmoded, artificial convention to establish a meaningful connection with their readers: "House property was the common ground from which the Edwardians found it easy to proceed to intimacy" (*E* 3: 431). Notably and to her credit Woolf does not advocate using any one particular form or a specifically experimental form, claiming in "Modern Fiction" that "Any method is right, every method is right, that expresses what we wish to express, if we are writers" (*CR* 1: 125). Second, Woolf not only criticizes the Edwardians' methodology, but she also definitely attacks their choice of subject matter, inextricably bound together as these are, a point ignored by most commentators on these essays. She indicts the Edwardians as materialists who "write of unimportant things" (*CR* 1: 210) such as houses and institutions, and who provide detailed social critiques. She wants them to deepen their insights into character and thus to expand the range of subject matter, concluding in "Modern Fiction" that "'[t]he proper stuff of fiction' does not exist; everything is the proper stuff of fiction, every feeling, every thought; every quality of brain and spirit is drawn upon; no perception comes amiss" (*CR* 1: 218). Third, Woolf employs, and does so consistently, "spiritual" or ethereal terminology rather than the terms of psychological realism, such as "stream of consciousness," to convey the element missing from Edwardian fiction.[3] Beginning in "Modern Novels," Woolf describes the "soul" of English fiction as benefiting from a rejection of the Edwardians, Joyce as "spiritual," and the Russians as revering the "human spirit." The chief task of the novelist is to convey "this incessantly varying spirit" (E 3: 33). In "Mr. Bennett and Mrs. Brown," Woolf introduces Mrs. Brown as the archetypal character or vision that the novelist attempts to capture. She is imaged as "a will-o'-the-wisp," a "flying spirit," and that imagery is developed further in "Character in Fiction" where she is "that surprising apparition" and "the spirit we live by, life itself" (E 3: 436). This imagery imbues Mrs. Brown with a supernatural quality.

Woolf's various motivations for writing the essays help explain some of these features. Though presented as literary history, these essays are not really concerned with accurate literary history at all. Bennett's type of realism had made her feel uneasy as early as 1916 (Daugherty 269), but from "Mr. Bennett and Mrs. Brown" on she was certainly reacting to Bennett's claim of her novel *Jacob's Room* that the characters do not vitally survive in the mind. As Daugherty has shown (273), she was also indirectly responding to sexist remarks made by Bennett. Not surprisingly, Arnold Bennett is the main target of her criticism, since as she admits in two versions the label of "materialist" strikes wide of the mark for both Wells and Galsworthy (E 3: 32; CR 1: 209).

It might also be argued that Woolf was championing Modernism as a whole, except that she provides few actual references to Modernist works and when she does, as with Joyce, she demonstrates considerable ambivalence towards his work, claiming in "Modern Novels" that it fails because of "the comparative poverty of the writer's mind" (E 3: 34). Astonishingly, she never allows that the Georgians have been successful, instead asserting in "Character in Fiction" that she has sought to excuse them and their presentation of the truth in a "rather an exhausted and chaotic condition" (E 3: 435).[4] Much more significantly, as I shall argue, Woolf was concerned with charting and to some extent defending her own individual approach to the writing of fiction. In doing this she most certainly succumbed to the anxiety of influence. Perry Meisel has made a convincing case that Woolf felt the anxiety of influence of Walter Pater, to whom she rarely refers in her work, and a similar sort of anxiety seems to permeate these essays. Not only does she fail to give adequate due to the Georgians she does mention, but she completely suppresses mention of more immediate, female rivals, including May Sinclair, who by 1919 was famous for her psychological novels and more recently for her experimentation with this form, Dorothy Richardson, and Katherine Mansfield. Crucial to this project is her exaggeration of the Georgians' break from the past[5] and her suppression of an alternative tradition that had begun to explore the semitransparent envelope of consciousness, as well as to expand its borders, from the late-Victorian era through the Edwardian age.

A significant number of late-Victorian and Edwardian writers *were* much more concerned with portraying the spiritual element of character than the material. Not only did they probe the dark places of psychology, but they explored extensions of the powers of the human mind in such phenomena as telepathy, hypnosis, extrasensory perception, prevision, and psychic possession. Furthermore, they often managed to do this convincingly within the conventional thirty-two chapter form of the novel, though some began to experiment with viewpoint. Among the many writers who began to tap this vein are Algernon Blackwood, Marjorie Bowen, Wilkie Collins, Walter de la Mare, William de Morgan, George Du Maurier, Lord Dunsany, Henry James, Rudyard Kipling, Vernon Lee, Arthur Machen, Elinor Mordaunt, Barry Pain, May Sinclair, and Oscar Wilde. A number of these achieved considerable prominence or popularity during their time.

This fiction was sometimes labelled "psychical" and was frequently considered to be a branch of supernatural fiction. An important influence on writers of it was the Society for Psychical Research, formed in 1882 by mainly Cambridge-educated intellectuals influenced by the revival of philosophical idealism in the 1870s. The Society's main aim was to test the hypothesis that personality survived bodily death, and it did so by examining the evidence from abnormal psychology on such topics as hysteria and hypnosis as well as psychical or supernatural phenomena. Through its *Journal* and *Proceedings* along with articles in the public press, the Society consequently introduced to a varied English audience the latest developments in psychiatry and psychology, including Pierre Janet's, William James's, Frederic Myers's, Freud's and Jung's, all of whom were members of the Society. Perhaps more importantly, it shaped the perceived significance and interpretation of this material. A number of the aforementioned novelists were introduced to psychological developments in the context of psychical research and thus did not make rigid distinctions between fields that have subsequently diverged significantly. Elsewhere I have suggested how Woolf might have become aware of some of these ideas through friends of her father Leslie Stephen and, later, her friendships with the Stracheys. It is worth mentioning here, though, that Leslie Stephen had been a member of the Society for Psychical Research before becoming an agnostic (Rosenbaum 110), and he remained a friend of several of its members, notably its

president, Henry Sidgwick, and secretary, Edmund Gurney. With characteristic ambivalence toward her father and his ideas, Woolf seems to have
adopted a position of agnosticism herself while tentatively exploring in her
essays and fiction psychical phenomena suggestive of a nonmaterial realm.
In this attitude she may have found a kindred spirit in James Strachey, who
had a considerable interest in psychical phenomena before taking up psychoanalysis. At the very least, Woolf shared an affinity with the psychical
novelists in that she blended the psychological and psychical, although she
preferred otherworldly language of ghosts, ghostliness, and spirits and even
diction with closer religious connotations such as spirit and soul over clinical
labels such as hysteria and shell shock. Though by definition the supernatural is that which transcends the natural, Woolf envisioned the supernatural
as integral to natural experience.

   That she was aware of the psychical tradition in literature cannot be
doubted after surveying her review essays, particularly those on psychical
subjects. Though Woolf demonstrated a good deal of ambivalence toward
contemporary fiction[6] and claimed that her knowledge of it was "perfectly
haphazard and nebulous" (E 2: 257), she displays an impressive knowledge
of the fiction of her immediate predecessors and contemporaries. In literally
dozens of reviews she assessed novelists ranging from the long-forgotten,
such as W. E. Tirebuck and W. E. Norris, to those now being rediscovered,
including Elizabeth Robins, from aging genre writers to emerging Modernists and canonized writers. More to the point, from 1907 on she reviewed
writers of psychical fiction, including Marjorie Bowen, Vernon Lee, Elinor
Mordaunt, Walter de la Mare, Oliver Onions, and Henry James (though not
necessarily their works of this nature) as well as demonstrating knowledge
of others such as E. F. Benson and Anthony Hope.

   The tradition of the supernatural overlapping with the fantastic has
typically been split off from the mainstream of English fiction and its importance suppressed, despite its being taken up by mainstream practitioners of
the novel from Charles Dickens to George Eliot to Henry James. It might be
argued that Woolf ignored this tradition in her attacks on the Edwardian novel
because of the tendency of critics to consider it in a separate category as genre
fiction, but if so Woolf was going against her own critical principles since she
disliked the rigid categorization of literature and criticized academics for
doing so in reviews of their books.[7] Three of her essays on supernatural topics
reveal more clearly her attitude toward fiction of the unseen and why she chose
not to bring it forward in her more famous essays on the novel.

   The first, a March 1917 review essay of Elinor Mordaunt's collection
of short stories *Before Midnight*, predates her polemical essays on the Edwar-

dians. Woolf's opening confession of "two, perhaps unreasonable, prejudices: we do not like the war in fiction, and we do not like the supernatural"
(E 2: 87) might suggest that there is no need to probe the influence any
further. However, a number of critics have shown the importance of the war
in her fiction and the same can and needs to be done for the supernatural.
Woolf goes on to suggest what she means by the supernatural, claiming,

> Nobody can deny that our life is largely at the mercy of dreams and
> visions which we cannot account for logically; on the contrary, if Mrs.
> Mordaunt had devoted every page of her book to the discovery of some
> of these uncharted territories of the mind we should have nothing but
> thanks for her. But we feel a little aggrieved when the writers who are
> capable of such delicate work resort instead to the methods of the
> conjuror and ask us to be satisfied with a trick. (E 2: 87)

By "methods of the conjuror" and "tricks" Woolf would appear to be
objecting to manifestations imposed on characters from the outside, plot
contrivances, *deus ex machina*, and the like. For example she criticizes the
dragging in of the god Pan in place of an analysis of the protagonist's state
of mind in one story. Her encouragement and praise is reserved for explorations of "uncharted territories of the mind," "those curious hidden things
in human life" naturally observed by Mordaunt (E 2: 87-88).

Woolf elaborates on the distinction in another piece predating her
"Edwardian" essays and just as crucial to understanding her aesthetic aims, a
January 1918 review entitled "Across the Border" of Dorothy Scarborough's
pioneering study, *The Supernatural in Modern English Fiction*. This book presents an
exhaustive survey of the rise of supernatural fiction from about 1887 on, though
it also sketches in earlier sources beginning with Gothic romance. The book is
organized according to subjects, which range from modern ghosts to the devil,
metempsychosis, dream-supernaturalism, hypnotism, spiritualism, and psychical research. In reviewing the book, Woolf took note that Scarborough
included "stories about abnormal states of mind" as well as those that are "strictly
supernatural" though, like Scarborough, she did not define "supernatural."
Unlike Scarborough, Woolf did, however, probe motivations for writing and
reading supernatural fiction. According to Woolf, "the fear which we get from
reading ghost stories of the supernatural is a refined and spiritualised essence
of fear. It is a fear which we can examine and play with. Far from despising
ourselves for being frightened by a ghost story we are proud of this proof of
sensibility, and perhaps unconsciously welcome the chance for the licit gratification of certain instincts which we are wont to treat as outlaws" (E 2: 218).

The attraction Woolf evinces here is for those stories which produce fear using the necessary element of reality and do not exaggerate their effects. Though the craving for the supernatural remains strong, the choice of subject matter and the means of evoking fear must change direction, toward "those ghosts which are living within ourselves. The great increase of the psychical ghost story in late years, to which Miss Scarborough bears witness, testifies to the fact that our sense of our own ghostliness has much quickened. A rational age is succeeded by one which seeks the supernatural in the soul of man, and the development of psychical research offers a basis of disputed fact for this desire to feed upon" (E 2: 218-19).

The strength of Woolf's conviction in these views is suggested in the fact that she takes issue with Henry James, whom she greatly admired, about the merits of the modern psychical story. Whereas he had disparaged its anesthetic quality, its respectable laboratory certification, she praises the new type, claiming that it "has justified its existence by rousing, if not 'the dear old sacred terror', still a very effective modern representative" (E 2: 219). Nevertheless, she omits to mention any examples more modern than Henry James's *The Turn of the Screw*. Instead Woolf continues to underline her main point, that it is not the external manifestations of ghosts that we are afraid of but the extension of our own fields of perception, "of a state of mind which is profoundly mysterious and terrifying" (E 2: 219). These statements suggest very strongly the focus of Woolf's attention—the ghosts of the mind and untracked desires—that she was beginning to transform into her own fiction. One of her concluding remarks in this essay makes the connection with her fiction even clearer. She says, "a vast amount of fiction both in prose and in verse now assures us that the world to which we shut our eyes is far more friendly and inviting, more beautiful by day and more holy by night, than the world which we persist in thinking the real world." This sentence alludes to the theme that Woolf was exploring in the writing of her second novel, and the phrasing even echoes its title, *Night and Day*. She adds that "there exists a group of writers who have the sense of the unseen" without employing mythological figures, but again, elusively and frustratingly, does not cite any names (E 2: 220).

This omission is striking since Scarborough's book would have introduced Woolf to most of her immediate predecessors working in the supernatural and psychical, including all of the writers mentioned above.[8] One cannot but wonder whether Woolf's curiosity would have been aroused by the discussion of spirits of dead mothers in the section on ghostly psychology (Scarborough 110). Also, among the numerous references to the highly regarded supernatural writer, Algernon Blackwood, is a discussion of his story "Clairvoyance" in which the protagonist sees his dead mother return to him among a multitude of spirits of unborn children (Scarborough 289). Woolf need have looked no further for Edwardian models of presenting the psychical in fiction than Blackwood, since his *The Centaur* (1911), for example, deals with a voyage undergone within the protagonist's mind. But she would also have learned of more famous examples (if she was not already aware of them), including the extent of H. G. Wells's contribution to "supernatural science" as Scarborough terms it and even a foray of Arnold Bennett's into the field, *The Ghost*, discussed in the context of fiction about jealous ghosts (Scarborough 117). Scarborough also presents evidence of the importance of findings of the Society of Psychical Research in this literature, claiming, for example, that Henry James's *The Turn of the Screw* was based on an incident reported to the Society (204). The tone of Woolf's review suggests that she felt an affinity with and may even have been influenced by Scarborough's belief that "[t]he sense of the unearthly is ever with us, even in the most commonplace situations,—and there is nothing so natural to us as the supernatural. Our imagination, coloured by our reading, reveals and transforms the world we live in. We are aware of unbodied emotions about us, of discarnate moods that mock or invite us" (3).[9] Woolf may also have taken heed of or at least have found agreement with Scarborough's statement that there is something ghostly in all great art: "In fact, without the sense of the marvellous, the unreal, the wonderful, the magical, what would poetry mean to us? So we should feel a keen loss in our fiction if all the vague elements of the supernatural were effaced. Absolute realism is the last thing we desire" (227).

Perhaps Woolf's most significant and telling omission of writers who could have and in fact did provide models of psychical fiction for the Georgians, notably Woolf herself, was Henry James, an almost exact contemporary of Thomas Hardy and W. H. Hudson, both of whom she does mention in her polemics on the Edwardians.[10] She might have eliminated James because of his foreign birth, as she did with Conrad, but instead she suppressed mention of him altogether; he is certainly a ghostly presence in these essays, though. Not only did James continue to write through the Edwardian period, but Woolf had certainly read James as early as 1897, highly praised his talents, and reviewed numerous books by or about him, beginning with a review of *The Golden Bowl* in 1905. That she felt some anxiety about his influence is suggested in a 1918 review in which she claims that "Henry James is much at present in the air—a portentous figure looming large and undefined in the consciousness of writers, to some an oppression, to others an obsession, but undeniably present to all" (*E* 2: 346). Interestingly, she also describes James, who had died two years previously, in spiritual terms: "Henry James, whatever else he may have been, was a great writer—a great artist. A priest of the art of writing in his lifetime, he is now among the saints to whom every writer, in particular every novelist, must do homage" (*E* 2: 348).[11]

James's influence on Woolf particularly in the area of fictional technique has been discussed at length, but that he loomed "large and undefined" in Woolf's own consciousness in other ways is further suggested by her review "Henry James's Ghost Stories." Woolf opens the essay by suggesting that James's prefaces should be neglected in order to "keep our own view more distinct" (*E* 3: 319). She illustrates her point by claiming that James's praise of his story "The Great Good Place" is wrong because it is a "failure." The weakness of the story derives from the supernatural, or at least James's sentimental use of it, as the other world into which the protagonist slips is about as exciting as "a celestial rest-cure establishment." One of the risks of using the supernatural is that "it removes the shocks and buffetings of experience," the contrasts and conflicts that generate interest (*E* 3: 320). Woolf suggests that she has become "fundamentally sceptical" of the supernatural but by the supernatural she refers to the old ghosts of Mrs. Radcliffe's novels. She goes on to suggest that new methods are necessary in order to penetrate "our armour of insensibility," and that James has succeeded in discovering them. Whereas a story of James's such as "Owen Wingrave" "misses the mark" because of its incongruous, violent, and sensational use of the supernatural,

> the stories in which Henry James uses the supernatural effectively are, then, those where some quality in a character or in a situation can only be given its fullest meaning by being cut free from facts. Its progress in the unseen world must be closely related to what goes on in this. We must be made to feel that the apparition fits the crisis of passion or of conscience which sent it forth so exactly that the ghost story, besides its virtues as a ghost story, has the additional charm of being also symbolical. (*E* 3: 324)

Woolf adds to this important prescription that "Henry James's ghosts have nothing in common with the violent old ghosts—the blood-stained sea captains, the white horses, the headless ladies of dark lanes and windy commons. They have their origin within us" (*E* 3: 324). She points out that both "Sir Edmund Orme" and *The Turn of the Screw* succeed according to these criteria. She also makes the interesting point that James's move from the natural to the supernatural is almost imperceptible since, for example, in his novel *The Wings of the Dove* Milly "goes on with her work after death" in the relationship of Kate and Densher: James's "characters with their extreme fineness of perception are already half-way out of the body" (*E* 3: 322). Woolf closes the essay by claiming, "We must admit that Henry James has conquered" (*E* 3: 325), and we would suggest that he had conquered Woolf's aesthetic sensibility as well. The supernatural element in James's late-Victorian and Edwardian novels and short stories in particular provided a model for Woolf. Her assessment of James's weaknesses and strengths in this genre provides insight into her early aims. She too portrayed inner ghosts and strove to slip imperceptibly over the border into the supernatural in her fiction. She did this only when the apparition fit the psychological "crisis of passion or of conscience which sent it forth" (*E* 3: 324) and when it contributed to the symbolism of her story. She also deplored and even satirized the crude scientific approach to the unseen, as did Henry James.

An analysis of the psychical aspect of the supernatural in Woolf's short stories "Kew Gardens" and "A Haunted House" and in an early novel *Night and Day*, as well as the Modernist experiment *Mrs. Dalloway*, confirms the extent to which Woolf's aesthetic of the unseen aligns with James's as well as the extent to which she drew on the supernatural tradition in general. "Kew Gardens," published as a separate pamphlet by Hogarth Press in May 1919, demonstrates her ambivalence toward the supernatural and reveals her trying out a new method of creating a disturbingly haunting atmosphere. On the surface, Woolf would appear to satirize belief in the supernatural through the cameo of the shaky old man named William who walks by, talking more to himself than to his younger companion: "He was talking about spirits—the spirits of the dead, who, according to him, were even now telling him all sorts of odd things about their experiences in Heaven." She mocks the experimental approach to making contact with the dead after the fashion of the Society for Psychical Research in his confused ramblings:

> a small electric battery and a piece of rubber to insulate the wire—
> isolate?—insulate?—well we'll skip the details, no good going into details
> that wouldn't be understood—and in short the little machine stands in
> any convenient position by the head of the bed, we will say, on a neat
> mahogany stand. All arrangements being properly fixed by workmen
> under my direction, the widow applies her ear and summons the spirit
> by sign as agreed. Women! Widows! Women in black—. (*CSF* 92)

The description evokes the charlatan who takes advantage of the grieving war widow, but the diversion of William's attention toward a woman in black at the close of the passage, followed by another diversion in which he seems to answer a voice speaking from a flower, intimates that his mind has become unhinged.

Nevertheless, the story as a whole more subtly suggests not only the ghostliness and insubstantiality of human beings but the ghostliness of reality altogether, leading Nicholas Royle to claim that "Kew Gardens" "is certainly a ghost story" (119). The idea is introduced casually into a conversation between a man musing about the woman he might have married and his wife, who responds, "Doesn't one always think of the past, in a garden with men and women lying under the trees? Aren't they one's past, all that remains of it, those men and women, those ghosts lying under the trees, . . . one's happiness, one's reality?" As if to reinforce the truth that those ghosts *are* all one's reality, the husband and wife themselves become the past, and insubstantial: they "soon diminished in size among the trees and looked half transparent as the sunlight and shade swam over their backs in large trembling irregular patches" (*CSF* 91). Woolf evokes the haunting atmosphere by using a linking device—a snail in a flower-bed—and by orienting the story from the creature's perspective. Although the snail is anthropomorphized, it is completely oblivious to the various groups that pass by it. The effect of this sense of oblivion is to make the people seem as if they are ghosts. As the piece draws to a close, the omniscient narration again suggests the temporality and immaterial nature of the people passing by: "Thus one couple after another with much the same irregular and aimless movement passed the flower-bed and were enveloped in layer after layer of green-blue vapour, in which at first their bodies had substance and a dash of colour, but later both substance and colour dissolved in the green-blue atmosphere" (*CSF* 95).

The title of "A Haunted House" immediately signals a more direct use of the supernatural than in "Kew Gardens," but in this brief lyrical piece Woolf subverts the conventions of the traditional haunted house story and also responds to and rewrites James's ghost stories, particularly *The Turn of the Screw*. Though the piece opens with the narrator commenting on the frequency of a door shutting in a house at night, there are apparently no direct ghostly sightings: "we see no lady spread her ghostly cloak" (*CSF* 123). Neither are there any unpleasant shocks nor "violent old ghosts," and the traditional effects of horror and terror are conspicuously absent. The narrative does not proceed to the traditional revelation of the crime or horror committed that brought the spirit into being nor to a final alteration of circumstances or expiation satisfyingly releasing the haunting presence. However, there is a "ghostly couple," whose movements are imagined by the narrator (and her partner). They seem to be on a quest for something that they have left behind, eventually described as "treasure buried" and finally revealed as their love, encapsulated in the closing phrase "The light in the heart." There is an echo of James's "The Friends of the Friends" in that the couple had been separated in the past and is now reunited in the spiritual realm. However, in James's story one of the pair is alive when he makes contact with his true love, whereas in Woolf's story it is the narrator who is alive and who senses the presence of the couple, both of whom already exist in the spiritual realm.

"A Haunted House" more strongly echoes several elements of *The Turn of the Screw*, especially atmosphere and setting. In her review essay on James's ghost stories Woolf claims that "it is the silence that first impresses us" in *The Turn of the Screw*, and she quotes the following passage: "I can hear again, as I write, the intense hush in which the sounds of evening dropped. The rooks stopped cawing in the golden sky, and the friendly hour lost for the unspeakable minute all its voice" (*E* 3: 325). In her much briefer story she creates a similar atmosphere of silence at twilight broken only by the cry of birds: "The shadow of a thrush crossed the carpet; from the deepest wells of silence the wood pigeon drew its bubble of sound. . . . A moment later the light had faded" (*CSF* 122). Woolf also draws attention to "the exquisite little beings who lie innocently asleep [and] must at all costs be protected" in *The Turn of the Screw* (*E* 3: 325), and in her own story she situates the living couple in their bed sound asleep as the ghostly couple observes them. Also, the possibility exists, as it does in *The Turn of the Screw*, that these ghosts do not have independent existence but have occurred through psychological projection or in a dream since at the close of the piece the narrator awakens and cries out her revelation. However, Woolf creates exactly the opposite effect to James's; she transforms the evil, the "unutterable obscenity" exuded in James's house into the comfort and security exuded by her house, whose heart beats "[s]afe, safe, safe" (*CSF* 123). Whereas James's ghosts strike terror, Woolf's "Seek their joy" and love, these positive feelings reinforced by the use of romantic imagery throughout the story. About James's story Woolf writes, "We are afraid of something, unnamed, of something, perhaps, in ourselves. In short, we turn on the light" (*E* 3: 325). In "A Haunted House" Woolf has the ghostly couple "turn the light" on the narrator at the close, and it provides for the narrator not fear but illumination about "[t]he light in the heart" (*CSF* 123).

In her second novel, *Night and Day* , Woolf does not as directly respond to the supernatural genre, but she suffuses the novel with metaphors of the supernatural and psychical. Fogel points out that of all Woolf's novels this is the one most pervasively influenced by James, but he restricts his discussion to techniques and strategies adopted by Woolf . He does not mention any influence of James's use of the supernatural; in fact he cites with approval Phyllis Rose's remark: "Critics have reached remarkable unanimity about the place *Night and Day* occupies in Virginia Woolf's career—it is her attempt to prove herself the master of the classical tradition of the English novel, to create solid characters and place them in realized settings, to have them speak to one another in credible dialogue and to advance the plot through dramatic scenes."[12] But Woolf did not aim at the materialism of the classical novel and subverted it here by creating a supernatural aura, partly drawing on what she had identified as James's use of inner ghosts.

Her assimilation of supernatural imagery serves several purposes. In the novel the past and particularly the illustrious ancestry of the protagonist Katharine is shown to be a continuing and important influence on present lives, a theme introduced through Mrs. Hilbery's musing: "'After all, what *is* the present? Half of it's the past, and the better half, too, I should say'" (*ND* 12). Woolf intimates the darker, oppressive side of that influence through a motif of characters being haunted by the ghosts of ancestors. Later in the novel Mrs. Hilbery feels driven to lay "the ghost of her parents' sorrow to rest" (*ND* 93) and is "haunted by the ghosts of phrases" (*ND* 283). Characters are affected by metaphorical ghosts of the more immediate past as well. Mary Datchet is in touch with the "ghosts of past moods" on a familiar walk, and Ralph Denham feels that his depression is "only a sentimental ghost" (*ND* 172, 205). But the supernatural plays a more positive role as well. Through this imagery Woolf suggests that the unseen world of thoughts and the unconscious, dreams and ideals, is far more significant and extensive than the material world of "reality." Woolf's title gives precedence to the night world, by which she means this insubstantial world, over the "day" or public world of social convention. Both Ralph and Katharine are frequent visitors to the unseen world, but at first their private worlds do not align. Ralph, for instance, concocts in his mind a "phantom Katharine" (*ND* 83) who is highly vital, imaginative, and sympathetic, and who does not correspond with the reality.

At times not only Katharine but her pending marriage with William Rodney seem unreal to Ralph: "at the moment, Rodney and Katharine herself seemed disembodied ghosts. . . . All things had turned to ghosts; the whole mass of the world was insubstantial vapour, surrounding the solitary spark in his mind, whose burning point he could remember, for it burnt no more" (*ND* 146). Katharine similarly experiences the unreality of the social world, which Woolf invokes using a metaphor of the survival of the personality beyond death. While at a party, Katharine isolates herself and hears the voices of the others

> as if they came from people in another world, a world antecedent to her world, a world that was the prelude, the antechamber to reality; it was as if, lately dead, she heard the living talking. The dream nature of our life had never been more apparent to her, never had life been more certainly an affair of four walls, whose objects existed only within the range of lights and fires, beyond which lay nothing, or nothing more than darkness. (ND 327)

However, as the intimacy between Katharine and Ralph develops, they are able to align their unseen, inner worlds, though only sporadically. Near the close of the novel while on one of many nocturnal walks, "they lapsed gently into silence, travelling the dark paths of thought side by side towards something discerned in the distance which gradually possessed them both" (ND 468). The sight of Mary Datchet's illuminated blinds leads to their sharing a vision, again imaged in supernatural terms: Katharine "felt him [Ralph] trying to piece together in a laborious and elementary fashion fragments of belief, unsoldered and separate, lacking the unity of phrases fashioned by the old believers. Together they groped in this difficult region, where the unfinished, the unfulfilled, the unwritten, the unreturned, came together in their ghostly way and wore the semblance of the complete and the satisfactory" (ND 470). Thus most importantly in this novel Woolf uses supernatural metaphor to invoke a sense of the limitless potential of the unseen, ghostly world that originates from within to dictate and transform the events of outward life.

Though Woolf found a more appropriate, Modernist form to express her belief in the psychical nature of reality in *Jacob's Room*, it is in *Mrs. Dalloway* that Woolf fully explores a number of facets of the supernatural within this form, and not surprisingly the impact of James's ghosts can be detected once again. Perhaps most importantly, the structure and unity of the novel depends upon the uncanny psychic connection between Mrs. Dalloway and the "mad" Septimus Smith, a connection that Woolf worried would not be recognized (D 2: 323). Woolf develops that link by revealing that both the war veteran Septimus Smith and Clarissa Dalloway have been profoundly changed through witnessing the traumatic deaths of someone very close to them (MD 78, 70). Whereas Clarissa subsequently has a horror of death, Septimus has a fascination with it (MD 135, 60). More importantly, their streams of consciousness overlap, and contain part of a line from *Cymbeline*, "Fear no more the heat o' the sun." Though Clarissa never meets Septimus, her uncanny sense of identification with him and the re-entry into her consciousness of this phrase when she hears of his death confirm their psychic connection (*MD* 165). Though it is Septimus who dies, Clarissa Dalloway is one of those Jamesian characters who are "already half-way out of the body" while living. Woolf expresses this in a number of ways, notably in Clarissa's feeling of insubstantiality, of being ghostlike: "she had the oddest sense of being herself invisible; unseen; unknown . . . " (*MD* 11).

Also, Clarissa's psychic sensitivity and moments of vision, comparable to Septimus's hallucinatory visions, help convey her ethereal nature. Like Septimus, she experiences the dark side of the visionary, expressed with supernatural imagery, as when Clarissa muses that Miss Kilman "had become one of those spectres with which one battles in the night; one of those spectres who stand astride us and suck up half our life-blood, dominators and tyrants; for no doubt with another throw of the dice, had the black been uppermost and not the white, she would have loved Miss Kilman! But not in this world. No" (*MD* 13). She has even evolved a theory to help account for her experience of the spiritual nature of reality, as Peter Walsh recollects: "Odd affinities [Clarissa] had with people she had never spoken to, some woman in the street, some man behind a counter—even trees, or barns. It ended in a transcendental theory which, with her horror of death, allowed her to believe, or say that she believed (for all her skepticism), that since our apparitions, the part of us which appears, are so momentary compared with the other, the unseen part of us, which spreads wide, the unseen might survive, be recovered somehow attached to this person or that, or even haunting certain places, after death. Perhaps—perhaps" (*MD* 135-36). Clarissa's "transcendental theory" bears a striking affinity with that of the psychical researchers. They too believed that the world imperceptible to the five senses was far more extensive than that perceptible to the senses and tried to prove the survival of the personality after death.

Woolf once again drew on the Jamesian ghost story in *Mrs. Dalloway*. One of the most striking instances of influence is from James's story "The Great Good Place," which is ironic since Woolf termed the story a "failure." Dane's escape from material reality in that story vaguely resembles the curious scene in which Peter Walsh slips into an uncanny dream state while sitting on a park bench beside a gray nurse, but Woolf rewrites the scene in accordance with her vision of the supernatural. Recall that Dane escapes to a blissful world criticized by Woolf in her review as being boring. The "great good place" is described by one of the brothers there as "a sort of kindergarten" and its nature is conveyed by an image of protection involving the baby-mother relation: "'The next thing you'll be saying that we're babes at the breast!' 'Of some great mild invisible mother who stretches away into space and whose lap's the whole valley—?' 'And her bosom'—Dane completed the figure—'the noble eminence of our hill?'" (James 593). In *Mrs. Dalloway* Woolf suggests that the gray nurse minding the baby next to Peter "seemed like the champion of the rights of sleepers, like one of those spectral presences which rise in twilight in woods made of sky and branches. The solitary traveller, haunter of lanes, disturber of ferns, and devastator of great hemlock plants, looking up suddenly, sees the giant figure at the end of the ride" (*MD* 52). This giant figure also has ambiguously maternal qualities: "this figure . . . had risen from the troubled sea . . . as a shape might be sucked up out of the waves to shower down from her magnificent hands, compassion, comprehension, absolution" (*MD* 52-53). However, Peter's spirit world is not as comforting as the great good place, as the reference during his dream to "the figure of the mother whose sons have been killed in the battles of the world" suggests (*MD* 53). Woolf criticized James's supernatural world because it "removes the shocks and buffetings of experience," but in Peter's dream world the shocks and buffetings do not disappear. Whereas Dane finds his soul in the great good place—"What had happened was that in tranquil walks and talks the deep spell had worked and he had got his soul again" (James 591)—Peter awakes from his dream of the solitary traveler exclaiming, "The death of the soul" (*MD* 53). Peter's uncanny vision more convincingly than Dane's arises from his troubled memories of Clarissa's crisis when her soul died at Bourton as well as of the larger crisis of the war.

Woolf returned to the possibility of the survival of personality and psychic communication in *To the Lighthouse* through Mrs. Ramsay's appearance after her death in a vision to Lily, and in several subsequent works, notably *The Waves*.[13] Woolf's early and persistent use of supernatural elements in aid of conveying the spiritual essence of reality suggests that the roots of this vision were deep. One would not want to exclude the contribution of biographical factors to the shaping of Woolf's vision. In his description of the Stephen family, Henry James sheds illumination in this well-covered terrain: "I liked being with them, but it was all strange and terrible (with the hungry *futurity* of youth); and all I could see mainly was the *ghosts*, even Thoby and Stella, let alone dear old Leslie and beautiful, pale, tragic Julia—on whom all these young backs were, and quite naturally, so gaily turned."[14] Ironically, James's own ghostly presence as well as the example of his ghostly tales more directly influenced Woolf's incorporation of the supernatural in her fiction. His absence, along with numerous other psychical and supernatural writers with whom Woolf would have become familiar through her review essays, haunts Woolf's essays attacking the Edwardians' materialism and claiming that in 1910 no models existed that could be used in probing the spirit and psyche of characters. These famous polemics need to be read for what they are—very clever strategic essays clearing the field of rivals in the psychological and psychical approaches she embraces—rather than as literary history, as they so often have been taken. The language of the spiritual employed by Woolf in these essays suggests the extent to which she viewed the world as spiritual reality. However, a more accurate and revealing picture of her spiritual aesthetic can be determined from her essays on supernatural topics, particularly on James's ghost stories. It is thus unfortunate that their significance has not been recognized by critics such as Fogel. Though Glen Cavaliero omits Woolf in his survey *The Supernatural and English Fiction*, she belongs to the tradition that most fully and, I would add, subtly integrates expression of the supernatural—the sacramental. Unlike the preternatural tradition, which shows the supernatural as an intrusion on or contrary to nature, or the paranormal tradition, which sees the supernatural as an extension of the natural and attempts to explain it, the sacramental "portrays the supernatural as the true province of the imagination" and envisions it (Cavaliero 21). For Woolf, metaphors of the supernatural helped to convey her conviction of the nonmaterial nature of reality and a sense of its vastness and mystery compared to the world of observable objects. As she says in "How It Strikes A Contemporary," "we do well to watch for" the "most brief apparitions" of the truth (*E* 3: 359). Through the spiritual and psychical dimension of her characterization and of the atmosphere of her fiction in general she sought to image something of that "will-o'-the-wisp" phantom Mrs. Brown, "to convey this varying, this unknown and uncircumscribed spirit" (*CR* 1: 213) of life and to avoid becoming mired in the materialist conventions of *some* of the work of *some* of her immediate predecessors.

Works Cited

Cavaliero, Glen. *The Supernatural and English Fiction*. Oxford: Oxford UP, 1995.

Daugherty, Beth Rigel. "The Whole Contention Between Mr. Bennett and Mrs. Woolf, Revisited." *Virginia Woolf: Centennial Essays*. Ed. Elaine K. Ginsberg and Laura Moss Gottlieb. Troy: Whitson, 1983.

Fogel, Daniel Mark. *Covert Relations: James Joyce, Virginia Woolf, and Henry James*. Charlottesville: UP of Virginia, 1990.

Hewitt, Douglas. *English Fiction of the Early Modern Period 1890-1940.* London: Longman, 1988.

James, Henry. *Stories of the Supernatural.* Ed. and Intro. Leon Edel. London: Barrie and Jenkins, 1971.

Johnson, George M. "'The Spirit of the Age': Virginia Woolf's Response to Second Wave Psychology." *Twentieth Century Literature* 40.2 (1994): 139-64.

Laurence, Patricia Ondek. *The Reading of Silence: Virginia Woolf in the English Tradition.* California: Stanford UP, 1991.

Lee, Hermione. "*To The Lighthouse.* Introduction." *Virginia Woolf. Introductions to the Major Works.* Ed. Julia Briggs. London: Virago, 1994.

Meisel, Perry. *The Absent Father: Virginia Woolf and Walter Pater.* London: Yale UP, 1980.

Rosenbaum, S. P. *Victorian Bloomsbury: The Early History of the Bloomsbury Group.* Vol. 1. Basingstoke: Macmillan, 1987.

Royle, Nicholas. *Telepathy and Literature: Essays on the Reading Mind.* Oxford: Basil Blackwell, 1990.

Scarborough, Dorothy. *The Supernatural in Modern English Fiction.* 1917. New York: Octagon, 1967.

Silver, Brenda R. *Virginia Woolf's Reading Notebooks.* Princeton: Princeton UP, 1983.

Woolf, Virginia. *The Complete Shorter Fiction of Virginia Woolf.* Ed. Susan Dick. London: Hogarth, 1989.

———. *The Diary of Virginia Woolf.* Ed. Anne Olivier Bell and Andrew McNeillie. 5 vols. London: Hogarth, 1977-1984.

———. *The Essays of Virginia Woolf.* Ed. Andrew McNeillie. 4 vols. to date. London: Hogarth, 1986-.

———. *Jacob's Room.* 1922. Harmondsworth: Penguin, 1968.

———. *The Letters of Virginia Woolf.* Ed. Nigel Nicolson. 6 vols. London: Hogarth, 1975-1980.

———. *Mrs. Dalloway.* 1925. London: Granada, 1983.

———. *Night and Day.* 1919. Harmondsworth: Penguin, 1969.

———. *To the Lighthouse.* 1927. New York: Harcourt, 1955.

———. *The Waves.* 1931. New York: Harcourt, 1978.

Notes

1. In one version Woolf does express gratitude to Hardy, Conrad, and W. H. Hudson but does not explain why ("Modern Novels," *E* 3: 31).

2. In another essay, "On Re-reading Novels," Woolf admitted that she found the term *form* "confusing" (*E* 3: 339).

3. This term had been applied to literature in an essay—May Sinclair's "The Novels of Dorothy Richardson"—that Woolf had taken notes on in preparation for writing "Modern Novels" (see Silver 18-19, 155-56).

4. See also the "profound dissatisfaction" she expresses with the Georgians in "How it Strikes a Contemporary" (E 3: 357).

5. She also argues this point in "How it Strikes A Contemporary" (E 3: 357).

6. In a review of W. L. George's A Novelist on Novels, she states, "For it is extremely difficult to take the writings of one's contemporaries seriously. The spirit in which they are read is a strange compact of indifference and curiosity. On the one hand the assumption is that they are certainly bad, on the other the temptation assails us to find in them a queer and illicit fascination. Between these two extremes we vacillate, and the attention we grant them is at once furtive, intermittent and intense" (E 2: 256).

7. See especially her review of Clayton Hamilton's Materials and Methods of Fiction, in which she criticizes him for his categorization of "romantic" and "realistic" fiction (E 3: 44).

8. About a week before the review was published, Woolf mentions in her diary she went to the London Library "to get a handful of stories on the supernatural," but we do not know what she obtained. At this time she also records listening to a friend John Mills Whitham, who had dabbled in spiritualism, talk about his experiences (D 1: 112-13, 114).

9. One even wonders whether the seed of the idea of the chauffeured car and airplane, used as transitional devices in Mrs. Dalloway, might have been planted by Woolf's reading of Scarborough's imaginative description of the mysterious and unearthly in the day-to-day world of people and modern technology: "That grey-furred creature that glooms suddenly before us in the winter street is not a chauffeur, but a were-wolf questing for his prey. Yon whirring thing in the far blue is not an airplane but a hippogriff that will presently alight on the pavement beside us with thundering hoofs to bear us away to distant lovely lands where we shall be untroubled by the price of butter or the articles lost in last week's wash" (3).

10. Like Hardy and Hudson, James was of her parents' and not her grandparents' generation.

11. In later essays she states, "If we wish to recall our happier hours they would be those Conrad has given us and Henry James" (E 3: 338) and she continues to praise James very highly, above all other Victorian novelists: "The novel is his job. It is the appropriate form for what he has to say. It wins a beauty from that fact—a fine and noble beauty—which it has never worn before" (E 3: 344).

12. Fogel 136-37.

13. Hermione Lee refers to *To The Lighthouse* as "a ghost story," but she does not situate it in the context of contemporary psychical fiction or ideas (179).
14. Fogel 55.

PART V

THE ESSAY AND FEMINISM

Refusing to Hit Back: Virginia Woolf and the Impersonality Question

Lisa Low

Impersonality is one of the central convictions of Modernism. In "Tradition and the Individual Talent," the key manifesto for impersonality in the modern period, T. S. Eliot claims that the personality of the artist has nothing to do with the art he or she creates. Instead, the artist's brain is a kind of petri dish in which chemicals combine, leaving only the impersonal integrity of art, all trace of the artist having been sublimed in the white heat of creation. In *Portrait of the Artist as a Young Man* James Joyce argues similarly that the impersonal artist sits sublimely apart, filing his nails like a god above the tormented passions of his protagonists. Virginia Woolf, too, recommends impersonality as an artistic goal. In "Women and Fiction," for example, Woolf writes that in the future "the greater impersonality of women's lives will encourage the poetic spirit," and that impersonality will lead women, hitherto focused solely on the personal life, to be "less absorbed in facts" and to look "to the wider questions which the poet tries to solve—of our destiny and the meaning of life" (GR 83).

A number of what this essay will call "identity feminists,"[1] among them Adrienne Rich, Elaine Showalter, and Tuzyline Jita Allan, have deconstructed this ideal of impersonal art, together with its cool posture of sexual neutrality, uncovering beneath the myth of the impersonal a patriarchal bias that reveres masculinist norms such as hierarchalization, artistic self-absorption, class stratification, and homogenization.[2] For Rich, Showalter, and Allan, all art is personal as well as political, and authors who claim to transcend themselves in the production of a supposedly universal work of art are really arrogant fantasists, arrogating to themselves supernatural powers they do not have and degrading others in their claim that more obviously personal art (written by uneducated outsiders) is not art at all but merely anecdote. According to Adrienne Rich and to the feminist movement that in many ways followed in her wake, a twentieth-century woman writer must rebel against this impersonal standard; she must learn "to do without authorities" (45), turning away from the tradition and writing instead from the point of view of herself using the first person I.

In recent decades identity feminists have accused Virginia Woolf of betraying feminism in her preference for impersonality in art, and especially for the suppression of anger that such a preference implies. Rich writes, for example, that Woolf tries "to sound as cool as Jane Austen, as Olympian as Shakespeare, because that is the way the men of the culture thought a writer should sound" (37). With less sympathy than Rich, Elaine Showalter argues that in A Room of One's Own Woolf chooses impersonality in a deliberate attempt to avoid "confrontation with her own painful femaleness" and to choke and repress "her anger and ambition" (264). Indeed for Showalter, Woolf is a dangerous model for feminists to follow since her repression of the feminine, and in particular her subsumption of feminist anger into the cool voice of impersonality, renders her suicidal. Allan takes Showalter a step further when she argues that Woolf's claim for impersonality, her suppression of the feminist I/eye is really a "fatal attraction" (140) to a dominant masculine discourse that forces women into the margins or, worse, into complete invisibility, an invisibility made even more problematic for the black woman writer. For each of these writers, Woolf betrays feminism by suppressing anger and adopting impersonality instead.

But however useful aesthetically, and especially politically, such critiques may be contested as oversimplifications. In the first place, there is a feminist difference between Woolf's version of impersonality and that of her male contemporaries; in the second, it is not true that Woolf identifies exclusively with an "impersonal" position; rather, throughout her life Woolf engages in constant and ultimately unresolved debate about the relative values of personality and impersonality, even as she constantly explores and redefines the feminine and masculine halves of the gender hierarchy; finally, what Allan calls Woolf's "depersonalization campaign" (136) is less a failure of feminist nerve than part of a larger, more theoretically complex attempt to redescribe the "cramp and confinement" (CR 1: 244) of familiar and deadening gender polarizations. Indeed, in the end, the identity-feminist position that Rich, Showalter, and Allan occupy has been critiqued by a post-Modernism that sees identity feminism as perpetuating the very ideals of a masculinist culture it strives to overthrow. Only by theorizing the self and problematizing gender, a problematizing that Woolf herself prophesied, can the inferiorization of woman be overcome.[3]

The connection between art and impersonality has a long history in the west that can be traced back through Augustinian and Pauline Christianity to the paganism of Plato and Socrates. In ideologies that may well be described as antifeminist, Christian and pagan philosophers alike have valorized the male-associated impersonal and transcendental over the personal and immanent with which women, especially because of their biological capacities, have been historically associated.

The Modernist pursuit of impersonality attaches itself to this misogynistic history even as, more locally, it rejects Romanticism. Modernists like Joyce, Hemingway, and Eliot, among others, reject what they perceive as the self-indulgence (and, it could be argued, the feminism[4]), of the Romantic cult of personality in favor of the cool remove and generalizing tendencies of a once-again valued neoclassicism.[5] The reaction against Romanticism is evident in art criticism as well, though ironically from a less conservative point of view. According to Roger Fry, personal art is biased as well as elitist since personality has to do with the advantaged perspective of a bourgeois viewer who wishes to fantasize possession of all he surveys. To make art abstract, to remove from it the personal, is to allow art to focus on purely formal elements such as color, line, symmetry, and proportion, emphases that theoretically move art away from the elitism of personal possession.[6]

It is clear that Woolf was early influenced by Bloomsbury-group conversations with Roger Fry, which she enjoyed, indeed, by which she was exhilarated,[7] and clear as well that she was influenced by the impersonality-touting T. S. Eliot who was a friend, intimate,[8] and rival. There can be no doubt that the high value she placed upon impersonality had at least in part to do with her attraction to the impersonality theory common to them and to her time. One can overhear Modernism's claims, for example, in Woolf's 1907 remark that Elizabeth von Arnim's *Fraulein Schmidt and Mr. Anstruther* "is merely a record of personal impressions" (*E* 1: 136) and in her 1918 description of Coleridge's hatred of "mere personality" (*E* 2: 222). But there is more in Woolf's "flight" into impersonality than a mere wish to be inoffensive or to concede to masculine norms. On the contrary, as this essay argues, Woolf uses impersonality to undermine historical divisions between male and female writing, connecting personal writing to both sexes, and to advocate impersonal writing—not for its authoritarian potential, as Eliot might, but because it is empathic and democratic.

Woolf's interest in impersonality is lifelong and haunts her writing throughout her career, from the early reference in 1905 to Baedecker's *Journeys in Spain* as "the most impersonal of books" (*E* 1: 44) to the late essay "Personalities," in which Woolf entertains an ultimately unresolved inquiry into the relative benefits of personality and impersonality (*M* 167-72). In between these two extremes impersonality can be detected in a variety of places: in her praise of Mrs. Gaskell as a more democratic author than Charlotte Brontë (Mrs. Gaskell may lack "personality" but her world, unlike Charlotte Brontë's, is "everybody's" [*E* 1: 342]); in her description of *Paradise Lost* as sublime but impersonal (*D* 1: 192); in her remark that the novels of Dorothy Richardson and James Joyce are flawed by the "damned egotistical self" (*D* 2: 14); in her theory of androgyny (which vitiates the purely feminine in favor of an ambivalence between masculine and feminine);[9] in her "self-expulsion" (Allan 132) from prose (in *A Room of One's Own*, for example, Woolf insists that the narrative "I" is fictive, "a convenient term for somebody who has no real being" [3]); in her pursuit, in *The Waves*, of an anonymous narrator ("Who thinks it?," she writes in her *Diary*, "And am I outside the thinker?" [*D* 3: 257]); in a 1933 letter to Ethel Smyth in which she admits that she deliberately avoided the "I" in *A Room of One's Own* to protect herself from critics who would delight in "how vain, how personal . . . women always are" (*L* 5: 195); in her description of an anonymous female "Outsiders' Society" in *Three Guineas*; and in the *Diary* entries for *Between the Acts* in which "I" is rejected in favor of "We" (*D* 5: 135). Common to each of these is Woolf's attempt to remove art from the merely personal.

According to Showalter such self-removals are escapist and even cowardly refusals to confront marginalized femininity in a competitive and male-dominated world. For Allan, Woolf's self-expulsions, even if they are deliberate, indeed, even if they are feminist strategies, are nevertheless problematic since they replicate the self-effacement that has historically proven fatal for women, and even more so for black women. But Showalter and Allan both almost completely ignore the antiauthoritarian politics of Woolf's self-denials. Indeed, Allan seems to equate Woolf with Eliot. The impersonal voice that is the underlying thesis of *The Common Readers*, for example, Allan claims is "Woolf's version of T. S. Eliot's dissociated sensibility" (133); and Woolf's "How it Strikes a Contemporary," the essay that closes the first *Common Reader*, replicates Eliot's call in "Tradition and the Individual Talent" for impersonal art in its phrase "the cramp and confinement of personality" (132). But as Teresa Heffernan points out, Woolf's "feminist texts cannot be slotted unproblematically" (20) among the Modernists.[10] Indeed, close inspection will show that "Tradition and the Individual Talent" and "How it Strikes a

Contemporary" reveal completely different visions of art, common readers, and the artist's relationship with tradition.

In "Tradition and the Individual Talent" Eliot argues that art does not condescend to enter the mainstream of life; that the artist of any present moment seeks conversation with the tradition directly; and, most importantly, that there is no relationship between the personal circumstances of the writer and the art he produces.[11] The problems of such a theory from a feminist standpoint are obvious and Virginia Woolf herself illuminates them in a variety of essays that stress more democratic principles, from one of her first published reviews, "The Feminine Note in Fiction," in which Woolf argues that the feminine voice is a direct result of feminine experience (*E* 1: 15-17), to the more explicitly radical vision of "The Leaning Tower," where Woolf argues, among other things, that players in the great tradition are highly educated well-to-do young men whose potential for canonization, far from being irrelevant, as Eliot claims, is a direct result of their middle class backgrounds and elite educations (*M* 153).[12]

Further, in "Tradition and the Individual Talent," Eliot conceives of the tradition, in terms completely different from Woolf's, as an exclusive conservatory of greatness past and to come, a kind of Egyptian pyramid in which great authors are sustained among the immortals above the reach of space and time. After the talented ephebe (by definition a highly educated and youthful male) enters into the sacred monument, the door shuts and the pyramid returns to silence. By implication others are forbidden entrance: the commoners, women, and pedestrians who pass may at best pay homage to the greatness within. Such is the library at the entrance of which the narrator was forbidden to pass at Oxbridge in *A Room of One's Own*.

This conception of the great tradition is the complete opposite of Woolf's. Where Eliot sees the canon in monumental architectural terms (in other words, in terms that reify stability and exclusivity), Woolf speaks in "How it Strikes a Contemporary" of "a ribbon which runs many miles" of which the present is "one inch" (*CR* 1: 245). The political implications of Woolf's presiding metaphor—a string of ribbon that runs for miles—are considerable. Unlike the masculine critic, who from Pope to Harold Bloom has seen the tradition Oedipally as a giant foot crushing a miniaturized present, Woolf sees art on a level with life, the past on a level with the future, and the artist and critic on a level with the commoner. She also sees the tradition as perpetually changing, as shifting sands rather than free-standing monuments built behind them, a position that, as Deborah Pope suggests, is fundamental to feminist canon-building. Indeed, Woolf increasingly emphasizes instability, describing civilization in "The Leaning Tower" as on the verge of collapse not with the demoralized tone of what must be restored, but with a sense that the future shall not only be different but better because all of us shall be readers and writers, the texts offering a place for the voice of the hitherto unwelcome outsider.

Heffernan's assertion that unlike her Modernist peers, Woolf perceived the fascist implications of the "unified autonomous ego" (24) is important to any interpretation of Woolf's use of impersonality. Indeed, Woolf's hatred of egotism and the authoritarianism that inevitably accompanies it is the underlying theme of all her work. For Woolf, egotism, whether in male or female, is in many ways the root of social conflict, for the ego, unbearably self-centered, is almost always fascistic: its desire, whether it arises as rage in the man or as bitterness in the woman, is to assert the self and ultimately to dominate. Such a desire inevitably undermines community. Male power and the ferocious will to maintain it, as well as female anger toward brute masculinity, alike distort art. Both insist on an assertion of the "I" that is to Woolf as "large, and ugly as could be" (L 5: 195).

Woolf's hatred of authoritarianism and her employment of impersonality as a means to oppose it are apparent in both *Common Readers*, in *A Room of One's Own* and *Three Guineas*, as well as in the novels, letters, and diaries. Allan writes correctly, for example, that both *Common Readers* have as their underlying premise the "disinterested" and impersonal voice of the critic (133). But Woolf's impersonal critic does not stand coldly removed, dispassionately assessing literature with the presumptuousness and arrogance bred by a Cambridge education. Rather, Woolf's impersonal critic is devoted to the democratic proposition that the common reader is preferable to the literary bully. For Woolf the irrepressible egotism of the university-educated critic falls like a shadow upon the literary page, blocking the reader's view. Trained in an academy that is itself corrupted by egotism, the pompous and self-important critic shouts "I, I, I." Rather than allowing literature to speak for itself, he speaks for the literature and so cramps and confines the common reader, taking away his or her intellectual liberty. The position is underscored in the epigraph on the title page of both *Common Readers*, from Johnson's *Life of Gray*:

> I rejoice to concur with the common reader; for by the common sense of readers, uncorrupted by literary prejudices, after all the refinements of subtilty and the dogmatism of learning, must be generally decided all claim to poetical honours.

With Johnson, Woolf predicts the final triumph of the common over the university-educated reader. In "How it Strikes a Contemporary," for example, Woolf cautions the critic "whose task it is to pass judgement" since in six months' time the "wreaths and coronets" will likely "get awry, and fade" (*CR* 1: 246); similarly, in "How Should One Read a Book?" Woolf asks each reader to decide the value of literature for him or herself and not "to admit authorities, however heavily furred and gowned, into our libraries and [not to] let them tell us how to read, what to read, what value to place upon what we read," since to do that "is to destroy the spirit of freedom which is the breath of those sanctuaries" (*CR* 2: 234).[13]

Woolf's abhorrence of egotism is the underlying theme of *A Room of One's Own* and is fundamental to her introduction of androgyny as an artistic ideal. In Woolf's analysis the suffrage movement has caused both men and women to become self-conscious and out of defensiveness to lay greater emphasis than necessary on one's sex: male writers insist on "I" and on male values to dominate and repress uppity women, and female writers insist on "I" and female needs to counteract domination and repression. To write effectively, to give full expression to one's genius, the mind needs to be free of bitterness; only then can poetry flow freely and can one ask the larger questions of human destiny, or get at "the common life which is the real life," for ultimately "our relation is to the world of reality and not only to the world of women and men" (*AROO* 124-25).

In their essays Showalter and Allan both grant that a significant element of Woolf's theory of literary impersonality entails Woolf's almost visceral hatred of masculine egotism. Showalter writes, for example, that "it is only fair to note that she found male writers ruined by exaggerated, or exacerbated, virility" (288). Similarly, Allan admits that Woolf's "feminist sensibilities recoiled from authority-wielding tendency" and that Woolf "abhors the overemphasis on self" which she "sometimes conflated with the male ego" (136, 143). Still, both Showalter and Allan grossly underestimate the importance of the antiauthoritarian politics in Woolf's use of impersonality. Showalter, for example, claims that Woolf disables feminism since she "developed a literary theory that made anger and protest flaws" (289).[14] But Showalter (demonstrating perhaps what Woolf might see as the characteristic imbalance of the feminist reader) all but completely ignores Woolf's repudiation of male as well as female anger.

In *A Room of One's Own* Woolf mocks male anger in chapter two, in which the narrator visits the British Museum and records the thoughts of a library full of male authoritarian pedants on women, and in chapter six, in which she analyzes the work of Galsworthy, Bennett, and Kipling, modern male authors who have been made self-conscious by the women's suffrage movement and who consequently pound their fists upon the table to insist that they are men and that as men they are superior to women. The male insistence on "I, I, I" barely disguises the fond wish that they and their male values be seen as superior to women. As a result their writing, which at first seems pleasingly self-confident, soon becomes boring. After a chapter or two a shadow lies across the page in "a straight dark bar" that is "shaped something like the letter 'I'." In the shadow of this infantile "I," "Alan . . . obliterate[s] Phoebe" and language becomes barren (*AROO* 109-10).

Woolf proposes androgyny as a solution to the barrenness that comes of anger in male and female writing. In androgyny, as in impersonality, the stridently male or female voice recognizes itself as part of a larger reality in which there is no "I." In *Moments of Being* Woolf retells an early childhood incident in which she has a revelation about the "I" as an obstacle: "I was fighting with Thoby on the lawn. We were pommelling each other with our fists. Just as I raised my fist to hit him, I felt: why hurt another person? I dropped my hand instantly, and stood there, and let him beat me." The refusal to hit Thoby leads Woolf to the realization that the ego is an obstacle; that "there is no Shakespeare, there is no Beethoven; certainly and emphatically there is no God" (God being the obnoxious assertion of the religious "I"); that we do not live solely in our bodies and that "we are the words; we are the music; we are the thing itself" (71-72). A number of critics have joined Showalter in criticizing androgyny on the grounds that, if theoretically ideal, androgyny has historically perpetuated not an equilibrium between the sexes but a repression of the female.[15] There may be some truth to this argument, but it is untrue that in proposing androgyny Woolf fled in cowardice from feminism; rather, in androgyny as in impersonality, Woolf attempts to move beyond binary constructions. Indeed, in theorizing androgyny Woolf antic-ipates the heterogeneity valorized by post-Modernism.

I shall return momentarily to binary constructions, but first I would like to say a word about *Three Guineas*, Woolf's most obviously political pamphlet. In *Three Guineas* Woolf exposes as evil the prevalent tyrannical belief, whether held by the private father or public tyrant, that one person has the right to dictate to others how they should feel and what they should do. In the essay's final image, Woolf imagines the fascist as

> Man himself, the quintessence of virility, the perfect type of which all the others are imperfect adumbrations. He is a man certainly. His eyes are glazed; his eyes glare. His body, which is braced in an unnatural position, is tightly cased in a uniform. Upon the breast of that uniform are sewn several medals and other mystic symbols. His hand is upon a sword. He is called in German and Italian Führer or Duce; in our own

language Tyrant or Dictator. And behind him lie ruined houses and dead bodies—men, women and children. (*TG* 142)

"Man himself, the quintessence of virility" is the military "I, I, I," the belligerent duce, the obnoxious domineering general who stirs the nationalism that is really only private egotism made gigantic and public. The duce (man himself) is the supreme egotist, imposing himself and his nation on men, women, and children, on farms and factories, on houses. He is hateful to Woolf, even more so because he effects politically the domination that the literary dictator only encourages; his self-conceit falls like a fatal shadow on soldiers, commoners, women, children, and civilization. Together the literary and military dictators insist upon the "I, I, I," the "damned egotistical self," the patriotic self-love in the shadow of which life is blotted out.

Instead of writing that expresses the personality, the voracious need for the assertion of self, Woolf strives to find a writing that expels the self.[16] In *The Waves* Woolf strives to be everywoman, nameless and removed; and in *Between the Acts* she writes a novel in which "I" might be ended in favor of the "We." In *A Room of One's Own* Woolf refuses to claim authorship or authority, stating that the "I" is a "convenient term" for one without being. Refusing to identify her voice with truth or to occupy the traditional shoes of authorial prerogative, Woolf steps, after every sentence in the opening pages of *A Room of One's Own*, into the margins, writing that there is no such thing as truth but only opinion, that she herself has merely a point of view, one of many, and that her personhood inevitably characterizes that point of view. In these and in other statements like them, Virginia Woolf expresses a lifelong quest to remove the personal element from her work, not because by impersonality she will transcend what is common, but because by being impersonal she will become common.[17]

Allan is eloquent in her descriptions of feminists who are "not too thrilled about [Woolf's] disappearing act." For Allan, Woolf's tactics of silence, self-marginalization, and the displacement of the "I" are "pyrrhic victor[ies]" in which her rights and visibility as a woman are sacrificed (132). Similarly, the nonviolent tactics Woolf recommends in *Three Guineas*—the erection of an Outsiders' Society; the refusal to assist men in any aspect of war; and the taking of vows of chastity, poverty, and integrity—may seem counterproductive since they seem to reinforce masculine descriptions of women as passive and to perpetuate norms that have historically silenced women in the first place. Women writers, the identity feminist claims, cannot afford to withdraw and can only find alienating this "modernist transmutation of the writerly self into an amorphous collective" (133).

In the end, however, such identity feminism (as Allan admits) may prove problematic since it clings to a dualist construction of the sexes. To focus exclusively on female experience without problematizing it, for example, to continue to speak in terms of male and female subjects without investigating what those terms mean is to risk perpetuating the hierarchalization that describes male as superior and female as inferior, even as it paralyzes the female subject into oppressive expectations (of nurturance, compassion, silence, and so on). The identity feminist assesses personal writing positively since it expresses the female (and even more so the black female) who has been absent from literary history. But does personality inhere to woman? Might not a woman be impersonal as well? In valorizing personality does the identity feminist, however inadvertently, perpetuate the misogynistic history that associates men with impersonality and women with personality?

In ways that are much more open and much less susceptible to the dogma and limitations of identity feminism, in ways, in fact, that anticipate post-Modernist and deconstructive thought, Woolf addresses these questions and more throughout her career. Indeed, not only in her radical problematization of the subject (the "I" is "a convenient term" for a person "who has no real being" [AROO 3]) and not only in her theory of androgyny, but in her redefinition of the terms "personality" and "impersonality," Woolf approaches the post-Modern, Derridian prophecy that women will eventually force men to founder on the shoals of western philosophy (Alcoff 307), as well as Julia Kristeva's request that women continue to say "'that's not it' and 'that's still not it'" to every male proposition (qtd. in Alcoff 308).[18]

Marder has argued that "while Virginia Woolf the controversialist is battling for certain reforms, the insidious voice of Virginia Woolf the artist keeps chiming in, implying that there is a higher reality, a realm which practical politics cannot enter" (155). From the point of view either of contemporary theory, cultural feminism, or identity politics alike, that claim is problematic. There is no "higher reality," no higher ground to which we can go to get past the ethnicities and personal details of our lives, past the bodies which we inhabit and the colors and fixtures that determine them. At the same time, Woolf asks us to get to such a place when she says that a writer should take no more notice of the color of her eyes than that she is a woman (E 2: 315), and when she says that our relationship is not only to men and women but to reality as well (AROO 125). For Woolf, feminism as a political movement reflects at best half the story, for the feminist cannot see beyond the egotistical need, however justified, of woman to defend herself. Is Woolf here, as Showalter would argue, bailing out on feminism, fleeing in fear from the consequences of being a woman in a misogynist society? Or is she recognizing what we too often overlook in the legitimate ferocity of our feminism: that the feminist vision is by definition partial, that it is overdetermined by the social conditions that have described women as inferior and by our desire for reform? What would society be if we achieved the equality we seek? What would it mean then to be a woman? What would it mean if the text for woman were not the anger she feels at injustice? When in *A Room of One's Own* Woolf looks forward to a time when we can look past Milton's bogey to a clear view of the sky, she is envisioning a time when our identity as females may no longer matter, when the word "female" may not be part of a polarization that inhibits both sexes, paralyzing their capacities.

Linda Alcoff describes the conflict between the identity feminist (Rich, Showalter, Allan) and the post-Modernist feminist as the difference between immediate political activism and long-term solutions. While identity feminism allows woman to act politically in the world, it is limited, since by default it accepts the historical definition of woman (as nurturer and compassionate empathizer and so forth). The post-Modern position of radical uncertainty (Woolf, for example, says she does not know what a woman is [DM 238]) is less immediately useful since it denies women political activism, but it may eventually, through Kristeva-like refutations of western male philosophy, undo patriarchal dualities.

It is clear that Woolf was drawn to the idea of impersonality as a counter to fascism. It is also clear that Woolf's quest for impersonality was not mere toadying to masculine norms. Stepping outside the "I" was not merely a formal exercise for Woolf, not merely an attempt to avoid the censure of her contemporaries, and certainly not, as the feminist critique has claimed, a turn-of-the-century bourgeois white woman's politesse. The displacements of the "I," the refusal of narrative voice, the leprechaunish disappearance of Woolf behind the text, the refusal to tell the truth, the assertion that all she can tell are lies because there is no truth fixable in the human mind, the seemingly "impersonal" but not indifferent remove of the pronoun "one"—are alike refusals to be authoritarian. Unlike the fascist, the university-educated literary critic, or the nineteenth-century novelist, Woolf refuses to tell people what they must think and do. In this, Woolf's quest for impersonality, far from a compromise with masculine norms as Showalter and Allan claim, represents a political position of heroic nonviolence not unlike Martin Luther King's.

In her late essay "Personalities," Woolf seems to rethink her lifelong attraction to the norms of impersonality. Mockingly, she writes, "yet the critics tell us that we should be impersonal when we write, and therefore impersonal when we read" (M 168). Surely "personality" improves upon impersonality: the common reader is intrigued by gossip, and writers are important to us insofar as we know something about their lives. The literature of the Greeks (who sit with long beards on marble plinths against the sky), however great and ancient, however loved by scholars, is in fact boring, lacking in personality. Surely human affairs have more heat and warmth than scholars conceive; surely human affairs are anything but impersonal.

But in midst of this meditation Woolf reverses her thesis, reiterating again a position that is the direct opposite of the identity feminist who claims that to declare the "I" in defiance is to avoid being left on the dump heap of history; and that to sink deeply into one's own shoes, digging one's heels in at "I," is preferable to wearing someone else's shoes, especially if that someone is the patriarch. In response Woolf argues that if it is important to sink into one's own shoes, it is important to walk in other people's as well. And that, Woolf argues, may be the ultimate objective: not to be able to see oneself clearly (however glorious that may be) but to see everyone, as Austen and Shakespeare were able to see everyone. For as soon as Woolf claims that personality is what is desired, she is reminded of those great writers (Shakespeare and Austen) who were so able to get the whole of themselves into what they wrote that they vanished completely, leaving no trace. As we read Austen and Shakespeare all egotism is transformed. Just as we think we see them clearly, we discover we are seeing ourselves instead. When personality is sublimed, in other words, one gets all personality, the ur-human, a mirror in which every human being can see him or herself, male or female, black or white. Perhaps this is something of what Maya Angelou means when despite her feelings of white betrayal she says she reads Shakespeare, finding in him a way to voice her blackness. Or perhaps in this Woolf sees in glimpses, behind ethnicities and personalities, some root of which we all partake, beyond all culturalizations, the being human in a world and over a stretch of time where human destiny may last no longer than a june bug.

Beth Carole Rosenberg argues that from Johnson Woolf learned not to seek truth but to entertain a play of ideas. Similarly, Phyllis Rose (188) has argued that Woolf's idea of androgyny is close to Keats's description of "negative capability," that state "when man is capable of being in uncertainties, Mysteries, doubts, without any irritable reaching after fact & reason" (Keats 1: 193). Heffernan writes similarly that in her theory of androgyny, Woolf was not trying to escape the consequences of being feminine; rather, she was trying to escape the binary construction of gender (24). Though it is the philosopher's burden to be a seeker after truth, in the end, like

Coleridge, "incapable of remaining content with half knowledge," Woolf rejects "truth." In this sense Woolf anticipates poststructuralist critiques not only of identity feminism but of western philosophy. In her use of "impersonality" Woolf is not finally definitive. Impersonality and personality are both good and bad, both valuable and deadly. The personal can be dangerous as well as effective. In the hands of the masculinist it has proved murderous. The "I" has blocked the page of literature. It has presented itself with swords and badges. Behind it "lie ruined houses and dead bodies—men, women and children" (*TG* 142). Impersonality is problematic as well. In male Modernist criticism, it reflects a terrifying coldness and remove, for human affairs are very rarely impersonal. And impersonality can be boring, part of the preserve of the canon in which men with very long white beards and white togas balance on marble plinths in the sky. By claiming impersonality, man has rendered himself gigantic and godlike, part of an odious pantheon of overseeing priests; through personality the male has made himself a menace. Similarly, women have defeated themselves through impersonality. Drowning in self-doubt, preferring anonymity to notoriety, women have subjected themselves to self-crippling and even fatal scrutiny, refusing to be published or heard. Through personality women have defeated themselves; they are too often trapped, for example, in the "merely personal" when there are global affairs and public life to be addressed. In the end Woolf will not define for us or for herself clearly what she means by impersonality and personality, for she means many things, and meaning, she suggests, like the definition of woman, is always evolving, is always contextual, is always to be explored, is always (though the identity feminist cannot think so or she would be rendered mute) fluid, flexible, unstable, untenable—mercury just out of reach.

Works Cited

Alcoff, Linda. "Cultural Feminism versus Post-Structuralism: The Identity Crisis in Feminist Theory." *Feminist Theory in Practice and Process.* Ed. Micheline R. Malson et al. Chicago: U of Chicago P, 1989. 295-326.

Allan, Tuzyline Jita. "A Voice of One's Own: Implications of Impersonality in the Essays of Virginia Woolf and Alice Walker." *The Politics of the Essay: Feminist Perspectives.* Ed. Ruth-Ellen Boetcher Joeres and Elizabeth Mittman. Bloomington: Indiana UP, 1993. 131-47.

Angelou, Maya. Speech at the Downtown Center for the Arts, Pace University, New York City, February 1993.

Bowlby, Rachel. *Virginia Woolf: Feminist Destinations.* New York: Basil Blackwell, 1988.

Caughie, Pamela L. *Virginia Woolf and Postmodernism: Literature in Quest & Question of Itself.* Urbana: U of Illinois P, 1991.

Eliot, T. S. "Tradition and the Individual Talent." *The Norton Anthology of English Literature.* Ed. M. H. Abrams et al. Vol. 2. New York: Norton, 1993. 2170-76.

Farwell, Marilyn. "Eve, the Separation Scene, and the Renaissance Idea of Androgyny." *Milton Studies* 16 (1982): 3-20.

Friedman, Susan Stanford. "Lyric Subversion of Narrative in Women's Writing: Virginia Woolf and the Tyranny of Plot." *Reading Narrative: Form, Ethics, Ideology.* Ed. James Phelan. Columbus: Ohio State UP, 1989. 162-85.

Groen, Hein. "The Problematic Nature of Feminist Criticism of Virginia Woolf." *Dutch Quarterly Review of Anglo-American Letters.* 16 (1986): 109-24.

Heffernan, Teresa. "Fascism and Madness: Woolf Writing Against Modernism." *Virginia Woolf Miscellanies: Proceedings of the First Annual Conference on Virginia Woolf.* Ed. Mark Hussey and Vara Neverow-Turk. New York: Pace UP, 1992. 19-27.

Keats, John. *The Letters of John Keats 1814-1821.* Ed. Hyder E. Rollins. Vol. 1. Cambridge: Harvard UP, 1972.

Leavis, F. R. *Revaluation: Tradition and Development in English Poetry.* 1935. Rpt. London: Chatto & Windus, 1956.

Liggett, P. A. "A Study in Modernism: Exploring the Relationship of T. S. Eliot and Virginia Woolf." *Yeats-Eliot Review: A Journal of Criticism and Scholarship* 9 (1988):165-68.

Marder, Herbert. *Feminism and Art: A Study of Virginia Woolf.* Chicago: U of Chicago P, 1968.

Pope, Deborah. "Notes Toward a Supreme Fiction: The Work of Feminist Criticism." *Women and a New Academy: Gender and Cultural Contexts.* Ed. Jean F. O'Barr. Madison: U of Wisconsin P, 1989. 22-37.

Rich, Adrienne. "When We Dead Awaken: Writing as Re-Vision." *On Lies, Secrets, and Silence: Selected Prose 1966-1978.* New York: Norton, 1979. 33-49.

Richardson, Alan. "Romanticism and the Colonization of the Feminine." *Romanticism and Feminism.* Ed. Anne K. Mellor. Bloomington: Indiana UP, 1988. 13-25.

Rose, Phyllis. *Woman of Letters: A Life of Virginia Woolf.* New York: Oxford UP, 1978.

Rosenberg, Beth Carole. *Virginia Woolf and Samuel Johnson: Common Readers.* New York: St. Martin's, 1995.

Showalter, Elaine. *A Literature of Their Own: British Women Novelists from Brontë to Lessing.* Princeton: Princeton UP, 1977.

Reed, Christopher. "Through Formalism: Feminism and Virginia Woolf's Relation to
   Bloomsbury Aesthetics." *Twentieth Century Literature* 38 (1992): 20-43.

Woolf, Virginia. *The Common Reader: First Series.* New York: Harcourt, 1953.

———. *The Death of the Moth and Other Essays.* New York: Harcourt, 1974.

———. *The Diary of Virginia Woolf.* Ed. Anne Olivier Bell. 5 vols. San Diego: Harcourt,
   1977-84.

———. *The Essays of Virginia Woolf.* Ed. Andrew McNeillie. 3 vols. to date. San Diego:
   Harcourt, 1986-.

———. *Granite & Rainbow.* New York: Harcourt, 1975.

———. *The Letters of Virginia Woolf.* Ed. Nigel Nicolson and Joanne Trautmann. 6 vols.
   New York: Harcourt, 1975-80.

———. *The Moment and Other Essays.* New York: Harcourt, 1974.

———. *Moments of Being.* Ed. Jeanne Schulkind. 2nd ed. San Diego: Harcourt, 1985.

———. *A Room of One's Own.* 1929. Rpt. New York: Harcourt, 1991.

———. *The Second Common Reader.* 1932. New York: Harcourt, 1960.

———. *Three Guineas.* 1938. New York: Harcourt, 1966.

Notes

1. This essay defines "identity feminists" as those who see feminist art as auto-
    biographical by definition.

2. See also Reed 21.

3. See Bowlby and Caughie among others. Bowlby writes, for example, that "in
    her novels [Woolf] attempts to shift the conventions that lay down the
    received distinctions" of masculine and feminine (35). In reference to *Orlando*,
    Caughie writes that Woolf's point is that masculine and feminine identity
    changes as we change clothes (79).

4. See Alan Richardson (13-22) for a discussion of the colonization of the
    feminine by Romantic writers.

5. For an example of the bias toward neoclassicism among the school of T. S.
    Eliot and the moderns, see F. R. Leavis. While he praises the line of wit headed
    by Jonson, Dryden, and Pope, for example, Leavis writes condescendingly
    that Shelley was "in some ways a very intelligent man" who was "peculiarly
    emotional" and whose poetry is "unreadable" in maturity (207-8; 204).

6. See Reed 27-28. The unfortunate consequence of this theory is the discon-
    nection between art and life; what began as a political movement to remove
    the bourgeois element in art ends in being itself elitist.

7. In her diaries Woolf records "taking a splendid flight above personalities" with Fry, as they "discussed literature & aesthetics" (D 1: 75, 80). Cited in Reed 24.

8. P. A. Liggett suggests intimacy between Eliot and Woolf (166).

9. See chapter six of A Room of One's Own.

10. Art critic Christopher Reed makes a similar point, arguing that Woolf used but ultimately mocked formalist claims in the early period's The Voyage Out and Night and Day, and that if cubist tactics were effected in the middle period in Jacob's Room, Mrs. Dalloway, and To the Lighthouse, it was to object to war. By the 1930s, as she grew increasingly impatient with—even disgusted by—formalism's separation of art and life, Woolf described her colleagues as "looking at pinks and yellows, and when Europe Blazes all they do is to screw up their eyes and complain of a temporary glare in the foreground. Unfortunately politics get between one and fiction" (qtd. in Reed 36).

11. T. S. Eliot writes, "The poet has, not a 'personality' to express, but a particular medium, which is only a medium and not a personality, in which impressions and experiences combine in peculiar and unexpected ways" (2174).

12. Woolf writes, "Also we must become critics because in future we are not going to leave writing to be done for us by a small class of well-to-do young men who have only a pinch, a thimbleful of experience to give us" (M 153).

13. The politics of "How Should One Read a Book" anticipate Woolf's late "The Leaning Tower" in which she undermines critical authority even more thoroughly: "It is time," she imagines the public library telling the common reader, "that even you, whom I have shut out from all my universities for centuries, should learn to read your mother tongue"; she urges commoners to "write daily; write freely" and to "trespass at once," for "literature is no one's private ground; literature is common ground. It is not cut up into nations; there are no wars there" (M 152-54).

14. Particularly galling to Showalter is Woolf's criticism of Charlotte Brontë. In A Room of One's Own, for example, Woolf writes that where Austen, like Shakespeare, miraculously writes without bitterness and protest, Brontë's work is "deformed and twisted" by a rage that makes us feel the "swerve" of the imagination (78, 75, 79).

15. See, for example, Farwell, who writes that in androgyny woman "symbolizes the lower side of the human being" (8) and that "because one of the most exclusive functions of the female in society is creation and reproduction, androgyny can be seen as a male attempt to appropriate the power of creation for himself" (8).

16. Friedman argues that nineteenth-century narrative is authoritarian and that the woman novelist's resistance to it is both Modernist and feminist (162-63).

17. This is, of course, a paradox. As Hein Groen says, feminists have claimed depersonalization as an attack on the male ego, and especially authoritarianism. But in this feminists are caught in a trap: to reify the feminine as absence is to stay marginalized; to become masculine is to reify what feminism seeks to destroy (117). Thus for Groen, Woolf's celebration of impersonality at the end of *A Room of One's Own* is "hardly reconcilable with feminist interests" (119).

18. According to Alcoff, Kristeva argues that "*a feminist practice can only be negative, at odds with what already exists so that we may say 'that's not it' and 'that's still not it'*" (Alcoff 308; emphasis in original).

"Que scais-je?": Virginia Woolf and the Essay as Feminist Critique

Catherine Sandbach-Dahlström

Before our century most essay writing defined itself as a male preserve. It re-presented an intimate cultural and cultured conversation between male subjects, conducted by the fireside or in the course of a long ramble in the countryside. The typical essayist is Montaigne's "honnête homme": an average decent man engaged in a measured conversation with his peers. In this spirit Lamb's bachelor, Elia, addresses a reader who has attended the same school or university, who moves in the same public world of commerce and who shares the essayist's ideological presuppositions. In Hazlitt's dialogue with his brother John on self-love and benevolence, in Arnold's assumption that the worlds of culture and politics are reserved for men alone, in Pater's fear that his writings will damage the minds of the young male, the pattern repeats itself. The essay is a conversation about men addressed to men: the canonical essay, in other words, is yet another nonfiction discourse—comparable to history, political science, or philosophy in which women are not present as subjects but are rendered invisible or marginalized—or even objectified as "the other."

Virginia Woolf's historicizing of the essay corresponds to this configuration. Fairly early in her writing career, in an essay entitled "Men and Women," she suggested that this androcentric discourse resembled a dance around the gold calf of the masculine ego, a feature of male culture that she was to critique so powerfully toward the end of her life in *Three Guineas*. Noting ironically that "the garrulous sex . . . is not the female but the male," she observes that "in all the libraries of the world the man is to be heard talking to himself and for the most part about himself" (*E* 3: 193). In this context of masculine exchange a woman, both as reader and writer of the essay, would be comparable to an interloper on the other side of the hedgerow or an eavesdropper outside the library door. Indeed, if a woman should dare to enter into the discourse, she would probably soon be silenced by the cacophony of male voices. Such a figuring of male domination is, however, an exaggeration. Though it would be hard to deny male hegemony in culture, feminist genealogy has revealed a greater female presence than has been historically generally recognized. Women were, of course, both the writers, the address-ees, and de facto readers of essays from the eighteenth century on. By the time Woolf started writing, the body of women's published writings (including journalism, history, biography, and even scientific work), as she presumably knew, was considerable. Thus, however effective Woolf's comment may be as a polemical statement, it apparently—despite the famous evocation of a female tradition in *A Room of One's Own*—represents a troubling tendency to underemphasize women's actual contribution to writing in general and to other texts than the fictional in particular.[1] "So if we may prophesy," she wrote characteristically in "Women and Fiction," "women in time to come will write . . . not novels only, but poetry and criticism and history" (*GR* 84). In view of Woolf's certain knowledge of the work of women journalists in the periodical press, and her acquaintance with the work of critics such as Gertrude Stein and Vernon Lee as well as with the work of Jane Harrison, this remark seems disingenuous to say the least.

Be that as it may, her apparent disregard for other women's nonfiction may be less an expression of personal jealousy than a deliberate political and didactic positioning.[2] Woolf's sometimes cavalier treatment of other women writers has been seen as confirmation of her avowed jealousy of potential rivals. But since the evidence for this is to be found primarily in the private writing, she was evidently aware of her own responses and capable of analyzing them and resisting her own ungenerous reactions to women competitors.[3] Moreover, while her representations of women's literary work as a task yet to be performed naturally highlight the signifi-cance of her own contribution to literature, her remarks could equally serve the purpose of persuading her audience of women's continued marginaliza-tion. They could encourage other women not to believe complacently that their place in literature was assured. It is in the light of this innate didactic component, designed to increase women's awareness of their tenuous relation to culture, that I will argue here for Woolf's use of the essay as a vehicle for her skeptical feminism.[4]

Much has been made of Woolf's rejection of the label of "feminism," but this seems to me to be primarily a rejection of all labeling. However, for all her sympathy for women's disabilities, her response to the organized women's movements was, paradoxically enough, consistently ambivalent. Feminism, for her, was never self-evident. Woolf's own feminism, in other words, is always engaged in a debate with its own political and intellectual difficulties. The essay genre, as Woolf understood it, provided her with a ready-made vehicle for the representation of just this type of indirect and questioning concept of feminism. Since the essay by definition is less constrained by conventions than other forms of nonfictional writing, it readily allows for the introduction of new perspectives; it admits the personal and encourages an open-ended discussion of whatever the topic at hand may be. Consequently, for all its presumed masculinity, the essay provided Woolf with a mode of writing well suited to a feminist critique of male culture. The lack of thematic constraints, the indeterminacy, and the self-reflexive nature of the form made it a suitable vehicle for her open-ended investigation of the accepted.[5]

In the introduction to their collection of modern essays, *The Politics of the Essay*, however, Joeres and Mittman argue the reverse; namely, that Woolf was an apolitical traditionalist for whom, as for Montaigne and many others, the essay merely provided "a space for contemplation, measured thinking, respite from the frenetic world" (14). It would be futile, of course, to deny that Woolf's texts invoke previous writers of familiar essays or that her critical method—particularly when dealing with individual authors—to a considerable extent resonates with the nineteenth-century mode of impressionist criticism practiced by her father Leslie Stephen, among others.[6] Moreover in both composition and subject matter Woolf's texts are, at least superficially, very similar to those of her contemporary and friend, Lytton Strachey. But to stress the debt to tradition is, I believe, to emphasize the formal element in the essays at the expense of conceptualization. On closer examination, it is apparent that Strachey's critique occurs from within tradition: his authorial position is determined by his status as a male subject with an Oxbridge education. In contrast Woolf's essayist, as we shall see, persistently places herself in the position of the skeptical outsider who questions the masculine bias of the culture of the past.

Elsewhere in *The Politics of the Essay*, Joeres asks what will happen when the essay is appropriated for radical feminist purposes. In view of Joeres's criticism of Woolf's traditionalism, it is ironic that Woolf adopted this most elastic of genres for her own purposes. In "Men and Women" she had suggested that women writers test the old forms before discarding those they found "unfit" (E 3: 195). Because it often conveys its concepts by means of open-ended exploration and indirectly through metaphor, "the essay," she wrote, "admits more properly than biography or fiction of sudden boldness and metaphor" (CR 1: 214).

Her use of metaphor, however, has proved troubling to some critics who experience this as evidence for conceptual confusion in Woolf's critical writing. In an otherwise acute analysis of "Modern Fiction," John Mepham, for example, takes Woolf to task for her failure to resolve the conflict she herself has constructed between materialism and the true purposes of fiction: between an attention to banal detail for its own sake on the one hand and the attempt to reproduce her vision of the essence of life itself in language on the other (66, 76). If, however, we consider Woolf's practice in the light of the theories presented here, we can see that far from representing confusion, this apparent failure makes perfect sense. The essay need not construct a strict logical argument that resolves all intellectual tensions in some form of closure. In fact Woolf's very inability to resolve the conflict between materialism and an ideal of fiction may well be the conceptual core, metaphorically speaking, of the essay: the idea itself. She is, in effect, making the point that in the creation of art there need be no opposition between features that might otherwise be regarded as incompatible, in this case the banal detail in coexistence with the visionary imagination.

In demanding the strict logic of closure of Woolf's analysis of fiction, Mepham also disregards another cardinal feature of the essay as she practiced it, namely its exploratory and skeptical nature. Historically speaking, and in the spirit of the Cartesian mode of philosophical speculation, the essay relentlessly questions its own status as a form of art and knowledge.[7] "And what are these things of mine, indeed," wonders Montaigne characteristically, "but grotesques and monstrous bodies, pieced together from sundry limbs, with no definite shape, and with no order, sequence, or proportion except by chance?" (91). Yet this statement is also an indication of how his essays differ from Cartesian thought insofar as they refuse to build new structures of knowledge or to claim a position of universal authority on the basis of experience. A similar refusal of authority infuses Woolf's first collection of essays, *The Common Reader*. As she apologetically explains in the introduction, the volume in hand is no more than a "rickety and ramshackle fabric" composed of the scraps that make up the amateur critic's own very personal and makeshift evaluative position (CR 1: 1).

Michael Hall has argued for a significant parallel between the essay and the voyages of discovery; the essay, he suggests, is "a product of the Renaissance idea of discovery as well as a response to it" (73). It thus seems fitting that Woolf should turn to the Elizabethan voyage as a means of exploring her own practice as a writer. In "The Elizabethan Lumber Room,"

she investigates the same issue of haphazard selection more extensively—
if also more indirectly (CR 1: 39-47). In this text writing and the voyages
of discovery are conflated by the controlling image of lumber; and
although the title apparently unites the various items collected by travelers
in an enclosed physical space (the room), the very concept of lumber—a
haphazard assembling of odds and ends from different places and times,
varying in quality and value—valorizes differentiation and dispenses with
unity. Differentiation is thematically expressed by the voyager's aimless
collection of these trophies, and differentiation is also reproduced in the
actual composition of the essay. The text proceeds by means of tenuously
related passages containing descriptions of items collected by Elizabethan
sailors, snippets of narrative sketching moments in their lives, and brief
critical statements outlining the storage of these items in the cultural
lumber room of Elizabethan writing. These fleeting insights combine at
last in the image of the bricolage of human knowledge as it manifests itself
in Browne's *Religio Medici* whereby lumber becomes a trope for the textual
configurations of both Woolf's own essay and the Elizabethan prose she
is describing.

The exploratory quality is often reenacted in Woolf's texts by the
disjunction created by a shift from the title towards a seemingly unrelated
topic. For instance, a personal essay entitled "Evening Over Sussex" is neither
a discussion of fading light nor the geography of southern England; rather,
it is a meditation on the nature of identity—of the self (DM 7-19). The
insights reached here as to the self's multiple and fragmented nature are,
moreover and significantly, a direct consequence of the space created in the
text by the metaphor of the journey; the car ride which encourages the
seemingly unitary self to split into various perceiving eyes/I's.

This vision of the essay as a metaphorical voyage or journey is also
reenacted in one of Woolf's best-known critical essays, "Character in Fiction." Here, appropriately enough, the actual venue is a vehicle, a railway
carriage. In a challenging analysis of this essay, Rachel Bowlby has remarked
that the text (and thus the carriage as a metaphor for writing, I would
suggest) is a kind of "literary Clapham Junction for the crossing and potential
collision of questions of representation, history, and sexual difference" (2).
The railway carriage reveals the sexual politics of writing as the male author
attempts to impose his own notions of form upon "character" in the form of
Mrs. Brown. She, however, remains obstinately a parodic Cleopatra; a
creature of infinite variety who appears differently at different times and to
different people. A lumberlike configuration, she demands through the
metaphor of her physical being (she is old; she is sad; she is poor, and her

parts and clothing are fastened, tied together, brushed up) toleration for the spasmodic, the obscure, and the fragmentary (E 3:91).

If Woolf saw the essay, then, as a vehicle for processes of exploration rather than determinacy, this evidently reflects upon her way of viewing her project. Her essays are a collage of vacillating viewpoints and shifting inconclusive perspectives imbued with their own ironic skepticism. To compose an essay is a way of both exploring a topic and exploring that exploration. In the essay on Montaigne, Woolf is characteristically prompted to a skeptical consideration of the essence of her enterprise. Considering Montaigne's experiment with his own soul through his "extraordinary volumes of short and broken, long and learned, logical and contradictory statements," she asks both herself and her reader, in the essay that bears his name, what impulse lies behind Montaigne's *essais:*

> But, as we watch with absorbed interest the enthralling spectacle of a soul living openly beneath our eyes, the question frames itself, Is pleasure the end of all? Whence this overwhelming interest in the nature of the soul? Why this overmastering desire to communicate with others? Is the beauty of this world enough, or is there, elsewhere, some explanation of the mystery? To this what answer can there be? There is none. There is only one more question: 'Que scais-je?' (CR 1: 67-68)

In thus recognizing through Montaigne, who is so close to her in spirit, that there are no certain responses to our existential questions and no final explanations for our aesthetic pleasures, Woolf indicates that skepticism is inherent in the essayist's way of viewing all art and knowledge. The voyage of discovery can generate only questions, never answers.

If the voyage of discovery conducted by the essayist is into the possibilities for a feminist critique, then, given the inherent skepticism of the form, questioning and resistance are inseparable. This is most evidently the case in a lesser-known essay entitled, "Why?" First published in 1934 in a short-lived Oxford magazine, appropriately named *Lysistrata* to denote rebellion against masculine norms, the text collapses literary and sexual politics and explicitly reenacts the parameters for skeptical resistance. It may consequently serve as a trope for Woolf's critical practice as a whole.

From the start of the essay the very act of asking a question is feminized through gender typing : "Questions, therefore, being sensitive, impulsive and often foolish, have a way of picking their asking place with care"(DM 227). Like women too they are confined, it seems, to the private sphere because they are too threatening to be allowed a hearing in public. "The little twisted sign that comes at the end of a question has a way of making the rich writhe; power and prestige come down upon it with all their weight" and the questions "shrivel up" in the face of patriarchy, or "power, prosperity, and timeworn stone" (*DM* 227-28). If, as the last images suggest, an ancient and immovable tradition is an obstacle to change, would not a woman's journal then provide a more sympathetic forum for skeptical debate? But even here there are sanctions; "the editor forbids feminism," the essayist tells us. And more damagingly, it would appear, for sexual politics, Woolf also refuses to answer the question "what is feminism?" by rapidly shifting her discourse to the seemingly innocuous question: "Why lecture, why be lectured?" (*DM* 228).

However, a reading of the whole essay suggests that this question is far from innocuous, and indeed serves to reintroduce sexual politics with a vengeance. For within the structure of the essay the lecturer, as well as the student of English literature, is gendered male whereas the listener or reader of dissertations is female. Moreover, both practices, lecturing and literary criticism, are subjected to feminine ridicule. In the first place, the lecturer is "a harried looking man, a man from whose face nervousness, vanity, or perhaps the depressing and impossible nature of his task had removed all traces of ordinary humanity" (*DM* 229). Secondly, the young literary critic, once a clever and sensitive reader, has, in the eyes of his woman editor, been reduced to a parrot whose texts are indistinguishable from anyone else's (*DM* 234).

What, then, in the light of this reenactment of a feminist position are we to make of the essayist's refusal to answer the question "what is feminism?" In *The Reading of Silence: Virginia Woolf and the English Tradition*, Patricia Laurence interprets the prevalence of silence—ellipses and omissions—as part of the feminist agenda in Woolf's fictional narrative structures. In this particular essay (itself couched in the form of a fictional narrative) silence is narrated by two dashes preceded by the words "a new." What new thing it is that feminism, women, or women's colleges will create is never spelled out. It is left to the reader to fill the gap, for, to quote Laurence further, "in narrating silences, Woolf implicates the readers . . . in new ways by creating a space for them to interpret" (12).

It seems, in fact, that by means of the unanswered question and the pregnant silence that concludes the essay, Woolf has evoked a response consistent with a phenomenological theory of reading whereby, as Iser writing of the "Interaction between Text and Reader" puts it, the reader is forced "to supply what is meant from what is not said" (111).[8] What can the reader supply here? The essay ends with the frustrated editor throwing the young man's sterile, many-page analysis of Shakespeare's sonnets across the room and breaking a teapot. In Woolf's feminist iconography, this particular piece of domestic equipment signifies the common failure of feminine courage, the semicowardice that makes women pander to male posturing over the tea table.[9] The reduction of the teapot to smithereens may thus well be read as the refraction of the famous inkpot thrown at the angel in the house, the ultimate feminist gesture. But the text ends with the essayist and her editor friend attempting to piece together the object that had belonged to a grandmother. It would appear that the feminine tradition destroyed by a violent expression of feminist rage is valuable nonetheless and should be restored. Or is this a comment on women's failure of nerve that leaves "the new" as yet unspoken and unfulfilled?[10]

If we regard this text, because of its ambivalent evocation of central feminist issues, as typical for Woolf's project, then we must read her work both for its sexual politics and for its skeptical approach to feminism itself. Both factors, I believe, inform the conceptualization and organization of her main collections of essays, the two *Common Readers*.[11]

As the first *Common Reader* increasingly took shape in 1923, Woolf paused to consider the course of the exploratory journey she was about to undertake. As she noted in her diary, she felt that in this collection she would "graze nearer [her] own individuality . . . [and] mitigate the pomposity & sweep in all sorts of trifles" (2: 261). Although the reference is unclear, Woolf evidently sees herself as working against a constricting tradition and her own earlier acceptance of it.[12]

Woolf's vehicle is the amateurish, unsystematic, ordinary common reader: her essayist persona. Since this figure occupies a female gender position, being without the usual trappings of power and cultural authority, she or he enables the infiltration of the "other point of view" into literary history. This applies both to the construction of the writing subjectivity and the choice of subject. Even if Woolf's common reader discusses some of the major literary figures of the past, and indeed literary movements in fairly conventional terms, reviews of this kind are juxtaposed against the representation of the "Lives of the Obscure." "It is one of the attractions of the unknown," the essayist remarks, that

> instead of keeping their identity separate, as remarkable people do, they seem to merge into one another, their very boards and title-pages and frontispieces dissolving, and their innumerable pages melting into continuous years so that we can lie back and look up into the fine mist-like substance of countless lives , and pass unhindered from century to century, from life to life. (CR 1: 108-9)

In representing the lives of these inhabitants of the cultural lumber room, Woolf implies that she is able to escape from the categories of literary history and the constrictions of linear time. Their inclusion also denaturalizes the public stance in favor of the private voice; it shifts attention from the superior qualities of the man of genius to the conditions of cultural production. In its turn this allows—in the famous essays on Jane Austen, Christina Rossetti and George Eliot, for instance—for a consideration of the particularities of the woman writer's situation. In other words, Woolf's redeployments in the *Common Readers* effectively domesticize, and thus by implication feminize, the writing of literary history.

In rewriting, the kind of obscure individual presented in "Dorothy Osborne's Letters" becomes a central figure in English literary history. The reason given is that her letters introduce domestic intimacy into the tradition: "for the first time in English literature" the reader, Woolf suggests, overhears the private conversation of "men and women talking together over the fire" (CR 2: 60). Furthermore Woolf figures this change as "rustlings in the undergrowth" (60), implying through this metaphor that the hitherto repressed and hidden secrets of the invisible groups in society will at last be voiced. The image indeed reproduces the spirit of both *Common Readers* with their privileging of the undergrowth of the private sphere over the tidy park land of public discourse.

A privileging of rustlings in the undergrowth that is the private life also applies to Woolf's representations of the great. In many essays on earlier prominent writers she evokes their private selves before their public personae. Moreover, true to the spirit of resistance to traditional modes of interpretation these representations are not projections of the deeper recesses of the artist's creative psyches but enactments of everyday flaws and weaknesses.[13] In Woolf's essay "Dorothy Wordsworth," Coleridge, filtered through Dorothy's subjectivity, is preserved for posterity in his private inglorious person. He is a man who cannot abide physical discomfort, who suffers unromantically from rheumatism in the joints, and who abandons a debate over the meaning of the sublime during a walk merely because it is cold (CR 2: 171). In "Cowper and Lady Austen" the poet is presented in equally unromantic terms, not as a significant poet but as an aging voyeur, an elderly gentleman looking out of his window in a village street at two women entering a draper's store (CR 2: 140). At one level, of course, this treatment of well-known writers is an expression of Woolf's received concern—whatever her theories of the impersonality of art—for the human consciousness behind the text. Nonetheless the iconoclasm of Woolf's portrayal of the great, here and elsewhere (we have but to think of her portrait of Pope in *Orlando* [202-9]) undoubtedly serves the purpose of mitigating an unthinking respect for authority.[14]

If this implicit questioning of the criteria for evaluating great writers succeeds in denaturalizing a primarily masculine tradition, there is a more overt sexual politics in the pervasive antimasculinism of Woolf's configurations of the critics. Several prominent male critics are, in fact, figured in her texts as sterile, pseudo-scientific or militaristic. In "On Re-reading Novels," Percy Lubbock figures typically with his desire to categorize, which imposes his analysis between literature and the reader like "an alien substance" (*M* 160). In contrast, in "The Art of Fiction," Forster is praised because as neither "a scholar" nor "a pseudo scholar" he approaches literature intimately as a lover (*M* 106).[15] The scientific approach to criticism is, in other words, not to be trusted since it effectively divorces the reader from the text. For example, in an earlier essay, "The Anatomy of Fiction," an American professor of literature (in the guise of a quack at a country fair) dissects the literary text as does the biologist a frog in a laboratory (*E* 3: 45). Science as a metaphor appears again in the first version of "On Reading Novels" when the critic's activity is compared to that of a radiologist: Mr. Lubbock applies his Roentgen rays to that "voluminous lady," fiction, and effectively deprives her of all her feminine charms and interesting diversity, "the smile and witchery, together with the umbrellas and brown paper parcels which she has collected on her . . . journey" through literary history (*E* 3: 341). The sexual politics of the image is clear: the critic's enterprise is an act of power against a female "other" designed to strip her down to a skeletal level where no enchantment is possible. Indeed, his theorizing functions as a further act of power since his type of criticism deprives the reader of a direct and natural response to the literary text.

More powerful even than these accusations of scientific sterility and of the unwarranted use of cultural power are the gendered associations of academic criticism with militarism. The horror with which Woolf's essayist in "All About Books" views the schooling of a new generation of readers in a masculinist tradition is movingly conveyed by the military language in which the representation is made.

> How orderly they come! One could swear that they are all arrayed in troops, and all march in step, and all halt, charge and otherwise behave themselves under the command of officers mounted upon chargers. . . .
> [T]here is not a single straggler or deserter among them; there is no dancing or disorder; no wild voice cries alone; no man or woman breaks the ranks and leaves the troop and takes to the wilderness stirring desire

and unrest among the hearts of his companions. All is orderly, all is preconcerted. If division there is, even that is regular. Camp is opposed to camp; the hostile parties separate, form, meet, fight, leave each other for dead upon the ground; rise, form and fight again. Classic is opposed to romantic; naturalist to metaphysic. . . . Never . . . were the young so well-equipped as at present. No more respectable army has ever issued from the portals of the two great Universities. . . . (CDB 123-24)

Given Woolf's postwar pacifism, the power of this critique is apparent. The evocation of recent history is striking. The images of war are highly reminiscent of the circumstances of young officers in the trenches during the first World War, where discipline was rigorously enforced, where deserters were shot in the back, and where the carnage of small-scale attacks into enemy territory was repeated again and again.

A similar tragic connection between critical failure and the recent history of war is made in the portrait of a great nineteenth-century critic, Walter Raleigh. In the course of his career, we learn in the essay bearing his name that he discovered that he preferred life to literature, soldiering to reading and writing (CBD 87-93). For him the debacle of 1914 was not a tragedy but a final chance to prove himself. "He did what a man of his age could do," remarks Woolf's essayist with biting irony, "He drilled. He marched. He wrote pamphlets. He lectured more frequently than ever; he practically ceased to read. At length he was made historian of the Air Force" (CDB 92-93). The irony is complete when we understand that sexual politics lies behind this defection: Raleigh has come to see the love of literature as effeminate and unrewarding—a concern merely for old maids.

Raleigh's realization that literature belongs to the feminine tallies with Woolf's own persistent gendering of literature and culture as feminine and the critical activity as appropriate. Not only does she represent Forster's approach to literature as that of a lover, but the same, we are told, is also true of another prominent nineteenth-century critic, Edmund Gosse: "Literature to him was an incomparable mistress and it was his delight 'to dress her charms and make her more beloved.'" In itself this impulse might be a fitting one on the part of the reader toward the literary work, but Gosse's love is unfortunately a sterile one. There will be no living children in the form of a vibrant and vital criticism, for, the reader is told, his masculinity inhibits true engagement. A captive to critical impartiality, he cannot risk "the agony of childbirth" that is a necessary condition of successful criticism (M 91).

The image of childbirth for the creative process is conventional, of course, but the effect of its use here is not simply to reclaim creativity for the feminine. The image is being used less commonly and most specifically for the consequences of a fertile relation between the critic and the object of desire, the literary text. This is a criticism that does not merely seek to master the other text. "[I]f we can imagine the art of fiction come alive and standing in our midst," writes Woolf in "Modern Fiction," "she would undoubtedly bid us break her and bully her." But although the will to power is present, it is an impulse that also recognizes the dignity, independence, and ultimate superiority of that other. For the critic must also "honor and love [fiction] for so her youth is renewed and her sovereignty assured (*CR* 1: 154). When this erotic connection is at its best, the critical essay as art may be conceived.

Woolf's skeptical feminism has thus far been represented as a mode of resistance to tradition and as a pervasive attack on masculinism. Other essays can be read in more positive terms, not merely as a critique of male culture but also as a valorization of the feminine. This endorsement of the feminine is conveyed, interestingly enough, through an evocation of the carnival spirit.

The first essay, "The Value of Laughter," written in 1905, ridicules male pomposity and the heavy-handedness of male attempts at humor. In contrast, the reader is told, it is women who truly possess "the comic spirit [which] concerns itself with oddities and eccentricities and deviations from the recognized pattern." This concern for what lies outside the familiar patterns is typical of carnival's recognition of otherness and its defamiliarization of established structures.[16] Women, we learn, like children such as the little boy in Andersen's tale, "The Emperor's New Clothes," have access to carnival because theirs is an undamaged perception allowing them to see phenomena and human beings with clarity, for "their eyes are not clouded with learning nor are their brains choked with the theories of books" (*E* 1: 60). In other words, they are able to see beyond traditional hierarchical notions of value to the essentials of character and situation.[17]

A carnival ability to ridicule the official structures of society is more extensively demonstrated in a much later essay, "Dr. Burney's Evening Party." This text reenacts the earlier insight into the quality of female humor and, moreover, provides an exemplary text for the points I have been making here. Not only does the essay evoke the qualities of the carnival, but its composition reproduces the nonhierarchical fusing of the conceptual and the aesthetic as outlined by theories of the essay genre. Moreover, the whole text may be read both as an extended critique of the relations of men and women in society and as an extended metaphor for the essay's own endemic skepticism.

Appearing in the second series of *The Common Reader*, this text offers its critique by penetrating to the heart of eighteenth-century London's cultural establishment in the shape of Dr. Johnson and his circle. Ostensibly a humorous narrative designed, as Woolf suggested the essay should be, as pure entertainment, this text also offers a thorough exposé of the power and dangers of female resistance to the norms of culture and society. As this exposé is realized through the mode if not the substance of fiction, an essayistic kaleidoscope suitably replaces the stringent argumentation that we would expect of a sustained polemical critique. The moment of criticism is signified not by ostensible logical presentation but by the aporia or tension between the seriousness of the tenor (the desire to resist the evils of patriarchal power) and the frivolity of the vehicle (the story of an evening party).

From the start the essay does not give its reader an impression of seriousness. Before even reaching its ostensible topic, the narrative meanders lightheartedly (in a way reminiscent of "The Elizabethan Lumber Room") through a number of domestic and private spaces: Fanny Burney's writing cabin at Lynn, Dr. Burney's study, the house in Portland Street, Daddy Crisp's house in a field, Fulke Greville's estate. Finally we arrive at Mrs. Thrale's house at Streatham where the essayist's project of domestication is completed by the image of Mrs. Thrale taming that ultimate representative of culture and literacy himself, the great Dr. Johnson. In fact, enclosed within this domestic space, the frivolous environment of a lady's drawing room, Dr. Johnson is not merely tamed, he is silenced. Without the appropriate stimulus, without the "other" man to converse with, without a Boswell prompting and hanging upon his every word, the doctor, far from expressing his opinion on every kind of topic in his usual manner, freezes into an "image of gravity, dignity, and composure" (CR 2: 124).

However, the reader is not to be left with the illusion that this silence necessarily embraces a profundity of thought. The narrator tells us that Johnson has turned to the capacious resources of his own mind for entertainment, but when we finally are made privy to one of Dr. Johnson's "starts of vision," its banality undermines our faith in his intellectual capacity. As it appears from his protest, "If it were not for depriving the ladies of the fire . . . I should like to stand upon the hearth myself," Dr. Johnson is primarily annoyed by the aristocrat Greville's appropriation of the best place in the room (CR 2:125). Even if the remark is fully justified and reflects the emotions of the other guests, and even though it is impossible to decide whether Johnson's chivalry is faked or not, there is no little doubt of the irony with which he is viewed.

This potentially anarchic humorous treatment of the great is reinforced in the narrative by Mrs. Thrale's behavior. True to the carnival spirit that sees "the entire world in its droll aspect" she is overcome by a wild impulse which prompts her to undermine the solemnity of the whole occasion (Bakhtin 11). While Signor Piozzi by singing tries to fill the gap in the conversation created by Johnson's silence,

> Giving rein to the spirit of recklessness which sometimes bubbled in her, she rose, and stole on tiptoes to the piano forte. . . . She began a ludicrous mimicry of his gestures: she shrugged her shoulders, she cast up her eyes, she reclined her head on one side just as he did. (CR 2: 123)

Although Dr. Burney intervenes almost at once to stop Mrs. Thrale, her conduct effectively reduces male authority and sets up a different set of values within the text. For her outburst is to be read as something more than a temporary aberration. It foreshadows her ultimate break with all decorum, namely her future marriage with Piozzi. This event, the narrator tells us, "drove her in ignomy from England" (CR 2:123). The informed reader will know, of course, that since she had been widowed there was no real crime in marrying Piozzi. Her "offence" was to break the barriers of nation and class by forming an alliance with a foreigner who was beneath her in social status. Her wild laughter, as well as her future life, is a demonstration of a radical resistance to patriarchy, for she is destined to defy both social mores in general and Dr. Johnson's fatherly patronage in particular. While the presentation of her behavior here is playful, the foreshadowing in the text is a reminder of the real seriousness behind the social game. When carnival becomes more than the accepted relief from the hierarchies of the everyday, it is no longer allowed. For what the decorum of the drawing room conceals is the cruel coercion practiced by a patriarchal society when it attempts to control women and anarchic female sexuality.

Insofar as this text demonstrates resistance to coercion, Woolf has recourse to multiple female subjectivities to represent the scene to the reader. In the first place, we owe the present text to the account of the events in Fanny Burney's diary. Secondly, we owe our vision of the ludicrous to Mrs. Thrale's perception, and finally, we are in debt to Woolf as essayist for the extended ridicule of male solemnity enacted in the essay. Instead of the egocentric male subject that usually lurks at the essay's center, here the reader meets a collective female perspective.

But as any reader of Woolf's writing knows, there is no perspective (single or collective) that may not be questioned or undermined within one text—or elsewhere. While this essay celebrates the anarchic and the carnivalesque, it also implicitly questions the value of these forces. Developments at Dr. Burney's party fill his guest with unease. For not only is gender hierarchy undermined, if briefly, but the structures of class society are also disturbed. Nor is the possibility of social disturbance limited to the fore-shadowing of Mrs. Thrale's defection as the narrative concludes with the defeat of the aristocracy (Greville) by the middle classes (Johnson, the son of a bookseller). When the evening was at last over, no one, we are told, "wished for its repetition" (CR 2: 125). For all its entertainment value, the possibility of anarchy is ultimately threatening.

It would seem, then, that in "Dr. Burney's Evening Party," as in "Why?," Woolf reproduced the classic feminist dilemma: a desire for change and an unease as to what change may bring with it.[18] On the one hand, where traditionally the essay is a conversation between male subjects, here, as in other essays, both the great critic himself and the controlling egocentric voice of the essayist have been silenced.[19] The reasonable utterances of Montaigne's "honnête homme" have been drowned by the titter of the party guests. In place of the male dialogue we hear a multiple feminine voice criticizing the sterility inherent in objectivity and impartiality, undercutting the sexual politics of culture, and mocking male pretensions and solemnity. On the other hand, however, this apparent victory of a wilder "other," this triumph of the carnivalesque, is not completely endorsed. In breaking the mold of tradition, something will be lost, or more precisely, perhaps, nothing will be gained.

Of course, given the indistinctness of the essayist's voice as a conse-quence of the merging of subjectivities here, it is impossible to determine whether the skepticism about the consequences of radical change is Woolf's or whether the criticism is being directed at women's—and by extension, feminism's—endemic failures of nerve. Change may be desirable, but women may lack the will to power that would bring it about. Woolf may thus merely be reporting Fanny Burney's unease at the turn events have taken. If, however, we read the essay generically as a skeptical meditation on itself, then it is probable that a more profound doubt as to the possibility or even desirability of effective resistance is being expressed. Not only does the society portrayed resist change, both in the gender system and in the fabric of the social body as a whole, but the controlling, if impersonal, narrative voice of the essayist cannot be allowed to valorize chaos by adopting a final or conclusive position. For to do so, even if it were but to embrace the carnivalesque as a consistent new mode of being, would inevitably and paradoxically be to introduce a new system of conventional wisdom. The essayist's voyage of discovery into the wild zone evoked by Mrs. Thrale's moment of rebellion is abandoned; the ship turns back into the harbor enthralled by its own self-doubt. The party is over and no one will ask for another like it.

What, then, is the purpose of the exploration: *Que scais-je?*

Works Cited

Adorno, Theodor. "The Essay as Form." Trans. Bob Hullot-Kenter. *New German Critique* 32 (1984) : 151-71.

Bakhtin, Mikhail. *Rabelais and His World.* Trans. Helène Iswolsky. Bloomington: Indiana UP, 1984.

Bauschatz, Cathleen M. "Montaigne's Conception of Reading in the Context of Renaissance Poetics and Modern Criticism." Suleiman and Crosman. 264-91.

Bowlby, Rachel. *Virginia Woolf: Feminist Destinations.* Oxford: Blackwell, 1988.

Good, Graham. *The Observing Self: Rediscovering the Essay.* London: Routledge, 1988.

Gordon, Lyndall. *Virginia Woolf: A Writer's Life.* Oxford: Oxford UP, 1982.

Hall, Michael. "The Emergence of the Essay and the Idea of Discovery." *Essays on the Essay.* Ed. Alexander J. Butrym. Athens and London: U of Georgia P, 1989. 73-91.

Hill, Katherine C. "Virginia Woolf and Leslie Stephen: History and Literary Revolution." *PMLA* 96 (1981) : 351-62.

Holquist, Michael. *Bakhtin and His World.* London: Routledge, 1990.

Humm, Maggie. *Feminist Criticism: Women as Contemporary Critics.* Brighton: Harvester, 1986.

Iser, Wolfgang. "Interaction between Text and Reader. " Suleiman and Crosman. 106-19.

Joeres, Ruth-Ellen Boetcher. "The Passionate Essay." *The Politics of the Essay.* Ed. Ruth-Ellen Boetcher Joeres and Elizabeth Mittman. Bloomington: Indiana UP, 1993. 151-71.

Laurence, Patricia. *The Reading of Silence: Virginia Woolf and the English Tradition.* Stanford: Stanford UP, 1991.

Lee, Hermione. *Virginia Woolf.* London: Chatto and Windus, 1996.

Meisel, Perry. *The Absent Father: Virginia Woolf and Walter Pater.* New Haven: Yale UP, 1980.

Mepham, John. *Virginia Woolf: A Literary Life.* London: Macmillan, 1991.

Montaigne, Michel de. "On Friendship." *Essays.* Trans. J. M. Cohen. Harmondsworth: Penguin, 1958. 91-105.

Rosenbaum, S. P. Introduction. *Women and Fiction: The Manuscript Version of* A Room of One's Own. By Virginia Woolf. Oxford: Blackwell, 1992. xiii-xiv.

Sandbach-Dahlström, Catherine. "Conversing about Collusion." *Pro Femina* 4 (1995/96): 145-53.

Sontag, Susan. "Against Interpretation." *Against Interpretation and Other Essays.* New York: Doubleday, 1993. 3-14.

Suleiman, Susan R., and Inge Crosman. *The Reader in the Text: Essays on Audience and Interpretation.* Princeton: Princeton UP, 1980.

Woolf, Virginia. *Articles, essays, fiction and reviews,* 1. Manuscript. Berg Collection. New York Public Library.

———. "A Sketch of the Past." *Moments of Being.* Ed. Jeanne Schulkind. London: Grafton, 1978. 71-162.

———. "A Society." *The Complete Shorter Fiction.* Ed. Susan Dick. London: Grafton, 1987. 168-85.

———. *The Captain's Deathbed and Other Essays.* 1950. New York: Harcourt, 1978.

———. *The Common Reader.* Ed. Andrew McNeillie. New York: Harcourt, 1984.

———. *The Death of the Moth and Other Essays.* New York: Harcourt, 1970.

———. *The Essays of Virginia Woolf.* Ed. Andrew McNeillie. 4 vols. to date. London: Hogarth, 1986-.

———. *The Diary of Virginia Woolf.* Ed. Anne Olivier Bell. Vol. 2. Harmondsworth: Penguin, 1983.

———. *Granite and Rainbow.* 1958. New York: Harcourt, 1975.

———. *The Moment and Other Essays.* New York: Harcourt, 1948.

———. *Orlando.* 1928. New York: Harcourt, 1956.

———. *The Second Common Reader.* 1932. Ed. Andrew McNeillie. New York: Harcourt, 1986.

———. *Three Guineas.* 1938. London: Hogarth, 1992.

Notes

1. The argument for looking back through our mothers is not particularly representative of Woolf's critical writing seen as a whole. Moreover, the lack of any clear narrative position in the self-deconstructing text of *A Room of One's Own* undermines the authority of the appeal to a female tradition.

2. There is a distinctly didactic trait in Woolf's critical and polemical writing that ill accords with the common image of the apolitical aesthete. For instance, the lecture that was to become *A Room of One's Own* was given with the express

purpose of awakening young women to the continuation of female subordination. See S. P. Rosenbaum xiii-xliv.

3.   Most important in this respect are the snide remarks about Katherine Manfield as a person and a writer in diary entries (for example, see *D* 2: 228-29). See Lyndall Gordon's comments on Woolf's relation to Mansfield (184-88) and John Mepham (56-58). Mepham makes the perceptive point that Woolf, for many years, had difficulty in identifying with any "outsiders" quite regardless of their gender identity. The latest contribution to the debate comes in Hermione Lee's biography where Woolf's complicated responses to Katherine Mansfield are explored in depth (386-401). It is apparent from Lee's analysis that Woolf's negative feelings about Mansfield were generated largely by differences of background and temperament rather than by professional jealousy.

4.   Woolf is known to have hoped that the lectures that became *A Room of One's Own* would make the young women there more aware of their own situation.

5.   Woolf's short story "A Society" from 1920 represents the first feminist impulse as a desire to investigate the mechanisms of an androcentric society.

6.   There has been considerable discussion of Woolf's relation to her father and to earlier criticism. See for instance, Katherine C. Hill (351-62) and Maggie Humm. For an extended discussion of Woolf's debt to Walter Pater, see Perry Meisel.

7.   Graham Good remarks that the essay's "starting point is like that of Cartesian philosophy: an isolated self confronting a world of which nothing is known for certain" (4).

8.   Iser actually cites Woolf's essay on Jane Austen as evidence for his theory. For an extended presentation of Woolf's theory of reading, see "How Should One Read a Book?" (*CR* 2: 258-70). The typescript drafts of this essay attribute even more to the active participation of the reader in the creation of meaning in fiction. For Woolf's debt to Montaigne in relation to the reader, see also Bauschatz (264-91).

9.   See Woolf, *The Pargiters*, xxxix, and "A Sketch of the Past," 150-51.

10.   One major problem of interpretation is the question of how Woolf actually understood the word "feminism." First to be found in the *OED* in 1894, the term usually applied to the struggle for equal rights. In 1934 it must have seemed to Woolf that this struggle had not produced any truly new structure in society in general and in the educational system in particular. Women's colleges existed entirely on male terms and their chances of being truly innovative were strictly limited. Her later rejection of the term in *Three Guineas* (117) should be understood in this context.

11. All the other collections are posthumous. Although Leonard Woolf's stated intention was to print essays of equally high quality as those in the *Common Readers*, some of the texts included are still only in draft form and the collections lack the chronological structure of the *Common Readers* that makes it possible to read them as literary histories.

12. Woolf had learned her trade as a journalist working within the framework of the *Times Literary Supplement*.

13. With this emphasis on the inglorious, Woolf is true to the spirit of the new "scientific" biography as theorized by André Maurois and practiced in England by her friend Harold Nicholson. In her own meditation on the topic, "The Art of Biography," Woolf defends the biographer's right to disregard pieties and present the less attractive sides of a personality. She also defends her "democratic" practice: "Is not anyone who has lived a life, and left a record of that life, worthy of biography—the failures as well as the successes, the humble as well as the illustrious?" (*DM* 195).

14. Even in her memorial essay on Conrad, whom she greatly admired, Woolf approaches the topic through the private person, the mysterious foreign gentleman, the recluse with perfect manners (*CR* 1: 223-30).

15. Forster belongs, of course, to a sexually ambiguous "modern mode" of writing if he is compared to the nineteenth-century critics and their spiritual heirs.

16. Cf. Holquist 89.

17. For the antihierarchical bias of carnival, see Bakhtin (10-16).

18. It would presumably be appropriate to define this dilemma as specific to liberal or moderate feminism. Radical feminists might argue that their aim is the complete dismantling of the structures of patriarchy on the grounds that no fundamental change at all is possible unless this occurs.

19. I have also argued for an ultimate pessimism about the possibilities of female resistance in "Conversing about Collusion."

Notes on Contributors

MELBA CUDDY-KEANE is Associate Professor of English and a Northrop Frye Scholar at the University of Toronto. She is past president of the Virginia Woolf Society and has published on Woolf and Joyce Cary in numerous journals, collections, and encyclopedias. She is currently writing a book-length study on Virginia Woolf's literary theory.

BETH RIGEL DAUGHERTY is Professor of English and Chairperson of the Integrative Studies at Otterbein College in Westerville, Ohio. She has published essays on "Mr. Bennett and Mrs. Brown," *To the Lighthouse,* and the *Common Reader* and has begun work on a study of Woolf and education.

JEANNE DUBINO is an Assistant Professor of English at Plymouth State College, New Hampshire. She has published essays on Virginia Woolf as well as essays on popular culture. In addition, she coordinated the Seventh Annual Conference on Virginia Woolf and serves on the editorial board for the *Woolf Studies Annual*

ANNE E. FERNALD teaches in the Expository Writing Program at Harvard University. She is the author of *"A Room of One's Own,* Personal Criticism, and the Essay," published in *Twentieth Century Literature* (Summer 1994).

SALLY GREENE is Lecturer in English and in Law at the University of Virginia. She has published in such journals as *Mosaic, Studies in American Fiction,* and *Studies in the Novel* on a broad range of authors including Woolf, Sylvia Plath, Charlotte Brontë, and Herman Melville. She is currently finishing her dissertation on Woolf and the Renaissance.

EDWARD A. HUNGERFORD has spent the last twenty-two years of his distinguished teaching career at Southern Oregon State College, where he is Professor Emeritus of English. He published the earliest version of "Byron and Mr. Briggs" in *The Yale Review* (1979) and has been a frequent contributor to the *Virginia Woolf Miscellany.* He is one of the founding members of the Virginia Woolf Society.

SALLY A. JACOBSEN is Professor of English at Northern Kentucky University. She has published a number of essays on Virginia Woolf and on Margaret Atwood. She is the co-editor, with C. R. Duke, of *Poets'*

Perspectives (Heinemann-Boynton/Cook, 1992) and is president of the Margaret Atwood Society. She is currently writing a book on the relationship between the stream-of-consciousness technique and Bloomsbury art in Woolf's aesthetics.

GEORGE M. JOHNSON won the Andrew J. Kappel Prize in 1994 from *Twentieth Century Literature* for his essay on Woolf's response to psychology. He has written a critical study of J. D. Beresford, contributed to the *Dictionary of Literary Biography*, and has edited *Late-Victorian and Edwardian British Novelists* (First and Second Series) and *British Novelists Between the Wars*. He teaches English at the University College of the Caribo in Kamloops, British Columbia.

MICHAEL KAUFMANN teaches literature and film at Indiana University–Purdue University, Fort Wayne. His book *Textual Bodies* (Bucknell UP, 1994) examines the innovative use of print in Modernist fiction. He has written on Eliot, Stein, Joyce, Pound, H. D., and other twentieth-century writers. Currently he is at work on a study of the ways Modernist writers and critics define their Modernism to their audiences.

LISA LOW is Associate Professor of English at Pace University in New York City. She is the author of a number of essays on early modern literature and is co-editor, with Anthony John Harding, of *Milton, the Metaphysicals, and Romanticism* (Cambridge UP, 1994). She is writing a book on Virginia Woolf's relationship to John Milton and is editing a collection of essays on Woolf and literary history.

CHERYL J. MARES, Professor of English at Sweet Briar College, has published articles and given papers on Virginia Woolf and Proust and on Woolf and the visual arts. She is currently completing a book to be entitled *Reading Woolf Reading Proust*.

ELEANOR MCNEES is currently Associate Professor and Chair of the English department at the University of Denver. She is the author of *Eucharistic Poetry* (Bucknell UP, 1992) and the editor of *Virginia Woolf: Critical Assessments* (Helm Information, 1994) and *The Brontë Sisters: Critical Assessments* (Helm Information, 1996). She is now editing *The Novel: Sources and Documents* (Helm Information).

BETH CAROLE ROSENBERG is Assistant Professor of English at the University of Nevada, Las Vegas, where she teaches courses in Modern British and women's literature. She is the author of *Virginia Woolf and Samuel Johnson: Common Readers* (St. Martin's, 1995) and has published articles on Woolf and eighteenth-century women writers. She is currently working on a full-length study of Modernism and anti-Semitism.

CATHERINE SANDBACH-DAHLSTRÖM is Reader in English literature in Stockholm. She is the author of *Be Good Sweet Maid: Charlotte Yonge's Domestic Fiction* and numerous articles on feminist criticism and Woolf. She is now working on a monograph entitled *Conversing with Feminism: Virginia Woolf's Sexual Politics* and the compilation of an anthology of feminist and antifeminist polemics.

KAREN SCHIFF is a doctoral candidate in Comparative Literature and Literary Theory at the University of Pennsylvania, where she is writing a dissertation tentatively titled, "Reading Volumes: Book and Book Art in an Electronic Age." She has published an essay on Virginia Woolf and encyclopedia entries on Alice Walker and Adrienne Rich.

Index